Implementation of the EU Preventive Restructuring Directive

Volume I

Edited by:
J.M.G.J. Boon
H. Koster
R.D. Vriesendorp

eleven

Recommended short citation: Boon, Koster & Vriesendorp, *Implementation of the EU Preventive Restructuring Directive, Volume I, BLRN No 1*, 2023.

Recommended full citation: J.M.G.J. Boon, H. Koster & R.D. Vriesendorp, *Implementation of the EU Preventive Restructuring Directive, Volume I, Business and Law Research Network Series No 1*, Den Haag: Eleven, 2023.

Published, sold and distributed by Eleven
P.O. Box 85576
2508 CG The Hague
The Netherlands
Tel.: +31 70 33 070 33
Fax: +31 70 33 070 30
e-mail: sales@elevenpub.nl
www.elevenpub.com

Sold and distributed in USA and Canada
Independent Publishers Group
814 N. Franklin Street
Chicago, IL 60610, USA
Order Placement: +1 800 888 4741
Fax: +1 312 337 5985
orders@ipgbook.com
www.ipgbook.com

Eleven is an imprint of Boom (Den Haag).

ISBN 978-90-4730-186-8
ISBN 978-94-0011-359-6 (E-book)

Table of Contents

Editors' Preface vii

Contributors ix

1 **Introduction** 1
Bob Wessels

2 **Austria** 7
Georg Wabl and Martin Trenker

3 **Denmark** 33
Line Langkjaer

4 **France** 45
Emilie Ghio

5 **Germany** 69
Stephan Madaus and David Ehmke

6 **Greece** 89
Yiannis Bazinas and Athanasios Paizis

7 **The Netherlands** 111
Gert-Jan Boon, Reinout Vriesendorp and Harold Koster

8 **United Kingdom** 141
Eugenio Vaccari and Jennifer Gant

9 **Conclusion** 175
Gert-Jan Boon, Harold Koster and Reinout Vriesendorp

Annex: Preventive Restructuring Directive 219

Editors' Preface

This is the first volume of the new book series of the Business & Law Research Network (BLRN), which is run by the Department of Company Law of the Leiden Law School, Leiden University. BLRN is a research and expertise network that focuses on a variety of aspects of doing business. Good corporate governance, sustainability, restructuring and insolvency are the main areas of focus. BLRN is created with the purpose of advancing company and insolvency law in a cross-disciplinary and comparative environment.

With this book series, BLRN aims to provide a new academic platform for research conducted at the intersection of business and law. The series will be available both in print and in digital form, presenting research aligning company law with socio-economic developments through continuous observation of interactions between law on the books and law in action. This book series begins with a first edited book on the implementation of Directive (EU) 2019/1023 on restructuring and insolvency (PRD 2019), a directive which operates at the intersection of restructuring and insolvency law, as well as corporate law.

In 2019 the European Parliament and the Council adopted the PRD 2019 (see Annex), which required all EU Member States to implement a preventive restructuring framework (PRF) into national law by ultimately 26 July 2022. Although not all EU Member States have already fully implemented the PRD 2019, most jurisdictions have taken steps by working on legislative drafts or partially implementing the PRD 2019, while several have already completed the implementation process. While the PRD 2019 provides only for minimum harmonization, it is ground-breaking as the first piece of EU legislation aimed to harmonize parts of substantive domestic restructuring and insolvency laws of financially distressed but viable debtors. Previously, the EU legislator restricted its efforts mostly to procedural matters of cross-border insolvency and only rarely and limitedly touched upon aspects of substantive restructuring and insolvency law. In these times of worldwide distress, driven by increased political and economic uncertainty, including the aftermath of the COVID-19 crisis and the war in Ukraine, the importance of the PRD 2019 and its domestic implementations can hardly be underestimated. Currently, Europe urgently needs efficient and effective restructuring tools to prevent capital destruction of viable enterprises due to imminent cash and liquidity shortages, and difficulties to obtain adequate financing due to over-indebtedness.

In light of this, editors of the Dutch online journal HERO (www.hero-online.nl), an acronym for "Herstructurering & Recovery Online", decided to publish a series of papers reporting on the implementation of the PRD 2019 in seven EU jurisdictions. In close cooperation with HERO and the involved authors, it was decided to collect all national contributions in a book, presenting a comprehensive overview of these national implementations. Some authors have adjusted their contribution for this book, by including more recent developments in their respective jurisdiction.

The distinguished authors have aptly described what the implementation of the PRD 2019 adds to their pre-existing national restructuring framework, in particular, by reviewing how national legislators have made policy choices from a vast array of options available under the PRD 2019. Based on an agreed template for ease of comparing the different jurisdictions, the authors dealt with the following topics in a concise manner: (i) overview of the domestic restructuring framework before implementing the PRD 2019, (ii) overview of the implementation process of the PRD 2019 and (iii) domestic implementation of the PRD 2019. With respect to the latter, this especially concerns the main features that have been introduced in the various national PRFs: objective and scope of the PRF, criteria/test to enter the PRF, the actors involved, the possibility of a stay, the plan (its contents, adoption and confirmation), the possibilities for a debt-for-equity swap, the effects of the PRF on executory contracts and jurisdiction and recognition of court decisions abroad. Since some of the domestic implementations have been transposed and have been in force for some time now, the authors also elaborate on (iv) current and/or envisaged focus points for furthering the domestic PRF and restructuring practice.

This is a first volume that focuses on the implementation of the PRD 2019 in the following jurisdictions: Austria, Denmark, France, Germany, Greece and the Netherlands. Because of its central role in cross-border restructuring, the United Kingdom is also included. We would like to thank the other authors – Ioannis Bazinas, David Ehmke, Jennifer L.L. Gant, Emilie Ghio, Line Langkjaer, Stephan Madaus, Athanasios Paizis, Martin Trenker, Eugenio Vaccari, Georg Wabl and Bob Wessels – for their insightful contributions. We also thank Sofya Chantladze for her assistance in compiling this volume. It is envisaged that contributions in a similar format relating to other EU Member States will appear digitally at HERO and physically in a second volume of the BLRN book series in the near future.

Gert-Jan Boon, Harold Koster & Reinout Vriesendorp
Leiden, September 2023

Contributors

EDITORS

Gert-Jan Boon LL.M MSc is a researcher and lecturer at the Department of Company Law at the University of Leiden, the Netherlands. His research focuses on turnaround, rescue and insolvency of financially distressed businesses and has a strong European/international character. Gert-Jan is writing a dissertation on the Debtor in Possession in restructuring of distressed businesses. He is chair of the Younger Academics Network of Insolvency Law (YANIL) of the INSOL Europe Academic Forum and adjunct secretary of the Conference on European Restructuring and Insolvency Law (CERIL) and a member of the Business & Law Research Network (BLRN). He publishes regularly in national and international journals.

Prof. **Harold Koster** is professor of company law at the University of Leiden, the Netherlands. He regularly publishes in Dutch and international journals.

Prof. **Reinout Vriesendorp** is part-time professor of insolvency law at the Institute of Private Law (Department of Company Law) and the Institute of Tax Law and Economics (Department of Business Studies) at Leiden University (the Netherlands). He was a partner at the Netherlands-based law firm De Brauw Blackstone Westbroek. His research is at the crossroads of private law, company law and business studies, mainly focused on legal norms (ex ante) and judgements (ex post) of the behaviour of directors, supervisors and other stakeholders in enterprises in financial distress. He regularly publishes in Dutch and international journals.

AUTHORS

Yiannis Bazinas is a PhD candidate at University College London, UK. His research focuses on cross-border restructurings and the interplay between restructuring law and traditional norms of private international law. Yiannis is also an associate for Bazinas Law Firm in Athens, Greece, where he specializes in the areas of international litigation, commercial contracts and insolvency. He has published articles in Greek as well as in English in a number of fields, including insolvency, private international law and intermediated securities. He is a member of INSOL Europe as well as the International Insolvency Institute's Next Gen Leadership Program.

Dr. Dr. **David Ehmke** is an associate in the Business Reorganisation & Restructuring Department of Willkie Farr & Gallagher LLP, focusing his practice on (cross-border) financial restructurings, insolvency and distressed transactions. David regularly publishes articles on insolvency and restructuring from a legal and economic perspective. He has spent several years of studies and research in the area of law and finance/economics at Humboldt-University of Berlin, University of Oxford, University of Pennsylvania and Columbia University.

Dr. **Jennifer Gant** is currently a senior lecturer in law at the University of Derby in the UK and is a supervising solicitor in the Business Law Clinic within the Student Legal Advice Centre in the law school. Her research interests are on the social policy issues present in insolvency and restructuring procedures globally with a focus on the application of vulnerability theory to issues of fairness, an area in which she has published extensively. She has been an active member of the INSOL Europe Academic Forum since 2015 and is currently the deputy chair. She is also a delegate of CERIL, and a member of the editorial board of Eleven International Publishing's series on European and International Insolvency Law Studies.

Dr. **Emilie Ghio** is a lecturer in corporate and insolvency law at the University of Edinburgh, Scotland, United Kingdom. She previously held positions at Edinburgh Napier University and Birmingham City University. She holds a Ph.D., LL.M., and LL.B. from University College Cork (Ireland), as well as an LL.B. from the University of Strasbourg (France). Emilie is actively engaged with INSOL Europe. She is a board member of the Younger Academics Network of Insolvency Law (YANIL); the co-editor of the Academic Forum Conference Proceedings; and she sits on the editorial board of the Yearbook. Emilie's research interests lie in the area of UK, French, and EU corporate insolvency law and theories. She has recently published *Redefining Harmonisation. Lessons from EU Insolvency Law* (EE, 2022) and *English Corporate Insolvency Law. A Primer* (EE, 2022, with E. Vaccari).

Dr. **Line Langkjaer** is an associate professor at Aarhus University, Denmark.

Prof. **Stephan Madaus** has held his chair at the Martin Luther University Halle-Wittenberg since April 2014, where he was the head of the Law School from 2016 to 2018. He teaches property law (including secured transactions), insolvency and restructuring law, as well as contract and tort law. Prof. Madaus is a Member of the European Commission's Expert Group on Restructuring and Insolvency. He also holds appointments at the International Insolvency Institute and at the Conference of European Restructuring and Insolvency Law (CERIL). His research interests are in dealing with debt burdens and consequently focus on insolvency and restructuring law, with a special focus on the comparative analysis of relevant regulatory approaches in jurisdictions worldwide as well as in the soft law of international organisations.

Dr. **Athanasios Paizis** is a qualified lawyer and works as a legal officer in the Company Law Department of the European Commission. He holds a PhD in law on the subject of EU insolvency of enterprise groups. He is also a postdoctoral researcher at the Law School of the University of Athens. His research focuses on cross-border company and insolvency law and the impact of new technologies. He regularly gives lectures on cross-border insolvency to the students of the master's programme of business law at the Athens Law School and publishes in Greek and international law reviews.

Univ.-Prof. Dr. **Martin Trenker** is head of the Institute for Civil Procedure at the University of Innsbruck (Austria). His research mainly focusses on civil procedural, insolvency and company law. Among others he is co-editor of the *Zeitschrift für Insolvenzrecht und Kreditschutz* (Austrian Journal for Insolvency Law and Creditor's Rights).

Dr. **Eugenio Vaccari** is a senior lecturer in law at Royal Holloway, University of London (UK). Eugenio is a qualified Italian lawyer specialized in corporate insolvency and bankruptcy law. Eugenio's main areas of interest are the theoretical and conceptual underpinnings of corporate insolvency law and abusive practices in insolvency, particularly in relation to the use of *ipso facto* clauses and the treatment of local public entities in distress. Eugenio is an active member of several leading institutions in the field, including III NextGen Class XI, the Insolvency Law Academy, INSOL International and INSOL Europe. He is co-chair of the Emerging Scholars Group at the Insolvency Law Academy.

Dr. Georg Wabl is partner at BINDER GRÖSSWANG Attorneys at Law in Vienna. He has extensive experience in national and cross-border restructurings, reorganizations and transactions in the crisis and insolvency context. Prestigious law firm directories call him a "Next Generation Partner" (The Legal 500, EMEA Edition 2023), "Up and Coming" (Chambers Europe 2023) and "Rising Star" (IFLR 1000, 33st Edition) in the Austrian market. He amongst others studied at Queen Mary University of London (LL.M. 2017), where he also worked as research assistant, and University of Vienna (Dr. iur. 2022), where he did his PhD focusing on EU harmonization in insolvency law. Georg teaches international insolvency law as a guest lecturer at Leiden University, The Netherlands.

Prof. em. **Bob Wessels** was a part-time professor from 1988 to 2014 at the Vrije University Amsterdam and at the University of Leiden (the Netherlands). He has over 45 years of business law experience, the last two decades as an independent counsel, acting as an expert witness in courts in over ten jurisdictions and as (international) arbitrator, mainly in the area of contract law, restructuring and insolvency law. He has been a consultant to the International Monetary Fund and the World Bank. From 1988 to 2016, he has served as Deputy Justice at the Court of Appeal, The Hague. Since 2010, he has been independent Expert Counsel to the European Commission in matters of restructuring and insolvency law and since 2016, he is Chairman of the independent European think tank Conference of European Restructuring and Insolvency Law (CERIL, www.ceril.eu).

1 Introduction

Bob Wessels

The Preventive Restructuring Directive (PRD 2019) aims to bring about a degree of minimum harmonization of substantive preventive restructuring law across the European Union (EU). By 17 July 2022, all EU Member States were required to have completed the implementation process.[1] While some twenty legislators have completed their implementation process, several reform processes, both in the EU and other European countries, are to start or are still pending. In this book, seven contributions will review the implementation of the PRD 2019 in Austria, Denmark, France, Germany, Greece, the Netherlands and the United Kingdom.

1 A Long European Journey

In the EU, for more than ten years, the various bodies of the EU (Parliament, Council, Commission) have been working to harmonize national insolvency laws. In 2011, the European Parliament gave its go-ahead by stating that there are certain areas of insolvency law where harmonization is useful and feasible, even where the creation of substantive insolvency law at the EU level itself is regarded as impossible.[2] A year later, the European Commission followed suit with a proposal to give companies a 'second chance' via modernization of their insolvency regimes.[3] This thought is at the forefront of the Commission's political agenda in promoting the functioning of the European internal market.

In 2014, a (non-binding) recommendation from the European Commission was a next step containing a new approach to business failure and insolvency.[4] However, the following years showed that EU Member States were not following up enough on the Commission's

1 In this book, implementation is used synonymously to transposition.

2 European Parliament resolution of 15 November 2011 with recommendations to the Commission on insolvency proceedings in the context of EU company law (2011/2006(INI)).

3 Communication from the Commission to the European Parliament, the Council, the European Economic and Social Committee and the Committee of the Regions, Single Market Act II, Together for new growth, 3 October 2012, COM(2012) 573 final.

4 Commission Recommendation on a new approach to business failure and insolvency, 12 March 2014, C(2014) 1500 final.

encouragement to introduce rules that enable viable companies in financial difficulties to be restructured at an early stage and to avoid formal insolvency.[5]

Then the panels slide. In 2015, with its Action Plan for Building a Capital Markets Union (CMU Action Plan), the Commission set course for European legislation in the field of "early restructuring and second chance policy".[6] Its original main policy objective to harmonize insolvency law becomes an accompanying measure to achieve another goal, namely the establishment of a EU's Capital Market Union (CMU). The CMU has the aim of circulating investments and savings between all EU Member States so that citizens, investors and companies can benefit, wherever they are located. In 2016, that policy goal is not yet very well distilled. A draft Directive on restructuring will be published, which has been adopted in June 2019 at the EU level as the PRD 2019,[7] to be implemented by July 2021. This Directive and its implementation across Europe is at the core of this book.

2 A Minimum Harmonization Framework for Preventive Restructuring

The Directive focuses on three topics, namely: (i) giving viable companies in financial difficulties access to a system that allows them to restructure their debts; (ii) giving entrepreneurs (natural persons) a 'second chance' by waiving their debt in full; and (iii) rules to make insolvency proceedings more efficient, in particular to shorten their duration. The PRD 2019 necessitates drafters of legislation, and their advisors, to think hard on some core and also new themes.

The main subject of the Directive has to be analysed and formulated: when a debtor is likely to become insolvent, he should be in the position to negotiate a restructuring plan with its creditors; a stay should be available to halt creditors exercising their rights; the creditors should be put in voting classes; a certain majority should adopt the plan; a court should cram down holdout creditors; specific new finance for the company should be

5 Directorate-General Justice & Consumers of the European Commission, 'Evaluation of the implementation of the Commission Recommendation of 12 March 2014 on a new approach to business failure and insolvency', 30 September 2015 at 2 and 5. This conclusion was reiterated in the Communication from the Commission to the European Parliament, the Council, the European Economic and Social Committee and the Committee of the Regions, Action Plan on Building a Capital Markets Union, 30 September 2015, COM(2015) 468 final, p. 25.

6 Communication from the Commission to the European Parliament, the Council, the European Economic and Social Committee and the Committee of the Regions, Action Plan on Building a Capital Markets Union, 30 September 2015, COM(2015) 468 final, at 6.

7 Directive (EU) 2019/1023 of the European Parliament and of the Council of 20 June 2019 on preventive restructuring frameworks, on discharge of debt and disqualifications, and on measures to increase the efficiency of procedures concerning restructuring, insolvency and discharge of debt, and amending Directive (EU) 2017/1132 (Directive on restructuring and insolvency).

protected; and the debtor in possession should be able to steer the whole process. It is certainly not easy to get this show on the road. With extreme legislative pressure due to the sudden need to adapt (amongst others) national insolvency legislation following the 2020 COVID-19 outbreak, it is not surprising that many EU Member States have requested the European Commission to extend the implementation period of the Directive until 17 July 2022.[8] In parallel, in some Members States, legislation had already been adopted to accommodate new restructuring modes following a global wave of legislative changes promoting business rescue over formal insolvency liquidation.[9]

This book dealing with preventive restructuring frameworks is very timely. The long history of enrolling the harmonization theme in the EU, the Member States' own strong and uncompromising views on several aspects of the theme, and the complexities of the many possible legislative options in the Directive itself call for an actual and comparative view on how other countries do have addressed these. When laying its groundwork and implementing its details, legislators should take into account that harmonization – in November 2021 once again acknowledged clearly by the European Commission announcing new legislative steps[10] – is a long and hard way to go.

3 The Next Harmonization Steps of the EU Legislator

By the way, the EU's policy theme CMU, that threw a spanner in the European harmonization's wheel of restructuring and insolvency law, has gradually lost its lustre. Nevertheless, five years down the road, the CMU politically got its booster with a new CMU Action plan launched in June 2020.[11] It certainly looks like the Commission is trying to get things out of the doldrums.

Insolvency law seems to be designated as a scapegoat. The divergent national insolvency law is a structural obstacle to cross-border investments and thus to the creation of an internal market for capital. In particular, cross-border investors find it difficult to estimate the duration and outcome of value recovery procedures, making it difficult to properly price risk, especially for debt instruments. The harmonization of certain targeted elements

8 For an overview of the implementation efforts of EU Member States, including whether they have requesting for an extension of the implementation, see the INSOL Europe Tracker on the Implementation of the EU Directive on Restructuring and Insolvency, available at: https://www.insol-europe.org/tracker-eu-directive-on-restructuring-and-insolvency.

9 See for instance, European Law Institute (ed Part I) and B. Wessels, S. Madaus & J.M.G J. Boon (eds Part II), *Rescue of Business in Europe*, Oxford: Oxford University Press 2020, p. 354 et seq.

10 European Commission, Communication from the Commission to the European Parliament, the Council, the European Economic and Social Committee and the Committee of the Regions, Capital Markets Union – Delivering one year after the Action Plan, 25 November 2021, COM(2021) 720 final, at 3.4.

11 High Level Forum, A New Vision for Europe's Capital Markets, Final Report of the High Level Forum on the Capital Markets Union, June 2020, available at: https://europa.eu/!gU33Hm.

of national insolvency rules or their convergence could improve legal certainty. To this end, the Commission presented in December 2022 its proposal on a new Directive to harmonize certain aspects of insolvency law. It is a proposal seeking harmonization in the areas of (i) avoidance actions, (ii) asset tracing, (iii) pre-pack proceedings, (iv) director's duty to file, (v) winding-up of insolvent microenterprises, (vi) creditors' committees and (vii) transparency of national insolvency laws.[12]

4 Comparative Perspectives: An Impulse for Legislators and Practice

This book allows to get clear and detailed insights in other countries' implementation of preventive restructuring solutions, as well as the restructuring's effects on matters of company law and general contract law. Practitioners, in their day-to-day practice, are further developing their know-how and expertise concerning matters as financial restructuring, corporate finance and reorganizing businesses. National implementations in a comparative perspective can certainly assist scholars to better understand any implemented tool and practitioners to raise their standards of know-how.

While several EU Member States' legislators have not yet completed the implementation, this book presents a selection of European jurisdictions that have already (partially) introduced new legislations drawing on the PRD 2019 of the ideas incorporated in this Directive. These jurisdictions include Austria, Denmark, France, Germany, Greece, the Netherlands and the United Kingdom. These chapters examine in detail how the reforms have impacted the national restructuring regime.

Although the Directive aims to improve the level playing field for restructuring in Europe, the chapters show that a significant diversity remains in how these preventive restructuring frameworks have been shaped. This includes the position of the debtor, type of practitioner(s) in the field of restructuring that are involved as well as their role, the scope of a restructuring plan, the grounds for confirmation including the applicable priority rule, as well the basis for jurisdiction and cross-border recognition of court decisions. This is not surprising, as many scholars critically reviewed the significant flexibility offered by the EU legislator itself. Even more, some authors are also expressing concerns, where the Directive, with around 70 options to implement its text into national legislation resulting in harmonized restructurings law "… might paradoxically result in actually disharmonising it."[13]

12 European Commission, Proposal for a Directive of the European Parliament and of the Council harmonising certain aspects of insolvency law, 7 December 2022, COM(2022) 702 final.

13 Reinhard Bork and Renato Mangano, *European Cross-Border Insolvency Law* (2nd ed.), Oxford: Oxford University Press, 2022, p. 38.

The coming years will remain extremely interesting. Not only because the implementation phase will come to a completion, but also to see what uptake these new frameworks will have. The economic turbulence of these very times is certainly a first test for all of them.

2 Austria

Georg Wabl and Martin Trenker[*]

1 Introduction

The Austrian implementation of the Preventive Restructuring Directive (PRD) 2019[14] was performed through the new Austrian Restructuring Code (*Restrukturierungsordnung*, ReO), Federal Law Gazette Nr. I 2021/147, which entered into force with effect from 17 July 2021. By now, it was broadly discussed whether the ReO is a real improvement within the existing Austrian restructuring and insolvency landscape. Especially practitioners remain critical or at least sceptical about the potential of the ReO. Nevertheless, this new law may, in our eyes, still provide tools and instruments which could help in the desired strengthening of a preventive restructuring and rescue culture.

This chapter tries to highlight the most promising aspects of the ReO and whether and how they may change existing dynamics. In order to set the frame, it will first briefly describe the Austrian restructuring and insolvency landscape existing prior to the ReO (Section 2) and then point out the main aspects and characteristics of the ReO (Sections 3 and 4).[15] The chapter will be rounded off with an outlook (Section 5) and a conclusion (Section 6).

2 Overview of the Austrian Pre-reform Restructuring and Insolvency Law Regime

2.1 *Long Tradition of Legislative Initiatives on Restructuring*

Restructuring culture is not new in Austria. Back in 1914 – actually, a comparable procedure had even already existed since 1862 – the Austrian legislator implemented the

---

* This chapter was finalized on 6 June 2022.

14 Directive (EU) 2019/1023 of the European Parliament and of the Council of 20 June 2019 on preventive restructuring frameworks, on discharge of debt and disqualifications, and on measures to increase the efficiency of procedures concerning restructuring, insolvency and discharge of debt, and amending Directive (EU) 2017/1132 (Directive on restructuring and insolvency), O.J. L 172, 13.

15 This chapter does only focus on the Austrian implementation of Preventive Restructuring Frameworks under Title II of PRD 2019. The implementation of other aspects of the PRD 2019 (such as the Title III on the Discharge of Debt and Disqualifications) are not addressed.

Austrian Settlement Code (*Ausgleichsordnung*, AO),[16] which allowed the debtor to restructure its debt in collective proceedings by reaching a settlement with the creditor majority. The AO provided for a concept of debtor in possession supervised by a court-appointed administrator, for a moratorium and a minimum quota of 40%. Unfortunately, and presumably due to the high minimum quota, such proceedings were rarely applied in practice. In 2010, the legislator replaced the AO through so-called rehabilitation proceedings with self-administration (see below Section 2.3.2).

In another legal initiative, the Austrian legislator introduced the so-called reorganization proceeding through the Business Reorganization Act (*Unternehmensreorganisationsgesetz*, URG) in 1997.[17] The URG was introduced to encourage timely and well-considered reorganization measures[18] by allowing for confidential reorganization proceedings of debtors facing reorganization need.[19] Despite the ambitions of the URG legislator, which are in its essence comparable to the idea standing behind the PRD 2019, reorganization proceedings under the URG have never been accepted in practice.[20] This is probably because the proceedings are arguably too costly and do neither provide for a moratorium nor for an option to force and cram-down dissenting (hold-out) creditors into restructuring measures (such as debt haircuts).[21] Nevertheless, the URG is still in effect.[22]

2.2 *Restructurings Mainly Performed Through Private Workouts*

Not least due to this lack of well-established formalized restructuring instruments, the vast majority of restructurings was (and still is) performed through private workouts. Such processes benefit from a by and large well-functioning Austrian out-of-court restructuring practice. Relevant 'players' such as banks, credit insurers and advisers mostly

16 National Law Gazette Nr. 1915/337.

17 Federal Law Gazette Nr. I 1997/114.

18 See Legislative Materials, *Regierungsvorlage* Nr. 734/XX. 10 June 1997, p. 75.

19 Such reorganization need is presumed (Section 22(1) n 1 URG) if certain financial figures are met (equity ratio according to Section 23 URG below 8% and fictional debt repayment period according to Section 24 URG exceeding 15 years).

20 See *e.g.* G. Wabl, 'Preventive Restructuring Mechanisms in Austria: More Flexibility Needed? A Practical Analysis of Existing Tools and Possible International Impacts', *International Corporate Rescue*, 2017, 14(4), p. 249.

21 These points were already raised in the legislative process preceding the URG (see Legislative Materials, above note 18, pp. 75-76); see also G. Wabl, above note 20.

22 Because of its very low practical relevance it was expected that the implementation of the PRD 2019 would either lead to an amendment or a repeal of the URG. Surprisingly, neither of that happened (this was criticized through the legislative process on the ReO *e.g.* by M. Trenker & M. Lutschounig, Statement of the University of Innsbruck, available at: https://www.parlament.gv.at/PAKT/VHG/XXVII/SNME/SNME_78341/index.shtml (last viewed 12 April 2022)).

act professionally, reasonably and in line with (non-binding) restructuring principles contributing to an established framework for successful restructurings.[23]

As such workouts must still rely on a contractual and consensual basis, risks of failure – especially due to hold-out creditors – can still not be excluded.[24] Other obvious disadvantages are avoidance/clawback risks and the lack of a moratorium, including liability concerns of the acting directors.[25] Therefore, also private workouts do not satisfy all aspects required for an effective (!) formalized restructuring process.

2.3 *Proceedings Available Under the Austrian Insolvency Code*

2.3.1 Structure of the Insolvency Code

The Austrian Insolvency Code (*Insolvenzordnung*, IO) has its origin in the Austrian Bankruptcy Code from 1914 (*Konkursordnung*, KO). It has been broadly updated during the last century with the most important reform in 2010 which merged and updated the KO and AO (see above Section 2.1) into one Code, the IO.[26] The IO now provides for three different types of insolvency proceedings for companies:

- Rehabilitation proceedings without self-administration (*Sanierungsverfahren ohne Eigenverwaltung*);
- Rehabilitation proceedings with self-administration (*Sanierungsverfahren mit Eigenverwaltung*), and
- Bankruptcy proceedings (*Konkursverfahren*)

All these proceedings can serve as a tool to restructure as well as to wind up/liquidate a business (even rehabilitation proceedings can in principle be used to wind-down a business).[27]

23 See *e.g.* G. Gassner & G. Wabl, 'The New EU Directive on Restructuring and Insolvency and Its Implications for Austria', *Insolvency and Restructuring International*, 13(2), p. 8. Such restructuring principles are based on eight principals on out-of-court restructurings basically comparable to the eight international associations of restructuring, insolvency and bankruptcy professionals (INSOL Global Principles for Multi-Creditor Workouts).

24 See further G. Wabl, above note 20, p. 247 et seq.

25 See for further considerations G. Wabl, above note 20, p. 251 et seq.

26 Insolvency Law Amendment Act 2010, Federal Law Gazette Nr. I 2010/29. A. Konecny, 'Das Verfahrensgebäude der Insolvenzordnung', in: A. Konecny (ed), *ZIK Spezial: IRÄG 2010*, Wien: LexisNexis, 2010, pp. 1-21 (pp. 5-6) ('*einheitliches Insolvenzverfahren*'); see also G. Kodek in: C. Koller, E. Lovrek & M. Spitzer (eds), *IO – Insolvenzordnung*, Wien: Verlag Österreich, 2022, IO § 1, Para. 14-15.

27 *E.g.* through a '*Liquidationstreuhandschaft*' (Section 157m IO), see S. Riel, 'Verfahrensrechtliche Fragen beim Treuhandsanierungsplan', *Österreichisches Bankarchiv*, 2015, 63(12), pp. 830-889 (p. 881); M. Trenker, *Treuhänderüberwachung der Sanierungsplanerfüllung*, Wien: Manz, 2017, pp. 219-220.

2.3.2 Rehabilitation Proceedings (Sanierungsverfahren)

Rehabilitation proceedings are addressed in Sections 166 et seq. IO and can only be applied by the debtor. The debtor must be either (i) imminently illiquid (*drohend zahlungsunfähig*) according to Section 167(2) IO or (ii) illiquid (*zahlungsunfähig*) according to Section 66 IO and/or (iii) over-indebted (*überschuldet*) according to Section 67 IO. At the core of every rehabilitation proceeding is the rehabilitation plan (*Sanierungsplan*). Depending on the conditions offered in this plan, the debtor can choose between rehabilitation proceedings with or without self-administration.

- If the debtor wishes to stay in possession and therefore applies for proceedings with self-administration, a rehabilitation plan with a minimum quota of 30% (leading to a debt haircut of up to 70%) to be paid to the creditors within two years at the latest must be presented together with a detailed set of further documents already together with the initial application (Section 169 IO). Still, a rehabilitation administrator (*Sanierungsverwalter*) must be appointed by the insolvency court, who must supervise the debtor and is in control of certain exclusive actions such as avoidance actions or the sale of certain assets, *e.g.* properties or the enterprise itself, to be approved by the insolvency court (Sections 171 et seq. IO).[28]
- An alternative are rehabilitation proceedings without self-administration which require a rehabilitation plan with a minimum quota of 'only' 20% (leading to a debt haircut of up to 80%) to be paid within at the latest two years (Section 167 IO in connection with Sections 140 et seq. IO). In such proceedings, an insolvency administrator (*Insolvenzverwalter*) is appointed who is fully in charge to administrate and dispose of the debtor's assets.[29]

Rehabilitation proceedings with self-administration are rather rare in practice, particularly because of related costs for preparation and the 30% minimum quota.[30] Rehabilitation proceedings without self-administration are commenced more often but are still relatively rare compared to the overall numbers of proceedings opened in Austria.[31] However, rehabilitation plans as such are still relatively common as such can also be applied in bankruptcy proceedings (see the following section).

---

28 See further G. Wabl, above note 20, p. 249 et seq.

29 Ibid.

30 Out of the 3,044 insolvency proceedings initiated in 2019 (last published statistics not influenced by the COVID-19-pandemic) as regards companies only a total of 32 were rehabilitation proceedings with self-administration (see KSV1870, Insolvenzentwicklung Unternehmen 2019, available at: https://www.ksv.at/KSV1870_Insolvenzstatistik_Unternehmen_2019_final (last viewed 12 April 2022)).

31 In 2019, the overall number of rehabilitation proceedings without self-administration was 342 (see ibid.).

2.3.3 Bankruptcy Proceedings (Konkursverfahren)

If the debtor does not apply for rehabilitation proceedings including a rehabilitation plan in its initial application, the insolvency proceedings are called bankruptcy proceedings. Such proceedings require material insolvency (*materielle Insolvenz*), *i.e.* illiquidity and/or over-indebtedness of the debtor (see for the relevant sections of the IO already above Section 2.3.2). Bankruptcy proceedings can be applied not only by the debtor (Section 69 IO) but also by its creditors (Section 70 IO). Together with the commencement order, the insolvency court appoints an insolvency administrator (in that case called a *Masseverwalter*) who – similar to that in rehabilitation proceedings without self-administration – takes control over the assets of the debtor.

Although bankruptcy proceedings originally aimed at liquidating the debtor's assets in order to satisfy the creditors, nowadays the IO encourages debtors to strive for a restructuring and rescue of the business even in bankruptcy proceedings. Therefore, the debtor can present a rehabilitation plan with a minimum quota of 20% to be paid within two years at the latest (see above Section 2.3.2. for rehabilitation proceedings without self-administration) at any time. What is not possible in bankruptcy proceedings is the subsequent approval of self-administration (this is only possible in rehabilitation proceedings with self-administration). Also, quasi as an alternative to a rehabilitation plan, the business (or at least viable business parts) can be rescued by selling it to a new entity (so-called *übertragende Sanierung*). Selling the business is even possible if the debtor has filed a rehabilitation plan as long as this option is more advantageous to the creditors.

3 PRD 2019: Implementation through the ReO

Kickstarter for the legislative initiative of the ReO was certainly the implementation need caused by the PRD 2019. As this came into effect more or less simultaneously with the outbreak of the COVID-19 pandemic, it was argued that the new law should also help in order to fight the economic effects of the pandemic.[32] In our eyes it still seems very unlikely that a comprehensive reform such as the ReO would have taken place without the external momentum such as the one caused by the PRD 2019.

32 See *e.g.* an interview given by the Austrian Minister of Justice, Ms. Alma Zadic, in October 2020, available at: https://www.wienerzeitung.at/nachrichten/wirtschaft/oesterreich/2080337-Justizministerin-will-Insolvenzrecht-bis-Ende-Jaenner-reformieren.html (last viewed 12 April 2022), according to which an 'overall reform of insolvency law' containing the requirements of the PRD 20119 should serve to avoid a 'wave of bankruptcies' caused by COVID-19.

The first legislative draft for the ReO was published on 22 February 2021[33] and led to around 50 published (partly very critical) statements during the six-week evaluation period.[34] Although the general idea of strengthening preventive restructuring and therefore also the initiative as such was broadly welcomed, strong criticism was voiced on the general structure of the law as well as in the details.[35] In the following, some particularly relevant reservations raised by experts from academia and practice are listed:

1. Structural and conceptual weaknesses[36] and generally the doubtful practical usability of the proceedings;[37]
2. Uncertainties on the scope of measures allowed under a restructuring plan;[38]
3. A missing link between corporate/company and insolvency law necessary for a well-functioning modern restructuring law;[39]
4. The lack of provisions of a debt equity swap or alternative shareholder contributions to the restructuring against the will of the shareholders;[40]
5. The continued application of the URG.[41]

Even international observers concluded that the Austrian legislator has shown no ambitions to join the European "competition of legislations".[42]

Although the legislator has considered some of the criticisms raised, the by now implemented ReO still largely corresponds with its first draft published in February 2021.[43]

33 See Ministerial Draft Nr. 96/XXVII. 22 February 2021; this was followed by a second draft Legislative Materials, *Regierungsvorlage* Nr. 950/XXVII. 16 June 2021.

34 The draft was the result of numerous meetings of a working group set up by the Austrian Ministry of Justice consisting of experts from the ministry, judiciary, academia and practice (see *e.g.* A. Konecny, 'ZIK AKTUELL', *Zeitschrift für Insolvenzrecht und Kreditschutz*, 2019, 25(5), p. 161).

35 The statements are publicly available on: https://www.parlament.gv.at/PAKT/VHG/XXVII/ME/ME_00096/index.shtml#tab-Stellungnahmen (last viewed 12 April 2022); see further G. Gassner, E. Welten & G. Wabl, 'Austrian Restructuring Code in force', *HERO* 2021/B-069 (18 August 2021).

36 M. Trenker & M. Lutschounig, above note 22, p. 2.

37 R. Wolff, Statement of the Austrian Bar Association (expert S. Riel), available at: https://www.parlament.gv.at/PAKT/VHG/XXV/SN/SN_00535/imfname_633912.pdf (last viewed 12 April 2022).

38 G. Wabl & G. Gassner, PRD-Implementation Act: Statement to the draft proposal, available at: https://www.parlament.gv.at/PAKT/VHG/XXVII/ME/ME_00096/index.shtml (last viewed 12 April 2022); M. Trenker & M. Lutschounig, above note 22, p. 2.

39 A. Isola, S. Weileder, D. Seidl & J. Schnur, Statement on the draft proposal 96/ME XXVII. GP, available at: https://www.parlament.gv.at/PAKT/VHG/XXVII/SNME/SNME_78259/index.shtml (last viewed 12 April 2022).

40 Ibid., p. 2 et seq; G. Wabl & G. Gassner, above note 38, p. 4 et seq.; M. Trenker & M. Lutschounig, above note 22, p. 66; similar also R. Wolff, above note 37, p. 20.

41 M. Trenker & M. Lutschounig, above note 22, p. 19.

42 S. Madaus, Österreichs Entwurf einer Restrukturierungsordnung – das Planverfahren der InsO 1999, available at: https://stephanmadaus.de/2021/02/24/oesterreichs-entwurf-einer-restrukturierungsordnung-das-planverfahren-der-inso-1999/ (last viewed 12 April 2022) (dealing the first draft of the ReO).

43 See G. Gassner, E. Welten & G. Wabl, above note 35.

Part of the criticism therefore still continues, and we address some of the most important aspects in the following.

4 MAIN FEATURES INTRODUCED BY THE REO

4.1 *Objective and Scope of the Proceedings*

The objective of the proceedings under the ReO is to allow companies and entrepreneurs to restructure in order to prevent illiquidity and ensure viability of the business (Section 1(1) ReO). The proceedings are basically available for all companies and entrepreneurs but exclude specific businesses such as financial institutions or insurance companies (Section 2(1) ReO) as well as non-entrepreneurs (Section 2(1) n 10 ReO).

There are no specific provisions for enterprise groups. A court-supported group restructuring therefore still requires separate restructuring proceedings for every affected group member. In contrast to other EU member states (such as *e.g.* Germany or the Netherlands),[44] Austrian law does further not offer options to include intragroup guarantees in the restructuring of the primary debtor.

The ReO allows the debtor to file for:

i. Regular restructuring proceedings (*ordentliches Restrukturierungsverfahren*);
ii. European restructuring proceedings (*Europäisches Restrukturierungsverfahren*);
iii. Simplified restructuring proceedings (*vereinfachtes Restrukturierungsverfahren*).

Regular and simplified restructuring proceedings are confidential, European restructuring proceedings are public. In Sections 4.2. to 4.9., the provisions of the regular proceedings are described. European and simplified restructuring proceedings are addressed separately in Sections 4.10. and 4.11.

4.2 *Criteria to Enter the Proceedings*

Restructuring proceedings can only be applied for by the debtor. In case of companies, the person(s) authorized to represent the company (*e.g.* director(s) of a limited liability

44 See further Chapter 5 for Germany and Chapter 7 for the Netherlands.

company) are entitled to apply for restructuring proceedings.[45] Creditors, shareholders (see on their role in Section 4.7 below) or others are not entitled to do so.[46]

The ReO (in particular Sections 6 to 8) provides for several criteria and formal requirements linked to the application for and the access to restructuring proceedings. The following aspects seem to be particularly relevant to us:

– **Likelihood of insolvency (*wahrscheinliche Insolvenz*):** the application requires the debtor's likelihood of insolvency which must be presented by the debtor in the initial application (Section 6(1) in connection with 7(1) ReO). A debtor is to be considered likely insolvent if its viability would be threatened without restructuring, in particular in case of imminent illiquidity (Section 6(2) ReO).[47] The likelihood of insolvency is assumed if the financial figures under Sections 23 and 24 URG are met (see Footnote 19 above). Although the ReO mentions the likelihood of insolvency as a requirement to access restructuring proceedings, its threshold is still rather low as the debtor is only obliged to present but not to evidence this requirement (Section 7(1) ReO). The court can only reject the application if the likelihood of insolvency is obviously not met (Section 7(3) ReO).[48]
– **Viability (*Bestandfähigkeit*):** the ReO does not provide for an explicit viability test. As the debtor must together with the initial application either present (i) a fully prepared restructuring plan including evidence on the viability of the debtor (see Section 4.5.1.) (Section 7(1) n 1 ReO) or (ii) at least a restructuring concept showing that the viability of the debtor can be achieved with such concept (Section 7(2) ReO),[49] the threshold to enter proceedings seems *prima vista* relatively high. But again, the application is only impermissible if the restructuring plan respectively the restructuring concept is obviously unsuitable to ensure the viability of the debtor. Only in such cases, the court can reject the opening of the proceedings because of non-viability (Section 7(3) ReO).[50]

45 M. Schimka, 'Gesellschaftsrechtliche Überlegungen zur Restrukturierungsordnung', *Der Gesellschafter*, 2021, 50(6), pp. 374-379 (p. 378); M. Trenker in: P. Fidler, A. Konecny, S. Riel & M. Trenker (eds), *ReO – Restrukturierungsordnung und die weiteren Bestimmungen des RIRUG*, Wien: Manz, 2022, ReO § 27, Para. 6; see also F. Mohr, 'Einleitung und Ablauf des Restrukturierungsverfahrens', in: A. Konecny (ed), *ZIK-Spezial: RIRUG – Neuerungen im Restrukturierungs- und Insolvenzrecht*, Wien: LexisNexis, 2021, pp. 67-84 (p. 70).

46 M. Trenker in: P. Fidler, A. Konecny, S. Riel & M. Trenker (eds), above note 45, ReO § 27, Para. 6.

47 Imminent illiquidity also allows the debtor to apply for rehabilitation proceedings (see Section 167(2) IO and above Section 2.3.2).

48 M. Trenker, 'Was will und kann die ReO? – Anwendungsbereich, Zweck und Mittel von Restrukturierungsverfahren', in: A. Konecny (ed), *ZIK-Spezial: RIRUG – Neuerungen im Restrukturierungs- und Insolvenzrecht*, Wien: LexisNexis, 2021, pp. 33-49 (p. 37).

49 If the debtor only presents a restructuring concept in the application for the opening of restructuring proceedings, a formalized restructuring plan is generally to be presented at the latest within 60 days after the opening of the proceedings (Section 8(2) ReO).

50 See for the relevance of the concept of viability in the ReO further M. Trenker, above note 48, p. 37.

- **No illiquidity** (***keine Zahlungsunfähigkeit***): the application for the opening of restructuring proceedings is in any case impermissible if the debtor is illiquid (Section 7(3) ReO). The liquidity of the debtor for at least the following 90 days of the proceedings must be presented by the debtor in the initial application through a liquidity plan (*Finanzplan*) (Section 7(1) n 2 ReO). Besides that, the court is not obliged to examine the liquidity of the debtor. It shall only reject the opening of the proceedings if the debtor is obviously illiquid (Section 7(3) ReO).

Nota bene: The debtor may still be over-indebted (*überschuldet*) within the meaning of the IO, provided that the restructuring proceedings can eliminate such over indebtedness.[51] Accordingly, the ReO provides, at least to some extent, an alternative to the IO for debtors which are already materially insolvent within the meaning of the IO.

The court has to examine all of these criteria – to the extent described above – *ex officio*. If the criteria are met, the court commences the restructuring proceedings. The commencement decision is not published because regular restructuring proceedings are, other than European restructuring proceedings, conducted *in camera*. Creditors are not entitled to challenge the commencement decision.[52]

4.3 Involved actors

The ReO basically follows the structure of the PRD 2019 leading to the following roles and positions:

- **The debtor (in possession)**: as a general rule, the debtor shall stay in possession and therefore keep control over the assets and the business operations (Section 16(1) ReO). There are still several exceptions to this rule as (i) certain tasks or responsibilities can be transferred to an appointed restructuring expert or (ii) the court can decide that certain measures are only allowed if the court or the restructuring expert consent (Section 16(2) ReO).[53] As the ReO provides for a large number of cases which require or allow the appointment of a restructuring expert (see the following section), we

51 Legislative Materials, above note 18, p. 1; M. Trenker, above note 48, pp. 38-39; D. Aigner in: D. Aigner, D. Gerstberger, N. Mooseder & T. Zeitler (eds), *Praxishandbuch Restrukturierungsordnung I ReO*, Wien: Linde, 2022, pp. 38-39.

52 Legislative Materials, above note 33, p. 7.

53 Section 16(2) last sentence ReO still makes clear that any restrictions ruled by the restructuring court may still not lead to the same extent of restrictions which are mandatory in Austrian bankruptcy proceedings (*i.e.* basically the replacement of the debtor by an administrator). For further details see S. Riel in: P. Fidler, A. Konecny, S. Riel & M. Trenker (eds), above note 45, ReO § 16, Para. 11; I. Kapetanovic in: S. Mock & M. Zoppel (eds), *ReO I Restrukturierungsordnung*, Wien: Linde, 2022, ReO § 16, Para. 14; S. Riel, 'Der Restrukturierungsbeauftragte', in: A. Konecny (ed), *ZIK-Spezial: RIRUG – Neuerungen im Restrukturierungs- und Insolvenzrecht*, Wien: LexisNexis, 2021, pp. 85-114 (p. 104).

expect that in practice the debtor in possession will not be applied as extensively as Article 5 PRD 2019 would have allowed.

- **Restructuring expert**: restructuring experts (*Restrukturierungsbeauftragte*) must be sufficiently experienced, including having special knowledge in restructuring and insolvency laws, business law and business administration (Section 11(1) ReO) which is why we expect that mostly lawyers will be appointed. Furthermore, restructuring experts must be independent (Section 11(2) ReO). The selection is done by the restructuring court and neither the debtor nor creditors have a formal right to influence the selection process. There is also a public list in which restructuring experts can be registered. The involvement of restructuring experts can be basically split into the following categories:
  - Appointment is mandatory to support the debtor as well as the creditors in the negotiations and preparations of the restructuring plan if one of the requirements in Article 5(3) PRD 2019 is met (the provisions are identically implemented in Section 9(1) ReO).
  - It is further mandatory if (i) there are circumstances which lead to the expectation that the debtor staying in possession may lead to disadvantages of the creditors, in particular if the debtor (ii) violates duties to collaborate and communicate, (iii) acts to the detriment of the creditors, (iv) the debtor or a member of its board of directors is subject to criminal proceedings related to the business operations, (v) the information in the liquidity plan must be tested in the interests of the creditors or (vi) the debtor does not pay liabilities occurred after the initiation of the proceedings (Section 9(2) ReO).
  - The court may finally appoint a restructuring expert if required, for instance (i) to examine whether to approve an interim or new financing, (ii) for a report about the expected results of an alternative insolvency proceeding (which shall likely serve as a basis for the determination of the best interest of creditors test as further addressed in Section 4.6.3.), (iii) in case of restrictions of the debtor in possession or (iv) to review creditor claims which have been contested (Section 9(3) ReO).

  With this list, the ReO legislator goes far beyond the list of the exceptions of the debtor in possession in Article 5(3) PRD 2019. This may be seen critically.

- **Restructuring court:** the court competent for restructuring proceedings is the same court that would be competent for insolvency proceedings under the IO (Section 4 ReO in connection with Section 63 IO). This is the first instance court where the debtor operates the business at the time of the application. This concept corresponds by and large to that of the centre of main interests (COMI) under Article 3 of the

European Insolvency Regulation (EIR 2015).[54] Still, practical problems may arise as Section 63(2) IO also allows the opening of proceedings where the debtor operates a branch or simply owns property.[55]

- **Creditors:** as mentioned previously, creditors are not entitled to file for restructuring proceedings or present a restructuring plan.[56] Creditors are still, of course, parties to the proceedings if they are affected by the restructuring plan (and can therefore *e.g.* exercise their right to vote according to Section 32(1) ReO). Creditors must be split in predefined creditor classes (see Section 4.5.2).
- **Workers:** claims of workers are excluded from restructuring proceedings (Section 3(1) ReO) and the rights of workers under individual or collective agreements under labour law may not be affected by the restructuring proceedings or the restructuring plan (Section 43 ReO). However, the debtor has to inform its employees' representatives according to Article 13 PRD 2019.[57]
- **Equity holders/shareholders:** although equity holders always play an important role for the success of restructuring proceedings under the ReO, the ReO only provides very few provisions addressing them (see details in Section 4.7.).
- **Directors:** in case of companies, the ReO also provides for specific duties of directors linked to the likelihood of insolvency (Section 1(3) ReO). Those duties broadly correspond to Article 19 PRD 2019. In the legislative materials, the legislator made it clear that with this provision no new liability framework should be implemented but rather existing company law principles for directors of limited liability companies should be concretized.[58] This means in a nutshell that in case of a likelihood of insolvency, directors must take steps to avoid insolvency and to ensure viability. The 'right' steps depend on the individual case and applying for restructuring proceedings under the ReO might but does not have to be the right choice (there is no automatism for restructuring proceedings).[59] It is therefore expected that this provision does not

54 Regulation (EU) 2015/878 of the European Parliament and the Council of 20 May 2015 on insolvency proceedings (recast).

55 Already criticized by M. Trenker & M. Lutschounig, above note 22, pp. 30-31.

56 The debtor has the monopoly on initiative (*Initiativmonopol*) (M. Trenker in: P. Fidler, A. Konecny, S. Riel & M. Trenker (eds), above note 45, ReO § 27, Para. 6; see further P. Fidler in: P. Fidler, A. Konecny, S. Riel & M. Trenker (eds), above note 45, ReO § 1, Para. 37; S. Mock in: S. Mock & M. Zoppel (eds), above note 53, ReO § 1, Para. 4).

57 M. Trenker in: P. Fidler, A. Konecny, S. Riel & M. Trenker (eds), above note 45, ReO § 43, Para. 6 et seq.

58 Legislative Materials, above note 33, p. 4.

59 G. Wabl & G. Gassner, 'Geschäftsleitung und Anteilsinhaber', in: A. Konecny (ed), *ZIK-Spezial: RIRUG – Neuerungen im Restrukturierungs- und Insolvenzrecht*, Wien: LexisNexis, 2021, pp. 201-219 (p. 206); P. Fidler in: P. Fidler, A. Konecny, S. Riel & M. Trenker (eds), above note 45, ReO § 1, Para. 62; M. Schimka, above note 45, p. 376.

lead to major changes in the Austrian legislative landscape, but it may raise further awareness amongst company directors.[60]

4.4 *Stay*

4.4.1 Stay of Individual Enforcement Actions (Vollstreckungssperre)

The provisions in Articles 6 and 7 PRD 2019 have been implemented through Sections 19 et seq ReO. A stay of individual enforcement actions is not granted automatically, but only upon application of the debtor. Creditors, the restructuring expert or others cannot apply for a stay.[61]

The stay shall support negotiations on a restructuring plan.[62] Therefore, the application for a stay is impermissible if the stay is not necessary to achieve the restructuring goal, not suitable to support the negotiations on the restructuring plan or if the debtor is illiquid (Section 19(2) ReO).

Similar to Article 6 PRD 2019, the stay can focus on individual creditors as well as creditor classes, who must in any case be informed about the stay (Section 21(2) ReO). The stay can include all kinds of creditors and therefore also secured creditors (Section 20(1) ReO). However, stronger requirements have to be met in order to also include secured creditors (Section 20(1) ReO in connection with Section 11(2, 3) IO). Furthermore, there is no stay for creditors whose claims cannot be part of the restructuring plan, *e.g.* workers' claims. A general stay is only possible in the so-called European restructuring proceeding (see on those proceedings below Section 4.10) and therefore requires publicity of the proceedings.

The application for a stay can be made together with the initial application for the proceedings as well as at a later stage.[63] The initial duration of the stay may not exceed three months (Section 22(1) ReO). Upon application of the debtor or the restructuring expert, the stay can be extended or also a new stay can be granted, as long as it does not exceed a total duration of six months (Section 22(2) in connection with (4) ReO).

---

60 See further including a critical assessment G. Wabl & G. Gassner, above note 59, pp. 201-202; for a general overview of the relevant aspects of the liability regime see already G. Wabl, 'Duties of Directors where there is a Likelihood of Insolvency – Results of an Empirical Survey of 107 Austrian Insolvency Administrators', in: J.L.L. Gant (ed), *INSOL Europe Booklet: Copenhagen*, Nottingham: INSOL Europe, 2018, p. 206 et seq.

61 A. Reckenzaun, 'Vollstreckungssperre und Insolvenzschutz', in: A. Konecny (ed), *ZIK-Spezial: RIRUG – Neuerungen im Restrukturierungs- und* Insolvenzrecht, Wien: LexisNexis, 2021, pp. 115-126 (p. 115).

62 Legislative Materials, above note 33, p. 11 (similar purpose as Art. 6 PRD).

63 A. Reckenzaun, above note 61, pp. 116-117; N. Mooseder & D. Gerstberger in: D. Aigner, D. Gerstberger, N. Mooseder & T. Zeitler (eds), above note 51, p. 159.

4.4.2 Insolvency Stay (Insolvenzsperre)

Further, the above-mentioned stay of individual enforcement actions – even if it is just granted against a single creditor[64] – leads to a limited insolvency stay. On the one hand, the duty of the debtor (respectively its directors) to file for insolvency (*Insolvenzantragspflicht*) linked to the insolvency ground of over-indebtedness is suspended (Section 24(1) ReO in implementation of Article 7(1) PRD 2019).[65] On the other hand, the insolvency court shall not decide upon creditor applications linked to the insolvency ground of over-indebtedness (Section 24(2) ReO in implementation of Article 7(2) PRD 2019). The Austrian legislator therefore made use of the option of Article 7(3) PRD 2019 and limited this insolvency stay to cases of over-indebtedness. The debtor's duty as well as the creditors' right to file for insolvency linked to illiquidity therefore remain untouched.[66] However, Section 24(3) ReO still provides that even in case of illiquidity the insolvency court can refrain from opening insolvency proceedings upon application of the debtor or a creditor if such opening would not be in the general interest of the creditors.[67]

4.4.3 Protection of Executory Contracts

Finally, in implementation of Article 7(4) and (5) PRD 2019, Section 26 ReO provides for a protection of executory contracts which shall secure the continuation of the debtor business.[68] The protection of executory contracts in Section 26(1) ReO is limited to essential executory contracts (*wesentliche, noch zu erfüllende Verträge*) which are defined as contracts necessary for the continuation of the day-to-day operations of the business (Section 26(2) ReO).[69] Besides, even essential contracts are only 'protected' if they (meaning the respective contractual claims standing behind) are at all subject to the stay.[70]

---

64 A. Konecny in: P. Fidler, A. Konecny, S. Riel & M. Trenker (eds), above note 45, ReO § 19, Para. 3 and 44; M. Simsa & C. Stegner in: S. Mock & M. Zoppel (eds), above note 53, ReO § 24, Para. 9.

65 In the context of to the suspension of a duty to file linked to over-indebtedness, Section 25(1) ReO provides for a further liability release for directors linked to the so-called payment ban (*Zahlungsverbot*) under Austrian corporate law, which ban shall ensure the equal treatment of creditors when a company is already materially insolvent; see G. Wabl & G. Gassner, above note 59, p. 212; see further P. Fidler in: P. Fidler, A. Konecny, S. Riel & M. Trenker (eds), above note 45, ReO § 25, Para. 5 et seq.; M. Trenker & M. Lutschounig, above note 22, pp. 52-53.

66 G. Wabl & G. Gassner, above note 59, p. 211; dissenting (in our eyes incorrectly) P. Fidler in: P. Fidler, A. Konecny, S. Riel & M. Trenker (eds), above note 45, ReO § 24, Para. 19.

67 P. Fidler in: P. Fidler, A. Konecny, S. Riel & M. Trenker (eds), above note 45, ReO § 24, Para. 22 et seq; M. Simsa & C. Stegner in: S. Mock & M. Zoppel (eds), above note 53, ReO § 24, Para. 16; A. Reckenzaun, above note 61, p. 123.

68 P. Anzenberger, 'Vertragsschutz und unwirksame Vereinbarungen nach der ReO', in: A. Konecny (ed), *ZIK-Spezial: RIRUG – Neuerungen im Restrukturierungs- und Insolvenzrecht*, Wien: LexisNexis, 2021, pp. 127-141 (p. 127).

69 The Austrian legislator therefore follows the understanding of essential executory contracts in Art. 7(4) PRD 2019.

70 M. Trenker in: P. Fidler, A. Konecny, S. Riel & M. Trenker (eds), above note 45, ReO § 26, Para. 8 et seq.

Creditors subject to this protection shall not be entitled to withhold performance or terminate, accelerate or in any other way modify such contracts to the detriment of the debtor solely because of debts not paid by the debtor deriving from the time prior to the stay. This provision can generally cover all types of contracts. Still, the debtor's right to claim disbursements of loans (Section 26(5) ReO) as well as contracts which are generally out of the scope of the ReO such as employment agreements are excluded.[71]

4.4.4 Ban on Ipso Facto Clauses (Not Linked to a Stay)

Finally, *ipso facto* clauses are unenforceable according to Section 26(3) ReO. The ReO provides for a list of impermissible clauses very similar to Article 7(5) PRD 2019. Although this provision is included in the fifth section of the ReO overall dealing with the stay, the impermissibility of ipso facto clauses applies notwithstanding whether a stay was granted to the relevant contractual party or whether a stay was granted at all.[72] It applies to all types of contracts and creditors except for the types listed in Section 26(4) ReO implementing the list also included in Article 7(6) PRD 2019 such as netting arrangements.

4.5 The Restructuring Plan

4.5.1 Formal Requirements

Only the debtor can present a restructuring plan to the restructuring court (see Section 4.2). The plan can be submitted either together with the application to the proceedings or within a deadline set by the court of no longer than 60 days (Section 27(1) in connection with Section 8(2) ReO). There is an extensive list of information which must be included in the plan (see Section 27(2) ReO) and which is similar to the list in Article 8(1) PRD 2019.

Besides the obvious necessity to list the terms of the plan (Section 27(2) n 7 ReO), another key information required is an explanation on how the plan is going to guarantee the viability of the business (*bedingte Fortbestehensprognose*) (Section 27(2) n 8 ReO). A remarkable, because in practice potentially costly (usually requiring the support of external advisors), invention of the ReO legislator is the requirement to compare the effects of the plan to (all?) alternative scenarios under the IO (Section 27(2) n 9 ReO).[73]

---

71 P. Anzenberger, above note 68, p. 131 with reference to Section 3(1) ReO.

72 P. Anzenberger, above note 68, p. 139; M. Trenker in: P. Fidler, A. Konecny, S. Riel & M. Trenker (eds), above note 45, ReO § 26, Para. 33.

73 M. Trenker in: P. Fidler, A. Konecny, S. Riel & M. Trenker (eds), above note 45, § 27 ReO, Para. 2 and 38.

4.5.2 Class Formation

Section 29 ReO provides a mandatory and conclusive[74] list of classes to be formed (if existing).[75] Such classes are:

- Secured creditors,
- Unsecured creditors,
- Bondholders,
- Vulnerable creditors (particularly such with claims of less than EUR 10.000) and
- Subordinated creditors.

Shareholders are not listed and their legal position can therefore not be affected by the plan without their consent (*see* Section 4.7).

If creditors belong to more than one creditor class (*e.g.* partly secured creditors), they can also be allocated to more than one class (Section 29(2) ReO). Within classes, the principal of equal treatment of creditors applies (Section 34(1) n 2 ReO).[76] Furthermore, the class formation must be appropriate (*sachgemäß*). However, the conclusiveness of the list makes it impermissible to form further classes of creditors within the existing classes (*e.g.* by splitting the unsecured creditors in classes of financial creditors and suppliers).[77] This rule restricts flexibility and may therefore be seen critically.[78]

SME debtors can choose whether to follow the above rules or whether to present a restructuring plan without creditor classes (Section 29(3) ReO).

4.5.3 Creditor Selection

The debtor can generally choose which creditors to include in a restructuring.[79] This gives some room for the debtor to find individualized solutions. Still, the selection of creditors to be included in the plan must be justified (Section 27(2) n 6 ReO) and appropriate

---

74 Legislative Materials, above note 33, p. 17; M. Trenker in: P. Fidler, A. Konecny, S. Riel & M. Trenker (eds), above note 45, ReO § 29, Para. 2, 6; M. Fellner in: S. Mock & M. Zoppel (eds), above note 53, ReO § 29, Para. 15.

75 If certain creditor classes are in the respective case not existing or shall not be affected by the plan, also no class for such creditors must be formed (M. Trenker in: P. Fidler, A. Konecny, S. Riel & M. Trenker (eds), above note 45, ReO § 29, Para. 7).

76 U. Reisch, 'Restrukturierungsverfahren – Planinhalte, Planwirkungen', in: A. Konecny (ed), *ZIK-Spezial: RIRUG – Neuerungen im Restrukturierungs- und Insolvenzrecht*, Wien: LexisNexis, 2021, pp. 143-162 (p. 149); M. Trenker in: P. Fidler, A. Konecny, S. Riel & M. Trenker (eds), above note 45 ReO § 28, Para. 44, § 34, Para. 13 et seq.

77 M. Trenker in: P. Fidler, A. Konecny, S. Riel & M. Trenker (eds), above note 45, ReO § 29, Para. 6; see also U. Reisch, above note 76, p. 149.

78 See *e.g.* M. Trenker in: P. Fidler, A. Konecny, S. Riel & M. Trenker (eds), above note 45, ReO § 29, Para. 6 referring to scenarios of different types of secured creditors.

79 Legislative Materials, above note 33, p. 2.

(*sachgemäß*) (Section 30(1) n 4 ReO).[80] This may be the case if only financial creditors are included in the plan and suppliers or customers shall remain unaffected by the plan.[81]

4.5.4 Pre-review of the Plan (Vorprüfungsverfahren)

Upon plan presentation, the court reviews whether the plan meets the formal statutory requirements as well as whether key requirements such as the class formation or the selection of creditors are met (see previous sections). The court can ask the restructuring expert or an external expert to review the plausibility of the plan's reasoning on the viability of the business (*bedingte Fortbestehensprognose*) (Section 30(1), last sentence, ReO). If the statutory requirements are not met, the court can set a deadline to the debtor to improve the plan (Section 30(2) ReO). This option to review the presented plan prior to the voting and confirmation decision shall allow to remove obstacles as early as possible and is therefore to be welcomed.[82]

Other than the Netherlands,[83] the ReO still does not provide for interim court decisions where (potential) disputes between parties can already be resolved before plan voting and confirmation.

4.5.5 Plan Measures

In terms of possible plan measures becoming effective solely as a result of the plan confirmation, the ReO is far more restrictive than the broad definition of restructuring included in Article 1(1) PRD 2019 (and also more restrictive than Section 1(2) ReO might indicate).[84] Only financial restructuring measures can be implemented against the will of dissenting parties through an intra-class and a cross-class cram-down mechanism.[85] Any other restructuring measures require the consent of the affected party (Section 39(3) ReO).

- **Financial restructuring measures:** plan measures under the ReO are basically focused on (I) the reduction (haircut) of creditor claims (Sections 28 sentence 1 and 4 ReO, 29(1) ReO) and (II) the amendment of (re-)payment modalities (Section 28 sentence 3 ReO), especially the granting of moratoria. In addition, interest provisions[86] can be

80 See M. Trenker in: P. Fidler, A. Konecny, S. Riel & M. Trenker (eds), above note 45, ReO § 30, Para. 15 et seq.

81 Partly critical M. Trenker in: P. Fidler, A. Konecny, S. Riel & M. Trenker (eds), above note 45, ReO § 30, Para. 16 with reference to Legislative Materials, above note 33, p. 16.

82 See also M. Trenker in: P. Fidler, A. Konecny, S. Riel & M. Trenker (eds), above note 45, ReO § 30, Para. 1.

83 See further Chapter 7.

84 See also M. Trenker in: P. Fidler, A. Konecny, S. Riel & M. Trenker (eds), above note 45, ReO § 28, Para. 4 (*Minimalkonzept*).

85 See for the general differentiation also M. Trenker, above note 48, pp. 41-42; M. Trenker in: P. Fidler, A. Konecny, S. Riel & M. Trenker (eds), above note 45, ReO § 27, Para. 9.

86 Legislative Materials, above note 33, p. 17.

amended or covenants[87] can be installed.[88] Further amendments of contractual terms such as a debt exchange (*e.g.* exchange offers) or a transfer of debts to another debtor/entity cannot be imposed through a restructuring plan and therefore still require the consent of the affected parties.[89]

- **Operational and other restructuring measures:** other measures such as the termination of (onerous) operational and other contracts, refinancing measures, capital increases, corporate law measures (including debt equity swaps, *see* Section 4.7) and many more can be included in the overall restructuring plan but still follow the general rules of contract (and if relevant corporate) law.[90] This very limited scope especially for operational restructuring measures will in our expectation lead to the fact that debtors requiring such measures (such as store closures and employment cuts) will either still restructure through (public) insolvency proceeding under the IO (see above Section 2.3.1)[91] or such measures will not be taken at all (especially if also the IO does not provide more options, which is the case for corporate law measures).
- **Interim and new financings:** interim and new financings can be mentioned in the plan. But same as the above-mentioned 'other measures', they do, of course, require an agreement with the financier (so there is no possibility to force or cram-down new financiers to grant a financing). To still enhance the willingness to grant interim and new financings, the Austrian legislator implemented the avoidance protection of Article 17 PRD 2019. However, the implementation was made in a very restrictive way.[92] Therefore, it is unlikely that this protection will stimulate the willingness of financiers to participate in a restructuring.

4.5.6 Permissibility of a Liquidation Plan Doubtful

The ReO does neither provide nor exclude the option of a so-called liquidation plan. Also, the legislative materials do not refer to such an option. Whether a restructuring plan may

87 Ibid., p. 4.

88 See in detail M. Trenker in: P. Fidler, A. Konecny, S. Riel & M. Trenker (eds), above note 45, ReO § 29, Para. 4, 6-7.

89 See also M. Trenker in: P. Fidler, A. Konecny, S. Riel & M. Trenker (eds), above note 45, ReO § 28, Para. 5.

90 See details M. Trenker, above note 48, pp. 48-49; M. Trenker in: P. Fidler, A. Konecny, S. Riel & M. Trenker (eds), above note 45, ReO § 27, Para. 9; M. Nitsche, Lexis Briefing Restrukturierungsplan, available at: https://360.lexisnexis.at/d/lexisbriefings/restrukturierungsplan/h_80004_6505619560836035860_e0781c3f81?searchId=20220413153542715&page=1&index=1&origin=rl (last viewed 12 April 2022).

91 See for considerations on the selection of the 'right' procedure also A. Isola, S. Weileder & D. Seidl, 'Strategische Sanierungsplanung – Kriterien für die Verfahrenswahl', in: A. Konecny (ed), *ZIK-Spezial: RIRUG – Neuerungen im Restrukturierungs- und Insolvenzrecht*, Wien: LexisNexis, 2021, pp. 19-32 (pp. 19-20).

92 See in detail M. Trenker in: P. Fidler, A. Konecny, S. Riel & M. Trenker (eds), above note 45, IO §§ 36a, 36b, Para. 16 et seq; see also C. Jaufer & A. Painsi, 'Restrukturierungsverfahren: (Neu-)Finanzierungen und Transaktionen', in: A. Konecny (ed), *ZIK-Spezial: RIRUG – Neuerungen im Restrukturierungs- und Insolvenzrecht*, Wien: LexisNexis, 2021, pp. 163-172 (pp. 167-168).

be used for the liquidation, respectively winding up of a debtor's business, remains to be seen. As every restructuring plan must mandatorily include a forecast on the viability of the business (*bedingte Fortbestehensprognose*), it is rather doubtful that the use of a plan for liquidation of the business is permissible.

4.6 *Adoption and Confirmation of the Plan*

4.6.1 Adoption

Voting on the restructuring plan is made in a court hearing to be scheduled 30 to 60 days after the debtor presented the plan (Section 31(1) ReO). The pre-review of the plan (see Section 4.5.4) has to be successfully concluded before such hearing. Furthermore, the debtor must send the restructuring plan to the creditors voting on the plan at the latest within two weeks before the restructuring plan hearing.

In the hearing, only affected creditors are entitled to vote. The voting right is calculated based on the claims included in the restructuring plan plus interest until the day the restructuring plan was presented (Section 32(1) ReO). Affected creditors can raise concerns (*Einwendungen*) against the voting rights of other creditors by contesting their claims included in the restructuring plan (Section 32(2) ReO). However, the court only decides on such contestations if the consideration of the contested claims would have an effect on the positive or negative outcome of the voting.[93] The court can appoint a restructuring expert to examine such concerns (Section 9(3) n 4 in connection with 32(3) ReO).

The plan is adopted by the creditors if in every creditor class, (i) the simple majority in number and (ii) a majority of at least 75% in value (both calculated based on the creditors present at the hearing) vote in favour of the plan (Section 33(1) ReO). If one or more creditor classes dissent, there is still the possibility to substitute their consent via a cross-class cram-down (see below Section 4.6.4).

4.6.2 Confirmation

When deciding on sanctioning the plan, the court must examine whether the statutory requirements such as (i) the above-mentioned majorities or (ii) the requirements for the class formation or the creditor selection are met, and (iii) whether none of the grounds for refusal (*Versagungsgründe*) according to Section 34(3) ReO apply. Such grounds for refusal correspond to the impermissibility reasons which are already relevant at the beginning of the proceedings, such as the fact that the plan is not suitable to ensure the viability of the

93 See in detail M. Trenker in: P. Fidler, A. Konecny, S. Riel & M. Trenker (eds), above note 45, ReO § 32, Para. 12; see further N. Mooseder & D. Gerstberger in: D. Aigner, D. Gerstberger, N. Mooseder & T. Zeitler (eds), above note 51, pp. 237-238.

business, the non-existence of likelihood of insolvency or the existence of illiquidity of the debtor (*see* Section 4.2).

Further particularly relevant confirmation requirements to be considered by the court *ex officio* are the equal treatment of creditors within every class (Section 34(1) n 2 ReO)[94] and the prohibition of special benefits (*Sonderbegünstigung*) granted to individual creditors in connection with the restructuring plan (Section 34(3) n 2 ReO).[95] To sum up, the list of possible grounds for refusal in Section 34 ReO is rather long. This might conflict with the principle of efficiency intended by the PRD 2019 and reduce the practical attractiveness of the ReO.[96]

4.6.3 Best Interest of Creditors Test

The best interest of creditors test (*Kriterium des Gläubigerinteresses*) is a further key confirmation requirement but must only be examined by the court upon application of a dissenting creditor (Section 33(2) ReO). The test is defined very similar to the PRD 2019 stating that a dissenting creditor shall not be treated worse than in the next best alternative scenario. This scenario can be a rehabilitation plan (*Sanierungsplan*) under the IO, the sale of the entire business or its liquidation in an insolvency proceeding.[97]

4.6.4 Cross-Class Cram-Down (Fairness Test)

If the required majority is not reached in every class, Section 36 ReO also allows for a cross-class cram-down (*klassenübergreifender Cram-down*). According to this provision, a plan can still be confirmed if (i) the majority of classes including the secured creditors or the majority of the 'in the money' classes voted in favour of the plan, and (ii) dissenting creditor classes are not treated worse than same ranking and treated better than subordinated classes.[98] In this context, the Austrian legislator has explicitly implemented the relative priority rule (and not the absolute priority rule) and justified this with the fact that already the IO allows for the relative priority rule when dealing with statutorily subordinated creditors.[99] Other than in other countries where a so-called relaxed absolute priority rule (meaning possible exceptions from the absolute priority rule)[100] is applied,

94 M. Trenker in: P. Fidler, A. Konecny, S. Riel & M. Trenker (eds), above note 45, ReO § 34, Para. 13

95 See in detail M. Trenker in: P. Fidler, A. Konecny, S. Riel & M. Trenker (eds), above note 45, ReO § 39, Para. 28-29.

96 M. Trenker in: P. Fidler, A. Konecny, S. Riel & M. Trenker (eds), above note 45, ReO § 34, Para. 4.

97 M. Nitsche, above note 90; U. Reisch, above note 76, p. 157; P. Fidler in: P. Fidler, A. Konecny, S. Riel & M. Trenker (eds), above note 45, ReO § 35, Para. 8 et seq, see particularly Para. 23-24; see also Legislative Materials, above note 33, p. 20.

98 The ranking follows the hierarchy in insolvency proceedings (Legislative Materials, above note 33, p. 20); see in detail M. Lutschounig in: M. Zoppel & S. Mock (eds), above note 53, ReO § 36, Para. 8-9.

99 Legislative Materials, above note 33, p. 20.

100 See *e.g.* for the Netherlands Chapter 7.

the ReO goes a different route setting the relative priority rule as the standard rule to be respected.

4.6.5 Appeals

If a dissenting creditor raises a breach of the best interest test or the fairness test (requirements of a cross-class cram-down) within or at the latest seven days after the restructuring plan hearing, the debtor's business must be evaluated in order to assess whether such breach does in fact exist (Section 38 ReO). The court can appoint an external expert or ask the restructuring expert to perform this evaluation (Section 38(2) ReO).[101]

If the court confirms the plan, any dissenting creditor can file an appeal against the decision which has as a general rule no suspensive effect (Section 40(2) ReO). The same applies for the debtor and any creditor voting in favour of the plan in relation to a negative court decision.

In case of a successful appeal against the sanctioned plan, the court can still uphold its decision if this is in the best interest of the creditors. However, in such a case, the debtor must pay compensation to the successfully challenging dissenting creditor (Section 40(5) ReO).[102] The option to uphold challenged court decisions is to be welcomed, but the way the ReO legislator has implemented it is partly inconsistent, for instance, why not generally give the restructuring court more flexibility in upholding decisions being in the best interest of creditors despite minor grounds for refusal? In addition, this approach will likely bring about more disputes (especially on the determination of the amount of compensation).[103]

4.6.6 Effects of a Restructuring Plan

The sanctioned and effective plan is binding on all affected creditors, regardless of their consenting or dissenting vote. As mentioned previously, only those creditors whose claims are reduced or extended may be referred to as affected creditors. Naturally, creditors not included in the plan are not bound by the plan (Section 39(1) ReO).[104]

Security granted by third parties is not affected and can also not be included in the plan against the will of the secured creditor. Still, from the perspective of the debtor, the

101 See P. Fidler in: P. Fidler, A. Konecny, S. Riel & M. Trenker (eds), above note 45, ReO § 38, Para. 33 et seq; M. Lutschounig in: M. Zoppel & S. Mock (eds), above note 53, ReO § 43, Para. 14.

102 The legal nature of this compensation is unfortunately not addressed in the ReO; for further reflections on this compensation see M. Trenker in: P. Fidler, A. Konecny, S. Riel & M. Trenker (eds), above note 45, ReO § 40, Para. 45-48.

103 See M. Trenker in: P. Fidler, A. Konecny, S. Riel & M. Trenker (eds), above note 45, ReO § 40, Para. 1-2.

104 See in detail M. Trenker in: P. Fidler, A. Konecny, S. Riel & M. Trenker (eds), above note 45, ReO § 39, Para. 1-2.

principle of single payment[105] applies, meaning that payment of the agreed restructuring plan quota by the debtor to its creditor also releases the debtor from recourse claims towards third-party guarantors, pledgors, etc. (Section 39(4) ReO in connection with Section 156(2) IO).

4.7 (Missing) Possibilities for a Debt-for-Equity Swap and Other Corporate Measures

The ReO does not provide for the option of a debt-for-equity swap against the will of the equity holders. Section 37 ReO more or less quotes Article 12 and recital 57 PRD 2019, stating that equity holders shall not be allowed to unreasonably prevent or create obstacles to the adoption and confirmation and implementation of a restructuring plan. At the same time, Section 37(1) ReO states that if the restructuring plan provides measures which require the consent of the equity holders, the provisions of corporate law must be respected. Only if the plan does not interfere with the legal or economic position (*rechtliche oder wirtschaftliche Stellung*) of the equity holder, the court can be asked to replace the consent of a non-consenting equity holder. In practice, most measures relating to the debtor company will directly or at least indirectly interfere with the legal or economic position of shareholders; in most of the cases, any restructuring may therefore be at the risk of the equity holders taking potential hold-out positions.[106] Furthermore, it remains uncertain if this replacement of the shareholders' consent is applicable to all individual plan measures or only to the initiation of restructuring proceedings.[107]

The lack of innovation of the ReO legislator has also been criticized during the legislative process.[108] This self-restraint was still not entirely surprising as already in the last large insolvency reform in 2010, the inclusion of a debt-for-equity swap was discussed and partly demanded, but at the end not implemented.[109] It remains to be seen whether and how this discussion will develop in future.[110]

---

105 M. Trenker in: P. Fidler, A. Konecny, S. Riel & M. Trenker (eds), above note 45, ReO § 39, Para. 18 (*Grundsatz der einmaligen Zahlungspflicht*).

106 G. Wabl & G. Gassner, above note 59, p. 213 et seq and p. 218 (also arguing that because of the very limited scope of the safeguards in Section 37 ReO the Austrian legislator might have failed the requirements of Art. 12 PRD 2019).

107 Whereas G. Wabl & G. Gassner, above note 59, p. 215 et seq, and P. Fidler in: P. Fidler, A. Konecny, S. Riel & M. Trenker (eds), above note 45, ReO § 37, Para. 50 et seq, argue that this provision applies to all corporate measures, Legislative Materials, above note 33, p. 21 indicate the latter; see also M. Trenker & M. Lutschounig, above note 22, p. 65; M. Lutschounig in: M. Zoppel & S. Mock (eds), above note 53, ReO § 37, Para. 14.

108 See sources above note 38.

109 At that time the legislator stated in the materials that there was no need for such debt equity swap in practice (Legislative Materials, *Regierungsvorlage* Nr. 612/XXIV. 21 April 2010, p. 3).

110 See also G. Wabl & G. Gassner, above note 59, p. 218.

4.8 Executory Contracts

As mentioned in Section 4.5.5 under plan measures, a restructuring plan cannot provide for a forced amendment and/or termination of executory contracts without the consent of the other party. Contract law still applies. On this point, Austrian law therefore lags behind other jurisdictions such as the Netherlands.[111] This was partly addressed throughout the legislative process[112] but as far as can be seen, no substantive discussion on the implementation of such termination rights has taken place yet.

4.9 International Jurisdiction and Recognition

4.9.1 Jurisdiction

As stated in Section 4.3, the jurisdiction for ReO proceedings follows the rules for insolvency proceedings (Section 4 ReO in connection with Section 63 IO). The competent court is therefore the court where the debtor operates its business at the time of filing the application. This rule determines the jurisdiction within Austria. Whether it also determines the international jurisdiction is not clear yet. The EIR 2015 is without any doubt not applicable to restructuring proceedings due to their confidentiality (except for European restructuring proceedings, *see* Section 4.10).[113] Still, it can be argued that the Brussels Ia Regulation[114] applies.[115] The opposite view denies the applicability of the Brussels Ia Regulation with good arguments and determines the international jurisdiction based on Austrian autonomous law.[116] In that case, international jurisdiction of Austrian

111 See *e.g.* Chapter 7 on the Dutch WHOA; see also G. Wabl & G.-J. Boon 'Das neue "Dutch scheme" – die Niederlande am Weg zum neuen Restrukturierungshub?', *Zeitschrift für Insolvenzrecht und Kreditschutz*, 2020, 26 (4), pp. 151-156.

112 See *e.g.* G. Wabl & G. Gassner, above note 38, p. 2 et seq.

113 R. Weber-Wilfert, 'Das Europäische Restrukturierungsverfahren', in: A. Konecny (ed), *ZIK-Spezial: RIRUG – Neuerungen im Restrukturierungs- und Insolvenzrecht*, Wien: LexisNexis, 2021, pp. 173-185 (pp. 181, 183); A. Konecny in: P. Fidler, A. Konecny, S. Riel & M. Trenker (eds), above note 45, ReO § 4, Para. 11 et seq, 14; M. Trenker & F. Loewit, 'Grenzüberschreitende präventive Restrukturierungsverfahren – Zuständigkeit, Anerkennung und anwendbares Recht bei Restrukturierungsverfahren mit Auslandsbezug (Teil 1)', *Juristische Blätter*, 2023, 145 (2), pp. 78-91 (p. 80).

114 Regulation (EU) 1215/2012 of the European Parliament and of the Council of 12 December 2012 on jurisdiction and the recognition and enforcement of judgments in civil and commercial matters (recast).

115 See *e.g.* D. Skauradszun, 'Die Restrukturierungsrichtlinie und das „verschwitzte" internationale Zivilverfahrensrecht', *Zeitschrift für Wirtschaftsrecht*, 2019, 40 (32), pp. 1501-1507 (p. 1503); J. Schmidt, 'Präventiver Restrukturierungsrahmen: Internationale Zuständigkeit, Anerkennung und anwendbares Recht', *Zeitschrift für das gesamte Insolvenzrecht*, 2021, 24 (13-14), pp. 654-661 (p. 656 et seq).

116 A. Konecny in: P. Fidler, A. Konecny, S. Riel & M. Trenker (eds), above note 45, ReO § 4, Para. 16; R. Weber-Wilfert, above note 113, p. 183; M. Trenker & M. Lutschounig, above note 22, p. 29 et seq; M. Trenker & F. Loewit, above note 113, pp. 81-85; see also C. Thole, 'Vertrauliche Restrukturierungsverfahren: Internationale Zuständigkeit, anwendbares Recht und Anerkennung', *Zeitschrift für Wirtschaftsrecht*, 2021, 42(42), pp. 2153-2162 (p. 2156).

courts is given if the debtor operates its business in Austria (Section 27a of the Austrian *Jurisdiktionsnorm* in connection with Section 63 IO).[117] Nevertheless, a clarification by the European Court of Justice seems necessary.

4.9.2 Recognition

The recognition of confidential restructuring proceedings in the EU is neither addressed in the ReO nor in the PRD 2019; especially the latter is hardly understandable to us. Similar to the international jurisdiction, the applicability of the Brussels Ia Regulation comes into question. Right now, as mentioned above, the tendency in the Austrian literature convincingly argues that confidential restructuring proceedings cannot fall within the scope of Brussels Ia based on the exception of Article 1(2) lit b of the Regulation.[118] As a result, recognition would depend on autonomous Austrian law and here most likely Section 240 IO applies *per analogiam*. Again, a clarification by the European Court of Justice seems unavoidable. Until then, in the Austrian context, significant uncertainty remains in confidential restructurings with cross-border implications.

4.10 European Restructuring Proceedings

In contrast to regular and simplified restructuring proceedings (on the latter, *see* Section 4.11) the initiation of so-called European restructuring proceedings (Section 44 ReO) is announced publicly upon request of the debtor.[119] The prevailing opinion is that the European restructuring proceedings are a separate type of procedure.[120] It may also offer several advantages to the debtor:

– To start with, the EIR 2015 is applicable in case of cross-border implications because the procedure is not conducted *in camera* (other than regular proceedings, *see* Section 4.2).[121] Meanwhile, the European restructuring procedure is already part of

117 R. Weber-Wilfert, above note 113, p. 183; A. Konecny in: P. Fidler, A. Konecny, S. Riel & M. Trenker (eds), above note 45, ReO § 4, Para. 16; M. Trenker & F. Loewit, above note 113, pp. 85-86.

118 R. Weber-Wilfert, above note 113, pp. 181-182; A. Konecny in: P. Fidler, A. Konecny, S. Riel & M. Trenker (eds), above note 45, ReO § 4, Para. 15; M. Trenker & F. Loewit, above note 113, pp. 86-90; for Germany see C. Thole, above note 116, pp. 2154-2155.

119 In this respect, the designation 'European' is misleading as a cross-border reference is not a procedural requirement; see A. Konecny, 'Die neuen Verfahrensgebäude im Restrukturierungs- und Insolvenzrecht', in: A. Konecny (ed), ZIK-*Spezial: RIRUG – Neuerungen im Restrukturierungs- und Insolvenzrecht*, Wien: LexisNexis, 2021, pp. 1-18 (p. 11); M. Trenker & M. Lutschounig, above note 22, pp. 18-19.

120 A. Konecny, above note 119, p. 6; A. Konecny in: P. Fidler, A. Konecny, S. Riel & M. Trenker (eds), above note 45, ReO § 44, Para. 1; dissenting R. Weber-Wilfert, above note 113, p. 174.

121 A. Konecny in: P. Fidler, A. Konecny, S. Riel & M. Trenker (eds), above note 45, ReO § 4, Para. 12; R. Weber-Wilfert, above note 113, pp. 179-180.

Annex A EIR 2015.[122] Therefore, European restructuring proceedings can be opened in Austria if the debtor has an Austrian COMI (Art. 3 Para 1 EIR 2015).[123] Consequently, an establishment in Austria also allows secondary/territorial proceedings (Art. 3 Para 2 EIR 2015). Moreover, automatic mutual recognition of (foreign) court decisions is guaranteed (see especially Art. 19 EIR 2015 et seq).[124]

- Furthermore, the debtor can ask the court to publish a request to the creditors to file their claims (*Forderungsanmeldung*) (Section 44 Para 4 ReO). Creditors who do not file their claim in time may not participate in the proceedings, yet the restructuring plan can be binding on them(!).[125]
- Also, a stay of enforcement actions may be extended to all creditors (Section 44 Para 3 ReO),[126] which is only permissible within this type of procedure (*see* Section 4.4.1).

4.11 Simplified Restructuring Proceedings

The arguably most innovative invention of the ReO legislator are the so-called simplified restructuring proceedings (*Vereinfachtes Restrukturierungsverfahren*) which are addressed in only Section 45. If only financial creditors are affected (the term may be interpreted in a broad way and can include any claims with financing nature such as *e.g.* supply loans),[127] most aspects of the regular proceedings can be short-tracked.

- Instead of the voting on a restructuring plan, the debtor shall already present a restructuring agreement signed by the necessary creditor majorities (Section 45(4) n1 ReO, see below).
- The proceedings are always debtor in possession, no restructuring expert can be appointed (Section 45(5) ReO).
- Safeguards such as the appropriateness of the class formation or the best interest test shall be ensured through an expert opinion confirming that all statutory requirements are met (Section 45(8) ReO).

122 See Regulation (EU) 2021/2260 of the European Parliament and of the Council of 15 December 2021 amending Regulation (EU) 2015/848 on insolvency proceedings to replace its Annexes A and B.

123 A. Konecny in: P. Fidler, A. Konecny, S. Riel & M. Trenker (eds), above note 45, ReO § 4, Para. 13.

124 R. Weber-Wilfert, above note 113, p. 179.

125 More detailed A. Konecny in: P. Fidler, A. Konecny, S. Riel & M. Trenker (eds), above note 45, ReO § 44, Para. 67 et seq.

126 See A. Konecny in: P. Fidler, A. Konecny, S. Riel & M. Trenker (eds), above note 45, ReO § 44, Para. 55 et seq.

127 Legislative Materials, above note 33, p. 25; W. Höller, M. Simsa & P. Wetter, 'Das vereinfachte Restrukturierungsverfahren', in: A. Konecny (ed), *ZIK-Spezial: RIRUG – Neuerungen im Restrukturierungs- und Insolvenzrecht*, Wien: LexisNexis, 2021, pp. 187-200 (p. 190); P. Fidler in: P. Fidler, A. Konecny, S. Riel & M. Trenker (eds), above note 45, ReO § 45, Para. 12 et seq.

- Through this slim process, such proceedings can in fact be fast-track proceedings; they can be performed and become legally effective within only a few weeks. Furthermore, the outsourcing of some criteria to an expert opinion might contribute to a higher planning (and deal) security. It therefore does not come as a surprise that the proceedings were also broadly welcomed, especially by practitioners, presumably closing a gap in private workouts and potentially taking the wind out of the sails of hold-out creditors.[128]

However, there are still some points worth criticizing:

- The majority requirements are higher than in normal proceedings as 75% of the claims in value in every creditor class must agree to the plan (Section 45(3) n 3 ReO). With this majority requirement in every class, the option of a cross-class cram-down is excluded for simplified proceedings.[129] This is not comprehensible, has also been criticized in the legislative process[130] and it may even be questioned whether this was in fact intended by the legislator.
- Simplified proceedings do finally not allow for a stay (Section 45(6) ReO), which may also be seen critically.[131]

Notwithstanding this criticism, we expect that the existence of the simplified proceedings can and will change the negotiation powers in restructurings, which is why this invention of the legislator is to be absolutely welcomed.

5 Outlook

All in all, the analysis made in this chapter shows that there is certainly need to still improve the ReO in several aspects. Nevertheless, there are also positive points. The fast-tack proceedings for financial restructurings show the innovative capacity of the Austrian legislator. Also, the pragmatic and clear commitment to applying the relative priority rule is, considering the partly controversial discussion amongst European scholars, in our eyes remarkable. In addition, the fact that debtors can choose between confidential (regular and fast-track) as well as published (European) proceedings brings more options and flexibilities to rescue businesses in financial difficulties.

128 G. Gassner, E. Welten & G. Wabl, above note 35; W. Höller, M. Simsa & P. Wetter, above note 127, pp. 187-188, 200.

129 W. Höller, M. Simsa & P. Wetter, above note 127, p. 193; P. Fidler in: P. Fidler, A. Konecny, S. Riel & M. Trenker (eds), above note 45, ReO § 45, Para. 51.

130 See G. Wabl & G. Gassner, above note 38, p. 8 et seq.

131 Ibid.

Still, the fact that the ReO legislator included partly unclear and in our eyes in some aspects also excessive protection mechanisms as well as cost-intensive documentation and examination requirements takes away the attractiveness of the ReO proceedings. This brings significant uncertainty for debtors and makes the proceedings at the same time costly, likely too costly for most of the SMEs.

Also, the limited scope of restructuring measures which can actually be imposed against dissenting creditors takes away a lot of flexibility. Finally, the more or less entirely missing link between the ReO and Austrian corporate law leads to the very unsatisfying result that in practice, restructurings must also in future still be structured around non-constructive equity holders,[132] who may even be able to get an unjustified 'free ride'.

Reading this, it may not come as a surprise that until the finalization of this chapter , not a single case of a restructuring proceeding under the ReO has come to light. The fact that generally also the number of insolvencies is just recovering from an all-time low caused by the public COVID-19 support measures may have contributed to this. Still, in summary we expect that at least the simplified restructuring proceeding will find its place in the market for financial restructurings. Furthermore, the mere possibility to cram-down dissenting creditors in formal restructuring proceedings might be useful to negotiate private workouts. Whether regular and European restructuring proceedings in the current form will be frequently used is, however, more than doubtful.

6 CONCLUSION

In summary, the Austrian implementation of the PRD 2019 through the ReO has brought out several aspects, which might facilitate the desired strengthening of a preventive restructuring culture as well as a general further development of relevant aspects of Austrian law. In order to become a success model and a real game changer, the ReO should still in the details be fundamentally revised, simplified and shortened. Otherwise, it is to be expected that for the large number of Austrian companies and entrepreneurs, the proceedings will be too complicated, uncertain and expensive, leaving the practical scope of application for larger and especially financial restructurings. The opportunity to implement proceedings practicable and attractive for the broader Austrian business landscape has therefore so far been missed.

132 G. Gassner, E. Welten & G. Wabl, above note 35.

3 DENMARK

Line Langkjaer[*]

1 INTRODUCTION

On 9 June 2022, the Danish Parliament adopted amendments to the Danish Bankruptcy Law[133] to implement the Preventive Restructuring Directive (PRD) 2019.[134] This new law entered into force on 17 July 2022, just in time for the implementation deadline of the PRD 2019. Denmark has opted out of the EU regulation concerning Justice and Home Affairs, which is why Denmark is among other things not bound by the European Insolvency Regulation (EIR) 2015.[135] The legal basis of the PRD 2019 is, however, Article 53 of the Treaty on the Functioning of the European Union (TFEU), dealing with the right to establishment. Therefore, for the first time in the history of Danish insolvency law, Denmark was obliged to implement EU legislation in the area of insolvency law.

This chapter is structured as follows. Section 2 presents an outline of the Danish pre-reform insolvency law regime. Section 3 elaborates on the implementation of a new preventive restructuring regimes in Denmark. Section 4 discusses the main features of the new preventive restructuring framework. Section 5 provides an outlook and concluding remarks.

2 OVERVIEW OF DOMESTIC PRE-REFORM INSOLVENCY LAW REGIME

Before 2022, only two collective insolvency procedures were available for a distressed business in Denmark. Both were (and are) governed by the Danish Bankruptcy Act (DBA), which originally dates back to 1977.[136] First, an insolvent debtor can enter into bankruptcy. Bankruptcy is a liquidation procedure in which the debtor's assets are

* This chapter only refers to material publicly available prior to the closing of the chapter on 15 October 2022.

133 L 181/2022 Lov om ændring af konkursloven.

134 Directive (EU) 2019/1023 of the European Parliament and of the Council of 20 June 2019 on preventive restructuring frameworks, on discharge of debt and disqualifications, and on measures to increase the efficiency of procedures concerning restructuring, insolvency and discharge of debt, and amending Directive (EU) 2017/1132 (Directive on restructuring and insolvency), O.J. L 172/18

135 Preamble 88 in Regulation (EU) 2015/838 of the European Parliament and of the Council of 20 May 2015 on insolvency proceedings (recast), O.J. L 141/19.

136 Consolidated Act No 775 2021, Bankruptcy Act, with later amendments, 'Danish Bankruptcy Act' ('*Konkursloven*') (DBA). Judicial debt relief is also available as a formal procedure for natural persons.

liquidated and the proceeds are distributed among the creditors based on the *pari passu* principle.[137] The overarching purpose of bankruptcy is to maximize the recovery rate for the creditors.

Second, an insolvent debtor can enter into restructuring. This procedure was introduced in 2011 and has been amended in 2021 and 2022. The purpose was to provide a court-regulated procedure for an insolvent debtor, making it possible to rescue an otherwise viable business through a restructuring plan.[138] Officially, the amendments in 2021 were triggered by the expected financial impact of the COVID-19 pandemic on the Danish businesses. However, the changes had already been recommended in 2015 by the Danish Bankruptcy Council (*Konkursrådet*), an advisory board for the government. They aimed to increase the efficiency of the Danish restructuring regime but were never put forward.[139] The 2021 amendments introduced a separate "fast-track restructuring procedure", under which the debtor was allowed to transfer his business without the need to hold formal meetings in court. In fact, the transfer was possible through an informal voting system based on deemed approval. Moreover, the former mandatory requirement of a court-appointed accountant was also abandoned to, principally, reduce costs. Prior to the 2021 amendments, approximately 97% of all formal insolvency procedures that were commenced in Denmark were bankruptcy procedures.[140] Stakeholders, including insolvency advisors and creditor organizations, had continuously questioned the efficiency of the restructuring procedure, highlighting that it is rigid, costly and inefficient compared to that of the bankruptcy procedure.[141] Based on this critique, it was the intention of the adopted amendments in 2021 that the restructuring procedure would become more flexible, cheaper and, therefore, more useful for insolvent (yet viable) debtors to overcome their financial difficulties.[142]

3 Implementing the PRD 2019 in Denmark

The implementation of the PRD 2019 brought significant changes in the existing regulation and introduced a completely new procedure. As mentioned above, implementing EU law in Danish insolvency law was a novelty. Moreover, the possibility of opening a procedure prior to the debtor's insolvency, along with a class voting system, was unfamiliar to Danish

137 Some claims are considered privileged, such as workers claim.

138 Indsæt konkursrådets udtalelse (COVID).

139 See more Betænkning nr 1555 om Ansattes retsstilling under insolvensbehandling, 190-200.

140 Ernst and Young: Rekonstruktion, Hvordan virker reglerne i praksis, September 2014.

141 See J. Paulsen, '5 år med rekonstruktionsbehandling', *Erhvervsjuridisk Tidsskrift* (2017), ET.2017.23; N. Vendelbo and M. Trabjerg Knudsen, 'Revision og Regnskabsvæsen' (2020), *R R online* 2020.09.0068, and J. Paulsen and I.M. Dam, 'Revision og Regnskabsvæsen' (2020), *R R* 2020.08.60.

142 Konkursrådets udtalelse af 3. juli 2020, p. 1. See also the public consultation to L65, FT 2020-21, Tillæg A.

law. It was, in fact, instantly met with some scepticism from various stakeholders. The governmental advisory body – Konkursrådet – even referred to the class system of the PRD 2019 as "unnecessarily complicated", and pointed out that it can "potentially lead to an increase in costs".[143] As also mentioned in Section 2, the amendments to the restructuring procedure were already introduced in 2021. Yet, the implementation of the PRD 2019 seems to introduce mandatory requirements put forward by the EU, but not necessarily tailored to the needs of Danish insolvency law. However, the PRD 2019s provisions on executory contracts provided an opportunity to fine-tune the existing Danish framework, for both the ordinary restructuring and the bankruptcy procedures, along of course with the newly introduced preventive restructuring procedure. These fine-tuning changes initiated by the PRD 2019 have been warmly received by the stakeholders in Danish insolvency law.

In October 2019, the Danish Ministry of Justice mandated the governmental advisory body – Konkursrådet – to consider the legal consequences of the PRD 2019 in Danish insolvency law. This was coupled with a mandate to propose new legislation that aimed to make Danish insolvency law compliant with EU law.[144] Due to COVID-19, the preparatory work of Konkursrådet was postponed, and in May 2021, the Ministry of Justice asked the EU Commission for a suspension on implementation until 17 July 2022, which was, subsequently, granted. In February 2022, Konkursrådet published its report on the implementation and a proposal for amendments to the Danish Bankruptcy Act. In March 2022, a public consultation was held, with mainly positive remarks towards the proposal put forward. However, it was also reiterated that the existing framework seemed to be efficient and to function overall well. In fact, some of the suggested provisions, specifically the voting system provisions based on Article 9 PRD 2019, were regarded as overcomplicating the existing process.[145] In the course of April-June 2022, the proposal went through the ordinary legislative process without any significant changes and was finally unanimously adopted on 9 June 2022.

4 Main Features Introduced by the Reform

4.1 *Objective and Scope of the Procedure*

The objective of the new preventive restructuring procedure is to provide not only insolvent debtors but also not yet insolvent debtors with a procedure to overcome or avoid

143 Betænkning 1579/2022, p. 137.

144 Ibid., p. 14.

145 Retsudvalget 2021-22 – L181, Bilag 1.

their insolvency. Only debtors that engage in commercial activities – meaning non-consumers – can use the procedure. Not providing the same opportunities for consumers is a novelty for Danish insolvency law, but it is reasoned by the purpose of the procedure, which is to rescue viable businesses. A debtor who has been placed in compulsory dissolution by a public authority cannot make use of the new procedure.

4.2 *Criteria/Test to Enter the New Procedure*

Before 2022, Danish insolvency law only operated with the legal concept of insolvency. According to Danish law, a debtor is insolvent when he is unable to meet his liabilities as and when they fall due, unless this inability is deemed to be temporary.[146] Unlike this insolvency standard, the likelihood of insolvency is not defined in Danish law. However, a debtor is assumed to be in a likelihood of insolvency when this is not disputed.

Since only the debtor – and not the creditors – can initiate the commencement of the procedure, it is expected that it will be very rarely questioned whether the debtor is in a likelihood of insolvency or not. The court is obliged to try if the condition is met if the circumstances of the case call for it and when disputed, the bankruptcy court will make a decision. The preparatory works provide eight examples of what is meant by likelihood of insolvency. A debtor could be considered in a likelihood of insolvency if he is "balance sheet insolvent" (liabilities exceed his assets) or when he is in a stage of temporary insolvency.[147] It is worth noticing, however, that according to the preparatory works, the threshold should not be set too high, and Konkursrådet also explicitly mentioned that they do not expect or even foresee events of abuse relating to the opening of the procedure.[148] In this regard, it is worth mentioning that the Danish legislator did not choose to implement a viability test at the opening of the procedure. If a court deems the procedure to be 'hopeless', the court could end it or refrain from opening it.[149]

4.3 *Involved Actors*

In accordance with PRD 2019, the starting point is that the debtor keeps full control over his assets and business as such. It is – unlike other insolvency procedures in Danish law – not mandatory for the court to appoint an insolvency practitioner (IP). However, if a debtor requires a stay, the appointment of an IP is mandatory and the debtor is no longer in full control, however still in general in possession of this assets. The IP facilitates, assists

146 Cf. DBA Section 17(2).
147 Betænkning, p. 96.
148 Ibid.
149 Cf. DBA Section 9 h.

and supervises the debtor in the procedure. Furthermore, a debtor is not entitled to enter into any transactions of *material significance* without the consent of the IP.

It is also possible for the court to appoint a restructuring accountant in supplement to the IP. The accountant would then prepare and approve financial and accounting records that could support the procedure.[150] While the debtor maintains the control, the creditor's role in the restructuring procedure sees only to the potential adoption of the restructuring plan in which only affected creditors, but not shareholders, are entitled to vote in order for the plan to become binding.

4.4 *Stay*

The PRD 2019s provisions on the stay of individual enforcement brought significant novelties to Danish insolvency law. First, the stay is now granted upon request of the debtor and therefore non-automatic. The only reason for the court to deny the stay is if the procedure cannot be continued, *i.e.* when the court considers it hopeless, and when the debtor is acting disloyal or has become solvent.[151] Therefore, the room for the court's discretion in granting the stay or not is quite limited. If the stay is granted, its scope includes all creditors, except the workers who have privileged claims.[152] The stay will initially last for 4 weeks, but can be extended by the bankruptcy court up to a year. If the debtor – after a preventive restructuring procedure – commences an ordinary restructuring procedure, the maximum duration of the stay during the latter procedure will be reduced, meaning that no creditors will be affected by a stay for more than a year in total.

4.5 *The Plan and the Adoption Hereof*

Before the amendments in 2022 – and still in effect regarding the ordinary restructuring procedure – the adoption of a restructuring plan had a two-stage process. First, the debtor and the practitioner in the field of restructuring (PIFOR) had to present a tentative plan 4 weeks after the commencement of the procedure, which was voted on by the creditors. The reason for this step was to provide a solid mandate for the PIFOR to continue its efforts (and for incurring the related costs) of rescuing the debtor's business, as well as engaging the creditors at a very early stage. If the tentative plan was not adopted, the restructuring procedure would be terminated, and bankruptcy would commence automatically. If, however, the tentative plan was adopted, the debtor and the PIFOR could

150 Cf. DBA Section 9 (b).
151 Cf. DBA Section 9 (h).
152 Cf. DBA Section 9 (d) (2).

continue the negotiations and take up the necessary steps in this regard, but no later than 6 months after the adoption of the tentative plan would the final plan then have to be presented and voted by the creditors.[153] To simplify the process, the first stage of this two-stage procedure has now been eliminated, when proposing a plan in the preventive restructuring procedure.[154] Only the final plan must now be presented to the creditors and will be voted on.

Prior to this, the 2022 proposed plan had to consist of either a compulsory composition or a sale of the business. If neither of these elements were present, the court could not confirm the plan. While it is still possible for the debtor to propose either a composition or a business transfer, this is no longer mandatory. Both in a preventive restructuring procedure and in an ordinary restructuring procedure the debtor is now free to propose any solution to the financial difficulties that will restore the debtor's solvency.[155] It is, however, still possible to propose a liquidation plan,[156] even though this does not necessarily restore the debtor's solvency.

To ensure that the basis for the creditor's decision is sufficient, the DBA consists of a fairly long list of mandatory information that must be provided to the creditors no later than 5 days before the creditors' voting meeting.[157] This includes accounting information, information on assets and liability, a statement from the PIFOR regarding the analysis of both the causes of the financial difficulties, as well as whether the proposed plan is fair and feasible.[158] These requirements were already in place before the implementation of the PRD 2019 and the legislator provided that the existing information requirements were in accordance with Article 8 PRD 2019, so the existing rules were not amended.[159]

At the creditors' meeting, the affected creditors must vote on the plan. The voting system and rules underwent significant changes due to the requirements of the PRD 2019. As mentioned before, class formation and voting did not exist in Danish law prior to 2022. The voting system was basically turned upside down. To reduce the differences between the preventive and ordinary restructuring procedures, the new voting system has also been introduced in the existing procedure. Prior to the implementation of the PRD 2019, a restructuring plan was approved if there was not a majority of creditors – based on the amount of the claims – who voted against the plan. This provided for a very flexible and efficient voting system, and often only a few – if any – creditors would be present at the voting meeting. It was – and still is – allowed to vote by proxy, and often the PIFOR would

153 Cf. DBA Section 13.
154 Cf. DBA Section 9 (f).
155 Cf. DBA Section 10.
156 Cf. DBA Section 10 (a).
157 Cf. DBA Section 13.
158 Cf. DBA Section 13 (b) (2).
159 Betænkning 1579/2022, p. 124.

do this on behalf of some of the major creditors. This 'deemed approval' system was rolled back, as the legislator explicitly mentioned that this was a requirement of Article 9(6) PRD.[160] It is therefore now required that a majority of the creditors present at the meeting based on the amount of their claims must vote in favour of the plan. When voting in classes, the creditors in each class will vote on the plan, and the creditors adopt the plan when the majority of the classes is in favour of the plan. The Danish legislator refrained from granting voting rights to equity holders, and exempted the related parties from voting plan as well.

Class voting was introduced in 2022 into the Danish insolvency law for the first time. The stakeholders in the area of insolvency law greeted the class formation and amendments of the voting system with some scepticism. Even Konkursrådet stated that the system was "unnecessarily complicated and could lead to further administrative costs".[161] Possibly due to this reluctance, the legislator allowed the SMEs to opt out of treating the affected creditors in different classes, in accordance with Article 9(4) PRD 2019.[162] SMEs are in the DBA undertakings which on their balance sheet dates do not exceed at least two of the three criteria: balance sheet total: EUR 20,000,000; net turnover: EUR 40,000,000; and average number of employees during the financial year: 250.[163] Since such undertakings in Denmark are fairly rare, it is expected that the class voting system will not be used frequently.

According to the DBA, the debtor is free to divide the creditors into different classes provided that the classes "reflect sufficient commonality of interest" of the creditors within each class.[164] The only mandatory requirement is that secured creditors must be placed in a class of its own. It is worth noticing, however, that the secured creditor can be placed in two different classes, since only the part of the claim that is secured needs to be put in a separate class.[165] The unsecured claim, therefore, should be placed in another class of unsecured claims. The preparatory works explicitly mention that the debtor is also allowed to divide unsecured creditors (who have the same rank in bankruptcy) into different classes, thus making it possible to place suppliers, public authorities and financial creditors into different classes. It is then the bankruptcy court that oversees whether the proposed

160 Betænkning 1579/2022 om revision af reglerne om rekonstruktion, herunder implementering af rekonstruktions- og insolvensdirektivet, p. 135.

161 Ibid., p. 137.

162 Cf. DBA Section 10(6).

163 In accordance with Directive 2013/34/EU of the European Parliament and of the Council of 26 June 2013 on the annual financial statements, consolidated financial statements and related reports of certain types of undertakings, amending Directive 2006/43/EC of the European Parliament and of the Council and repealing Council Directives 78/660/EEC and 83/349/EEC Text with EEA relevance, Art. 3(3) and Årsregnskabslovens § 7.

164 Cf. DBA Section 13 (d) (5).

165 Betænkning 1579/2022 om revision af reglerne om rekonstruktion, herunder implementering af rekonstruktions- og insolvensdirektivet, p. 338.

class formation is in accordance with the law. The court's decision on this cannot be appealed.[166]

Despite the flexibility in the class formation, it must be noted that it is not possible to propose different solutions to these classes, since the plan must not propose elements that are in breach of the insolvency equality principle.[167] Creditors – who are protected by the same rank in the bankruptcy procedure, *i.e.* all unsecured creditors – must be treated in the same way. The Danish implementation, therefore, is founded on the absolute priority rule. However it is implemented in the voting rules and not in the confirmation rules, as discussed below.

4.6 *Confirmation of the Plan*

The bankruptcy court must confirm a plan.[168] However, there are five grounds where the court must reject the plan: (1) in the event of formal mistakes in the adoption process and where this has had an effect on the outcome of the voting; (2) if the plan is not in accordance with the law, *i.e.* if the plan writes down privileged debt; (3) if a third party or the debtor, in order to influence the voting, have granted benefits to a voting creditor outside the plan; (4) if the plan discharges debt of a natural person, the plan may not be a circumvention of the requirement laid down in the Danish discharge procedure;[169] and finally, (5) if the plan does not meet the best interest test. The best interest test had to be fulfilled before 2022 as well. However, now, in accordance with the PRD 2019, the wording in the DBA Section 13 e was made more precise. It was made evident that decisive is whether a creditor – who has not consented– would be worse off under a restructuring plan compared to the normal ranking in case of liquidation.[170] It is, however, worth noticing that the plan should be compared to the potential future outcome of a liquidation (bankruptcy) procedure. In this regard, the Danish legislator has opted not to implement the possibility of comparing the

166 Cf. DBA Section 249. Whether this limitation of appeal is in accordance with Art. 16 PRD 2019 could be discussed. However, it is a judicial authority and not an administrative authority – the bankruptcy court – which is competent to decide on the class formation.

167 Cf. DBA Section 10 c.

168 Cf. DBA Section 13 (e), in accordance with Art. 9 PRD.

169 This requirement is the result of a debate initiated by a few judgements from the Supreme Courts in 2018 and 2019. The Supreme Court found it necessary to reject confirmation of a plan based on a doubtful legal interpretation of the existing confirmation rules when it was obvious that the debtor would not have met the criteria for a discharge in the ordinary discharge procedure, *i.e.* if the debt was based on criminal acts. See further U 2018. 3090H and U2019.1859H.

170 Betænkning 1579/2022 om revision af reglerne om rekonstruktion, herunder implementering af rekonstruktions- og insolvensdirektivet, p. 157.

restructuring plan to the next best alternative.[171] The court's confirmation or rejection of the plan can be appealed to the Danish High Courts.[172]

4.7 *Possibilities for a Debt-for-Equity Swap*

The possibilities of pursuing a debt-for-equity swap under the preventive and ordinary restructuring procedure has been amended quite dramatically with the implementation of PRD 2019. This was done explicitly because of the wording of Article 12 PRD, which states that EU Member States "shall ensure by other means that those equity holders are not allowed to unreasonably prevent or create obstacles to the adoption and confirmation of a restructuring plan". This has led the Danish legislator to introduce the possibility to write-down equity without consent of the shareholders *and* without having to go through the ordinary procedure of a company's general meeting, as provided by the Danish Company Act. The DBA now allows that a company can fully write-down the existing shares (1) if the company is illiquid – thus requiring cash flow insolvency, and (2) if the company's liabilities exceed the value of the assets – thus requiring balance sheet insolvency.[173] Both forms of insolvency must be proven to legitimize a forced write-down. If this is the case, the write-down can be part of the plan, on which the creditors vote. Basically, this means that it is in the hands of the creditors, not the shareholders whether there will be a write-down. Precisely because the company is insolvent, it is not regarded a problem that the shareholders cannot vote on the plan. They are not affected financially since their shares do not hold any financial value. If the company does not meet the double insolvency test, the write-down cannot be forced by this provision and the creditors must rely on regular company law.

The company must fulfil the 'minimum shares requirement' laid down in Danish law requiring that the write-down of existing shares must be followed by the issuance of new shares. The new shares cannot be issued directly in a debt-for-equity swap since the law requires that the issuance of new shares must be paid in cash.[174] However, as mentioned by the legislator, it is possible to write-down existing shares in combination with writing down debt for some creditors, so long as these creditors pay the minimum cash capital requirement. In this way, the plan can *de facto* provide for a debt-for-equity swap.[175]

171 Art. 2(1)(6) PRD 2019.
172 Cf. DBA Section 249.
173 Cf. DBA Section 10(8).
174 Ibid.
175 Betænkning 1579/2022 om revision af reglerne om rekonstruktion, herunder implementering af rekonstruktions- og insolvensdirektivet, p. 127.

4.8 *Executory Contracts*

As required by Article 7(4) PRD 2019, Danish law provides that creditors are not allowed to withhold performance, terminate, accelerate or, in any other way, modify essential executory contracts to the detriment of the debtor during a stay. Technically, this has been done by copying the existing regulation on executory contracts for application in the preventive restructuring procedure. This was done with some modifications because a debtor might not be insolvent yet.[176] When a stay is granted, the debtor is allowed to 'continue' his executory contracts on the same terms as before the commencement of the procedure.[177] The right to choose which contracts should be continued is entrusted to the debtor, as the debtor-in-possession. However, the appointed IP must give his consent to the continuation of the contract.[178] When the debtor chooses to continue a contract, the rights and liabilities will remain the same and the claims arising from such a contract will be treated as preferential claims according to the DBA Section 94.[179] Thus, the debtor and its creditors can only amend and terminate the contract in accordance with Danish contract law. It is worth noticing that the creditor's contractual right to terminate the contract due to a delay in (or lack of) payment of the debts, that came into existence prior to the commencement of the stay, is not prohibited.[180]

To reduce the obstacles to continuation of the debtor's operations, and more specifically, to protect the debtor's cash flow during the restructuring procedure, the DBA also prohibits the counterparty to demand additional security. This includes demanding provision of security for performing according to the contract, withholding its performance or demanding performance prior to its due date.[181]

4.9 *Jurisdiction for and Recognition of Court Decisions in Europe*

Denmark is not bound by the EIR 2015.[182] Under Danish insolvency law, a debtor must file for the preventive restructuring procedure at the bankruptcy court where he engages in

---

176 One example of modification is the fact that the right for the debtor to re-establish already terminated contracts has not been transferred to the new framework. Contrary to DBA Section 12o.

177 Cf. DBA Section 9 (e).

178 DBA, Section 12 o (1) See further on the requirements of consent: K. Jensen, R. Bank-Pedersen, H. Christensen, S. Jensen, J. Madsen & A. Mylin, *Rekonstruktion – teori og praksis* (2nd ed.), Copenhagen: Jurist- og Økonomforbundets Forlag, 2020, pp. 357-358 and DBA, Section 12 o (3).

179 DBA Section 9 (e) and 12 (p). There are limits on the preferential treatment of claims in continuous contracts, cf. DBA Section 12 p (2).

180 DBA Section 9 (e) (2) with reference to DBA Section 58(2) If this is in accordance with the wording of Art. 7(4) PRD 2019 could be challenged.

181 DBA, Section 12 (q) (1).

182 Cf. Arts. 1 and 2 of Protocol No 22 on the position of Denmark annexed to the Treaty on European Union and the Treaty on the Functioning of the European Union and EIR 2015 preamble 88.

financial activities.[183] This requirement bears similarities to the centre of main interests (COMI) assessment, as the place of the debtor's central administration is usually where he engages in financial activities.[184] Contrary to Article 3(2) EIR 2015, it is not possible to file for preventive restructuring when the debtor only has an establishment in Denmark.

The literature has discussed whether preventive restructuring procedures can be covered by the Brussels Ibis Regulation,[185] especially if the procedure is non-public or based purely on company law.[186] In case a preventive restructuring procedure will be covered by Brussels Ibis, it will also be recognized in Denmark. Looking at the Danish preventive restructuring procedure, it is non-public until the time where a stay is established or a proposal for a plan is presented. The legislator has refrained from stating whether the preventive restructuring procedure could then be considered to be covered by Brussels Ibis. This remains to be decided on by the courts.

5 Outlook and Conclusion

As already mentioned, some of the elements of the changes have been met with certain scepticism by both practitioners and lawmakers. Most of the concerns regard the scope of application of the preventive restructuring procedure and its actual usefulness. Danish law already allows a debtor to file for insolvency procedures before he is illiquid, when there is some evidence of such a prospect. Although there is sympathy for the reasoning behind the PRD 2019 and its scope of applicability, the success of getting a debtor to deal with his financial difficulties at an earlier time than is now the case most likely depends on a change in culture. Another point is how the new adoption and confirmation system will be dealt with in practice. Will judges and practitioners continue to see the new preventive restructuring procedure as unnecessarily complicated, or will they discover new ways of getting the deal through? Not much guidance is provided for the stakeholders in this regard, and it will be interesting to follow if practice will work around the new procedure or work with the new procedure.

183 Cf. DBA Section 3.

184 See more on this, L.H. Langkjær, *De danske domstoles internationale kompetence på det konkursretlige område – i lyset af EU's insolvensforordning*, Copenhagen:Karnov Group, 2019.

185 Regulation (EU) No 1215/2012 of the European Parliament and of the Council of 12 December 2012 on jurisdiction and the recognition and enforcement of judgments in civil and commercial matters, *OJ L* 351/1.

186 CERIL Report 2022-2 on Cross-Border Effects in European Preventive Restructuring, 6 July 2022.

4 France

*Emilie Ghio**

1 Introduction

This chapter contains an analysis of the most recent reforms in French insolvency law, following the passing of the Ordinance of September 2021[187] which transposed the Directive on Restructuring and Insolvency (PRD 2019).[188] France has traditionally been known for its pro-debtor nature and the rather low involvement of creditors in preventive restructuring proceedings. The Ordinance of September 2021 transposing PRD 2019 has made significant changes to French restructuring and insolvency law, hopefully making France more attractive to financial investors. While the attractiveness of preventive measures for debtors has been strengthened, in particular conciliation proceedings with the improvement of the grace period mechanism and accelerated safeguard proceedings with the introduction of automatic constitution of classes and cross-class cram-down mechanism increased the protection that is now offered to secured creditors.

This chapter is structured as follows. First, the French preventive restructuring regime is described, against the background of PRD 2019 (Section 2). Second, an analysis of the main features introduced into French insolvency law by the Ordinance of September 2021 is provided. In particular, Section 3 discusses the adoption of the conciliation and accelerated safeguard proceedings as the main French reference preventive framework, the conditions for the adoption of the restructuring plan and the substitution of creditors' committees for *classes* of creditors, as well as the introduction of a cross-class cram-down mechanism into French law. Finally, Section 4 complements the discussion by examining the changes in the mechanisms in place for the detection and prevention of business difficulties, as well as the additional distinctions between the safeguard and rehabilitation proceedings which have been introduced by the Ordinance of September 2021.

---

* This chapter covers the law, case law and literature as of 31 May 2022. The author wishes to thank Dr. Paul Omar for casting an eye over a late draft and suggesting some amendments, as well as Vasile Rotaru for his useful insights.

187 Ordinance No. 2021-1193 of 15 September 2021.

188 Directive (EU) 2019/1023 of the European Parliament and of the Council of 20 June 2019 on preventive restructuring frameworks, on discharge of debt and disqualifications, and on measures to increase the efficiency of procedures concerning restructuring, insolvency and discharge of debt, and amending Directive (EU) 2017/1132, O.J. L 172/18.

2 OVERVIEW OF THE FRENCH INSOLVENCY LAW REGIME

2.1 *A Brief Historical Perspective*

French insolvency law has a long and ancient history, dating back from Roman law. Before the introduction of the Commercial Code in 1807, insolvency law was mostly coercive and punitive, with procedures consisting of arresting and imprisoning the defaulting debtor. In 1880, the liquidation procedure was introduced, which ran alongside the coercive bankruptcy procedure. It was available to honest bankrupts who could save their businesses through debt forgiveness from their creditors.

It took until the 1950s[189] and 1960s[190] for insolvency law, as we know it today, to develop. In particular, the Laws of 20 July 1955 and 13 July 1967 considerably transformed the corporate insolvency landscape, notably by introducing the first rescue procedure known as rehabilitation proceedings (*redressement judiciaire*). At that stage, therefore, a 'twin-track' system was established, whereby a company could either be liquidated or rescued. The first pre-insolvency process was subsequently introduced in 1984.[191]

The year 2000 marked the promulgation of the new Commercial Code, which consolidated insolvency laws. Since then, the French legislator and government have been prolific at reforming and modernizing the insolvency regime at regular intervals, with substantial reforms taking place every few years. This continuous reform activity has been partly caused by regular economic crises, which have led to an increase in the number of insolvency cases, and partly due to consideration that previous reforms had fallen short of success. Most reforms have been rooted in the idea that corporate difficulties should be dealt with upstream, in order to preserve the value of the assets of the company and facilitate a successful restructuring.

2.2 *The Current French Insolvency Regime*

In 2005, the safeguard procedure (*procédure de sauvegarde*) was instituted, introducing a debtor-in-possession process into French insolvency law. It was designed to encourage upstream rescue, since companies can avail of it before becoming officially insolvent. In the wake of the global economic and financial crisis from the late 2000s, variations of the safeguard procedure were created: the expedited financial safeguard (*sauvegarde financière*

189 Decree-Law No. 55-583 of 20 July 1955.
190 Law No. 67-563 of 13 July 1967.
191 Law No. 84-148 of 1 March 1984.

accélérée) in 2010[192] and the accelerated safeguard (*sauvegarde accélérée*) in 2014,[193] which drew on the practice of pre-packs.

French insolvency law was once again reformed in 2014, with the aim of promoting preventive measures, strengthening the efficiency of pre-insolvency proceedings and increasing the rights of creditors in insolvency proceedings.[194] In 2016, the Law on the Modernization of 21st Century Justice again focused on the promotion of the rescue culture, the enhancement of confidentiality during proceedings, the ring-fencing of new monies during restructuring, and the improvement in transparency and impartiality.[195]

Finally, in 2019, the French legislator passed the so-called 'Pacte Law' (*Plan d'Action pour la Croissance et la Transformation des Entreprises*).[196] The law had two main objectives: (i) business growth and job creation; and (ii) the redefinition of the place of the company in society with a view to better involving employees in the life of the company.[197] In order to achieve these aims, the Pacte Law tasked the French government with transposing the provisions of the EU Directive on Preventive Restructuring by means of an Ordinance. The latter came out in September 2021.[198]

Thanks to these regular reforms and the long-standing corporate rescue culture of France, French insolvency law is now equipped with a comprehensive body of procedures, all governed by Title VI of the Commercial Code (*Code de Commerce*). The current corporate insolvency law system is comprised of the following procedures:

1. Ad hoc mandate (*mandat ad hoc*);[199]
2. Conciliation (*conciliation*);[200]
3. Safeguard (*sauvegarde*);[201]
4. Accelerated safeguard (*sauvegarde accélérée*);[202]
5. Judicial rehabilitation (*redressement judiciaire*);[203] and
6. Liquidation.[204]

192 Law No. 2010-1249 of 22 October 2010.
193 Ordinance No. 2014-326 of 12 March 2014.
194 Ibid.
195 Law No. 2016-1547 of 18 November 2016.
196 Law No. 2019-486 of 22 May 2019.
197 See the Report of the French Council of Ministers of 18 June 2018, available at: https://www.assemblee-nationale.fr/dyn/15/dossiers/alt/Croissance_transformation_des_entreprises.
198 Ordinance No. 2021-1193 of 15 September 2021.
199 Governed by Arts. L611-1 to L611-16, Commercial Code.
200 Ibid., Arts. L611-1 to L611-16.
201 Ibid., Arts. L620-1 to L627-4.
202 Ibid., Arts. L628-1 to L628-8.
203 Ibid., Arts. L631-1 to L632-4.
204 Ibid., Arts. L640-1 to L645-12.

3 The PRD 2019 and the French Preventive Restructuring Regime

The preventive focus of the Directive on Preventive Restructuring 2019 (PRD 2019) is clearly articulated in its early recitals. For example, the PRD aims to ensure that: "viable enterprises ... that are in financial difficulties have access to effective national preventive restructuring frameworks which enable them to continue operating" (Recital 1); and "debtors [are able] to restructure effectively at an early stage and to avoid insolvency" (Recital 2).

While the Directive is the result of the codification of over 420 inputs on existing European practices received during the trilogy process, the influence of French law is rather noticeable. This is not surprising considering that the prevention of business failure and the possibility for debtors to restructure at an early stage is not new to France, a jurisdiction which has long been known for its "restructuring-biased" insolvency law regime,[205] given its history of promoting the rescue of businesses at an early stage, especially with a view to preserving employment.[206]

3.1 Out-of-Court, Amicable, Preventive Proceedings

The ***ad hoc* mandate** is an out-of-court procedure opened by the President of the competent court at the request of the debtor who is experiencing legal, economic or financial difficulties but who is not yet insolvent. An *ad hoc* representative is appointed to assist with the negotiations between the debtor and their principal creditors,[207] though the debtor remains in full possession of its assets and management of its company.

Principal creditors are invited to consider debt rescheduling and/or cancellation and/or the injection of new money into the business with a view to ensure the sustainability of the business, the pursuit of its economic activity and the preservation of employment.[208] Major shareholders can be invited to negotiate and potentially re-capitalize the company. A debt restructuring agreement cannot be imposed on dissenting creditors or creditors who have not participated in the negotiations, as the process is consensual, contractual and no cram-down is possible. There is no stay on enforcement proceedings and the procedure is fully confidential.

---

205 M. Adalet McGowan & D. Andrews, 'Insolvency Regimes and Productivity Growth: A Framework for Analysis', OECD Economic Department Working Papers No. 1309, 2016, p. 18.

206 See R. Parry, 'Introduction', in: K. Gromek Broc & R. Parry (eds), *Corporate Rescue in Europe: An Overview of Recent Developments from Selected Countries in Europe*, Deventer: Kluwer Law International, 2004, p. 1.

207 Ibid., Art. L611-7.

208 The court can sanction the agreement through homologation only if certain conditions are met, including that the provisions of the agreement aim to ensure the viability of the going concern of the company: Art. L611-8, Commercial Code.

Conciliation is also an out-of-court procedure opened at the request of the debtor. The debtor must face legal, economic or financial difficulties but cannot have been insolvent for more than 45 days.[209] A conciliator is appointed by the court for a duration of 4 months with a view to reaching an agreement between the debtor and their main creditors.[210] The objective is to put an end to the debtor's difficulties and/or prepare a plan for the sale of the business.[211]

Conciliation proceedings are confidential in nature as long as the agreement reached by the debtor and their creditors is not sanctioned by the court (*homologation*). A debt restructuring agreement cannot be imposed on dissenting creditors or creditors who have not participated in the negotiations, as similarly to *ad hoc* mandate proceedings, the process is consensual, contractual and no cram-down is possible (unless accelerated safeguard proceedings are subsequently opened). The debtor remains in control of its assets and the management of the company's activities, and there is no automatic stay on enforcement actions. However, the judge may issue a debt deferral for up to 2 years against certain creditors at the request of the debtor. The debtor may also, in case of refusal of the creditor of a waiver request submitted by the conciliator, ask for the suspension of payments in respect of that creditor's outstanding claims during conciliation proceedings.[212] Parties to a conciliation agreement sanctioned or approved by the court are barred from initiating legal proceedings against the debtor.[213]

The main difference between the *ad hoc* mandate and the conciliation procedures, therefore, is that a conciliation agreement is ratified by the court at the request of the debtor. The court can either approve the agreement (*constatation*), which means that the confidentiality of the procedure is preserved, or it can sanction the agreement (*homologation*), which involves publicizing the judgement.[214] In the latter case, the adverse effect of publicity is mitigated by the fact that the sanctioning confers more legal advantages than a mere approval in the event of subsequent insolvency proceedings being opened.

In particular, if the conciliation proceedings are later converted into restructuring proceedings, new money providers will benefit from a protection for new financing (*privilège de conciliation*).[215] This benefit is granted to investors who have provided new money, goods or services during conciliation proceedings with a view to ensure the continuation of the business and aims to secure the repayment of this new debt in the event of subsequent restructuring proceedings. A claim benefitting from a new money

209 Art. L611-4, Commercial Code.
210 Ibid., Art. L611-6.
211 Ibid., Art. L611-7.
212 Ibid., Art. L611-10-1.
213 Ibid., Art. L611-10-1.
214 Before the court sanctions an agreement, it must hear the debtor, the creditors who are parties to the agreement, the conciliator and some representatives of the company: Art. L611-9, Commercial Code.
215 Arts. L611-11, L626-20 and L626-30-2, Commercial Code.

privilege may be given a different treatment from old money in any subsequent court-supervised procedure. The new investors will enjoy a priority of payment over all pre-commencement and post-commencement claims (subject to some exceptions, especially with respect to employment claims and procedural costs). Claims benefitting from this new money privilege are not to be rescheduled or written off under a safeguard or rehabilitation plan without their holders' consent, not even through a (cross-class) cram-down process.

3.2 *Court-Assisted Preventive Proceedings*

The **safeguard** procedure was introduced by the law of 2005 and subsequently reformed in 2008, 2014 and 2016. Modelled on Chapter 11 of the United States (US) Bankruptcy Code, the procedure was originally introduced as an insolvency procedure where the debtor was required to show that it was facing "difficulties that it was not able to overcome" and which would lead to a payment failure situation (*cessation des paiements*). The Ordinance of 2008 relaxed this criterion, making the safeguard available to a debtor who is encountering difficulties and is not in a position to overcome, while not yet in a payment failure situation. It thus transformed the safeguard procedure into a hybrid mechanism, which can also serve as a preventive restructuring process.

Compared to the *ad hoc* and conciliation procedures, the safeguard exhibits characteristics closer to formal insolvency proceedings. It is a court-supervised procedure, aimed at alleviating a debtor's financial difficulties. It is opened at the sole request of the debtor and is only available to solvent companies experiencing difficulties that they cannot overcome.

An administrator (*administrateur judiciaire*) is appointed by the court who supervises and/or assists the debtor or its management, the latter remaining in control of the company and its assets.[216] The court also appoints one or more creditors' representative(s) (*mandataires judiciaires*) to represent creditors' interests and assess proof of claims, as well as a supervising judge (*juge-commissaire*) who supervises the procedure.[217]

Following the opening judgement, an observation period starts (*période d'observation*), which lasts for 6 months, renewable once for a further 6 months.[218] The observation period imposes an automatic stay on all actions against the debtor who is also prevented from repaying pre-petition claims.[219] The debtor and the administrator prepare a safeguard plan during the observation period. The content of the plan is flexible and can include the

216 Ibid., Art. L622-1.
217 Ibid., Art. L621-4.
218 Ibid., Art. L621-3.
219 Ibid., Art. L622-7.

rescheduling of debts, write-offs, debt-for-equity swaps, etc. It is voted on by creditors who may be grouped within classes. If the debtor fails to comply with the terms of the plan or becomes insolvent, the court may convert the safeguard procedure into rehabilitation proceedings (*redressement judiciaire*) if rescue remains possible, or liquidation proceedings if rescue is manifestly impossible.

In the immediate wake of the global financial crisis of the mid-2000s, developments in legal practice prompted further reforms in France. Debtors wishing to benefit from an arrangement similar in structure to a pre-pack[220] were negotiating an agreement before formally entering into safeguard proceedings. The agreement negotiated would then be adopted in the form of a safeguard plan.[221] To codify existing practices, the accelerated financial safeguard was introduced in 2010 as a 'pre-pack' variant of the safeguard.[222] In 2014, following the prolonged devastating effects of the crisis on the French economy, the second variant of the safeguard – the accelerated safeguard – was created.[223] While the accelerated safeguard offers a means for the debtor to enter into negotiations with all his creditors, the accelerated financial safeguard only affected financial creditors. Following the transposition of the PRD into French law, the two accelerated safeguard proceedings have been merged into the accelerated safeguard.

The **accelerated safeguard** is therefore a court-supervised procedure which can be opened at the sole request of a debtor who is not insolvent, or has not been insolvent for more than 45 days prior to the request to open the conciliation procedure that preceded the accelerated safeguard proceedings.

The debtor remains in control of its assets and management of the company, and the proceedings come with a stay on creditor enforcement actions, which is limited to 4 months from the date of the opening judgement.

Accelerated safeguard proceedings are not a standalone procedure. Rather, a company must:

1. Have opened conciliation proceedings;
2. Have negotiated a restructuring plan with the creditors later involved in the accelerated version of the safeguard; and

---

220 F.-X. Lucas, 'Le plan de sauvegarde apprêté ou le prepackaged plan à la française', *Cahier Des Entreprises*, 2009, dossier 28; A. Besse & N. Morelli, 'Le prepackaged plan à la française: pour une saine utilisation de la procédure de sauvegarde', *JCP, E No. 25* (18 June 2009), p. 1628.

221 Y. Le Gales, 'Comment fonctionne la procédure de sauvegarde financière accélérée', *Le Figaro* (11 January 2011).

222 Law No. 2010-1249 of 22 October 2010. See also P. Omar, 'Preservation and Pre-Packs à la Française: The Evolution of French Insolvency Law after 2005', *International Company and Commercial Law Review*, 2011, 8, p. 258; L.-C. Henry, 'La sauvegarde financière accélérée ou les leçons de la pratique', *Les Petites Affiches*, 2010, No. 232, p. 4; T. Monteran & M. Mieulle, 'Le vade-mecum du plan de cession « prepack »', *Bulletin Jolly Entreprises en Difficulté*, 2015, No. 3, p. 164.

223 Ordinance No. 2014-326 of 12 March 2014.

3. Be able to demonstrate to the court that the plan will receive the support of the creditors involved.[224]

The objective is for the debtor to reach an agreement with its creditors in a speedy fashion. The attractiveness of the accelerated safeguard procedure is that they combine confidentiality and contractual flexibility during the conciliation phase with:

1. The protection of new financing brought forward during the conciliation phase;[225] and
2. The possibility for the court to bind dissenting creditors via a cross-class cram-down in the accelerated safeguard phase of the procedure.[226]

3.3 *Improving French Preventive Restructuring Law*

Regrettably, French insolvency law has traditionally been known for being too favourable to debtors and "unreasonably averse to creditors".[227] While regular reforms over the years reinforced the prerogatives of creditors in insolvency procedures,[228] French insolvency law has continued to rank relatively low regarding the "strength of its insolvency framework" in international and comparative studies,[229] because of the limited role of creditors in restructuring proceedings,[230] especially compared to the protection of other stakeholders' interests.[231] Therefore, while the transposition of the Directive was not expected to deeply upset the rather sophisticated existing French preventive restructuring system, it has nonetheless provided a unique occasion for France to reform its preventive restructuring

224 Art. L628-1, Commercial Code.

225 Ibid., Art. L611-11.

226 Ibid., Arts. L628-8 and L626-31, as amended by Art. 37, Ordinance of 15 September 2021.

227 F. Pérochon, *Entreprises en difficulté*, Paris: Librairie Générale de Droit et de Jurisprudence, 2014, p. 205.

228 Law No. 2005-845 of 26 July 2005; Ordinance No. 2008-1345 of 18 December 2008; Ordinance No. 2014-326 of 12 March 2014; Law No. 2015-990 of 6 August 2015; Law No. 2016-1547 of 18 November 2016.

229 See, for example, World Bank, *Doing Business Report*, available at: https://www.doingbusiness.org/en/methodology/resolving-insolvency, which states the recovery rate of creditors in a fictitious case under consideration is estimated at 74.8%, while it is well above 85% in other European countries, such as Denmark, Finland, Ireland, the Netherlands, Norway, Slovenia and the United Kingdom. See also S. Davydenko & J. Franks, 'Do Bankruptcy Codes Matter? A Study of Defaults in France, Germany and the UK', *Journal of Finance*, 2008, 63, p. 565.

230 A. Epaulard & C. Zapha, 'Distressed Firms: How Effective Are Preventive Procedures?', *France Stratégie*, La Note D'Analyse No. 84 (February 2020), p. 2, available at: https://www.strategie.gouv.fr/sites/strategie.gouv.fr/files/atoms/files/fs-na-84-procedures-preventives-anglais.pdf.

231 G. Plantin, D. Thesmar & J. Tirole, 'Reforming French Bankruptcy Law', Les notes du conseil d'analyse économique, No. 7 (June 2013), p. 1, available at: https://www.cae-eco.fr/staticfiles/pdf/cae-note007-en.pdf; L. Spizzichino, S. Gorrias, H. Bourbouloux & M. Menjucq, 'Les perspectives d'évolution du rôle des créanciers en droit des entreprises en difficulté', *Revue des Procédures Collectives*, 2019, No. 3, p. 1.

landscape, notably by rebalancing the protection afforded to different stakeholders' interests.[232]

The transposition of PRD 2019 into French law has followed a two-step process. First, on 11 April 2019, the so-called 'Pacte Law' relating to the growth and transformation of companies was passed.[233] The Law had three main stated objectives:

1. To grow businesses and to create jobs;
2. To redefine the place of the company in society and to better involve employees in the life of the company; and
3. To transpose the PRD 2019.[234]

Second, the Pacte Law tasked the French government with achieving these listed objectives by adopting an executive ordinance within two years. On 15 September 2021, the government adopted Ordinance No. 2021-1193,[235] which made few, yet substantial changes to Book VI of the French Commercial Code dealing with insolvency and restructuring procedures. Indeed, while the premise of the PRD 2019 mirrors that of the French regime, the conditions for drawing up and adopting the restructuring plan under the Directive are inspired by Anglo-American law, notably by Chapter 11 of the US Bankruptcy Code, as well as the British scheme of arrangement. Consequently, key changes introduced into French insolvency law by the transposition of the PRD 2019 have included:

1. The endorsement of the reference preventive framework, *i.e.* conciliation followed by accelerated safeguard proceedings;
2. The shift from *committees* to *classes* of creditors; and
3. The introduction of a cross-class cram-down mechanism.

4 An Analysis of the Main Features Introduced into French Insolvency Law by the Reform

While the reform brought about by the Ordinance of September 2021 did not introduce any new (preventive) restructuring procedure into Book VI of the French Commercial Code, significant changes have nonetheless been introduced, which apply to proceedings opened from 1 October 2021.

232 Recital 35, PRD 2019.

233 Law No. 2019-486 of 22 May 2019.

234 See the Report of the French Council of Ministers of 18 June 2018, available at: https://www.cae-eco.fr/staticfiles/pdf/cae-note007-en.pdf.

235 Ordinance No. 2021-1193 of 15 September 2021, later supplemented by Decree No. 2021-1218 of 23 September 2021.

4.1 *The French Reference for Preventive Frameworks: Conciliation and Accelerated Safeguard Proceedings*

The French government has transposed the Directive *de minimis*, by retaining existing preventive restructuring procedures. In particular, the combination of the conciliation and accelerated safeguard proceedings was preserved and endorsed as the reference preventive framework within the meaning of the Directive, through the reinforcement of the effects of conciliation proceedings and the facilitation of the adoption of restructuring plans in case of opposition by dissenting creditors.

4.1.1 Step 1: Conciliation Proceedings

French insolvency law, through its *ad hoc* mandate and conciliation, has been a forerunner with respect to preventive restructuring frameworks, as they have proven to be rather effective tools over the years. The conciliation procedure has thus only been slightly altered by the Ordinance of September 2021. Therefore, the transposition of the Directive has resulted in a marginal strengthening of conciliation proceedings only, mostly through the modification of the procedure allowing the debtor to obtain a stay on enforcement actions and grace periods.

Conciliation proceedings are voluntary, flexible and to some extent, confidential, proceedings which aim to facilitate the negotiation of a restructuring agreement (*accord de conciliation*) between a company and its creditors under the supervision of a court-appointed conciliator (*conciliateur*). It is available to debtors that:

1. Encounter legal, economic or financial difficulties, actual or anticipated; or
2. Are not insolvent, or have been insolvent (*i.e.* in a payment failure situation (*cessation des paiements*)) for less than 45 days.

Articles L611-4 and L611-5 specify that a 'debtor' includes any natural and legal person who carries out a commercial or artisanal activity. These will include limited companies, closed corporations, partnerships, limited liability companies or individuals conducting a commercial or trade activity. Debtors carrying out an agricultural activity are excluded from the scope of the procedure.[236]

The opening of conciliation proceedings follows a judicial decision by the President of the competent court (*i.e.* the commercial or judicial court (*tribunal judiciaire*)) located where the debtor has its registered office.[237] A conciliator (*conciliateur*) is appointed, who oversees the procedure and makes any proposal relevant for the preservation of the

236 For the procedure applicable to agricultural tradespersons, see Arts. L.351-1 to L.351-7, Rural and Fisheries Code.

237 Art. L611-5, Commercial Code.

business, its activity and employment. The conciliation procedure cannot exceed a duration of 4 months, which may be extended by the court for a maximum of 1 month.[238]

The conciliation is a debtor-in-possession regime. The conciliator does not assume any management responsibility and there are no restrictions on trade activities. While the opening of conciliation proceedings does not trigger any automatic stay, Article L611-7 of the Commercial Code allows the debtor to petition the judge to suspend enforcement actions under certain conditions.

Until the implementation of the Directive, the debtor could only petition for a stay against creditors attempting to enforce their due and payable claims while conciliation proceedings were ongoing. In such circumstances, the judge could grant grace periods (*délai de grâce*) for up to 2 years, in accordance with Article 1343-5 of the Civil Code. This was considered rather "excessive, allowing for a substantial transfer of wealth benefitting the shareholders and carrying very costly effects for credit institutions since their debt [would] become … almost automatically non-performing".[239] Although such long stays were seldom granted by the court in practice, their mere prospect had an impact on the negotiations during the conciliation procedure, and were therefore heavily criticized for being a "formidable threat to the benefit of the debtor".[240]

The Ordinance of 15 September 2021 has since amended Article L611-7, enshrining a measure initially adopted in the context of the COVID-19 pandemic under the Ordinance of 20 May 2020.[241] Under the new rules, the debtor can petition the judge who opened the conciliation procedure to:

1. Stay enforcement actions and reschedule claims, that are due and payable, for a maximum of 2 years with respect to creditors attempting to enforce their claims or that have not granted a consensual standstill requested by the conciliator during the negotiations (but without any need for prior enforcement attempts by the creditor in the latter case); and
2. Reschedule claims, that are not yet due and payable, for the duration of the ongoing conciliation procedure (*i.e.* for a maximum of 5 months) in relation to creditors who have not granted a standstill requested by the conciliatory during the negotiations.

---

238 Ibid., Art. L611-6.

239 V. Rotaru, 'The Restructuring Directive: A Functional Law and Economics Analysis from a French Law Perspective' (30 September 2019), Para. 97, available at: https://papers.ssrn.com/sol3/papers.cfm?abstract_id=3461716; A. Pietrancosta & S. Vermeille, 'Le droit des procédures collectives à l'épreuve de l'analyse économique du droit. Perspectives d'avenir?', *Revue Trimestrielle de Droit Financier* 2010, No. 1, p. 15, available at: https://droitetcroissance.fr/wp-content/uploads/2015/04/1.-Le-droit-des-proc%C3%A9dures-collectives-%C3%A0-l%C3%A9preuve-de-lanalyse-%C3%A9conomique-du-droit.pdf.

240 V. Rotaru, above note 239, Para. 98.

241 Ordinance No. 2020-596 of 20 May 2020.

While the debtor's bargaining position seems to be reinforced following the reform, it should be noted that some French courts have rejected petitions, where it appeared that the requested suspension or rescheduling would be used as a way to force creditors to negotiate, rather than as a way to stay enforcement actions.[242]

A stay is also effected, yet this time automatically, as per Article L611-10-1, while the conciliation agreement is being carried out, provided that the agreement is sanctioned (*homologation*) by the court. The sanctioning of the conciliation agreement by the court suspends any legal action against the debtor and prohibits any individual enforcement action against the debtor's estate with respect to claims covered within the agreement.[243]

The reforms introduced by the 2021 Ordinance have improved the effectiveness of the conciliation phase of the conciliation agreement by broadening the participating creditors. The conciliator is tasked with promoting the conclusion of a restructuring agreement between the debtor and its main creditors (and, where applicable, his main co-contractors).[244] As a result, it is up to the debtor and conciliator to determine which creditors should be included in the negotiations. However, bearing in mind that, if conciliation proceedings are subsequently followed by accelerated safeguard proceedings, the decision as to which creditors to involve during the conciliation phase is therefore an important one.

At the end of the negotiation process, the conciliation agreement is approved by the court. The court can either approve the agreement (*constatation*) or sanction the agreement (*homologation*). If the agreement is merely approved, it is neither subject to publication nor to appeal. However, at the request of the debtor, the court can sanction the agreement if the following conditions are met:

1. The debtor is not in a payment failure situation or the agreement concluded puts an end to it;
2. The terms of the agreement are such as to ensure the sustainability of the company's activity; and
3. The agreement does not impact the interests of non-negotiating and non-signatory creditors.[245]

Approval of the agreement puts an end to the conciliation procedure, as well as the automatic stay.

242 Commercial Court, Nanterre, Order of 17 May 2021.

243 Art. L611-10-1, Commercial Code.

244 Ibid., Art. L611-7.

245 Ibid., Art. L611-8.

4.1.2 Step 2: Accelerated Safeguard Proceedings

The Ordinance of September 2021, transposing PRD 2019, made the accelerated safeguard procedure the core framework of preventive restructuring within the meaning of the Directive. It meets the European legislator's expectations of ensuring a vote on a restructuring plan in a short time frame, thanks to the compulsory passage through conciliation first. With a maximum duration of 4 months (2 months which can be extended by another 2 months at the request of the debtor or the administrator), accelerated safeguard proceedings are now available to all companies, regardless of their size, which was not the case before October 2021. The objective of the accelerated safeguard procedure is, therefore, to preserve the company's value within the framework of a so-called pre-pack, where a restructuring plan can be adopted by affected creditors.[246]

Importantly, the accelerated safeguard is not a standalone procedure. Rather, accelerated safeguard proceedings are opened at the request of a debtor who can demonstrate that:

1. They are engaged in conciliation procedure;
2. A conciliation agreement has been drawn up, aimed at ensuring the sustainability and rescue of the company; and
3. The agreement must be likely to receive support from the affected parties within 2 months of the opening judgement.[247]

Subject to some variations, found in Chapter VIII of Book VI of the Commercial Code, the accelerated safeguard is subject to the rules applicable to the traditional safeguard.[248] The first substantial condition for opening accelerated safeguard proceedings is that the debtor must be engaged in conciliation proceedings.[249] The fact that the debtor is in a payment failure situation does not preclude the opening of accelerated safeguard; the same criterion is used as that of the conciliation, *i.e.* the debtor must not have been in a payment failure situation for more than 45 days.[250] The decision to open accelerated safeguard proceedings is taken by the court on the basis of the report prepared by the conciliator, expressing their own opinion on the likelihood of the restructuring plan being adopted by the creditors concerned.[251]

246 The replacement of the concept of committees by *classes* of creditors, as discussed in Section 4.2, led to the disappearance of the accelerated financial safeguard because the committee of credit institutions no longer exists. However, it is still possible to limit the effect of accelerated safeguard proceedings to financial creditors only (Art. L628-1, Commercial Code).

247 Art. L628-1, Commercial Code.

248 Governed by Arts. L620-1 to L627-4, Commercial Code.

249 Ibid., Art. L628-1.

250 Ibid., Art. L628-1.

251 Ibid., Art. L628-2.

The plan is therefore prepared during conciliation proceedings and it must be likely to receive the approval of affected parties against which the procedure will take effect. The attractiveness of the two-stage approach of the conciliation and accelerated safeguard preventive restructuring framework is that it combines confidentiality and contractual flexibility during the conciliation phase with the possibility for the court to bind dissenting creditors in the safeguard phase of the procedure through a cross-class cram-down process.[252] It also protects new financing brought forward during the conciliation process (*privilège de la conciliation*), if the conciliation agreement has been sanctioned (*homologation*) by the court. Investors will enjoy a priority of payment over all pre- and post-commencement claims in the event of subsequent court-administered proceedings. Such claims benefitting from this new money privilege cannot be rescheduled or written off by a safeguard or rehabilitation plan (*plan de sauvegarde/plan de redressement judiciaire*), without their holders' consent, not even through cram-down or cross-class cram-down.

Overall, the voting conditions and adoption of the plan by the classes of affected parties are defined within the framework of the traditional safeguard, which remains the flagship of Book VI of the Commercial Code. The specificities of the accelerated safeguard, therefore, lie in the compulsory constitution of classes of affected parties and the imposition of a short deadline, since the plan must be adopted within 2 months of the opening judgement, otherwise the procedure is closed, without possible conversion.[253]

4.2 *Adoption of the Plan and the Introduction of Classes of Creditors*

Article 9(6) of PRD 2019 gave Member States some leeway in setting up the creditors' voting majority:

> Member States shall lay down the majorities required for the adoption of a restructuring plan. Those majorities shall not be higher than 75% of the amount of claims or interests in each class or, where applicable, of the number of affected parties in each class.

French insolvency law complied with Article 9(6) of the PRD 2019, since Article L626-30-2 of the Commercial Code already required that two thirds in value of each class of creditors must approve the plan.

252 Ibid., Arts. L628-8 and L626-31.

253 Ibid., Art. L628-8.

Article 9(2) of PRD 2019 also provides that "all affected parties have a right to vote on the adoption of a restructuring plan", while parties not affected by the plan should not vote on it. Before transposing the Directive, French law already aligned with this first element of Article 9 PRD 2019 as only creditors affected by the plan could vote on it.[254] The Commercial Code also explicitly excluded some creditors from voting on the plan:

1. Those not affected by the restructuring plan;
2. Those who benefit from a trust agreement (*bénéficiaires d'une fiducie*); and[255]
3. Social and taxes authorities, invited to take part in the negotiations and able to agree to debt cancellations or rescheduling without being members of any committees.[256]

The formation of classes of creditors as per Article 9(4) PRD 2019 was one of the main sticking points of the 2021 reforms, since the French Commercial Code did not provide for actual classes of creditors, but rather grouped creditors within *committees*. While the EU legislator expected Member States to ensure that "affected parties are treated in separate classes, which reflect sufficient commonality of interest [and as] a minimum, creditors of secured and unsecured claims should be treated in separate classes",[257] the Commercial Code grouped creditors within committees depending on their *institutional* nature, as opposed to the *nature of their claims*.

Until the Ordinance of September 2021 transposing PRD 2019, Article L626-30-2 provided that creditors be grouped within the three following committees:

1. Credit institutions;
2. Main suppliers; and
3. Bondholders.

The French position had been heavily criticized by commentators[258] over the years for its lack of homogeneity of interests, with senior, junior, privileged and unsecured creditors

254 Ibid., former Art. L626-30-32.

255 Ibid., former Art. L626-30-32. See also former Art. L626-32. A *fiducie* is defined by Art. 2011, Civil Code as 'the operation by which one or more persons transfer assets, rights or security interests, or a set of assets, rights or security interests, present or future, to one or more trustees who, holding them separate from their own assets, act for a specific purpose for the benefit or one or more beneficiaries.'

256 Ibid., Art. L626-6.

257 See also, Recital 44, PRD 2019: 'To ensure that rights which are substantially similar are treated equitably and that restructuring plans can be adopted without unfairly prejudicing the rights of affected parties, affected parties should be treated in separate classes … "Class formation" means the grouping of affected parties for the purposes of adopting a plan in such a way as to reflect their rights and the seniority of their claims and interests. As a minimum, secured and unsecured creditors should always be treated in separate classes.'

258 See for example R. Dammann, 'L'introduction des classes de créanciers dans l'optique d'une harmonisation franco-allemande des procédures d'insolvabilité', in: *Mélanges en l'honneur du Professeur Claude Witz*, Paris: LexisNexis, 2018, p. 223; R. Dammann & M. Boché-Robinet, 'Transposition du projet de directive sur

being grouped in the same committees[259] and for not meeting international standards when complex financing schemes involving different layers of debt were involved.[260]

In the period leading to the transposition of PRD 2019, debates around class formation were numerous. Some authors proposed that the formation of these classes be done ahead of the opening of accelerated safeguard proceedings, during the conciliation phase.[261] However, conciliation proceedings are contractual in nature and do not normally abide by the voting mechanism envisioned by the Directive. Others suggested that classes could be divided into sub-categories based on a commonality of interest, as is the case in Chapter 11 of the US Bankruptcy Code and in German insolvency law.[262] The possibility for the government to introduce a specific class for new money providers during conciliation proceedings or a one-person class comprising of one creditor only was also mentioned,[263] as well as a classes grouping all shareholders who could vote on the safeguard plan but could also be cram-downed with a view to deter them to "unreasonably prevent or create obstacles to the adoption … of a restructuring plan".[264]

First, in introducing classes of creditors, the Commercial Code has also introduced a difference between safeguard and accelerated safeguard proceedings. In the latter, the formation of classes is compulsory for all debtors.[265] For safeguard proceedings, the new class system is not mandatory, except for companies which meet the following thresholds:

1. They employ over 250 employees and have a turnover greater than EUR 20 million; or
2. They have a turnover of over EUR 40 million.[266]

This threshold is higher than those applying to the former creditors' committees and, therefore, it is anticipated that their formation will remain relatively marginal in number. The thresholds reflect delicate political choices between equal access to restructuring tools and greater or lesser complexity of the procedures depending on the size of the debtor.[267] At the request of the debtor, the supervising judge (*juge-commissaire*) may nonetheless

l'harmonisation des procédures de restructuration préventive en Europe. Une chance à saisir pour la France', *Recueil Dalloz*, 2017, No. 22 (22 June 2017).

259 V. Rotaru, above note 239, Para. 12: 'current French law provides, contrary to any common sense, that any safeguard plan must be voted on by creditors organized in three separate bodies.'

260 R. Dammann & M. Boché-Robinet, above note 258.

261 Ibid.

262 A. Droege Gagnier & A. Dorst, 'France: quo vadis? France Is Keen to Reform Its Security and Insolvency Law', *Insolvency and Restructuring International*, 2018, 12, p. 25.

263 See R. Dammann & A. Alle, 'Directive 'Restructuration et Insolvabilité': l'introduction des classes de créanciers en droit français', *Recueil Dalloz*, 2019, p. 2047 et seq.

264 Art. 12, PRD 2019.

265 Art. L628-4, Commercial Code.

266 Ibid., Arts. L626-29 and R626-52.

267 O. Buisine & V. Rousseau, 'L'efficacité des procédures de restructuration, d'insolvabilité et de seconde chance: commentaire du titre IV de la directive Restructurations préventives', *Revue Procédures Collectives*, 2020, No. 2, study 10.

constitute classes of affected parties for debtors that fall below the threshold. The decision is a measure of judicial administration and is not subject to appeal.[268]

Second, considerable leeway is left to the insolvency practitioner (*administrateur judiciaire*) who will group creditors within classes representative of a sufficient commonality of economic interests (*communauté d'intérêt économique suffisante*). This will therefore vary depending on the typology of the company's liabilities and its activity. At the very least, however:

1. Creditors whose claims are secured by security interests *in rem* and other creditors (such as unsecured ones) shall belong to different classes;
2. The class formation shall comply with subordination agreements entered into before the commencement of proceedings;
3. Equity holders shall make up one or more classes; and
4. In relation to creditors secured by a trust (*fiducie*) granted by the debtor, only the amount of their claims not secured by such security is considered.[269]

Public creditors such as tax and social creditors benefit from a preferred status, while claims resulting from employment contracts, as well as pension rights acquired under an occupational pension scheme and maintenance claims are considered not to be affected by the plan.[270]

The administrator notifies each affected party of their grouping and class.[271] In the event of disagreement concerning the affected parties, the methods of distribution into classes and the calculation of the votes, each affected party, the debtor, the public prosecutor, creditors' representatives or the administrator may petition the supervising judge.[272]

The composition of classes, presence of equity holder classes and the supervised flexibility left to the administrator in their composition should allow for the emergence of greater options and solutions while better protecting secured creditors' rights. The introduction of classes, coupled with the cross-class cram-down mechanism, thus contributes to reinforcing France's attractiveness, particularly for foreign investors.

268 Arts. L626-29 and R626-54, Commercial Code.
269 Ibid., Art. L626-30.
270 Ibid., Art. L626-30-IV.
271 Ibid., Art. R626-55.
272 Ibid., Art. R626-58-1.

4.3 The Introduction of a Cross-class Cram-Down Mechanism into French Law

With the introduction of the possibility to cross-class cram-down dissenting creditors during safeguard or accelerated safeguard proceedings came the introduction of protections ensuring that all parties are treated fairly, especially creditors.

First, the debtor's consent is compulsory for the court to cross-class cram-down creditors.[273] Second, France has adopted the absolute priority rule, which means that creditors of a class that voted against the plan must be fully repaid when a lower ranking class is entitled to be paid or retains an interest. However, the court may make exceptions to this requirement (*e.g.* in the case of strategic suppliers, tort claimants or equity holders), if such exceptions are deemed necessary to achieve the plan's objectives and if the plan does not excessively affect the rights or interests of impaired parties.[274] Third, in order to adopt a restructuring plan despite the negative vote of one or several classes of creditors, and therefore effect a cross-class cram-down, the court must verify that one of the following two criteria is met:

1. A majority of the classes of impaired parties voted in favour of the plan, provided that at least one of those classes is a secured creditors' class or is senior to the ordinary unsecured creditors' class;[275] or
2. At least one of the classes of affected parties has voted favourably, *i.e.* a class other than an equity holders' class or any other class which is 'out of the money' (*i.e.* which, after determining the value of the debtor as a going concern, could reasonably be expected not to be entitled to any payment or retain any interest while applying the normal distribution order as would be the case in liquidation proceedings or a sale plan (*plan de cession*)).[276]

Finally, the court must ensure that when affected parties have voted against the draft plan, none of these affected parties is in a less favourable situation because of the plan, than that which they would be in in a liquidation or sale of the company.[277]

When one or more classes of equity holders have been constituted and have not approved the plan, a cross-class cram-down may only be implemented if:

1. The debtor exceeds a certain threshold (*i.e.* 150 employees or more or a turnover of EUR 20 million or over);
2. The equity holders of one or several dissenting classes are not 'in the money';

273 Ibid., Art. L626-32.
274 Ibid., Arts. L626-32-I-3° and L626-32-II.
275 Ibid., Art. L626-32-I-2°-(a).
276 Ibid., Art. L626-32-I-2°-(b).
277 Ibid., Art. L626-31.

3. If the plan provides for a capital increased subscribed by cash contribution or by set-off against receivables, the shares issued are offered in priority to the shareholders, *pro rata* their existing shareholding; and
4. The plan does not provide for the transfer of all or part of the rights of dissenting class(es) of equity holders.[278]

5 Other Features Adopted within the French Insolvency and Restructuring Regime

Besides the conciliation/accelerated safeguard reference preventive framework, the Ordinance of 15 September 2021 has also amended the other two restructuring procedures, the safeguard and the rehabilitation processes, as well as upstream early warning tools (*procédure d'alerte*).

5.1 *Mechanisms for Detecting and Preventing Business Difficulties*

Recital 22 of PRD 2019 states that:

> early warning tools should … be put in place to incentivise debtors that start to experience financial difficulties to take early action. Early warning tools which take the form of alert mechanisms that indicate when the debtor has not made certain types of payments could be triggered by, for example, non-payment of taxes or social security contributions. Such tools could be developed either by Member States or by private entities, provided that the objective is met.

Internal early warning tools already existed in France (*procédure d'alerte*),[279] intended to promote a dialogue within the management of the company before the difficulties encountered become overwhelming. The triggering initiatives belongs to the auditor, the social and economic committee or the shareholders. The alert process is divided into several steps. First, the entity that has triggered the alert requests the company's management to explain the economic and financial situation in which the company is. Secondly, if the manager fails to respond or if the continuity of the operation remains compromised, a special report is drafted and a copy sent to the president of the court. Other external warning mechanisms now also exist, notably triggered by the President of

278 Ibid., Art. L626-32-I- 5°.
279 Governed by Arts. L234-1 to L234-4, Commercial Code.

the relevant court (commercial or judicial court) or from approved risk management agencies (*groupements de prévention agréés*).

Article L611-2 of the Commercial Code states that the President of the relevant court may summon the directors of the debtor company, when it is revealed, from any act, document or procedure that they are experiencing difficulties which are likely to jeopardize the continuity and sustainability of the business. The objective of this provision is to make managers aware of, and react to, the difficulties which their company is experiencing, in order to prevent insolvency. Originally available only to the President of the commercial court, this preventive mechanism has since been extended to the judicial court as well (*tribunal judiciaire*).

This detection mechanism is relatively straightforward. The President of the relevant court summons the company's directors for an interview to discuss the implementation of necessary measures with a view to avoid insolvency. Before the Ordinance of September 2021 transposing PRD 2019, managers were merely summoned to attend this meeting but were not sanctioned in case of absence. Article L611-2 of the Commercial Code has therefore been amended to provide that the President of the court may obtain any information likely to give them some accurate representation of the economic and financial situation of the debtor, from the auditors, members of the social and economic committee, public administrations, social security and welfare organizations, as well as the financial risks and payment incidents services *(services chargés de la centralisation des risques bancaires et des incidents de paiement)*.

In relation to detection by approved risk management agencies, Article L611-1 of the French Commercial Code states that, when the agency identifies signs of difficulty, it informs the manager of the debtor and can suggest the intervention of an expert. The detection criterion ('signs of difficulty') is therefore broad and there is no legal precision as to what it entails. In practice, these risk management agencies tend to look at accounting and financial documents communicated by the debtor, as well as any other information brought to their attention such as the loss of contracts or conflicts between equity holders.

5.2 *The 'Post-money' Privilege*

The ordinances implemented in response to the COVID-19 pandemic were in some way inspired by PRD 2019, a 'post-money' privilege which did not exist until then and which has been embedded in the Ordinance of September 2021. This privilege benefits to claims arising from a cash contribution to the debtor:

1. During the observation period, authorized by the supervisor judge; and/or
2. For the implementation of the safeguard (or rehabilitation) plan adopted by the court; or

3. For a modification of the plan, adopted by the court.[280]

Just as in the case of claims benefitting from the new money privilege (*privilège de conciliation*, discussed in Section 2.1), claims guaranteed by the 'post-money' privilege (*privilege de post money*) cannot be subject to write-off or postponements, which are not agreed by their holders in the event of subsequent restructuring proceedings. During restructuring proceedings, therefore, these claims can only be overridden by certain specific claims, such as the super-priority granted to wages, legal fees, new money privileged claims and post-petition claims of the National Wage Guarantee Fund (*Association pour la Garantie des Salaires* (AGS)).

5.3 *Additional Distinctions between Safeguard and Rehabilitation Proceedings*

While rehabilitation proceedings follow the rules of the safeguard procedure with some departures, the main difference between the safeguard and rehabilitation procedures lies in the nature and severity of the difficulties encountered. For rehabilitation proceedings to be opened, the company needs to be in a payment failure situation, which amounts to difficulties which are more severe than the possible momentary cash flow problem under safeguard.

Similar to the safeguard, when the debtor is insolvent and rescue does not seem unlikely, the management of the distressed company can request the opening of rehabilitation proceedings no later than 45 days from the date on which it becomes insolvent, provided that conciliation proceedings are not pending.[281] Any unpaid creditor or the public prosecutor may also request the court to open rehabilitation proceedings against the debtor.[282] Similar to the safeguard, the objectives of rehabilitation proceedings are to allow the company to keep trading, preserve employment and pay off the company's liabilities. It gives rise to a plan sanctioned by a court at the end of an observation period and, where appropriate, to the constitution of classes of affected parties.[283]

As a result, although the safeguard proceedings are available to solvent debtors and rehabilitation proceedings to insolvent ones, the similarities of these two regimes meant that very comparable restructuring tools were applied to companies in very different situations (solvent or insolvent). The Ordinance of September 2021 has slightly modified these proceedings, as the government opted to use the accelerated safeguard as the main

280 Ibid., Art. L622-17.
281 Ibid., Art. L631-4.
282 Ibid., Art. L631-5.
283 Ibid., Art. L631-1.

vessel for the transposition of the PRD. However, since safeguard proceedings are in practice often used defensively to protect a company facing financial difficulties, or as a threat in upstream negotiations, the French government has chosen to introduce additional distinctions between the safeguard and rehabilitation procedures:

1. The maximum duration of safeguard proceedings has been lowered to 12 months, whereas rehabilitation proceedings can last for up to 18 months;[284]
2. While the safeguard rules also apply to creditors' voting and classes, differences have now been introduced to the rehabilitation procedure:
   a. if the debtor does not meet the required thresholds, the authorization to form classes of affected parties may be requested by the administrator, without the debtor's approval;[285]
   b. any affected party may submit a draft restructuring plan to the vote of the classes;[286]
   c. if the plan has not been approved by all classes of affected parties, the court can decide to apply the cross-class cram-down mechanism at the request of the debtor or any affected party (in safeguard proceedings, cross-class cram-down can be implemented by the court with the approval of the debtor only);[287] and
   d. if the approval of the plan through the class-based consultation procedure (whether by regular approval by the classes of affected parties or by a cross-class cram-down) is not achieved, the approval may occur through individual consultation of the creditors.[288]
3. Finally, where the plan is not approved by the requisite classes, including through a cross-class cram-down, the court's power to reschedule the debtor's liabilities by up to 10 years (also known as 'term-out') is no longer available in safeguard proceedings[289] but remains available in rehabilitation proceedings. This is however subject to a minimum instalment of 10% after the fifth years, thereby providing debtors with stronger leverage in restructuring discussions.[290]

6 CONCLUSION

For years, France has been internationally known for its pro-debtor nature and the rather low involvement of creditors in preventive restructuring proceedings. The Ordinance of September 2021 transposing PRD 2019 has made significant changes to French

284 Ibid., Art. L631-7 and Art. L621-3 for the safeguard.
285 Ibid., Art. L631-1.
286 Ibid., Art. L631-19.
287 Ibid., Art. L631-19.
288 Ibid., Art. L631-19.
289 Ibid., former Arts. L621-62 et seq.
290 Ibid., Art. L626-18.

restructuring and insolvency law, making France more attractive to financial investors. While the attractiveness of preventive measures for debtors has been strengthened, in particular conciliation proceedings with the improvement of the grace period mechanism and accelerated safeguard proceedings with the introduction of the constitution of classes and cross-class cram-down mechanism increased the protection that is now offered to secured creditors.

Although this situation is welcomed, the implementation of the new provisions in practice largely rests on insolvency practitioners, whose responsibility is now to make sense of the system of classes of creditors, which turns out to be rather technical. Since the legislator did not strictly regulate the grouping of affected parties into classes, the number and types of classes will therefore depend on the assessment of the administrator. The judge will also have to apprehend new concepts with caution, as they are significant and complex. Concepts such as 'affected parties', 'best interest of creditors test', 'commonality of interests', as well as the criteria for cross-class cram-down are subtle and of variable geometry.

5 GERMANY

Stephan Madaus and David Ehmke[*]

1 INTRODUCTION

The new German preventive restructuring law (*Unternehmensstabilisierungs- und -restrukturierungsgesetz, StaRUG*)[291] of 2021 introduced, for the first time in Germany, a statutory procedure that debtors can use to bind dissenting parties to a restructuring plan outside a formal insolvency procedure. The restructuring procedure offers three distinct advantages for debtors when compared to the insolvency procedure: (i) control, (ii) flexibility and (iii) reputation.

Control: The restructuring procedure is generally designed to be controlled by the debtor with light-touch involvement of the court. This gives directors and possibly even the equity holders an incentive to start the restructuring procedure early and as soon as developments that could jeopardize the existence of the debtor's business have been detected. The debtor will retain the control over the business as well as the restructuring procedure itself. In case the debtor's directors and shareholders see a high chance for a turnaround as well as a good prospect to share in the future success of the business, this is the best possible argument to incentivize an early restructuring.

Flexibility: The restructuring procedure follows a modular approach, *i.e.* any restructuring instrument such as a stay, court examination of specific question, or a plan cram-down or cross-class cram-down confirmation can be selected and requested individually and combined with other restructuring instruments. The court will only order (coercive) restructuring instruments upon the debtor's request. This gives the debtor great flexibility to adjust the procedure to the specific challenges of the restructuring case. The procedure does not require any active court involvement at all if all parties consent to the plan. The debtor also has a bargaining chip in negotiations for a consensual adoption of the plan without court involvement and cram-down confirmations because the debtor can potentially request a (cram-down) confirmation at a later point in time so that creditors know that there is no advantage in opportunistically holding out. Eventually, the debtor may select who shall be affected by a stay or by the plan.

---

* The closing date of this chapter is 30 May 2022.

291 A non-official English translation of the statute can be accessed here (from p. 179), available at: https://www.schultze-braun.de/fileadmin/de/Fachbuecher/Insolvenzjahrbuecher/Insolvenzjahrbuch_2021/Insolvency_and_Restructuring_2021_rz.pdf?_=1618475256 (last viewed 30 May 2022)

Reputation: As insolvency is still often associated with the stigma of a failed debtor, any insolvency process can have a serious negative impact on the debtor's relationship with its business partners, customers and employees. Given that debtors in an already serious liquidity crisis generally do not qualify for restructuring but for insolvency,[292] the average debtor in restructuring can be expected to be in a better financial situation and to have a higher chance to continue trading than the average debtor in insolvency. Also given the flexibility of the restructuring procedure, the procedure may only be as invasive or coercive as is necessary to reach the restructuring goal, *e.g.* concentrated on a financial restructuring, leaving customers and suppliers unaffected and, thus, causing less disruption to the debtor's operative business. A favourable selection of debtors and the opportunity of target-oriented minimal-invasive restructuring measures can help debtors in restructuring to preserve and promote their reputation.[293]

In this chapter, we shall explain and analyse the key features and restructuring instruments of the German restructuring procedure in Section 4, after an overview of the pre-reform situation in insolvency and restructuring in Section 2 and a brief summary of the debate on the implementation of the Preventive Restructuring Directive (PRD 2019)[294] in Germany by StaRUG in Section 3. Where appropriate, we will highlight key differences to the German insolvency procedure. In Section 5, we will conclude with an outlook and suggestions for further improvements to the present restructuring law.

2 Overview of Domestic Pre-reform Restructuring and Insolvency Law Regime in Germany

The last two decades have seen significant reforms on the path towards a restructuring-friendly law and business culture. Already the enactment of the German Insolvency Code (InsO) in 1999 was a major step towards the direction of a more rescue-oriented environment. The InsO was inspired by the US Bankruptcy Act of 1978 and thus comprised a Chapter 11-type plan process. The plan procedure intended to offer the debtor a second chance instead of being primarily a tool for the debtor's liquidation and distribution of liquidation proceeds. In practice, however, the InsO only in part met these expectations. The reasons for the rather moderate success are manifold. German practice was used to

292 See Section 4.2.

293 See Section 2, D. Ehmke & A. Wolf, 'From Bankruptcy and Insolvency, from Restructuring to Resolvency', manuscript, forthcoming 2022; B. de Bruyn & D. Ehmke, 'StaRUG & InsO: Sanierungswerkzeuge des Restrukturierungs- und Insolvenzverfahrens', *NZG*, 2019, pp. 661-672, Section 6.

294 Directive (EU) 2019/1023 of the European Parliament and of the Council of 20 June 2019 on preventive restructuring frameworks, on discharge of debt and disqualifications, and on measures to increase the efficiency of procedures concerning restructuring, insolvency and discharge of debt, and amending Directive (EU) 2017/1132 (Directive on restructuring and insolvency), O.J. L 172/18.

sell viable businesses in an insolvency liquidation as a going concern. Courts and legal practitioners would thus be rather cautious to make use of the full spectrum of newly available restructuring instruments whereas creditors and business partners of a debtor were often sceptical about supporting an insolvent debtor. Directors fearing the stigma of insolvency had an incentive to avoid or to postpone insolvency procedures for as long as possible. Accordingly, many debtors only filed for an insolvency procedure at a point of time where the debtor's course of action could not be reversed anymore (because of a lack of funds to successfully implement reorganization strategies). As a result, the much-feared stigma of insolvency often turned into a self-fulfilling prophecy.[295]

In 2012, substantial reforms of the German InsO with a view to facilitate the restructuring of distressed companies and to promote the transformation of insolvency practice towards rescue culture came into effect (the so-called 'ESUG reforms'). The debtor-in-possession (DIP) option was strengthened, as well as the barriers to enter the self-administration/DIP procedure were lowered. A so-called 'protective shield procedure' was introduced for the debtor to prepare an insolvency plan before the insolvency-opening, the federal states were encouraged to establish centralized insolvency courts and the insolvency plan option was expanded (*e.g.* modification of equity claims, to allow for debt-to-equity swaps and the transfer of ownership interests). The goal of the reform was to enhance the effectiveness of early restructurings and to make it more appealing for debtors and directors to take actions for an early restructuring procedure.[296]

Another step towards a rescue culture was made with the claw-back reforms in 2017 which were sought to increase the chances of a successful turnaround outside formal insolvency. Against the background that the German insolvency law provides for a comparatively quite broad mechanism for insolvency contesting, the powers of the insolvency administrator to reverse transactions and claw-back assets were tightened by the 2017 reform. While claw-back can certainly ensure equal and fair treatment and disincentivize fraudulent or biased transactions, powerful claw-back rights are particularly burdensome for debtors trading in an already financially difficult situation. Business partners are more reluctant to trade with a distressed debtor if they need to give due consideration to the additional risk of extensive contesting rights resulting in a claw-back of the business partner's settled receivables. The 2017 reform, thus, was intended to avoid such negative side effects of extensive claw-back rights for debtor's trading in difficult times.

295 See D. Ehmke & A. Wolf, above note 293.

296 See F. Jacoby, S. Madaus, D. Sack, H. Schmidt & C. Thole, 'Evaluierung – Gesetz zur weiteren Erleichterung der Sanierung von Unternehmen (ESUG) vom 7. Dezember 2011', BT-Drs. 19/4880 available at: https://dserver.bundestag.de/btd/19/048/1904880.pdf (last viewed 30 May 2022) for a legal and practical evaluation of the ESUG-reforms, commissioned by the German government, and presented by the research group on 30 April 2018.

The efforts made by the German legislator to reform the insolvency procedure always intentionally fell short of any type of statutory procedure for an orderly restructuring outside insolvency law. Out-of-court restructurings would always require unanimous consent in the form of a workout. This approach followed a decision of the German Federal Court of Justice in 1991 when the Court ruled that no dissenting party is under any civil law obligation to cooperate and consent to a restructuring plan,[297] even if the restructuring plan is in the best common interest of all creditors.

Out-of-court restructurings could, thus, only be arranged as informal workouts. A rather concentrated lending structure in Germany with professional repeat players as lenders in regularly long-established lending relations with the debtor would indeed often enable such informal workouts. The increasing importance of debt instruments such as bonds, debt trading, and consequently a rather dispersed and less related creditor structure, however, would confront debtors with new challenges such as the individually rational but collectively destructive incentive of creditors to hold-out and free ride on the concessions of other creditors.[298] The old German Bond Law (SchVG) of 1899 was not equipped for this task. Substantial amendments of payment terms by a binding majority vote were prohibited under the old SchVG until its reform in 2009.[299] Absent such contractual provisions, the rule remained – until the introduction of the new restructuring procedure – that debt restructurings would always require individual and unanimous consent.

3 THE INTRODUCTION OF THE STARUG AS PART OF THE IMPLEMENTATION OF THE PRD 2019

The introduction of the new German restructuring law – the StaRUG – has principally been welcomed by academics and practitioners alike as a useful addition to the spectrum of restructuring and insolvency options. Especially, the mere availability of a statutory procedure outside formal insolvency to restructure corporate debt was acclaimed by many. Already the pace of the legislative procedure, with the first draft being presented on 19 September 2020 and the law coming into force on 1 January 2021, highlights the legislator's ambition for implementing the new tool.

Nonetheless, the specific features of the then draft restructuring law were subject to a heated debate in 2020. Criticism came from two angles: while some had hoped for a more

297 Federal Court of Justice, decision of 12 December 1991 – IX ZR 178/91 = NJW 1992, pp. 967-971.

298 See D. Skeel, 'An Evolutionary Theory of Corporate Law and Corporate Bankruptcy', *Vanderbilt Law Review*, 1998, 51, pp. 1325-1398 on the impact of dispersed versus concentrated lending and ownership structures.

299 See D. Ehmke, *Bond Debt Governance*, Nomos: Baden-Baden, 2019, pp. 279-294.

courageous approach, others were rather sceptical as to whether the law would lay the ground for misuse and mismanagement. In line with the traditional German approach in insolvency "not to put the fox in charge of the henhouse", the sceptical commentators advocated a stronger role for the practitioner in the field of restructuring (PIFOR), less powerful instruments for the debtor, more intense oversight and stricter requirements to be tested before the debtor could make use of the restructuring instruments. As a result of the debate, two major changes to the draft of the restructuring law stand out.

The first major amendment was the cancellation of rules which would have established a shift of the directors' fiduciary duties towards the creditors in the vicinity of insolvency and declared shareholder resolutions contradicting the creditor's best interest irrelevant. This would have basically entitled directors to enter the restructuring procedure without the shareholder's consent and, thus, would have been a game changer for the German restructuring business, because a voluntary insolvency application always (at least according to a decision of the Appellate Court of Munich) requires a qualified shareholder resolution. In fact, directors not seeking such shareholder resolution could be held liable by the debtor's shareholders should their ownership interest in the debtor be devalued in insolvency, which is quite likely.[300] The same principle will probably be adopted for the restructuring procedure so that a solo run of the management to initiate the restructuring procedure without the shareholders' support is rather unlikely.

The second major change was the cancellation of the debtor's right to terminate executory contracts and modify debt arising from such contracts, as discussed in Section 4.8. This amendment significantly reduced the attractiveness of the restructuring procedure for debtors with long-term liabilities (*e.g.* such as lease and supply contracts) and makes the procedure less useful for operative restructurings.

4 MAIN FEATURES OF A StaRUG RESTRUCTURING

4.1 *Objective and Scope of the StaRUG*

The main objective of the new restructuring procedure, as stated in the explanatory memorandum to the government draft of the restructuring law, is to increase the chance for an early restructuring outside formal insolvency. This statement is rather surprising given that the restructuring law is not available for debtors, unless they also qualify for a voluntary insolvency application.[301] To this extent, the German legislator has forgone the

300 OLG München, decision of 21 March 2013 – 23 U 3344/12 = NZI 2013, pp. 542-546.

301 For a comparison of restructuring and insolvency procedure in Germany see B. de Bruyn & D. Ehmke, above note 293.

chance to make the restructuring procedure available for a truly early (solvent) restructuring. Yet, it is to be expected that the new restructuring route will be beneficial for debtors as well as creditors and thus provide a real alternative to the existing insolvency procedures, especially for the purpose of financial restructurings.

As to the personal scope, the restructuring procedure is available for any entrepreneur or corporate debtor having debts stemming from entrepreneurial activity, provided in each case that the debtor is expected to encounter a liquidity crisis within the next 24 months (prospective insolvency – *drohende Zahlungsunfähigkeit*).[302]

As to the duration, the restructuring procedure expires 6 months after the initial motion unless it is extended for another 6 months.[303] In practice, the time frame mostly depends on how fast an agreement on the restructuring plan can be reached with the key players. On a practical note, a debtor who requires the protection of a stay should have concluded the procedure in under 8 months, which corresponds with the maximum duration of a stay.

4.2 Criteria/Test to Enter the StaRUG

The German legislator decided to translate the 'likelihood of insolvency' threshold in Article 4(1) of PRD 2019 into the insolvency law definition of "imminent or prospective insolvency" in the InsO. Pursuant to that definition, a debtor qualifies as imminently or prospectively insolvent if it is more likely than not that the debtor will not be able to cover all debts once they fall due with the available liquidity within a forecast period of 24 months.[304] The forecast period may be more or less than 24 months with proper case-specific justification. As a result, debtors considered to be prospectively insolvent may choose to voluntarily access the StaRUG restructuring procedure, the insolvency procedure or to use no statutory procedure at all for a turnaround.

The access to the restructuring option is denied, however, if debtors are already unable to pay their debts as they fall due[305] or over-indebted.[306] Directors of such corporate debtors

302 See Section 4.2.

303 Section 31, Para. 4 no. 4 StaRUG. For a practical example of a restructuring procedure concluded in approximately 2 months, see G. Bernau, H. Beyer, N. Raiß & M. Hofmann, 'Früh, schnell und fast geräuschlos', *INDat Report*, 2021, 9, pp. 10-25.

304 Section 18 InsO.

305 Section 17 InsO. As defined in case law, a debtor is considered unable to pay their debts if the debtor cannot pay over 90% of liabilities falling due within a period of 3 weeks with the liquidity available during that period.

306 A debtor is over-indebted if (i) the liabilities exceed the assets and if (ii) it is more likely than not that the debtor will experience a liquidity shortage within the next 12 months pursuant to Section 19 InsO. The statutory definition of 12 versus 24 months was introduced with the same reform as the restructuring procedure and relates to a proposal by M. Brinkmann, 'Die Antragspflicht bei Überschuldung – ein

are obliged to file for insolvency procedure and otherwise face civil liability and criminal sanctions for a delayed filing for insolvency.[307]

If the debtor was able to access the restructuring procedure before they become insolvent, the directors' obligation to file for insolvency is suspended. They are, however, required to inform the court should the debtor become unable to pay their debts or should the debtor become over-indebted.[308] In such case, the court will generally terminate the restructuring procedure unless the debtor can show that the restructuring is likely to succeed and that the restructuring procedure is in the best interest of creditors.[309] This opens a window of opportunity for well-prepared debtors, especially in case that they have already advanced negotiations with their creditors, to initiate the StaRUG procedure even though they know internally that they might become insolvent immediately after due to stakeholder actions. This does not change the fact, however, that any debtor who initiates the restructuring procedure must present a liquidity forecast in good faith that shows that the debtor will not run out of cash within the next 12 months but will probably become illiquid sometime during the next 13 to 24 months. If this projection proves wrong later in the procedure, the case is dismissed unless the debtor is able to convince the court that a highly advanced negotiation status justifies the continuation of the restructuring procedure for the sake of all creditors.

Differently from an insolvency procedure, there is no formal opening procedure during which the court must decide based on a report submitted by a court-appointed examiner as to whether the debtor qualifies for the procedure. The debtor, however, must formally notify the court of its restructuring intent in order to apply for restructuring instruments. The formal notification by the debtor shall be submitted along certain mandatory information. Importantly, the debtor shall report about the status of negotiations and submit a draft of the restructuring plan or, absent a draft plan, at least a restructuring concept, in which the debtor elaborates on the reasons of the debtor's (financial/economic) crisis, the restructuring goal and measures to be taken to reach the restructuring goal.[310] A test of the entry criteria of imminent insolvency becomes relevant only once the debtor requests the use of a restructuring instrument such as a stay or a plan confirmation.[311]

---

notwendiges Korrelat der beschränkten Haftung', in: W. Ebke, C. Seagon & A. Piekenbrock (eds), *Überschuldung: Quo Vadis*, Nomos: Baden-Baden, 2020, pp. 67-78.

307 See especially Section 15a and 15b InsO.

308 Section 42 StaRUG.

309 Section 33, Para. 2 no 1 StaRUG. Cf. District Court of Dresden, decision of 7 June 2021 – 574 RES 2/21 = NZI 2021, 893.

310 Section 31 StaRUG.

311 See Section 51, Para. 1 no 3 StaRUG (for a stay) and Section 63, Para. 1 no 1 StaRUG (for a plan confirmation).

4.3 Involved Actors

The DIP principle has been strictly translated into the new restructuring procedure. The debtor's management retains control of all business decisions, with the exception that the restructuring court can appoint a PIFOR and bestow the power upon him to approve or disapprove exceptional payments[312] (but not to interfere with the debtor's day-to-day business).[313] Importantly, the debtor is the main actor of the procedure. Only the debtor is entitled to initiate the procedure, to propose a restructuring plan (thereby excluding competing plans by creditors or the PIFOR), and to ask the court to order a stay or confirm the restructuring plan in a (cross-class) cram-down decision. It follows that the right of initiative is the debtor's prerogative. Neither the PIFOR, restructuring court nor creditors take a proactive role in the restructuring procedure.

The PIFOR advises the debtor, monitors the restructuring procedure and assists the competent restructuring court by making reports. There are certain limited cases in which a PIFOR must always be appointed while typically the appointment of a PIFOR only happens if requested by the debtor (or creditors) and in cases in which the court decides in its own discretion that the appointment of a PIFOR is necessary to advance the procedure in all parties' best interest.

To fulfil his duty to advise, monitor and report, the PIFOR may access the debtor's business records, request insider information from the debtor/the debtor's management and review the debtor's financial situation, compliance with procedural rules and the plan.[314] The PIFOR may also preside over the voting procedure.[315]

In the spirit of a true DIP procedure, the court also does not assume a proactive role. The court will answer at the debtor's initiative and typically will rely for its decision on information provided by the debtor, unless creditors or the PIFOR bring circumstances to the court's attention upon which the court may reject or suspend a restructuring instrument that has been requested by the debtor.

The creditors' main right is to approve or disapprove the plan and to appeal to the restructuring court should their rights be violated.[316] Creditors can also influence the appointment of a PIFOR,[317] but the debtor's proposal for a PIFOR takes precedence over the creditors' proposal.[318] The most powerful tool of individual and organized creditors

312 Section 76, Para. 2 no 3 StaRUG.

313 The court may also order that any payments to the debtor shall be collected by the PIFOR, see Section 76, Para. 2 no 2 lit. b. StaRUG.

314 Section 76, Para. 2 no 2 lit. a, Para. 4 StaRUG.

315 Section 76, 77, Para. 2, 79 StaRUG.

316 See Section 17 et seq StaRUG for the voting procedure.

317 Section 74, Para. 2 sent 3, 77, 93, Para. 2 StaRUG.

318 See Section 74, Para. 2 sent 2 StaRUG.

with a significant share of voting rights to affect the course of the restructuring procedure is, therefore, their hold-out position as a bargaining chip in negotiations with the debtor.

4.4 Stay

A key instrument of the procedure is a stay, which prevents creditors from enforcing their claim[319] or from realizing an asset pledged as collateral.[320] A stay can be ordered by the court upon the debtor's request and the debtor can request that the stay should apply to all or only to selected creditors.[321] Given that every party affected by the stay needs to be informed, a stay applicable to (almost) all business parties, such as suppliers, can cause quite a turmoil and rather worsen than improve the debtor's situation so that absence of an automatic stay and the flexibility to target only specific creditors can be considered a strength of the restructuring procedure.

A stay will initially be ordered for up to 3 months with a possible 1-month extension conditional upon that the debtor has presented a plan to the creditors. Once the voting has taken place and the debtor has requested a court confirmation, an extension for an additional 4 months is possible until the plan has been confirmed and a final judgement has been entered.[322]

During a stay, a creditor may not withhold performance, terminate or modify the contract, because the debtor did not perform the contract as agreed before the stay was ordered.[323] This rule provides broader protection during the stay as the prohibition of *ipso facto* clauses which invalidate contractual clauses to modify or terminate a contract because of the mere fact that a debtor has entered the restructuring procedure or made use of its instruments.[324] Petitions to open an insolvency procedure by creditors are also suspended during the stay.[325] Given that the stay does not come with a moratorium, the debtor remains obliged to perform contracts as contractually agreed during the stay.

4.5 The Plan

The restructuring plan must contain an informative part and a part in which the terms of the plan, *i.e.* the modifications to debt, equity and collateral, are proposed. The first part of

319 Section 49, Para. 1 no 1 StaRUG.
320 Ibid.
321 Section 50, 51 StaRUG.
322 Section 52, 53 StaRUG.
323 Section 53, Para. 1 StaRUG. The counterparty, however, may demand adequate protection should they be obliged to provide their performance in advance to the debtor according to Section 55, Para. 3 StaRUG.
324 Section 44 StaRUG.
325 Section 58 StaRUG.

the restructuring plan is informative and shall enable the affected parties to make an informed decision and evaluate as to whether the plan is in their best interest. For this purpose, the plan needs to describe the reasons for the debtor's current situation and describe how the plan shall help to overcome the debtor's financial crisis.[326] A key component of the informative part is the comparative calculation, in which it shall be presented how the parties would stand with and without the plan's confirmation. The calculation based on an alternative liquidation scenario requires special justification.[327] In a case decided by the District Court Dresden, the debtor, for instance, could show that there was no investor available to acquire the debtor's business and that there was no prospect to continue the business in an insolvency procedure because the debtor was highly dependent on public clients who were not allowed to place an order with an insolvent debtor for regulatory reasons. The alternative no-plan scenario, thus, was the liquidation of the debtor's assets.[328]

In the second part, the plan defines how the rights of (secured) creditors and equity holders shall be modified.[329] Debt claims may be postponed, reduced or swapped into equity. Equity claims may be cancelled or diluted, with or without compensation. Secured creditors may have to give up or exchange their collateral. The plan would, moreover, define the conditions of new financing.[330]

To this extent, the restructuring plan equals the insolvency plan, however, with two important differences. First, the restructuring plan may involve the modification of non-payment terms of multi-party agreements,[331] such as bond contracts. Different from an insolvency plan, for which all debt claims are considered due and payable[332] and are therefore subject to ratable satisfaction, this is not necessarily the case in a restructuring plan. The contractual relation between a debtor and bond creditors might very well be continued, especially in case of only minor adjustments to the bond contract. The restructuring plan may not even entail a haircut for the bond creditors but require the suspension of negative covenants which would otherwise prohibit transactions essential for the restructuring; for instance, a distressed M&A with a change of control or the assumption of new (senior) debt. With the suspension or modification of non-payment terms, the debtor can avoid default under the bond contract and possibly the acceleration of debt repayment obligations and a subsequent cross-default under other debt contracts.

326 Section 6, Para. 1 StaRUG.

327 Section 6, Para. 2 StaRUG.

328 District Court of Dresden, decision of 7 June 2021 – 574 RES 2/21 = NZI 2021, 893. See also District Court of Hamburg, decision of 12 April 2021 – 61a RES 1/21 = NZI 2021, 544.

329 Section 7, Para. 1 StaRUG.

330 Section 12 StaRUG.

331 Cf. District Court of Cologne, decision of 3 March 2021 – 83 RES 1/21 = NZI 2021, 433 on the amendment of a syndicated loan agreement and a restructuring agreement.

332 Section 41, Para. 1 InsO.

Second, the debtor has quite some flexibility to select the parties affected by the plan and may even treat creditors with an equal rank in insolvency differently, conditional upon that the debtor can show reasonable (economic) grounds for this decision. The right of the debtor to treat creditors of equal rank differently follows naturally from the right to select the parties affected by the plan.[333] Given that the debtor in principle has the right to exclude trade creditors based on the argument that their inclusion would harm the business, the debtor is effectively entitled to treat the claims of trade creditors more favourably if needed.

Like the insolvency plan, a restructuring plan is not an instrument to restructure the debt of a corporate group as a whole. It cannot work as a group restructuring plan across group entities. But the new German law enables both the restructuring and the insolvency plan to carry a single point of entry for the financial restructuring of the group. The plan of one debtor/legal entity as part of a corporate group is now able to modify the principal loan or bonds agreement and encumbered rights in down-, side- or up-stream collateral of affiliated companies with their consent and conditional upon adequate compensation to affected creditors in order to disentangle intercompany relations.[334] This enables the debtor and affiliated companies to either restructure the group's financing or prepare the business for a fresh start without intercompany obligation, *e.g.* for a sale of only the debtor's business.

Any performance or debt modification pursuant to a court-sanctioned restructuring plan is protected against any claw-back based on bad faith in a possible future insolvency. This safe harbour is meant to incentivize parties to support a reasonable plan offer made by a debtor in distress. As the distress is disclosed in a restructuring the insolvency administrator in a potential later insolvency procedure could avoid transactions made with this knowledge pursuant to Section 133 InsO, including plan-related transactions, for a period of 4 (to 10) years. The much-needed claw-back privilege comes however, with significant exceptions. Importantly, if a plan determines the transfer of (almost) all of the debtor's assets, the claw-back protection will typically not apply unless the adequate compensation of parties not affected by the plan is guaranteed, *i.e.* that they are not left behind.[335] To incentivize new financing, which is often vital for a successful restructuring and therefore in the best interest of all creditors, it is necessary to extend such privilege to new financing, as it is explicitly required by Article 17(1) PRD 2019.[336]

333 Sections 9, 28, Para. 1 StaRUG with the corresponding explanation in the explanatory memorandum of the government draft of SanInsFoG/StaRUG.

334 See Section 2, Para. 4 StaRUG and Section 217, Para. 2 InsO in connection to Section 15 Stock Corporation Law (AktG).

335 See Section 90, Para. 2 StaRUG.

336 Absent an explicit rule claw-back protection of new financing in the German restructuring law, German courts should be expected to apply such privilege under the existing rules in conformity with the PRD 2019. See S. Madaus, 'Die begrenzte Insolvenzfestigkeit des Restrukturierungsplans, der Planleistungen

4.6 Adoption and Confirmation of the Plan

All parties directly affected by the plan are entitled to vote on the plan for its adoption. Voting takes place in classes of rights as constructed by the debtor. A plan is adopted by a class if parties in this class representing at least 75% of the nominal debt or equity value accepted the plan. No headcount majority is required.[337]

In case all classes have accepted the plan by the required majority, the court may confirm the plan over the dissent of individual creditors and shareholders in a class, provided that the plan meets all legal requirements. The restructuring court will review as to whether the debtor is still imminent insolvent, as to whether the debtor has complied with the rules governing the plan regarding content, procedure and adoption, and as to whether the plan does not obviously lack prospect of success.[338] In case of new financing, the court will also review the soundness of the underlying restructuring concept, *i.e.* the measures taken to reach the restructuring goal as defined by the debtor and thus the prospect that new financing can be repaid. Facts which should raise doubts about the restructuring concept will only be considered as far as such facts are positively known to the court. Otherwise, the court will rely on the information provided by the debtor.[339] Upon the objection of dissenting parties, the court also considers whether the plan sees those worse off than they would be in the next best alternative scenario (best interest test).[340] In case of a complex restructuring, it is very likely that the court will appoint a PIFOR in its own discretion to assist the court in providing an informed opinion on the restructuring plan.[341] In case of a cross-class cram-down, a PIFOR will be appointed to comment on the restructuring plan.[342]

If the plan is not adopted by all classes, the debtor can request a cross-class cram-down confirmation, which requires a more intense court review. The court will also assess as to whether the dissenting class as a whole receives a fair share in the value distributed under the plan (plan value). For this purpose, the court will apply a non-discrimination test and a (relaxed) absolute priority rule. This requires the equal treatment of the dissenting class with consenting classes of equally ranking rights in an insolvency liquidation[343] and that

sowie unterstützender Rechtshandlungen während der Restrukturierungssache', *NZI-Beilage*, 2021, pp. 35-37.

337 See Section 24, 25 StaRUG.

338 See Section 63, Para. 1 StaRUG.

339 See Section 63, Para. 2 StaRUG.

340 See Section 64, Para. 1 StaRUG. Cf. Higher Regional Court of Dresden, decision of 1 July 2021 – 5 T 363/21 = ZIP 2021, 2596 (appeal against District Court of Dresden, decision of 7 June 2021 – 574 RES 2/21).

341 Section 73, Para. 3 no 2 StaRUG.

342 Section 73, Para. 2 StaRUG.

343 See Section 27, Para. 1 no 3 and Para. 2 no 2 StaRUG.

classes of lower ranking rights, especially shareholders, shall not receive any value[344] unless the specific needs of the restructuring case justify the discrimination or deviation under the plan.[345] Differently and more flexible than in an insolvency plan, creditor classes of equal rank may thus be treated differently if there is a justifying economic reason.[346]

These deviations contain some important new exceptions to the traditional absolute priority rule: shareholders of the debtor may participate in the distribution of plan value, *i.e.* retain ownership in the going-concern business of the debtor, without further justification or contribution if the plan entails only minor adjustments to the creditors' rights (*e.g.* postponement of repayment for up to 18 months).[347] This possibility provides an incentive for early restructurings which should often require less harsh measures than late restructurings. Further, a sole shareholder or a shareholder class may also retain value (their shares) if the shareholder's continued engagement is essential for the going concern of the debtor,[348] *e.g.* because of the shareholder's input as manager, key person or creative mind. To bind such individually important shareholders, their participation in the plan value will be conditional upon their commitment to the debtor for as long as required to reach the restructuring goal but for a maximum period of 5 years.

4.7 *Possibilities for a Debt-for-Equity Swap*

One possibility to restructure debt and distribute the company's value to creditors is a debt-for-equity swap. Such a debt-for-equity swap requires the individual consent of the relevant creditors to become shareholders of the company.[349] In practice, this is a significant obstacle because many creditors, such as banks or trade creditors, have no interest in accepting shares, especially in private companies.

The only relevant objection to a plan proposing a debt-for-equity swap is that the plan is not in the best interest of existing creditors or shareholders, for which they must prove that an alternative scenario outside a formal restructuring would have promised a higher value for them.

While the debt-for-equity swap is a helpful tool to restructure the debtor's liabilities without draining the company of cash, it may also be used for loan-to-own strategies by investors who have bought debt, possibly in a distressed situation, with the ultimate

344 See Section 27, Para. 1 no 2 StaRUG. Under this provision, the plan does not provide for any value if rights retained or value received is adequately compensated under the plan ('new money / value exception').

345 See Section 28 StaRUG.

346 See Section 28, Para. 1 StaRUG and District Court of Hamburg, decision of 12 April 2021 – 61a RES 1/21 = NZI 2021, 544.

347 See Section 28, Para. 2 no 2 StaRUG.

348 See Section 28, Para. 2 no 1 StaRUG.

349 Section 2, Para. 3, Section 7, Para. 4 StaRUG.

intention to acquire the company. For shareholders, this constitutes a threat to their ownership of the company – a threat, however, which is mitigated by the fact that directors run the risk of personal liability should they initiate the restructuring procedure without the shareholders' approval.[350]

An alternative to the debt-for-equity swap is the direct transfer of shares to a third party under the plan, *i.e.* to a new outside investor. The advantage of this option is that the debtor's equity can be offered to a strategic investor who can extract the most value from the debtor's business. Practical experience from the ESUG reform, which introduced the option to modify rights in equity with an insolvency plan, showed that a share transfer is more frequently used than a debt-for-equity swap.[351]

4.8 *Executory Contracts*

While the most recent draft of the new restructuring law contained the debtor's right to terminate executory contracts, this right was removed at the last minute from the restructuring procedure by the legislator. Consequently, the debtor is left with no other choice than to perform executory contracts, *i.e.* only the already outstanding obligations of the debtor for which the counterparty's consideration has already been provided are subject to modification. Future (mutual) obligations, however, remain unaffected by the restructuring procedure.[352] The termination right or the debtor's choice to perform economically favourable contracts and terminate unfavourable contracts is key to many insolvency laws and an important instrument in German insolvency law.[353] The availability of such an instrument in the restructuring procedure has been criticized by politicians, lobbyists and academics alike. It was argued that a termination right outside formal insolvency would contradict the principle *pacta sunt servanda* and that it could potentially cause a chain reaction of financial distress, *e.g.* the landlord's distress following the tenant's distress.[354] Both arguments are not compelling.

The principle *pacta sunt servanda* is certainly affected if contracts can be terminated and future (mutual) obligations can be suspended in a statutory procedure but the same is

350 See Section 3.

351 See F. Jacoby, S. Madaus, D. Sack, H. Schmidt & C. Thole, above note 296, Zweiter Teil, C II. Tab. 16.

352 Section 3, Para. 2 StaRUG.

353 See Section 103 et seq InsO.

354 See, for instance, the statement of the German Federal Council to proposed German restructuring law pointing out that, that the debtor's termination right would (i) constitute a fundamental violation of the principle pacta sunt servanda, (ii) cause significant economic damage, and (iii) overwhelm restructuring courts which would have to decide on complex economic issues: Bundesrat Drucksache 619/20 at no. 3 and 13, available at: https://www.bundesrat.de/SharedDocs/drucksachen/2020/0601-0700/619-20(B).pdf;jsessionid=0FDB98DE17FF84A92647B8A32CA2FE3B.2_cid391?__blob=publicationFile v=1 (last viewed 30 May 2022).

true in a (cross-class) cram-down for past obligations. The expectation of a dissenting lender that the loan will be repaid in full when it is due is similarly disappointed in a restructuring as the expectation of a landlord that the full contractual period for the lease will be honoured should the tenant make use of a restructuring instrument to terminate the contract or to choose non-performance. From an economic perspective, the only difference is that a lender (or similarly the landlord, supplier, etc. with past/outstanding claims) has already sunk their investments in advance while the counterparty of an executory contract has not yet provided their own corresponding consideration. Whether this should be considered as a good argument to reject the termination right seems rather questionable given that the counterparties of executory contracts have at least the advantage that they can try to offer their performance to the market, *e.g.* the landlord can still look for another tenant. Should the new lease agreement offer less value, the landlord could claim damages from the debtor subject to modification by the plan.

While it is debatable under what requirements the debtor should be entitled to choose non-performance of a contract, the cancellation of the termination right has burdened the German restructuring procedure with a distinct disadvantage to the German insolvency procedure and the Dutch restructuring procedure (*Wet homologatie onderhands akkoord*, WHOA). The latter does not only offer a termination right but also a low entry barrier for foreign debtors, thus setting an incentive for forum shopping. The latest draft version of the German restructuring law required the restructuring court to review the economic question as to whether the termination of the contract is appropriate to benefit the restructuring concept, *i.e.* the restructuring plan and further measures to be taken to reach the restructuring goal. This approach is flawed since insolvency courts in Germany would typically not deal with such kind of questions and because the question what is appropriate to benefit the restructuring concept is primarily determined by the restructuring concept itself.[355] Put differently, if the financial creditors take a huge haircut, the debtor might be able to pay the full rent of an uneconomic lease. If the burden of restructuring is shared equally by financial creditors and the counterparties of executory contracts, the termination of uneconomic contracts and the modification of damage claims which arise from such contracts is always appropriate. This leads to the fundamental question as to whether a termination or modification of debts arising from executory contracts should be permitted: how shall the burden of restructuring be distributed?

Eventually, the risk of a chain reaction should claims arising from executory contracts be subject to modification is similarly not convincing. Debtors entitled to enter the restructuring procedure are similarly entitled to voluntarily enter into the insolvency procedure. Should non-performance of executory contracts be required, the insolvency

355 See M. Hofmann, 'Vertragsbeendigung nach §§ 49 ff. StaRUG-E – praktisches Sanierungstool oder untaugliches Ungetüm?', *NZI*, 2019, pp. 871-874.

procedure offers this opportunity. As initially discussed, insolvency might not be the best value-preserving option if compared to a restructuring. The cancellation of the termination right, thus, rather incentivizes debtors who are reluctant to make use of the insolvency option to delay an early restructuring and likely enter insolvency at a later point in time with an even less satisfactory quota for the counterparty of the executory contract. The potential chain reaction is not avoided; it is just delayed.

One of the authors has suggested in a parliamentary hearing to make future obligations of the debtor subject to a modification under the restructuring plan. The counterparties of the debtor in an executory contract would vote in a distinct class on the plan and potentially be crammed-down (in a cross-class cram-down). They could reject the plan and claim to be worse off than in a no-plan scenario or discriminated in the burden sharing under the plan compared to other classes. If bound by the plan, they would still be entitled to terminate their contract and, thus, not be bound to offer their performance for the debtor's consideration for the reduced/modified price as defined by the plan, which in turn incentivizes the debtor to offer market terms in the plan.[356] This proposal borrows from the practice of the UK company voluntary arrangements as it has been used by debtors in the retail sector who have suffered severely under the retail crisis in UK's city centres due to changing shopping habits and the shift towards online shopping.

4.9 *Jurisdiction for and Recognition of Court Decisions in Europe*

Starting from 17 July 2022, German debtors can request a public restructuring procedure. Differently from a private (or confidential) procedure, the public procedure is publicly announced so that also parties which might not yet be affected by the procedure will have an opportunity to learn about them. Only the public procedure was added to Annex A of the European Insolvency Regulation 2015 (EIR 2015)[357] so that the COMI principle applies according to Article 3(1) EIR 2015, and German restructuring law according to Article 7 EIR 2015, and recognition within the EU follows from Articles 19 et seq, and in particular Article 32 EIR 2015 for court-confirmed restructuring plans and court-ordered stays.

The matter of international jurisdiction and cross-border recognition for private restructuring procedures within the EU remains unclear. The same is true for all types of (private and public) restructuring procedures in relation to third countries. While the German courts will probably accept international jurisdiction for such restructuring

356 See S. Madaus, 'Stellungnahme zum Regierungsentwurf eines Gesetzes zur Fortentwicklung des Sanierungs- und Insolvenzrechts (SanInsFoG) sowie zum diesbezüglichen Antrag der Fraktion der FDP', Deutscher Bundestag – Anhörung des Ausschusses für Recht und Verbraucherschutz, 12 November 2020, Section 3 (c).

357 Regulation (EU) 2015/838 of the European Parliament and of the Council of 20 May 2015 on insolvency proceedings (recast), O.J. L 141/19.

procedures if the debtor's COMI is in Germany,[358] the question of the applicable law and of recognition across Europe and in third states is uncertain.[359]

For contracts governed by German law, it is likely that the modification of the debt claim arising from such contract in the course of a StaRUG procedure should be recognized across the EU also under the Rome I Regulation.[360] For contracts governed by foreign law, neither German[361] nor EU law provides specific answers to the question of the law applicable to a modification and whether modifications in a German restructuring plan will be recognized in foreign (EU and third country) countries. As things currently stand, it is particularly uncertain that restructuring plans adopted and confirmed in private restructuring procedure would receive recognition in fellow EU Member States pursuant to the Brussel Ibis Regulation due to its Article 1(2)(b).[362]

The German restructuring law is surprisingly silent when it comes to matters of international jurisdiction and recognition. Therefore, debtors with debt contracts in significant volume governed by foreign law of other EU jurisdictions are currently best advised to request a public procedure considering that absent recognition under the EIR 2015, they will have to cope with substantial legal uncertainty, *i.e.* they might have to deal with lawsuits and enforcement for full repayment.

Still, the use of a public procedure to overcome cross-border uncertainties has relevant limitations too. First, a public procedure requires the debtor's COMI to be found in Germany. Second, the framework of the EIR 2015 envisions the ability to limit the effects of main procedure by initiating secondary procedures. Third, the EIR 2015 contains a number of mandatory provisions, *e.g.* for the filing of claims or the hotchpotch rule in Article 23 EIR 2015, that are not easy to apply in restructuring procedures.

358 Section 35 StaRUG determines jurisdiction of regional restructuring courts within (!) Germany (venue) based on the COMI principle. It is argued that Section 35 StaRUG should be applied in analogy to determine jurisdiction in private procedures also to determine international jurisdiction based on the COMI principle.

359 See for private procedure *e.g.* C. Schlöder, J. Parzinger & L. Knebel, 'Der Restrukturierungsplan nach dem StaRUG im Lichte grenzüberschreitender Restrukturierungen – praxistaugliches Anerkennungsregime oder ein Fall für die obersten Gerichte?', *ZIP*, 2021, pp. 1041-1051 (p. 1043) on the applicability of the Brussel I Regulation (EU) No 1215/2012 on jurisdiction and the recognition and enforcement of judgements in civil and commercial matters. See also Thole, 'Vertrauliche Restrukturierungsverfahren: Internationale Zuständigkeit, anwendbares Recht und Anerkennung', *ZIP*, 2021, pp. 2153-2162, 2154 et seq.

360 See D. Skauradszun, 'Restrukturierungsverfahren und das Internationale Privatrecht', *NZI*, 2021, pp. 568-572, 570 et seq on recognition under the Rom-I regulation (EC) No 593/2008 on the law applicable to contractual obligations (Rome I).

361 See D. Skauradszun, above note 360, p. 571 et seq. argues in favour of German restructuring law to apply in analogy to Section 335 et seq InsO.

362 See *e.g.* C. Thole, above note 359, p. 2154.

5 Outlook and Conclusion: Focus Points for Domestic Practice

The PRD 2019 gave the EU Member States ample flexibility for implementing the restructuring procedure.[363] A cautious or traditional approach would have meant high barriers, little powers for debtors, and strict oversight and control by restructuring courts and a PIFOR. A rescue- and debtor-friendly approach would have meant the exact opposite. Some national lawmakers were surprisingly courageous. The Netherlands, for example, which has not had an effective plan procedure before, made a bold move with the Dutch restructuring procedure offering flexible restructuring plan options with a comparatively low entry barrier for foreign debtors. The German implementation of the PRD 2019, especially the first drafts, was similarly a surprisingly fresh breeze of a new restructuring-friendly culture. Yet, the enacted German restructuring law is significantly more cautious. It is, nonetheless, fair to say that the positive attitude towards debtors as leading actors of their own reorganization and restructuring, worthy to be given a second chance, is also signalled by the new restructuring law. It is the first time that there exists a guarantee for debtors to remain in possession of their business and achieve a restructuring outside formal insolvency with the support of the majority of their creditors, though without unanimous consent.

The practice test of the German restructuring procedure in large scale is still outstanding. Since the restructuring procedures' enactment, insolvency business has been rather quiet in Germany. Insolvency case numbers declined during the COVID-19 pandemic by 15.5% in 2020 compared to 2019. With the onset of the COVID-19 pandemic, the German government has rolled out massive support programmes and government-co-sponsored loans have been readily available.[364] Thus, many debtors might already be over-indebted on the balance-sheet but with sufficient cash to cover expenses for at least the next 12 if not 24 months, whereas those debtors entering insolvency are often already deeply troubled, so not exactly the candidates for a restructuring procedure. The German restructuring procedure has received much credit upfront so far and proven successful in a handful of financial restructurings.[365] The coming months and years to come will tell us as to whether such credit is deserved.

363 See D. Ehmke, J. Gant, G.-J. Boon, L. Langkjaer & E. Ghio, 'The European Union Preventive Restructuring Framework', *International Insolvency Review*, 2019, 28(2), pp. 1-26.

364 Press release No. 161 by on 31 March 2021 by German statistical Bureau, available at: https://www.destatis.de/DE/Presse/Pressemitteilungen/2021/03/PD21_161_52411.html (last viewed 30 May 2022).

365 See for successful examples the following practice report by G. Bernau et al., above note 303 (bond and 'Schuldschein' restructuring). See also the case heard by the District Court of Hamburg, decision of 12 April 2021 – 61a RES 1/21 = NZI 2021, 544 (shareholder loan restructuring) and the case decided by the District Court of Dresden, decision of 7 June 2021 – 574 RES 2/21 = NZI 2021, 893 (financial restructuring of a smaller group entity).

While the introduction of the German restructuring procedure was certainly a big step forward and a valuable addition to the German restructuring toolbox, there are some areas for reform that could significantly increase the attractiveness of the restructuring procedure, also in cross-border institutional competition. Three areas for reform we like to point out are the entry test, the treatment of executory contracts and the internationality of the restructuring procedure.

First and foremost, the entry test for the restructuring procedure is the same as for voluntary insolvency procedures. The self-proclaimed goal set by the legislator to encourage early restructurings outside formal insolvency would suggest that an earlier entry is possible. While it is understandable that modifications to debt and equity claims without the parties' individual consent should be well justified, procedural rules such as a qualified majority vote, equal treatment and best interest tests can assure that only well justified modifications are possible. Comparable to the solvent UK scheme of arrangements, the German restructuring procedure could allow for cram-down confirmations in a restructuring plan for solvent debtors. Proof of the debtor's imminent insolvency could be required for more invasive cross-class cram-down confirmations. Because the German restructuring procedure follows a modular approach anyhow, it would be a step towards more flexibility and accessibility should different instruments be made available under different requirements.

Second, the cancellation of the termination right without an alternative, such as the option to modify future claims, makes the procedure significantly less attractive if not useless for debtors with constantly arising liabilities from unprofitable contracts. As discussed in Section 4.8, the arguments against the cancellation of the termination right are not convincing at all, especially considering that a debtor can currently enter the insolvency procedure voluntarily and choose as DIP to perform or not perform executory contracts which are exempt from any modification in the restructuring procedure. Thus, it would be most sensible for a truly competitive restructuring procedure to re-install an option allowing for the modification of future claims.

Third, the German restructuring law is determined by a very national perspective. In the interest of legal certainty and institutional competition, the future restructuring law should allocate jurisdiction to German restructuring courts based on a sufficient connection test in private procedures and establish rules on the applicable law and the recognition of foreign procedures, which are not part of Annex A of the EIR 2015.[366] For the time being, cross-border effects of German restructuring procedures are guaranteed only for plans modifying German law-governed debt and for public restructuring procedures. The effects of private procedures in other countries depend on the choice of law and cross-border recognition rules applicable.

366 See S. Madaus, above note 356, Section 3 (d).

With a few but substantial amendments, the German restructuring law stands in a great position to offer a revolutionary restructuring procedure which can be understood as a collective decision-making mechanism. In particular, the availability of an inter-class cram-down mechanism accessible for debtors with a sufficient connection to Germany without an entry test, such as the likelihood of insolvency, would demonstrate that restructuring is not just a light-touch insolvency procedure but a unique tool for collective decision-making designed to preserve and increase value in the common best interest of all parties affected.

6 Greece

*Yiannis Bazinas and Athanasios Paizis**

1 Introduction

The legal framework in Greece for insolvency and restructuring has witnessed several significant reforms in the last 20 years. It should therefore not be surprising that the introduction of the Preventive Restructuring Directive (PRD 2019) came at a time when the domestic insolvency framework was, once again, in the midst of a major reform process. Nevertheless, as will be analysed, Greece managed to utilize this window of opportunity to implement the stipulations of the PRD 2019, to the extent that they did not already form part of the legal framework, and fine-tune existing procedures. While several issues remain to be clarified by practice, the end result is nevertheless a comprehensive preventive restructuring process that goes a long way to conform to European benchmarks and principles and has the potential to contribute in resolving the country's growing problem of private debt.

The following chapters will consider, in particular, the new rehabilitation procedure, as has been amended by the most recent insolvency legislation[367] and consider how its provisions fit within the framework established by the PRD 2019. Section 2 discusses briefly the history of the Greek insolvency and restructuring framework. Section 3 elaborates on the implementation of the PRD 2019 in the Greek Insolvency Law (GIL). Section 4 discusses the main features of the new rehabilitation proceeding in the GIL. Section 5 provides an outlook and concluding remarks.

2 Brief History of the Greek Insolvency and Restructuring Framework

For the better part of its modern lifetime, Greece lacked a comprehensive insolvency framework. The Commercial Law, which can be traced its ancestry to the Napoleonic Code de Commerce of 1807, contained certain provisions on insolvency issues, but

* The views are of the authors only and cannot in any circumstances be attributed to the institutions for which they work, in particular to the European Commission. The closing date of this chapter is 10 June 2022.

367 An English translation of the Greek Insolvency Law, including the provisions of the rehabilitation procedure can be accessed online at: https://www.bazinas.com/media/616d81aae21c4.pdf.

restructuring tools were severely underdeveloped.[368] During the 20th century, mechanisms to facilitate the rescue of troubled enterprises were introduced by means of specialized legislation, which operated in parallel to insolvency law and often pursued different policy objectives.[369] This mosaic of legal provisions was eventually revamped in 2007, by the introduction of the Greek Insolvency Code (GIC),[370] which replaced all erstwhile legislation and created a modern framework for insolvency and restructuring. In addition to significantly reforming the framework for insolvency, the GIC also introduced formal restructuring processes by enabling creditors to agree, after the commencement of insolvency, to a plan of reorganization, as opposed to a piecemeal liquidation of the debtor's assets.[371] Perhaps more importantly, the GIC also envisaged a pre-insolvency procedure, the so-called 'conciliation procedure' (often referred to simply as 'Article 99'), which enabled business rescue before the onset of insolvency and quickly became the procedure of choice for distressed debtors.[372] Unfortunately, conciliation was routinely abused during the first years of its implementation, as its attraction owed more to the liberal tendency of courts to grant interim relief orders (precluding enforcement against the debtor's assets), rather than the efficiency of its restructuring tools.[373] Despite these growing pains, the introduction of these new restructuring tools created high hopes that a rescue culture could eventually develop.

Unfortunately, the genesis of the GIC came at an inopportune time. Greece soon spiralled down an unprecedented economic crisis, which led to the failure of numerous businesses and the accumulation of non-performing loans on bank balance sheets in gargantuan proportions. In this context, the insolvency framework came under scrutiny as a means to address the growing problem of private debt. As a result, the GIC entered into a cycle of successive reforms, undergoing five major amendments in a decade, which completely transformed its original provisions and mechanisms.[374] Conciliation was replaced by a new rehabilitation procedure, which was purported to place stricter requirements on interim relief; rehabilitation however was also remodelled successively and was eventually transformed into a strictly pre-packaged procedure. This constant

368 L. Kotsiris, *Insolvency Law*, Athens: Sakkoulas, 2017, p. 23 (in Greek).

369 During the 1980s, the rehabilitation of troubled enterprises was utilized to increase the state's control over distressed firms in certain crucial economic sectors (Law 1386/1983). Under Law 1892/1990, this approach was reversed and reorganization measures became tools for achieving the privatization of distressed enterprises that had been brought under public control.

370 Law 3588/2007, State Gazette (SG) A' 153/10.7.2007.

371 Art. 107 GIC.

372 L. Kotsiris, above note 368, p. 580.

373 Y. Sakkas & Y. Bazinas, 'The Greek Insolvency Code: An Over-Reformed Law', *Pratt's Journal of Bankruptcy Law*, 2018, 14(5), p. 223.

374 Ibid., p. 225.

reform of restructuring mechanisms,[375] however, significantly undermined their effectiveness and fuelled a general perception about their inadequacy among market participants. At the same time, specialized legislation also introduced several quasi-restructuring procedures that directly antagonized reorganization and rehabilitation under the GIC.[376] In the end, less than 15 years after the introduction of the GIC, the Greek insolvency framework found itself once again in a state of fragmentation and had lost much of its original appeal in the eyes of debtors and creditors alike.

3 The New Greek Insolvency Law

In the face of this unstable setting, the introduction of PRD 2019 and the need for national implementation provided an opportunity to reconsider the country's insolvency and restructuring framework and address the deficiencies that had accumulated during the previous decade. As a result, the GIC was replaced by a completely new piece of legislation, the new GIL, under the aspiring name "Debt Settlement and Facilitation of a Second Chance".[377] The main objective of the reform was to consolidate, once again, in a single piece of legislation all procedures relating to the treatment as well as the prevention of insolvency.[378] While this was a noble goal that gathered support from the academic community and legal practice, the GIL also introduced more fundamental and controversial changes to Greek insolvency and restructuring law, the most striking of which was the extension of insolvency eligibility to consumers.[379] This marked a sharp break from the previous framework, which relied on a strict conceptual distinction between merchants and non-merchants as regards their eligibility for insolvency but more importantly extended the favourable discharge provisions of the GIL[380] to millions of individuals, who comprised a significant part of the banking system's non-performing exposures. As expected, debates on such fundamental aspects of the new regime dominated the policy dialogue surrounding the introduction of the new law.[381]

375 A special liquidation procedure was introduced in 2012 as a means to encourage going concern sales, only to be dropped a few years later after minimal (if any) application.

376 Such procedures included special administration (Art. 68 Law 4307/2014), whose main objective was to enable large businesses to restructure their bank debt, and an automated out-of-court workout mechanism (Law 4469/2017), that appealed to corporate as well as consumer debtors and would enable them to write down their bank, tax and social security obligations. Although special administration yielded some high-profile successful restructurings, the OCW mechanism, despite high aspirations failed to provide any noticeable results.

377 Law 4738/2020 SG A 207/27.10.2020.

378 Y. Sakkas & Y. Bazinas, 'The New Greek Insolvency Law: A Turning Point', *Eurofenix*, 2022, 86, p. 22.

379 Art. 76 GIL.

380 Art. 192 GIL.

381 Kathimerini, Greece Says New Insolvency Code Gives 'Second Chance' to Debtors, available at: https://www.ekathimerini.com/economy/256313/greece-says-new-insolvency-code-gives-second-chance-to-

Nominally, the alignment of the Greek insolvency and restructuring framework to the stipulations of the PRD 2019 was an additional important impetus behind the latest reform.[382] This is reflected in the new GIL embracing early warning mechanisms as well as a novel framework for debt discharge. On the issue of preventive restructuring frameworks, however, the constant remodelling of the GIC over the preceding years had already provided numerous opportunities to adjust the framework to the European paradigm as these norms were developing. As early as 2016, the explanatory report to law 4446/2016, the last major overhaul of the GIC, referred to the need to incorporate the provisions of the Commission Recommendation of 2014 on a new approach to business failure and insolvency.[383] The Greek restructuring framework thus already included a preventive restructuring framework, the rehabilitation procedure, which, to a large extent, already conformed to the main stipulations of the PRD 2019. Still, the GIL elevated rehabilitation as the sole fully fledged restructuring mechanism in Greece, as formal reorganization, after the declaration of insolvency, was abolished owing much to its lack of utilization by debtors and creditors alike.[384] In addition, the rehabilitation procedure was further streamlined, and additional reforms were introduced to ensure that it fully complied with the PRD 2019. In the broader context, the implementation of the PRD 2019 in Greece, unlike other EU jurisdictions, constituted only a sideshow of a wider and major reorientation of the domestic insolvency and restructuring framework.

4 MAIN FEATURES OF THE REHABILITATION PROCEDURE

4.1 Objective and Scope of the Rehabilitation Procedure

The rehabilitation procedure is the main preventive restructuring framework under the GIL and in fact the only available procedure that can result, as stated by GIL, in the preservation, utilization, restructuring and recovery of the debtor's business.[385] It is available only to debtors engaged in a business activity, whether legal or natural persons; consumers are thus excluded from its scope.[386] There are no special provisions on enterprise groups but it is generally conceded that eligibility is assessed by reference to legal personality and therefore groups cannot access rehabilitation as distinct entities from

debtors/ (last viewed 28 August 2022).

382 Explanatory Report to Law 4738/2020.

383 Commission Recommendation of 12 March 2014 on a new approach to business failure and insolvency (2014/135/EU).

384 Y. Sakkas & Y. Bazinas, above note 378.

385 Art. 31 GIL.

386 S. Psychomanis, *Insolvency Law*, Athens: Sakkoulas, 2021, p. 112.

their comprising members.[387] The guiding principle of the rehabilitation procedure is the 'no-creditor-worse-off' principle, which stipulates that all creditors (unless they agree otherwise) must receive at least what they would receive in the context of insolvency.[388] On a conceptual level, the rehabilitation procedure is strictly a pre-packaged procedure, meaning that the procedure is commenced by the filing of a rehabilitation agreement that is already signed by the requisite creditor majorities for ratification.[389] Thus, the negotiations for the formulation of a rehabilitation agreement take place out of court. Once the plan is filed and the procedure is commenced, the GIL stipulates that a hearing on ratification shall be held no later than 2 months after the date of the filing.[390] In general it is envisaged that the rehabilitation procedure should be completed within a few months as of the date of filing the agreement.

4.2 *Criteria to Enter the Rehabilitation Procedure*

4.2.1 Competent Persons to Initiate a Rehabilitation Procedure

The initiation of the pre-insolvency procedure for the ratification of a rehabilitation agreement may be commenced either by the debtor[391] or by anyone of the contracting creditors.[392] A debtor is defined as a natural or legal person engaged in a business activity having its centre of main interests (COMI) in Greece. Although this was not expressly mentioned in the law, the term 'business activity' falls within the definition set by national tax law, as a series of economic transactions with the purpose of obtaining profit, thus excluding consumers or, more generally, non-business entities from the scope of the rehabilitation procedure.[393] COMI, on the other hand, is defined in GIL[394] in a way that follows the definition set by EIR 2015.[395]

387 A. Paizis, *The Treatment of Cross-border Insolvency in Groups of Companies in the EU* Athens: Nomiki Vivliothiki, 2019, pp. 137-142 (in Greek).

388 Art. 31 GIL.

389 The relevant application should be filed before the Multimember Court of First Instance in the district where the debtor has its COMI (procedure of voluntary/non-contentious jurisdiction).

390 Art. 49 GIL.

391 Art. 32(1) GIL.

392 Art. 44(1) GIL.

393 E. Perakis, Insolvency Law, Athens: Nomiki Vivliothiki, 2021, p. 73 (in Greek), who refers to Arts. 21 and 47 Law 4172/2013.

394 Art. 78(3) GIL.

395 Art. 3(1) EIR 2015, see also G. Michalopoulos, *European Cross-border Insolvencies*, Athens: Nomiki Vivliothiki, 2007, pp. 110-129, A. Paizis, above note 387, pp. 42-86 and G. Michalopoulos & L. Athanasiou (eds), *European & International Cross-Border Insolvency Law*, Athens: Nomiki Vivliothiki, 2020, pp. 165-188.

The debtor may submit a request for the ratification of a rehabilitation agreement.[396] However, it is possible that creditors (amounting to the requisite majorities) conclude the rehabilitation agreement on their own without the participation of the debtor. In this case, the GIL allows contracting creditors to commence rehabilitation by filing such inter-creditor agreement for ratification in order to better serve the objectives of this pre-insolvency procedure.[397] An important question is therefore who should be considered a creditor for the purposes of the rehabilitation procedure. GIL does not provide for a definition of the term 'creditor'. However, it is provided that together with the application for the ratification of the agreement, a list should be submitted with all the creditors' claims against the debtor irrespective of their class or potential securities. These claims should be evidenced by the accounting records of the debtor or acknowledged/presumed by a court decision.[398] Any creditor holding such a claim participating in this agreement may apply to the competent court for the ratification of the rehabilitation agreement.

4.2.2 Criteria for Opening a Rehabilitation Procedure

GIL provides for certain flexibility in relation to the criteria for the opening of a rehabilitation procedure. They range from likelihood of insolvency to a general and permanent cessation of payments. In particular, GIL provides for the following: present (not permanent) inability to fulfil pecuniary obligations in a general way (hereinafter 'present inability'), potential inability to fulfil pecuniary obligations in a general way (hereinafter 'potential inability'), likelihood of insolvency and general and permanent cessation of payments. The first two existed already under the GIC,[399] whereas the last one seems to have been adjusted during the recent reform and the likelihood of insolvency was introduced in the reform of 2015 in order to transpose in Greek law the principles described in the Commission Recommendation 2014.[400] They have been designed in order to provide restructuring solutions to debtors from an early stage of their financial difficulties to the vicinity of insolvency.

Chronologically, potential inability precedes present inability. Present inability refers to a present cessation of payments towards the creditors affecting all the obligations of the debtors, which has not become permanent yet. This implies that the financial distress of the debtor can be remediated with the appropriate restructuring tools. Potential inability corresponds, in practice, to a debtor's financial forecast in relation to its own financial status. The debtor predicts – based on the current and expecting cash flows as well as on the current and expecting obligations – that it will not be able to pay such obligations as

396 Arts. 34(2) and 44(1) GIL.
397 Art. 31 GIL.
398 Art. 34(3) GIL.
399 Law 3588/2007, SG A 153/10.7.2007.
400 Law 4336/2015, SG A 94/14.08.2015.

they fall due.[401] In both cases, inability needs to be general, meaning that it should cover all or most of the financial obligations of the debtor in a way that once expressed it may harm the debtor's market reputation.[402]

The third criterion is likelihood of insolvency.[403] Interestingly, likelihood of insolvency is not defined in Greek law, although its meaning was ambiguous.[404] An explanation for this absence could be found to its purpose. A definition could limit the scope of this criterion and consequently, the cases to which debtors could involve likelihood of insolvency in order to achieve an early-stage rehabilitation agreement.[405] In the insolvency spectrum, likelihood of insolvency happens before any present or potential inability incidents can be confirmed.[406] However, the absence of a definition does not allow for a clear boundary delimitation between likelihood of insolvency and the other criteria. Likelihood of insolvency is based on a reasonable suspicion that insolvency might occur in the future allowing for an early intervention before the financial problems become definite. In theory, such financial problems should not be sufficient to evidence a present or potential inability, but they should be able to present certain financial impact in order to avoid the abusive use of this criterion.[407] In practice, present or potential inability and likelihood of insolvency may overlap.[408] For this reason, it cannot be excluded that, in future, the latter might absorb the former.

Apart from the above-mentioned criteria, it is also possible to request the opening of a rehabilitation procedure when the debtor is already in a situation of general and permanent cessation of payments. This option could be seen as the link between the preventive restructuring measures and the insolvency framework allowing a last attempt to save the business or permit the smooth transition if restructuring cannot prevent insolvency. GIL clearly provides for this possibility in case of an inter-creditor's agreement without the participation of the debtor.[409] In this case, the applicant creditor should also submit a petition for the declaration of the debtor's insolvency.[410] A more thorough reading of the relevant provisions reveals that it might also be possible for the debtor to submit a ratification application, while being already in a cessation of payments.[411] However, the

401 S. Psychomanis, above note 386, p. 60.

402 A. Paizis, 'Likelihood of Insolvency as a Criterion for the Opening of a Rehabilitation Procedure: First Interpretation Approach', *DEE*, 2016(1), p. 12 (in Greek).

403 In line with Art. 4(1) PRD 2019.

404 S. Psychomanis, above note 386, p. 73.

405 A. Paizis, *The Problematic Implementation of 'likelihood of insolvency' in the Greek Legal Order, Annual Business Law Conference*, Athens: Nomiki Vivliothiki 2018, pp. 420–423 (in Greek).

406 Art. 2(2)(a) PRD 2019.

407 E. Perakis, above note 393, p. 75.

408 A. Paizis, above note 405, p. 13.

409 Art. 34(2) GIL.

410 Art. 47(1) GIL.

411 E. Perakis, above note 393, p. 79.

internal coherence of the relevant chapter seems unbalanced on this matter. There are only two references to such possibility with no clear connection to the criteria for the opening of the rehabilitation procedure: one in the provisions related to the review of the ratification application[412] and another in the final provisions of the chapter.[413] For coherence reasons and considering that the objectives of the law allow such interpretation, we should accept that this option is also open to the debtor.

4.3 *Involved Actors*

4.3.1 DIP and PIFOR Appointment

Rehabilitation is fundamentally a debtor-in-possession (DIP) procedure. However, the insolvency court may, following the application of anyone having a legitimate interest, appoint (after the submission of the application to ratify the rehabilitation agreement) a practitioner in the field of restructuring (PIFOR) (under the GIL this actor is called a special mandate holder) with the authority to exercise certain or all the powers of the debtor's administration.[414] This power is discretionary but may be exercised in particular where the debtor has delayed the filing of an insolvency application or has intentionally caused the insolvency, where there have been fraudulent transfers of assets or in cases where the debtor abusively refuses to participate in negotiations for a rehabilitation agreement. These instances do not necessarily align with the circumstances set out in Article 5(3) PRD 2019 regarding the mandatory appointment of a PIFOR. Still, the interests of creditors are safeguarded by the requirement that a rehabilitation plan is accompanied by an expert report, which expresses an opinion regarding the fulfilment of the conditions for the ratification of the rehabilitation agreement (including the requirements for a cross-class cram-down) and also certifies the accuracy and validity of the list of creditors that accompanies the rehabilitation agreement.[415] Yet, such an expert report is not a PIFOR within the meaning of the PRD 2019. A PIFOR may nevertheless be appointed after the ratification of the rehabilitation agreement for the performance of special acts, as specified by the court, such as the safeguarding of the debtor's assets or the execution of agreements implementing the terms of the rehabilitation agreement.[416]

---

412 Art. 54(4) GIL.

413 Art. 74(1) GIL.

414 Art. 51 GIL.

415 Art. 48(1) GIL. The expert, who is usually a certified accountant, is selected jointly by the debtor and the contracting creditors or only by the latter, where the application is only filed by creditors Art. 48(2) GIL.

416 Art. 55 GIL.

4.3.2 The Rights of Shareholders in a Rehabilitation Procedure

As regards shareholders, it should be noted that their role in the rehabilitation procedure is limited. As a general matter, shareholders do not need to consent, as a class, on the rehabilitation agreement. As already noted, a rehabilitation agreement requires the debtor's consent, unless the latter is in cessation of payments, in which case the rehabilitation agreement may be concluded by creditors only.[417] In the case of legal persons, such consent may be provided by the board of directors.[418] As a result, the board of directors may consent to an agreement that significantly prejudices shareholder rights, by agreeing *e.g.* to a debt-for-equity swap. Things, however, become more complicated, when the debtor's Articles of association require the approval of a rehabilitation agreement at a shareholders' meeting. In these cases, the GIL stipulates that the consent of the shareholders' meeting is not required, if the expert report concludes that the shareholders would have no residual claim against the debtor.[419] As a result, shareholders have very limited options to prevent the conclusion of a rehabilitation agreement that is detrimental to their interests.

A related issue concerns the possibility that the rehabilitation agreement may, at the stage of implementation, mandate the adoption of measures that require a decision of the shareholders meeting, under the provisions of company law (*e.g.* share capital increases, exclusion of pre-emption rights, etc.). The GIL clarifies that such decision of the shareholders meeting is not required, in cases when the debtor's consent for the conclusion of a rehabilitation agreement is not required, most notably when the debtor is already in cessation of payments. When this is not the case however, and provided that the shareholders have no residual claim against the debtor's business, the GIL adopts a scheme to ensure that shareholders do not prevent the implementation of a rehabilitation plan. In particular, the insolvency court, with its decision on the ratification of the rehabilitation agreement, may order the appointment of a special proxy, with the power to convene a shareholders' meeting and exercise the right to attend and vote for the debtor's shareholders or partners who do not cooperate.[420] In principle, the special proxy may overrule the objections of the shareholders and ensure that the rehabilitation agreement is carried through.[421] In this way, the Greek legislator ensured that equity holders are not allowed to unreasonably prevent or create obstacles to the ratification and implementation of the rehabilitation agreement.[422]

---

417 Art. 54(1) GIL.

418 Art. 35(1) GIL.

419 Art. 35(2) GIL.

420 Art. 35(3) GIL.

421 However, according to Art. 35(3)(c) GIL, the non-cooperating shareholders maintain their right to compensation against the company and the creditors in the event that it is later proven that they would have had a residual claim after liquidation.

422 Art. 12(1)(2) PRD 2019.

4.4 *Stay*

4.4.1 Stay at the Negotiating Stage

In accordance with the provisions of Article 6 PRD 2019, the GIL provides that a court may, at the application of the debtor or a creditor, order provisional measures even before the submission of the application to ratify a rehabilitation plan. Such measures may include a stay, similar to the one that takes effect after the filing of the application. The requirements for such a stay at the negotiating stage are the existence of special urgency or imminent danger as well as a written statement by creditors representing at least 20% of the debtor's overall liabilities, stating that they participate in the negotiations for the conclusion of a rehabilitation plan.[423] Any such stay shall remain in force until the filing of the application for ratification and in any case for a maximum duration of 4 months after the lapse of which it shall cease automatically. In exceptional circumstances, the stay may be extended provided that there is progress in the negotiations, the continuation of the stay does not unduly infringe on the rights of any party, no insolvency petition against the debtor has been heard and the total duration of the stay, including the renewal, does not exceed 6 months.[424]

The court has a broad discretion to order any measure that would automatically enter into force upon the filing of the application for the ratification of a rehabilitation plan. These could, for instance, be a stay of individual enforcement measures, whether already pending or not, relating to all types of claims. In addition, they could include collective enforcement measures, such as the filing and hearing of insolvency applications, as well as provisional measures, such as conservative arrests or attachments, unless such measures purport to prevent the transfer of the business' movable assets and the depletion of the value of the debtor's business.[425] Still, there are some limits to the scope of the stay. For instance, such a stay cannot infringe on rights from financial collateral arrangements or financial leases, as well as the right to terminate and request the surrender of leased property, provided that the debtors is in arrears of rent for 6 months or more.[426] More importantly, employees' salary claims are not covered by the provisional measures, unless the court also extends them to such claims for cause and for a set period, specifically mentioned in the decision.[427]

423 Art. 53(1) GIL.

424 Art. 53(2) GIL.

425 Art. 50(1) GIL. If there is a specific business or social justification, the court may extend the application of such stay to the debtor's guarantors or other co-obligors see Art. 50(5) GIL.

426 Art. 52(2) GIL.

427 Art. 52(5) GIL.

4.4.2 Stay after the Filing of the Application for Ratification

As a general matter, a stay will automatically be put in place after the filing of an application to ratify a plan of rehabilitation.[428] As already mentioned, such a stay will preclude individual and collective enforcement actions as well as provisional measures, whereas employees will similarly be excluded from its scope, as set out above. The duration of the automatic stay remains a mystery; in theory, it remains in place until the court issues its judgement on the ratification of the rehabilitation agreement but at the same time it may not exceed a period of 4 months.[429] Things are further complicated by the stipulation that, after the lapse of the initial 4 month period, the court may, at the application of any interested party, order any additional stay at its own discretion.[430] It seems from the above that, although the initial 4 month stay is automatic, if a judgement on the ratification of the rehabilitation agreement has not been issued within such period, the debtor will need to apply to the court for an extension of the stay.[431] Although it is not entirely clear, it seems that the duration of such stay, taking into account any extensions may not extend beyond a period of 12 months.[432]

4.5 *The Rehabilitation Agreement*

4.5.1 Scope of the Rehabilitation Agreement

The rehabilitation agreement aims at the preservation, utilization, restructuring and recovery of the debtor's business.[433] Hence, it may include all necessary measures affecting any asset and liability of the business that could positively contribute to the restructuring of the debtor and the prevention of insolvency. All affected creditors may be included in this agreement irrespective of their class or potential securities as long as there is a claim evidenced by the debtor's accounting record or being acknowledged/presumed by a court decision.[434] As already noted, the plan may also affect shareholder rights.

4.5.2 Persons Able to Propose an Agreement

Considering that rehabilitation is strictly a pre-packaged procedure, there is no actual distinction between the person who can propose a plan and the person who can request for the opening of the rehabilitation procedure. Therefore, the debtor or its creditors may propose a plan that should be submitted for ratification by the court in order for the

428 Art. 50(1) GIL.
429 Art. 50(2) GIL.
430 Art. 50(3) GIL.
431 S. Psychomanis, above note 386, p. 150.
432 Art. 52(1) GIL.
433 Art. 31 GIL.
434 Above note 398.

rehabilitation procedure to be initiated.[435] In any case, it must be remembered that the agreement will need to have the support of the required creditor majorities, as well as the debtor's consent, unless the debtor is already in cessation of payments.

4.5.3 Content of the Verification Application/Rehabilitation Agreement

In Greek law, the rehabilitation agreement is annexed to the application for its ratification together with other required documents.[436] The content of the application is described in Article 45(1) GIL, which transposed (almost word by word) Article 8(1) PRD 2019.[437] On the contrary, the content of the rehabilitation agreement includes only the various measures agreed between the parties for the restructuring of the business and the prevention of insolvency. In this context, Article 39 GIL provides for an indicative set of measures that could be included in the rehabilitation agreement, but the parties may agree on different measures.

On the one hand, the content of the application must include all the necessary information for the identification of the debtor, the elements of its estate, affected parties and their classes, the special mandate holder (if appointed) and the terms of the restructuring plan.[438] On the other hand, the rehabilitation plan constitutes essentially a private agreement (or a notarial deed if required by law),[439] which is submitted for ratification to the court in order to be able to produce *erga omnes* effects.[440] As such, the parties may agree and include any term they deem necessary or appropriate. This applies when the agreement is concluded between the debtor and the creditors, or only by the creditors with the consent of the debtor. In case of an inter-creditor agreement without the consent of the debtor, the agreement cannot create new obligations for the debtor, but it

---

435 Section 4.2.1.

436 Art. 46 GIL. The other documents are: debtor's financial statements, creditors' list, expert's report confirming that all requirements for the ratification of the agreement are met, a certificate of the obligations to the State and social security institutions issued within 1 month prior to the submission of the application for ratification.

437 Art. 45(2) GIL provides that if any of the elements of the application are not known to the person filing the application, especially when this person is a creditor, the application must contain the reasons for which such information is not known and the relevant estimations even if these are by approximation or presumptions.

438 The restructuring plan must include: the proposed settlement of the debtor's assets and liabilities, the duration of the proposed rehabilitation measures as applicable, the way of informing and consulting with the employees' representatives, to the extent required under EU and national law, any general consequences regarding employment, such as redundancies, part time employment or similar, every financing expected in the context of the rehabilitation agreement and the reasoning necessitating the new financing for the implementation of the rehabilitation plan and the reasons justifying why the rehabilitation agreement has a reasonable prospect to ensure the viability of the business as well as the necessary conditions for the success of the rehabilitation plan. Art. 45(1) GIL.

439 Art. 42 GIL.

440 Art. 41 GIL. However, the parties may agree to apply certain terms between them even without ratification.

might refer to inter-creditor agreements in relation to priority, measures to support the business and other relevant measures.[441] Despite the large flexibility of the parties based on the principle of the freedom to contract, the law provides indicatively for a potential content of such an agreement, which ranges from simple modifications of debtor's obligations to the sale of its entire business.[442]

In particular, the rehabilitation agreement may describe the alteration to the terms in relation to the debtor's obligations. This may consist in an alteration to the time of the fulfilment of claims, including the modification of the terms under which early repayment of such claims may be requested, the alteration to the interest rate, the replacement of the obligation to pay interest with the obligation to pay part of the profits, the replacement of claims with convertible or non-convertible bonds issued by the debtor, or the obligation of creditors with security *in rem* to accept a change in the mortgage or lien rank in favour of the debtor's new creditors.

In addition, a debt-for-equity swap option can be part of the agreement as well as the reduction in creditors' claims, the assignment of the administration of the debtor's business to a third party, the suspension of individual and collective actions by creditors for a set period after the ratification of the agreement,[443] new financing[444] for the debtor and other measures. Liquidation measures were also considered by the Greek legislator. The law provides for the liquidation of debtor's individual assets or even the transfer of all or part of the debtor's business to a third party or to a company belonging to creditors given that the subject of the restructuring is the business and not the debtor itself. This transfer will take the form of an asset deal.

It should be mentioned that the rehabilitation agreement is mandatorily accompanied by a business plan with a duration equal to that of the agreement, which should be approved by the contracting parties.[445] The business plan describes the operation and the prospects of the business taking into consideration the terms of the rehabilitation agreement. It provides indicators related to the viability of the business assisting not only creditors with their decisions on the measures for the recovery of the business but also the court to form a reasoned opinion on the viability of the business. In a debtor-creditor agreement, the business plan is drafted by the debtor and due to its importance it is required to be clear and specific.[446] In an inter-creditor agreement, on the other hand, the

441 E. Perakis, above note 393, pp. 90, 92.
442 Art. 39 GIL.
443 The suspension shall not bind a non-contracting creditor as well as the creditors whose consent is presumed for a period not exceeding 3 months as of the ratification of agreement.
444 As defined in Art. 2(1)(7) PRD 2019.
445 Art. 43 GIL.
446 E. Perakis, above note 393.

business plan is prepared by the creditors but must still meet the same requirements of clarity and specificity.

4.5.4 Verification of the Information Provided

The information provided for both the ratification application and the rehabilitation agreement is not subject to any kind of verification or review by the affected parties after its submission to the court and there is no legal basis for others to request additional information related to this agreement. Such verification, review or request for additional information can be discussed in the context of the negotiations for the conclusion of the rehabilitation agreement and only between the participants. However, together with the rehabilitation agreement an expert report should be submitted.[447] The objective of this report is to confirm the accuracy and correctness of the list of creditors as well as the debtor's list of assets,[448] and conclude on whether the application meets the ratification requirements.[449]

Once the rehabilitation agreement is finalized, it should be submitted to the court, which is competent to verify, review or ask for additional information within the limits set by law. The role of the court is limited and it has no discretion to amend the agreement or partially ratify it. This means that the court can either approve or reject the application. The law provides the court with two alternatives in case certain elements are missing from the application and/or the submitted documents. The first is to defer the issuance of a final decision and order the debtor to provide to the appointed expert all the necessary information for the application to be complete within 1 month as of the issuance of its non-final decision.[450] The second is to set a deadline, which cannot exceed a period of 20 days, for the parties to submit any missing document or amend the agreement as necessary.[451]

4.5.5 Formation of Classes

Article 9(4) PRD 2019 provides that affected parties should be grouped into separate classes in order to reflect commonality of interests based on verifiable criteria. The same article provides that as a minimum, creditors of secured and unsecured claims shall be treated in separate classes for the purposes of adopting a restructuring plan. The Greek legislator transposed this article opting for the minimum by separating the creditors into

447 According to Art. 48(2) GIL, the expert is selected among the persons registered with the Registry of Experts of Art. 65, jointly by the debtor and the contracting creditors, and only by the contracting creditors in case of an inter-creditors' agreement.

448 Art. 48(1) GIL.

449 For the minimum content of the expert's report, Ministerial Decision n. 26400 EΞ 2001, SG B 865/05.03.2021.

450 Art. 47(2) GIL.

451 Art. 54(5) GIL.

two classes, namely creditors with secured claims and creditors with unsecured claims.[452] There is no provision for further optional or mandatory division of classes in relation to the adoption of the rehabilitation agreement. Despite the formation of classes, the Greek legislator chose to offer the contracting parties the option to include in their negotiations the relationship between creditors after the ratification of the agreement, including matters of priority.[453] Different treatment between creditors in a class is thus conceptually possible and practically relevant for the unsecured creditor class. The limits to such different treatment are set by the principle of the equal treatment of creditors. It should be noted that if business or social reasons can be presented, GIL allows a deviation to the principle of equal treatment. Indicatively, labour claims or claims essential for the maintenance of the creditor and his family may receive a favourable treatment under GIL.

4.6 *Adoption and Ratification of the Plan*

4.6.1 The Consent of the Debtor

Once the rehabilitation agreement is concluded between the parties, it should be submitted to the court for ratification. In order for the court to ratify, it should conduct a series of assessments. First, the court shall verify whether the agreement is signed by at least the debtor and the majority of participating creditors from both classes.[454]

If the debtor is a legal person, then the administration or the managing body has exclusive competence to provide debtor's consent for the rehabilitation agreement.[455] However, certain measures/operations included in the rehabilitation agreement (such as capital increase) may require the consent of the shareholders. Considering the risks that such operations may hold for them (*e.g.* dilution of shares), it is likely that they vote against.[456] Therefore, GIC provides for deadlock prevention measures that are discussed in Section 4.3.2.

4.6.2 The Consent of the Creditors

In relation to participating creditors, it is required to obtain the consent of affected creditors representing more than 50% in value of secured claims and more than 50% in value of the remaining claims of the affected creditors.[457] The law clarifies when a creditor

452 Art. 34(1) GIL.

453 Indicatively, among other terms, the rehabilitation agreement may provide that a class of creditors may not request the repayment of claims of it before the full satisfaction of another class, Art. 31(c) GIL.

454 Art. 35(1) GIL.

455 Ibid.

456 S. Potamitis & A. Rokas, 'Debt-to-equity Swap as a Measure for the Rehabilitation of Businesses and the Methods to Bypass Shareholders Will', *Company Law Review*, 2017(3), p. 379 (in Greek).

457 In compliance with principle outlined in Art. 9(2) PRD 2019.

is considered as an affected one by determining who is not affected. Thus, a creditor's claim is deemed not to be affected when its legal position prior to the ratification of the agreement is not affected by the agreement. A claim is not affected if not only the total amount of the claim has not been modified but also any essential term such as the date when the claim becomes due. The consent of the creditors[458] can be evidenced either by their signature on the rehabilitation agreement or by electronic voting.[459]

4.6.3 Cross-Class Cram-Down

GIC provides, in line with Article 11 PRD 2019, for a cross-class cram-down mechanism allowing the court to ratify the agreement under certain conditions even if the majority of one of the two classes is not consenting to that agreement.[460] In particular, the requirements to be satisfied are the following:

1. The agreement has been approved by creditors representing more than 60% of the debtor's total claims and more than 50% of the secured claims.
2. The non-consenting affected creditors are treated more favourably than each creditor whose claims has a lesser repayment priority, where this is evident based on their ranking in insolvency liquidation.[461] Although the explanatory note of the law clarifies that this is a transposition of Article 11(1) PRD 2019, the provision does not make reference to classes but to individual creditors. Therefore, either the Greek legislator did not want to have a clear-cut option between absolute and relative priority rule or the transposition does not reflect its full intention.
3. No class of affected creditors can, under the rehabilitation agreement, receive more than their total claim against the debtor.
4. Finally, it is additionally required that the agreement is proposed by the debtor or has the debtor's consent. This requirement implies that an inter-creditor agreement without the consent of the debtor cannot use the cross-class cram-down mechanism.

4.6.4 General Ratification Requirements

In both a classic ratification scenario and in a cross-class cram-down situation, the court should proceed *ex officio* to the assessment of whether the agreement respects certain general principles:[462]

458 The law provides for specific rules for the consent of public administration or public entities in Art. 37 GIL.

459 Art. 34(1) GIL.

460 Art. 54(1) GIL.

461 It refers to Art. 167(2) GIL.

462 Art. 54(2) GIL.

1. It is presumed that the rehabilitation agreement has a reasonable prospect of ensuring the viability of the debtor's business.[463] The assessment of the viability will be carried out on the basis of the agreement, the business plan and the expert report.
2. It is presumed that the no-creditor-worse-off principle is satisfied.[464] This principle is satisfied if the rehabilitation agreement:[465]
   a. places none of the non-consenting creditors or a creditor whose consent is presumed by law in a worse economic position than would have been in the event of the debtor's insolvency; and
   b. does not result in any non-consenting creditor, who has ownership of an asset or is the assignor of claims with the right to satisfy its claims against the debtor from the said assets, being compelled to receive less than he would receive or will receive by exercising his contractual rights over the said assets.
3. In order to ascertain this condition, the court will need to refer to the expert report, which will include an opinion on whether the no-creditor-worse-off principle is satisfied (in practical terms this will involve a valuation of the firm). The satisfaction of this criterion is required to be examined only in relation to creditors whose consent is presumed or may be presumed and those who oppose the ratification of the agreement in any way available by law. This means that creditors, who have consented to the plan actively (*i.e.* not presumably), may receive less than they would receive in the event of insolvency.
4. The rehabilitation agreement is not the outcome of malicious intent and does not breach compulsory law provisions, especially of competition law.
5. The rehabilitation agreement treats creditors of the same position on the basis of the principle of equal treatment of creditors. Divergences from the principle of equal treatment among creditors are allowed for a business or social cause, which is specifically described in the decision of the court or if the affected creditor consents to that divergence.[466]
6. The debtor consents in the case of an application for the ratification of an inter-creditor agreement. The debtor's consent is deemed to have been given if the debtor has not lodged an intervention against its acceptance of the application for ratification by the time of the hearing. The court may proceed to such an assessment also *ex officio*.[467]

463 As provided in Art. 10(3) PRD 2019.
464 It refers to the best-interest-of-creditors test within the meaning of Art. 2(1)(6) PRD 2019.
465 Art. 31(a)(b) GIL.
466 Indicatively, creditors' claims may receive favourable treatment when they are labour claims or their non-satisfaction might essentially harm debtor's business reputation.
467 E. Perakis, above note 393, p. 106.

The insolvency court should not ratify the rehabilitation agreement if it is presumed that the implementation of the rehabilitation agreement will not stop the cessation of payments. In this case, and if an insolvency petition is pending, the court declares the debtor's insolvency.[468]

4.6.5 Objections against the Agreement before Ratification

In an inter-creditor agreement, the debtor may intervene against the acceptance of the application for the ratification. However, this does not preclude the ratification of the agreement by the court, provided that it follows from the application and particularly from the expert report that the rehabilitation agreement will not put the debtor in a worse legal and financial position than it would have been without the agreement.[469] For example, if creditors agreed for an extension of deadlines for payments followed by an increase to the interest rates, this agreement could be challenged by the debtor.

In both debtor/creditor and inter-creditor agreements, any non-consenting affected creditor may also intervene and object on the ratification of the agreement. Otherwise, a third-party opposition is possible after the ratification.

If no such objection is presented before the court and the requirements presented above are met, then the rehabilitation agreement may be ratified and produce legal effects as per the terms of the agreement against all the affected creditors and the debtor.[470]

4.6.6 Amendment of the Ratified Rehabilitation Agreement

The ratified rehabilitation agreement may be amended once with a subsequent agreement of all contracting parties, which is submitted to the court for ratification by the debtor or any of the contracting creditors. In this case, the amended agreement will be ratified by the court if the following cumulative conditions apply:[471]

1. The amendment concerns the time and manner of the repayment of claims or the type of the respective considerations or the amount of the claims for repayment.
2. The amended agreement does not prejudice the principle of equal treatment of creditors and does not result in the non-satisfaction of the no-creditors-worse-off principle in relation to creditors opposing the ratification of the amendment agreement. The benchmark taken into consideration is the recovery value in case of the debtor's insolvency at the time of the conclusion of the amended agreement.
3. A supplementary report of the appointed expert on the amended terms should be provided with the pleadings.

468 Art. 54(4) GIL.

469 Art. 54(3)(e) GIL.

470 Art. 60 GIL transposing Art. 15 PRD 2019.

471 Art. 59(1) GIL.

4.6.7 Third-Party Opposition

A third-party opposition against the ratifying judgement may be lodged before the court by a person who did not attend the hearing and had not been duly summoned, within an exclusive deadline of 30 days as of the publication of the ratification judgement.[472] If the court accepts the third-party opposition, it cancels the agreement only if it is not possible to maintain it by recalculating the amounts that the person who filed the third-party opposition is entitled to receive.[473]

4.7 *Possibilities for a Debt-for-Equity Swap*

A debt-for-equity swap was provided by GIC since 2007. The numerous reforms since then maintained this possibility with certain variations. GIL also provides for this possibility allowing to pursue a debt-for-equity swap in the context of the rehabilitation agreement.[474] The law does not set specific requirements for the use of this tool other than what is agreed between the parties. However, certain safeguards are in place in line with the PRD 2019 in order to ensure the effectiveness of the restructuring process.[475] As discussed in Section 4.6.1, the GIL includes provisions that make it possible to overcome difficulties caused by a shareholders' holdout. In addition to that, the law provides for the possibility to proceed to a decrease of the share capital, prior to the debt-for-equity swap, for the amortization of losses in any case, or for the purposes of forming a reserve.

At the same time, to secure the effectiveness of the restructuring process, it is also required to consider the role of the guarantors. In the case of a debt-for-equity swap, the guarantor may be released since the creditor becomes a shareholder and the debt no longer exists. Such release could be demotivating for creditors to enter into the rehabilitation agreement.[476] In this regard, the options proposed by the Greek legislator are either a prior agreement between the creditor and the guarantor or the sale from the creditor to the guarantor of the share resulting from the debt-for-equity operation.[477] Although the second option may raise issues on when the guarantor should be released, both options seem reasonable from a practical perspective since the guarantor is usually the majority shareholder of the debtor, member of the same group or member of the family of a person controlling the debtor.[478]

472 Art. 57(1) GIL.
473 Art. 57(2) GIL.
474 Art. 39(1)(b) GIL.
475 Recital 96 PRD 2019.
476 E. Perakis, above note 393, p. 89.
477 Art. 39(1)(j)(jb) GIL.
478 A. Paizis, 'Insolvency Announcement and the Fate of the Personal Guarantor', *DEE*, 2014(11), p. 1040 (in Greek).

4.8 *Executory Contracts*

As a general matter, executory contracts remain in force in the context of a rehabilitation procedure. In particular, the GIL states that the filing of an application to ratify a rehabilitation plan or to request provisional measures (including the granting thereof) does not constitute grounds for the termination or modification of executory contracts in a matter that is detrimental to the debtor.[479] This suggests that any *ipso facto* clauses are inoperative and may not be exercised by contractual counterparties. Still, counterparties are able to terminate or modify executory contracts if such termination or modification rests on other grounds.[480] Even in these cases, however, the court may, as a provisional measure, either at the negotiating stage or after the filing of an application for ratification, forbid the termination of agreements that it considers material for the operation of the business until the ratification or the rejection of the rehabilitation agreement.[481]

4.9 *Jurisdiction for and Recognition of Court Decisions in Europe*

The Greek legislator has not requested any new procedures to be added to Annex A of the EIR 2015. The implementation of the PRD 2019 occurred by reforming the rehabilitation procedure, which already existing at the time of adoption of the European Insolvency Regulation (EIR) 2015. Therefore, it was already included in Annex A. As a result, the legal basis for assuming jurisdiction and recognition of court decisions in cross-border cases in the EU is the EIR 2015.

5 Outlook and Concluding Remarks

Overall, the legal practice has exhibited a lukewarm approach to the new GIL. As regards the rehabilitation procedure, the overall impression is that there have been no fundamental changes. Still, the law lacks clarity in a number of respects and several issues would thus need to be clarified by practice. The application of the stay as well as the protection of dissenting creditor interests in the context of the rehabilitation agreement are likely to attract the most attention in the application of the new law. Since the law has been completely overhauled, one additional challenge for legal practice will be to draw insights from the pre-existing framework and the case law that had been developed in order to address any gaps and deficiencies in a systematic and coherent way. In addition, the

479 Art. 44(2) GIL.
480 S. Psychomanis, above note 386, p. 153.
481 Art. 52(2) GIL.

success of certain tools is, to some extent, dependent on the organization and workload of the court system, which may create obstacles in their efficiency. Nevertheless, despite certain inadequacies, the GIL largely conforms to the PRD 2019 and can thus be regarded a success, as far as the implementation of the PRD 2019 is concerned. It still remains to be seen whether the new framework will prove up to the task of addressing the issues faced by debtors and creditors and the economy at large.

7 The Netherlands

Gert-Jan Boon, Reinout Vriesendorp and Harold Koster[*]

1 Introduction

Dutch restructuring and insolvency law has long been characterized by the absence of an effective preventive restructuring framework. Consequently, restructurings had to take place either in an out-of-court debt restructuring or – especially when creditor holdouts could not be resolved – a going-concern sale in *faillissement* (bankruptcy). Whereas bankruptcy has been used to restructure successfully in many cases, it also leaves ample room for hold-out strategies hindering timely restructurings to prevent debtors from bankruptcy.[482] Only abuse of law could deter creditors from pursuing a hold-out strategy. This has changed with the entry into force of the *Wet homologatie onderhands akkoord* (Act on the confirmation of a private restructuring plan, WHOA) on 1 January 2021. This Act introduced a flexible framework for proposing restructuring or liquidating plans to (a part of) the debtors' creditors and shareholders, which upon court confirmation will also be binding on the absent or dissenting creditors and shareholders who were included in the plan.

The WHOA, the result of a long-running legislative process, has been characterized to not only be flexible but also to introduce an effective tool for both domestic and cross-border restructurings.[483] The Dutch legislator has developed the WHOA in particular in line with Chapter 2 of the Preventive Restructuring Directive 2019 (PRD 2019).[484] Within the parameters of the PRD 2019, the Dutch legislator has developed a flexible framework apt to the restructuring needs of a case at hand. Furthermore, the WHOA process could

---

* This chapter states the law as per 1 January 2023, all sources have been checked on the same date.

482 *Kamerstukken II* 2018/19, 35 249, nr. 3 (Explanatory memorandum to the WHOA), pp. 1-3.

483 Dominic Lawson, 'New Dutch Scheme Hailed as "Perfect"', *GRR*, 2019, available at: https://globalrestructuringreview.com/new-dutch-scheme-bill-hailed-perfect.

484 Directive (EU) 2019/1023 of the European Parliament and of the Council of 20 June 2019 on preventive restructuring frameworks, on discharge of debt and disqualifications, and on measures to increase the efficiency of procedures concerning restructuring, insolvency and discharge of debt, and amending Directive (EU) 2017/1132 (Directive on restructuring and insolvency), O.J. L 172/18. Several remaining discrepancies with the PRD 2019 have been addressed with Act Implementing the PRD 2019 (*Implementatiewet richtlijn herstructurering en insolventie*), which entered into force on 1 January 2023. See *Implementatiewet richtlijn herstructurering en insolventie* (*Stb.* 2022, 491); *Besluit van 5 december 2022 tot vaststelling van het tijdstip van inwerkingtreding van de Implementatiewet richtlijn herstructurering en insolventie* (*Stb.* 2022, 492).

take form as a light-touch corporate restructuring where the court is only involved once confirmation of a plan is requested. However, given the modular approach of the WHOA, a process may come with features such as a temporary stay, interim decisions, bespoke measures, a safe harbour for interim financing and/or involvement of a restructuring expert to draft a plan. Moreover, a statute provides for a WHOA process to be either public or private; this allows for amendments or termination of executory contracts and accommodates for restructuring of enterprise group financing arrangements.

This chapter discusses the current Dutch corporate restructuring framework, with a focus on the WHOA. Section 2 provides an overview of the domestic restructuring and insolvency regime as it was available before the WHOA entered into force. Section 3 discusses the legislative background of the WHOA. Section 4 provides an overview of the key features of this new restructuring framework. Section 5 discusses some experiences with the WHOA, along with an outlook on furthering the WHOA process. Section 6 concludes with some observations on what the future may hold for this new instrument in the Dutch restructuring toolbox.

2 Overview of the Pre-reform Dutch Restructuring and Insolvency Regime

In the Netherlands, matters of restructuring and insolvency are dealt with primarily in the *Faillissementswet* (Dutch Bankruptcy Act, DBA). The DBA provides two corporate restructuring and insolvency proceedings: bankruptcy[485] and *surseance van betaling* (suspension of payments).[486] As opposed to bankruptcy, which is a liquidation-oriented proceeding, suspension of payments can be considered a preventive restructuring proceeding. Both proceedings come in addition to the limited possibilities that Dutch contract law used to offer to bind dissenting creditors in an out-of-court debt restructuring, before the WHOA entered into force.

485 Art. 1 DBA et seq. The DBA is in force since 1 September 1896. Subsequently, various amendments have been included in the DBA, see further: B. Wessels, *Insolventierecht, Faillietverklaring (Deel I)* (5th ed.), Deventer: Wolters Kluwer, 2019, Paras. 1051-1053c.

486 Art. 214 DBA et seq. The DBA also provides for the *schuldsanering natuurlijke personen* (debt restructuring for natural persons) which is open only to natural persons who do not exercise a business (Art. 284 DBA et seq).

2.1 Suspension of Payments

Suspension of payments – a proceeding that is available to both corporate debtors and natural persons running a business[487] – aims at facilitating the continuation of imminent insolvent, but viable companies.[488] A suspension of payments is a public and voluntary proceeding, which is only available at the debtor's request.[489] Commencement of a proceeding, in principle, brings about only an automatic stay of the unsecured and non-preferred creditors,[490] and provides debtors with time to prepare a restructuring plan and/ or to reorganize the business in order to regain viability. The suspension of payments can be requested when debtors expect (or foresee) an inability to continue paying the debts as they fall due.[491]

In a suspension of payments, a court will appoint a *bewindvoerder* (joint administrator) and a *rechter-commissaris* (supervisory judge). Joint administrators are tasked with the joint administration – together with a debtor – of a debtor's assets and affairs.[492] In particular, debtors require the consent of joint administrators in every part of administering their assets and affairs.[493] Debtors are not rendered legally incompetent in a suspension of payments. As opposed to bankruptcy, they continue the business and do not lose their power to dispose of assets belonging to the estate, albeit subject to the authorization of the joint administrator. When debtors act without or in violation of this consent, their actions can be reversed by joint administrators.[494] Consequently, debtors are effectively partially in possession in suspension of payments. Furthermore, proceedings will typically involve a supervisory judge, who in suspension of payments is tasked only with advising a joint administrator and to hear – at the request of a joint administrator – witnesses and experts.[495]

Upon filing for suspension of payments, a court will readily grant debtors a temporary suspension. This can later be converted in a permanent suspension of payments, which, in principle, can run for up to 1.5 years.[496] In addition to creating a breathing space for a

---

487 Compare Art. 214(4) DBA.

488 B. Wessels, *Insolventierecht, Surseance van betaling* (5th ed.), Deventer: Wolters Kluwer 2021, Para. 8003 and 8005.

489 Arts. 214(1) and 22a(1)DBA.

490 Arts. 230(1) and 231 DBA. An additional stay (*afkoelingsperiode*) may be requested to stay enforcement actions of secured creditors (Art. 241a DBA).

491 Art. 214(1) DBA.

492 Art. 215(2) DBA.

493 Art. 228 DBA.

494 Art. 228(1) DBA. Furthermore, Art. 228(2) DBA determines that a debtor's estate is not bound by a legal act as long as a joint administrator does cooperate, unless the legal act is in the interest of the debtor's estate.

495 Arts. 223a and 223b DBA.

496 Arts. 215(2) and 223 DBA, from which it follows that a suspension can also be extended also after the first 1,5 years.

debtor by suspending payments and suspending attachments, a suspension of payments provides a framework to adopt a restructuring plan (also referred to as a composition). A restructuring plan affects, in principle, only claims of unsecured and non-preferred creditors. It must be adopted in a creditors' meeting by a majority of the affected creditors that are present, which represents a majority of the claims in value. Confirmation by a court will make a restructuring plan binding on all absent or dissenting unsecured and non-preferred creditors.[497]

Although a suspension of payments is designed as a preventive restructuring proceeding, in practice, it is often perceived as a forerunner of filing for bankruptcy proceedings.[498] In particular, different from bankruptcy, there is no statutory law requiring a board of directors to obtain prior approval of the General Assembly before applying for suspension of payments.[499] This proceeding may therefore be an alternative option for the board of directors to deal with financial distress in a situation that shareholders are unwilling to approve a bankruptcy filing. Typically, such debtors are in too much financial distress to be able to continue paying debts as they fall due. In turn, this is a mandatory ground for joint administrators to request a court to terminate a suspension of payments and declare a debtor bankrupt.[500]

2.2 *Bankruptcy*

Bankruptcy – the most used proceeding in the DBA – is primarily aimed at liquidation of a debtor's assets. It is open to all debtors who are unable to pay their debts as they fall due, including legal and natural persons, whether or not they run a business or profession.[501] A bankruptcy proceeding can be voluntary when a debtor himself requests for commencing the proceeding, or involuntarily when a request for bankruptcy is made by one or more creditors.[502] In either case, upon declaring a debtor bankrupt, the court will appoint a *curator* (liquidator) and a supervisory judge. In a bankruptcy proceeding, debtors are out of possession while liquidators are tasked with the administration and liquidation of the debtor's assets.[503] Supervisory judges are appointed to supervise the liquidator's conduct during the proceeding.[504]

497 Art. 252 DBA et seq.

498 See for instance *Kamerstukken II* 2001/02, 24 036, nr. 238, p. 1.

499 See Arts. 2:136 (public companies) and 2:246 (limited liability companies) DCC.

500 Art. 242(1), (2) and (4) DBA.

501 Arts. 1 and 6(3) DBA.

502 Art. 1(1) DBA.

503 Arts. 23 and 68(1) DBA.

504 Art. 64 DBA.

In practice, liquidators will consider the opportunities for restructuring in bankruptcy as this may result in maximizing the value of the estate. For instance, liquidators will pursue a (partial) going-concern sale when the business is still (partially) viable and when this is in the best interest of the general body of creditors. This can also be pursued by means of pre-packaged bankruptcy.[505] Also, the involved debtor and creditors could agree to a restructuring plan in bankruptcy. When the quorum is met (a majority of the creditors present, representing at least 50% of the value of the claims), and the restructuring plan is confirmed by the court, it becomes binding on all ordinary, unsecured creditors, also those absent or dissenting.[506]

2.3 *Out-of-Court Debt Restructuring*

Before filing for suspension of payments or bankruptcy proceedings, viable debtors will typically propose to (a part of) their creditors a *buitengerechtelijk akkoord* (composition). In principle, this out-of-court debt restructuring takes places informally without any court involvement. In practice, this will require the support of all affected creditors, which may easily be interfered with by creditors taking a hold-out position to the proposed composition, whether for rational or strategic reasons.[507]

In case law, a small window has emerged to bind dissenting creditors to an otherwise out-of-court composition. When a hold-out strategy constitutes abuse of power, the court may overrule the decisions of creditors to reject the proposed composition. The abuse of law exception is only available under exceptional circumstances. A situation in which a creditor is aware of a pressing financial situation of a debtor, or an imminent bankruptcy will, in general, not constitute abuse of power. The fact that a majority of creditors accept

505 The Dutch pre-pack has been developed in practice, however, in recent years it has been used limitedly. This was due to growing legal uncertainty on the position of employees in such cases, in particular following preliminary questions raised to the CJEU. The most recent decision (CJEU 22 April 2022, ECLI:EU:C:2022:321 (*Heiploeg*)) has brought some clarity in this regard. Currently, a legislative proposal is pending to establish a legal basis for the pre-pack, see bill for the *Wet continuïteit ondernemingen I* (Business Continuation Act I; WCO I), which is pending with the Senate, available at: https://www.eerstekamer.nl/wetsvoorstel/34218_wet_continuiteit.

506 See Art. 138 DBA et seq. This concerns only unsecured creditors, in addition, a debtor may pursue a consensual agreement with secured or preferential creditors. Upon confirmation of a restructuring plan, a (corporate) debtor will not be dissolved (Art. 2:19(1)(c) Dutch Civil Code (DCC)) and its creditors will not regain their rights of foreclosure (Art. 195 DBA is not applicable in case of a restructuring plan).

507 See further also European Law Institute (ed Part I) and B. Wessels, S. Madaus & J.M.G.J. Boon (eds Part II), *Rescue of Business in Europe*, Oxford: Oxford University Press, 2020, p. 153 et seq.

an out-of-court composition is not sufficient reason to characterize the rejection of the composition by a creditor as an abuse of power.[508]

3 Towards the Dutch WHOA

3.1 *Historic Views on Plan Proceedings*

The introduction of the WHOA is preceded by a long-running discussion on the introduction of a legal instrument that provides for confirmation of extrajudicial restructuring plans (plan proceedings). Although such plans were forbidden in 1540, over time local statutes and practices evolved which increased the scope for adoption of a restructuring plan.[509] With the introduction of the so-called *Desolate boedelskamers* (Chambers of Empty Estates) in several Dutch cities such as Amsterdam, Dordrecht and Middelburg, debtors could apply for sequestration (*sekwestratie*). This was a proceeding in which a plan could be negotiated with the creditors in order to avoid bankruptcy.[510] Later, when the Netherlands had been annexed to France, the French Code de Commerce as applicable from 1811 and subsequently the Dutch Code of Commerce of 1838 introduced uniform insolvency proceedings in the Netherlands. Consequently, this removed the prior local frameworks for plan proceedings.[511]

Discussions on whether statutory provisions on a plan proceeding should be introduced have since continued, including by means of several (draft) legislative texts. This was the case in the late 19th century in the parliamentary discussion prior to the adoption of the DBA in 1893 and continued in the 20th and 21st centuries.[512] A plan proceeding was argued for to avoid bankruptcy proceedings for honest but unfortunate debtors, and as a

508 Supreme Court 12 August 2005, ECLI:NL:HR:2005:AT7799 (*Payroll*), at 3.5.2 and 3.5.3. Furthermore, the Supreme Court has ruled that the abuse of power standard also applies when a creditor (whilst rejecting the composition) seeks to obtain payment of a larger part of his claim from the debtor than what other creditors obtained under the out-of-court composition (Supreme Court 24 March 2017, ECLI: NL:HR:2017:485 (*Mondia/V D*), at 3.4.3 and 3.4.4).

509 A. Mennens, *Het dwangakkoord buiten surseance en faillissement*, Onderneming en Recht, nr. 118 (diss. Nijmegen), Deventer: Wolters Kluwer, 2020, p. 41 et seq.

510 A. Noordam, *Schuldsanering en goede trouw* (diss. VU Amsterdam), 2007, p. 131 (footnote 92). See for a legal historic analysis of this proceeding: M. den Hollander, *Stay of Execution. Institutions and Insolvency Legislation in Amsterdam* (diss. Tilburg), 2021, Chapters 3-5. See also B. Wessels, *Rembrandt's Money: The Legal and Financial Life of an Artist-entrepreneur in the 17th Century Holland*, Deventer: Wolters Kluwer, 2021, pp. 389-390.

511 A. Mennens, *Het dwangakkoord buiten surseance en faillissement*, Onderneming en Recht, nr. 118 (diss. Nijmegen), Deventer: Wolters Kluwer, 2020, p. 42.

512 N.W.A. Tollenaar, *Het pre-insolventieakkoord. Grondslagen en raamwerk* (diss. Groningen), Deventer: Wolters Kluwer, 2016, Para. 1.2; A. Mennens, *Het dwangakkoord buiten surseance en faillissement*, Onderneming en Recht, nr. 118 (diss. Nijmegen), Deventer: Wolters Kluwer, 2020, p. 43 et seq.

consequence, not only to prevent the detrimental effects of collective liquidation but also to prevent creditors from pursuing hold-out strategies. However, successive academic and legislative proposals for plan proceedings were critiqued on substantive grounds. A plan proceeding would be unfair, violate ownership rights and be a source of legal uncertainty.[513] However, as was the case with the 2007 pre-draft for a new Dutch Insolvency Act (DIA) that included a proposal for a plan proceeding, it could also be macroeconomic and political reasons which prevented the adoption of such proposals.[514]

3.2 *Towards a Dutch Plan Proceeding: The WHOA*

The initiative for what eventually became the WHOA was part of the 2012 Dutch legislative programme to recalibrate Dutch bankruptcy law (*wetgevingsprogramma herijking faillissementsrecht*).[515] One of the three so-called 'pillars' of this initiative deals with strengthening the restructuring capacity of businesses.[516] The legislative reforms in this pillar aim to promote that businesses will not enter bankruptcy proceedings unnecessarily, especially when creditors frustrate an out-of-court debt restructuring. The legislative reforms should ensure that a restructuring plan can also be adopted outside bankruptcy, while simultaneously providing for continuation of the debtor's business.[517]

Building on the Draft DIA 2007 and (comparative) studies,[518] the Minister proposed several legislative reforms. One of these reforms includes the introduction of a preventive restructuring framework enabling viable debtors to continue in possession while preparing a restructuring plan, which became the WHOA.[519] A golden thread for this pillar, and for

513 A. Mennens, *Het dwangakkoord buiten surseance en faillissement*, Onderneming en Recht, nr. 118 (diss. Nijmegen), Deventer: Wolters Kluwer, 2020, p. 43 et seq.

514 S.C.J.J. Kortmann & N.E.D. Faber (eds), *Geschiedenis van de Faillissementswet, Deel 2-IV Voorontwerp insolventiewet*, Deventer: Kluwer, 2007. Part 7.1 introduces a framework for concluding a composition outside insolvency, for a debtor that faces impending insolvency, and with a view to prevent its insolvency. In 2010, it was announced that due to the 2008 Global Financial Crisis, an overhaul of the DBA with introduction of a new Insolvency Act was undesirable, see *Kamerstukken II* 2010/11, Aanhangsel nr. 1014, p. 5.

515 *Kamerstukken II* 2012/13, 29 911, nr. 74, p. 2 et seq.

516 *Kamerstukken II* 2012/13, 29 911, nr. 74, p. 2, the other pillars concern modernization of the DBA and prevention of fraud in insolvency.

517 *Kamerstukken II* 2012/13, 29 911, nr. 74, pp. 2-3; *Kamerstukken II* 2012/13, 33 695, nr. 1, pp. 2 and 4; Kamerstukken II 2013/14, 33 695, nr. 3, pp. 3-4.

518 See, for instance, P.M. Veder, T.E. Booms & N.B. Pannevis, *Rechtsvergelijkende verkenning in het kader van het programma herijking faillissementsrecht* (WODC Rapport 2315), Nijmegen: Radboud Universiteit Nijmegen – Onderzoekcentrum Onderneming & Recht 2013, available at: http://hdl.handle.net/20.500.12832/2037; R.M. Hermans & R.D. Vriesendorp, 'Het dwangakkoord in het insolventierecht: vrijheid in gebondenheid?', *TvI* 2014/10.

519 *Kamerstukken II* 2012/13, 33 695, nr. 1, p. 5. This pillar had three legislative proposals: (i) the Business Continuation Act (*Wet continuïteit ondernemingen*, WCO) I, for a codification of pre-packaged bankruptcies, (ii) the WCO II for a preventive restructuring framework, which was later called the WHOA,

the WHOA, has been the objective to strengthen the ability for businesses to restructure. In particular, individual creditors should be prevented from pursuing strategic hold-out positions which could frustrate the adoption of a plan and a timely attempt to prevent bankruptcy.[520] Over the course of the lengthy legislative process, the Minister has drawn on the evolving EU initiatives, including a Commission Recommendation on a New Approach to Business Failure and Insolvency from 2014[521] and the PRD 2019.[522]

In July 2019, the WHOA bill was introduced in Parliament. This bill followed an extensive public consultation consisting of two prior draft bills.[523] Although public consultations resulted in extensive responses with substantive critiques on parts of the draft bills, most of which were incorporated in subsequent drafts, it was also clear that – maybe for the first time in the Netherlands – there was broad support from practice and academia for introducing a plan proceeding. Consequently, the lengthy legislative process has also allowed for detailed consideration and refinement of the implications for (legal) practice.[524]

In the final stage of the drafting process, there were extensive discussions in Parliament on the position of secured and unsecured creditors and the distribution of reorganization value under a plan. Some parliamentarians raised concerns that under the relaxed Absolute Priority Rule (APR) and the so-called 'cash-out option', secured creditors had too much control over a WHOA process and would take a disproportionately high part of the (reorganization) value, leaving unsecured creditors basically empty-handed. On the one hand, amendments were adopted that improved the protection of unsecured small- and medium-sized enterprise (SME) creditors by requiring that they should receive at least 20% of their claim under the plan, even when higher ranking classes of creditors are not

---

and (iii) the WCO III for a more effective winding-up of a bankruptcy estate, which has later been called Act to further the effectiveness of bankruptcy procedural law (*Wet bevordering doelmatigheid van het faillissementsprocesrecht*) (*Kamerstukken II* 2013/14, 33 695, nr. 3, p. 3; *Kamerstukken II* 2016/17, 33 695, nr. 14, p. 2).

520 See, for instance, *Kamerstukken II* 2013/14, 33 695, nr. 5, pp. 4-5; *Kamerstukken II* 2015/16, 33 695, nr. 10, p. 2; *Kamerstukken II* 2016/17, 33 695, nr. 14, p. 2; *Kamerstukken II*, 35 249, 2018/19, nr. 3, p. 1.

521 Commission Recommendation on a new approach to business failure and insolvency, 12 March 2014, C(2014) 1500 final.

522 See *Kamerstukken II* 2012/13, 33 695, nr. 1, pp. 7-8; *Kamerstukken II* 2013/14, 33 695, nr. 5, pp. 4, 7-8; *Kamerstukken II* 2016/17, 33 695, nr. 14, pp. 6-7; *Kamerstukken II* 2018/19, 33 695, nr. 17, p. 4; Kamerstukken II 2018/19, 33 695, nr. 18, p. 3. See further Explanatory memorandum to draft bill WCO II, 2014, pp. 4-6; *Kamerstukken II*, 35 249, 2018/19, nr. 3, pp. 3-4. See also: N.W.A. Tollenaar, *Het pre-insolventieakkoord. Grondslagen en raamwerk* (diss. Groningen), Deventer: Wolters Kluwer, 2016, Para. 1.3.

523 In 2014 a first draft bill was presented, the *Wet continuïteit ondernemingen II* (Business Continuation Act II). The public consultation led to ample response and led to a revised draft bill – the WHOA – that was made available for a public consultation in 2017. This draft WHOA and an explanatory memorandum are available at: https://www.internetconsultatie.nl/wethomologatie.

524 *Kamerstukken II* 2018/19, 35 249, nr. 3 (Explanatory memorandum to the WHOA), pp. 3 and 23-25; A.M. Wolffram-van Doorn, 'Inleiding ter gelegenheid van de indiening bij de Tweede Kamer van het wetsvoorstel betreffende de Wet homologatie onderhands akkoord', *FIP* 2019/212, pp. 4 and 7.

satisfied in full.[525] On the other hand, amendments have limited the rights of secured creditors in two respects. Firstly, contrary to other creditors, certain secured creditors are not entitled to a cash-out option, which allows a creditor to ask the debtor to pay in cash the liquidation value of its claim, instead of what has been offered under the plan.[526] Secondly, an amendment introduced bifurcation of the claims of secured creditors. Their claims are placed in a class of secured creditors in accordance with the extent that their claim – in case of liquidation – is covered by security. For the remaining part of their claim, they are placed in a class of unsecured creditors.[527]

With these amendments,[528] the House of Parliament and the Senate adopted the WHOA bill,[529] which entered into force on 1 January 2021.[530] Because the WHOA implemented the PRD 2019 only in part, the Act Implementing the PRD 2019 – which entered into force on 1 January 2023 – has implemented the remaining parts of the PRD 2019, which also introduced some changes to the WHOA.[531]

4 Main Features of the WHOA

4.1 *Objective and Scope of the Framework/Process*

The WHOA introduces a legal framework to the DBA, which provides for confirmation of extrajudicial plans.[532] The legislator has drawn inspiration from features of the US

---

525 *Kamerstukken II* 2019/20, 35 249, nr. 25; Art. 384(4)(a) DBA. SME creditors are in general small entities with no more than 50 employees.

526 *Kamerstukken II* 2019/20, 35 249, nr. 24; Art. 384(4)(d) DBA.

527 *Kamerstukken II* 2019/20, 35 249, nr. 14; Art. 374(3) DBA.

528 In addition to the aforementioned three amendments, a fourth amendment introduced a mandatory evaluation of the WHOA 3 years after its entry into force (*Kamerstukken II* 2019/20, 35 249, nr. 8. See Art. IIA Wet homologatie onderhands akkoord (*Stb.* 2020, 414).

529 *Handelingen II*, 2019/20, 74, item 17; *Handelingen I* 2020/21, nr. 4, item 5.

530 *Wet homologatie onderhands akkoord* (*Stb.* 2020, 414); *Besluit van 26 oktober 2020 tot vaststelling van het tijdstip van inwerkingtreding van de Wet homologatie onderhands akkoord* (*Stb.* 2020, 415). Unofficial translations have been prepared by several law firms, see for instance: www.debrauw.com/cerp.

531 *Implementatiewet richtlijn herstructurering en insolventie* (*Stb.* 2022, 491); *Besluit van 5 december 2022 tot vaststelling van het tijdstip van inwerkingtreding van de Implementatiewet richtlijn herstructurering en insolventie* (*Stb.* 2022, 492). With this act, the legislator deviates from the earlier plan where the PRD 2019 would be implemented primarily by amending the suspension of payment, see: *Kamerstukken II* 2018/19, 35 249, nr. 3 (Explanatory memorandum to the WHOA), p. 4. See also *Kamerstukken II* 2018/19, 33 695, nr. 18, p. 3. For a comparative review of the WHOA and the suspension of payments in light of the PRD 2019, see: Gert-Jan Boon, 'Mapping Preventive Restructuring Frameworks and the EU Preventive Restructuring Directive for the JCOERE Project, Country Report The Netherlands', JCOERE Project, May 2020, available at: http://www.ucc.ie/en/media/projectsandcentres/jcoereproject/bannerimages/TheNetherlands_FINAL_PDF.pdf.

532 This Section presents an overview of some of the main features of the WHOA, however, it does not yet include an extensive discussion with respect to the treatment of, in particular, *ipso facto* clauses, third-party

Chapter 11 Bankruptcy Code (Restructuring Proceeding) and the UK Scheme of Arrangement.[533] However, first and foremost, the WHOA is a new Dutch pre-insolvency[534] or also preventive restructuring framework implementing in part the PRD 2019. Although the WHOA has been introduced as a part of the DBA, it is not to be categorized as a 'bankruptcy proceeding'. In fact, the WHOA has been subsumed under Title IV of the DBA, entitled "outside bankruptcy and suspension of payments".[535]

The WHOA's primary aim is to prevent financially distressed debtors from entering bankruptcy proceedings due to hold-out creditors that prevented debtors from successfully pursuing a plan. This can be done by means of either a restructuring or a liquidating plan. A restructuring plan is geared towards securing the viability of debtors and their business. A liquidating plan is aimed at the winding-up of debtors with unviable businesses. In comparison with bankruptcy proceedings, a liquidating plan should still result in a more favourable outcome for the affected creditors.[536] Although statutory law hardly introduces any differences for either type of plan, unless stated otherwise, the following will focus on a WHOA process that is directed to confirmation of restructuring plans. Although it is a single framework, the legislator introduced a dual track for the WHOA processes, either public or private. In the case of public WHOA process, the hearings will be heard in public and registered in the public registers. By contrast, for private WHOA processes the hearings will be *in camera* and the process will not be registered in the public register. The choice regarding either track must be made at the start of the judicial process and cannot be changed afterwards.[537]

releases and enterprise groups. See also other publications in English reviewing aspects of the WHOA, including: M. Noldus, 'Creditors' Rights under the New "Dutch" Scheme', *International Corporate Rescue*, 2021, 10(1), p. 17 et seq; R.A.G. de Vaan & G.J. de Bock, 'Rapidly Implemented Amidst COVID Crisis, New Dutch Restructuring Procedure Offers Relief to Business and Organizations Struggling with High Debts', *European Company Law Journal*, 2021, 18(3), pp. 106-112; V.J.M van Hoof, 'The Continue Use and Disposal of Encumbered Assets during the Restructuring Directive's Stay', *European Insolvency and Restructuring Journal*, 2021(4), Paras. 3.3.2-3.3.3, available at: https://eirjournal.com/article/view/15087; S. Pepels, 'Third Party Releases under Dutch Law since the WHOA – a Warm Welcome for a Very Limited Number of Guests Only?', in: *Third Party Releases by Means of Bankruptcy Law Guarantees and (Mass) Tort*. Preadviezen/Reports 2022 (Netherlands Association for Comparative and International Insolvency Law), Den Haag: Boom Juridisch (forthcoming).

533 *Kamerstukken II* 2018/19, 35 249, nr. 3 (Explanatory memorandum to the WHOA), pp. 3-4, 17 and 65; N.W.A. Tollenaar, *Het pre-insolventieakkoord. Grondslagen en raamwerk* (diss. Groningen), Deventer: Wolters Kluwer, 2016, Para. 1.3; A.M. Wolffram-van Doorn, 'Inleiding ter gelegenheid van de indiening bij de Tweede Kamer van het wetsvoorstel betreffende de Wet homologatie onderhands akkoord', *FIP* 2019/212, p. 6.

534 Compare European Law Institute (ed. Part I) and B. Wessels, S. Madaus & J.M.G.J. Boon (eds Part II), *Rescue of Business in Europe*, Oxford: Oxford University Press 2020, p. 160 et seq.

535 The heading of Title IV will be introduced to the DBA as part of the bill WCO I, see Art. I bill WCO I.

536 *Kamerstukken II* 2018/19, 35 249, nr. 3 (Explanatory memorandum to the WHOA), pp. 1-2.

537 Art. 369(6) AND (9) DBA; *Kamerstukken II* 2018/19, 35 249, nr. 3 (Explanatory memorandum to the WHOA), pp. 6-7 and 31-32.

The personal scope of the WHOA includes, in principle, debtors that are both natural and legal persons, regardless of their legal form. However, excluded from the scope are those natural persons that do not conduct a profession or business, and debtors that qualify as banks or insurers.[538] Alternative debt restructuring or rescue mechanisms are available to these debtors; therefore, they are excluded from the scope of the WHOA.[539] Furthermore, as is the case with other restructuring and insolvency processes, the WHOA also takes an entity-by-entity approach when debtors are part of an enterprise group.[540] However, there are two exceptions to this default approach. When a restructuring plan involves adjustment of debts for which an enterprise group member provided a guarantee, subject to certain requirements, a debtor may extend a restructuring plan to also include this guarantee within its scope.[541] In addition, the WHOA provides for a form of procedural consolidation. In WHOA processes involving multiple members of an enterprise group, the debtors can file their petitions simultaneously to be heard by a single court in the Netherlands.[542]

In regard to the material scope of the WHOA, the framework can be accessed by debtors that are in a situation in which it may reasonably be assumed that they will become unable to pay their debts as they fall due (the so-called 'pre-insolvency' or 'light insolvency' test).[543] Furthermore, the WHOA process is not necessarily collective. In fact, it is up to the proponent of a plan to determine which creditors and shareholders will be affected and who will accordingly be involved in the process and vote on the plan. This may involve all or just part of a debtor's creditors and shareholders.[544]

The WHOA is designed as a time- and cost-efficient process and is characterized by a high degree of flexibility for debtors. Therefore, the statutory time frames are limited to promote a straightforward process. For instance, a stay can have a maximum duration of 8 months.[545] Also, courts are required to act swiftly; they are urged to handle requests for interim decisions during one hearing, to decide as soon as possible when they will hear a

538 Art. 369(1), first sentence, DBA.

539 *Kamerstukken II* 2018/19, 35 249, nr. 3 (Explanatory memorandum to the WHOA) pp. 29-30; Arts. 212g et seq, 213 et seq and 284 et seq DBA.

540 Art. 370(1) DBA; *Kamerstukken II* 2018/19, 35 249, nr. 3 (Explanatory memorandum to the WHOA), p. 10. Nonetheless, the WHOA gives certain consideration to groups in some provisions, compare in particular Arts. 369(8), 371(15) and 372 DBA.

541 Art. 372 DBA.

542 Art. 369(8) DBA. Although the legislator has argued that may also apply when some enterprise group members have their centre of main interests outside the Netherlands (*Kamerstukken II* 2018/19, 35 249, nr. 3 (Explanatory memorandum to the WHOA), p. 32), this has been disputed (see for instance W.J.E. Nijnens, 'De WHOA en het internationaal privaatrecht inclusief de herstructurering van groepen', in: C.M. Harmsen & M.L.H. Reumers (eds), *De WHOA: van wet naar recht, (Recht & Praktijk, nr. InsR18)*, Deventer: Wolters Kluwer, 2021, Paras. 12.3.5 and 12.6).

543 Arts. 370(1) and 371(3) DBA, see further Section 4.2 below.

544 Arts. 369(2) and 381(2) DBA. See further, Section 4.5 below, discussing the scope of a plan.

545 Art. 376(2) and (5) DBA.

request for confirmation of a plan (which should be within 8-14 days after the request for confirmation was submitted).[546] Although there is no set duration for the completion of the WHOA process, it can be completed within 6 weeks.

4.2 *Commencing a WHOA Process*

A WHOA can be commenced by debtors as well as individual creditors, shareholders, Works Councils or an Employee Representative Body (*personeelsvertegenwoordiging*).[547] Debtors can do so by submitting a commencement statement (*startverklaring*) with the registrar of the court, which indicates when debtors have commenced the process and whether it is a public or private process.[548] When debtors are legal entities, their boards of directors do not require approval from the General Assembly or a specific class of shareholders to offer its creditors and shareholders a restructuring plan.[549] Individual creditors, shareholders, a Works Council or an Employee Representative Body can commence a process by requesting courts to appoint a restructuring expert (*herstructureringsdeskundige*). This expert has the primary task of preparing a plan that will be submitted to the affected creditors and shareholders of a debtor.[550] In addition to depositing a commencement statement, debtors may also request appointment of a restructuring expert at the start or later during the process.[551]

Debtors can enter a WHOA process when they are in a situation in which it can reasonably be assumed that they will be unable to continue paying their debts. This pre-insolvency test also requires that debtors are still able to pay their current obligations,[552] while it is foreseeable that they will not be able to do so in future and that this – if debts would not be restructured – would result in their insolvency.[553] The legislator has not given a specific definition or description of a time frame for determining the pre-insolvency situation; however, it has been indicated that this may include situations where debtors

546 Arts. 378(3), 383(4) and (5) DBA.

547 Arts. 370(1) and 371(1) DBA.

548 Art. 370(1) and (3) DBA. A uniform commencement statement has been drafted by the Dutch Judiciary and is annexed to the national court procedural rules for WHOA cases (*Landelijk Procesreglement WHOA zaken rechtbanken*, version of 1 February 2022, available at: https://www.rechtspraak.nl/SiteCollectionDocuments/procesreglement-whoa-p-2022.pdf). A commencement statement is not mandatory to commence preparations for a restructuring plan, except when debtors want to make to the court, such as for requesting a stay or a bespoke measure.

549 Art. 370(5) DBA. This also applies to the debtor's performance of the plan.

550 Art. 371(1) DBA.

551 Art. 371(1) DBA.

552 *Kamerstukken II* 2018/19, 35 249, nr. 3 (Explanatory memorandum to the WHOA), p. 33.

553 Ibid., pp. 33-34.

foresee being unable to repay loans in the coming 6-12 months.[554] The pre-insolvency test will be applied by a court when it is faced for the first time with a request in a WHOA case. This may be as early as a request to appoint a restructuring expert[555] or a stay.[556] However, this will not be reviewed by the court when debtors submit a commencement statement.[557] Courts will ultimately examine the pre-insolvency test when they are presented with a request to confirm a restructuring plan.[558]

4.3 *Involved Actors*

The WHOA introduces new actors and roles in the DBA. The two new actors are the restructuring experts and observers, who can be appointed by courts on a case-by-case basis in WHOA processes. Furthermore, specific roles have been allocated to debtors and courts. The WHOA does not contain statutory provisions dealing with (creditor's) committees.

4.3.1 Debtor-in-Possession

In a WHOA process, a debtor remains in full control, and is therefore also referred to as 'debtor-in-possession' (DIP). However, statutory provisions do not refer to the debtor as a DIP. It is only in the parliamentary history that the legislator makes mention of a DIP, notably in conjunction with the respective provision on the DIP in the PRD 2019.[559] The commencement of a process itself does not result in an automatic divestment of the debtor, nor does it create a separate estate as is common in bankruptcy proceedings. The WHOA introduces a process which, in principle, leaves debtors in the same situation as they were before the process was commenced. This is due to the fact that upon a successful restructuring, a debtor will also continue its business 'as usual'. Debtors maintain full

554 Ibid. Compare also Germany with a more articulated pre-insolvency test in the StaRUG, see Chapter 5, Sections 4.1 and 4.2.

555 Art. 371(3) DBA.

556 This does not follow literally from the DBA, but the pre-insolvency test has been applied by some courts, see for instance District Court Midden-Nederland 13 January 2021, ECLI:NL:RBMNE:2021:392, at 4.8; District Court Limburg 11 February 2021, ECLI:NL:RBLIM:2021:8854, at 3.2; District Court Zeeland-West-Brabant 12 February 2021, ECLI:NL:RBZWB:2021:6911, at 3.4; District Court Gelderland 4 March 2021, ECLI:NL:RBGEL:2021:1126, at 3.4-3.5; District Court Den Haag 5 August 2021, ECLI:NL:RBDHA:2021:15535, at 3.4; District Court Oost-Brabant 17 September 2021, ECLI:NL:RBOBR:2021:5058, at 3.4-3.5. Some courts have not done so, see for instance, District Court Rotterdam 8 March 2021, ECLI:NL:RBROT:2021:1887; District Court Amsterdam 26 May 2021, ECLI:NL:RBAMS:2021:2815, District Court Amsterdam 13 September 2021, ECLI:NL:RBAMS:2021:6771; District Court Overijssel 12 October 2021, ECLI:NL:RBOVE:2021:3891.

557 Art. 370(3) DBA.

558 Art. 384(2)(a) DBA.

559 *Kamerstukken II* 2018/19, 35 249, nr. 3 (Explanatory memorandum to the WHOA), pp. 27, 38 and 60; *Kamerstukken II* 2019/20, 35 249, nr. 6, p. 5; Art. 5 PRD 2019.

control over their assets and affairs.[560] In a voluntary WHOA process, it will be the debtor – or if appointed, the restructuring expert – who will draft, negotiate, and offer its creditors and shareholders a restructuring plan.[561] As the Advocate General De Bock has stated (freely translated):

> during the entire process, a debtor maintains its powers to administer the estate and take legal actions. A debtor undergoes an extrajudicial … restructuring in which the WHOA merely facilitates the debtor where necessary.[562]

Still, debtors subject to a WHOA process may experience some impact on their duties. The severity of the debtor's financial distress will determine the extent to which debtors – in case of a sole proprietorship the entrepreneur and in case of a legal person primarily the directors – need to take into account the interests of creditors, which will limit the discretionary space for taking legal actions. They may risk liability claims based on tort, in particular for director's liability. Furthermore, measures adopted during a WHOA process may impact the debtor's role. In particular, a stay will impose restrictions on debtors to use the assets subject to a stay outside the ordinary course of business, and while safeguarding the interests of the third parties affected by the stay.[563] In addition, courts may impose measures, which could limit the discretionary space of debtors during a WHOA process.[564] Importantly, a court appointment of a restructuring expert or observer does not affect the formal rights and duties of debtors in a WHOA process; their appointment does not divest debtors.[565]

4.3.2 Restructuring Experts and Observers

In WHOA processes, courts may appoint either a restructuring expert or an observer (*observator*) on a case-by-case basis. Restructuring experts can be appointed not only at the request of individual creditors, shareholders, Works Councils or Employee Representative Bodies, but also – typically when debtors consider this helpful in

560 *Kamerstukken II* 2018/19, 35 249, nr. 3 (Explanatory memorandum to the WHOA), p. 27; J.M.G.J. Boon, 'Actoren in de WHOA: herstructureren met de schuldenaar (debtor in possession), herstructureringsdeskundige en observator', in: C.M. Harmsen & M.L.H. Reumers (eds), *De WHOA: van wet naar recht, (Recht & Praktijk, nr. InsR18)*, Deventer: Wolters Kluwer, 2021, Para. 5.3; Opinion AG De Bock 6 December 2021, ECLI:NL:PHR:2021:1152, at 3.16.

561 Art. 370(1) DBA.

562 Opinion AG De Bock 6 December 2021, ECLI:NL:PHR:2021:1152, at 3.16.

563 Art. 377(1) and (2) DBA.

564 Arts. 377(3) and 379(1) DBA.

565 Compare Art. 371(1) and 380(1) DBA; Opinion AG De Bock 6 December 2021, ECLI:NL:PHR:2021:1152, at 3.16.

strengthening the support of affected parties in the process – by debtors.[566] To appoint restructuring experts, courts must be satisfied that the pre-insolvency test has been met and that such appointment will not be detrimental to the interests of the general body of creditors.[567] In addition, the person to be appointed must be sufficiently qualified and possess a level of expertise.[568] If the debtor is an SME debtor,[569] and no WHOA process had been commenced yet, appointment of a restructuring expert also requires the approval of the debtor.[570]

Once appointed, restructuring experts are primarily tasked with drafting and negotiating a restructuring plan. They do this either to prepare a standalone plan – separately from the debtor – or to assist debtors who are preparing such a plan themselves.[571] When a restructuring expert is appointed, a debtor can only submit its plan to the affected creditors and shareholders through the restructuring expert. As such, during a WHOA process two competing restructuring plans may be put forward, one prepared by a debtor and one prepared by a restructuring expert. When both plans are adopted by the required majority,[572] confirmation can be requested by the restructuring expert for both plans.[573] In these cases, the court will, in principle, first consider for confirmation the plan prepared by the debtor.[574] Furthermore, restructuring experts are tasked with supervision of the debtor's conduct, which can be derived from their position in WHOA processes. Once a restructuring expert is appointed, courts can no longer appoint or continue the appointment of an observer, who has the explicit task to supervise

566 Art. 371(1) DBA; *Kamerstukken II* 2018-19, 35 249, nr. 3 (Explanatory memorandum to the WHOA), pp. 40-41.

567 Art. 371(3), a similar provision applies to observers, see Art. 381(1) DBA.

568 See further: Art. 371(3) and (6) DBA; Guidelines on appointment of restructuring experts and observers in the WHOA (*Richtlijnen aanwijzen en aanstellen herstructureringsdeskundigen en observatoren in de WHOA*), version 1 January 2023, available at: https://www.rechtspraak.nl/SiteCollectionDocuments/richtlijnen-aanwijzen-aanstellen-%20herstructureringsdeskundigen-observatoren-whoa-0101-2023.pdf.

569 Art. 369(1), second sentence, DBA. The Dutch legislator has adopted the EU definition of an SME: '... enterprises which employ fewer than 250 persons and which have an annual turnover not exceeding EUR 50 million, and/or an annual balance sheet total not exceeding EUR 43 million' (Art. 2(1) of the Annex to Commission Recommendation of 6 May 2003 concerning the definition of micro, small and medium-sized enterprises (Text with EEA relevance) (notified under document number C(2003) 1422)). See also: *Kamerstukken II* 2018/19, 35 249, nr. 3 (Explanatory memorandum to the WHOA), p. 66.

570 Art. 371(15) DBA. If the debtor has shareholders, they are not permitted from unreasonably preventing the board from giving such permission, neither is the board permitted to withhold its permission without good reasons.

571 Art. 371(1) DBA; *Kamerstukken II* 2018/19, 35 249, nr. 3 (Explanatory memorandum to the WHOA), p. 38; *Kamerstukken II* 2019-20, 35 249, nr. 7, pp. 2-3; *Kamerstukken II* 2021/22, 36 040, nr. 3, p. 24.

572 See Section 4.6.2 below.

573 This is a deviation introduced by the Act Implementing the PRD 2019 and the common practice for suspension of payments and bankruptcy where confirmation can be requested only for one plan, that is prepared by the debtor.

574 Arts. 381(1), third sentence, and 384(1), third and fourth sentence, DBA; *Kamerstukken II* 2021/22, 36 040, nr. 3, pp. 25-28, 92-93 and 94.

debtors.[575] In order to supervise debtors, restructuring experts have strong rights to acquire information from both debtors and their employees.[576] Given their position in a WHOA process, courts will hear restructuring experts before taking most of their decisions.[577]

As previously mentioned, another actor introduced by the WHOA is the observer. An observer can be appointed by the court upon request of a debtor or *ex officio*.[578] However, observers can only be appointed if no or as long as no restructuring expert is appointed.[579] The observer's task is to supervise the preparation of a restructuring plan and consider the interests of the general body of creditors.[580] In some cases the court may or must appoint an observer, for instance to secure the creditors' interests when a stay has been granted or prior to the confirmation hearing when the confirmation involves a cross-class cram-down.[581]

Notably, both restructuring experts and observers have an auxiliary role in a WHOA process. They do not divest or replace debtors in WHOA processes; instead, they have a supportive role to promote a successful outcome of the process, by furthering adoption of a restructuring plan and/or consider the interests of affected parties.

4.3.3 Courts

The WHOA is considered an *ultimum remedium*, the legislator attempts to facilitate that debtors will be able to better succeed with out-of-court debt restructuring as parties will be aware that hold-out strategies can also be overcome in a subsequent WHOA process.[582] Also, a WHOA process is designed to promote negotiations between a debtor, the affected creditors, and shareholders, and – if appointed – a restructuring expert. In this context, the court's role is limited; it can be characterized as a remote facilitator (or the 'stick') to assist a fair restructuring plan when no consensus can be reached.[583]

---

575 Art. 380(1) and (3) DBA. See further J.M.G.J. Boon, 'Actoren in de WHOA: herstructureren met de schuldenaar (debtor in possession), herstructureringsdeskundige en observator', in: C.M. Harmsen & M.L.H. Reumers (eds), *De WHOA: van wet naar recht (Recht & Praktijk, nr. InsR18)*, Deventer: Wolters Kluwer, 2021, Para. 5.4.1; M.R. Schreurs, 'Het rechtskarakter van de herstructureringsdeskundige', in: L.J.J. Kerstens, B. Rikkert, M.A. Broeders & R.F. Feenstra (eds), *Wet Homologatie Onderhands Akkoord*, Insolad Jaarbundel, Deventer: Wolters Kluwer, 2021, p. 120 et seq.

576 Art. 371(7) DBA.

577 Arts. 371(5), 376(11), 377(3), 378(8), 379(2) and 384(7) DBA.

578 Art. 380(1) and 379(1) DBA.

579 Art. 380(3) DBA.

580 Art. 380(1) DBA.

581 Arts. 376(9) and 383(4) DBA; *Kamerstukken II* 2018/19, 35 249, nr. 3 (Explanatory memorandum to the WHOA), pp. 36 and 67.

582 *Kamerstukken II* 2018/19, 35 249, nr. 3 (Explanatory memorandum to the WHOA), pp. 1-2.

583 Although court involvement is limited, the Dutch Judiciary has formed a pool of judges and legal aids from all district courts who will exclusively deal with all WHOA cases. They will hear requests in a three-judge

At the very least, courts will be involved – when a WHOA process has been commenced by a debtor – when it is seized of a request for confirmation of a restructuring plan.[584] However, there may be involvement at an earlier stage, for instance, courts may be seized of requests to appoint a restructuring expert or observer,[585] grant a stay,[586] take bespoke measures to secure the interests of creditors and shareholders,[587] or give interim decisions on (potential) disputes in a WHOA process.[588]

Notably, court involvement is limited because of the general ban on legal remedies in WHOA processes, which prevents parties from appealing against court decisions.[589] Courts may, however, at request or on their own initiative ask preliminary questions to the Dutch Supreme Court.[590] In addition, court decisions may still be appealed in case of one or more specific grounds developed in case law to override this ban, such as when statutory provisions have been wrongly applied in WHOA processes.[591]

4.4 *Stay*

Article 376 DBA provides for a temporary stay of individual enforcement actions by third parties during a WHOA process. This is a non-automatic stay that may be granted by courts solely at the request of a debtor or a restructuring expert. When a debtor requests a stay, a restructuring plan must have already been submitted to the affected creditors or shareholders, or a debtor must promise to do so within 2 months.[592] Courts may grant a stay only when two requirements are met. Firstly, a stay must be necessary to continue the debtor's business during the drafting and negotiations on a plan.[593] Secondly, a court

---

panel and are an important pillar towards knowledge building by the judiciary to handle WHOA cases (*Kamerstukken II* 2018/19, 35 249, nr. 3 (Explanatory memorandum to the WHOA), p. 20).

584 Arts. 383 and 384 DBA.

585 Arts. 371(1) and 380(1) DBA.

586 Art. 376 DBA.

587 Art. 379 DBA.

588 Art. 378 DBA allows a debtor or a restructuring expert to obtain prior approval of matters relevant for the adoption and confirmation of the restructuring plan, such as, the class formation and allocation of value under a plan.

589 Art. 369(10) DBA. There is one statutory exception to this ban on legal remedies, see Art. 371(14) DBA.

590 *Kamerstukken II* 2018/19, 35 249, nr. 3 (Explanatory memorandum to the WHOA), pp. 17-18. A preliminary question may delay continuation of a WHOA process and can hamper timely confirmation of the plan. However, in the first case where this was an issue, it was resolved by a settlement agreement entered into by the debtor and creditor involved in the dispute on how to deal with the possible consequences of a decision of the Dutch Supreme Court (District Court Amsterdam 21 December 2021, ECLI:NL:RBAMS:2021:7533, at 1.8-1.9, 2.3-2.4, 4.9-4.11), This enabled the district court to confirm the plan while the preliminary question was still pending with the Supreme Court.

591 See further A. Mennens, *Het dwangakkoord buiten surseance en faillissement*, Onderneming en Recht, nr. 118 (diss. Nijmegen), Deventer: Wolters Kluwer, 2020, p. 595.

592 Art. 376(1) DBA.

593 Art. 376(4)(a) DBA.

should reasonably be convinced that a stay serves the interests of the general body of creditors while not substantially harming the interests of third parties affected by a stay.[594]

Courts will initially grant a stay for up to 4 months, which can be extended multiple times up to a maximum duration of 8 months.[595] As far as third parties have been informed of a stay or that a debtor is subject to a WHOA process, they are not able to enforce their claims for the duration of the stay on a debtor's estate without prior approval of a court.[596] If requested, a court may lift any attachments on assets belonging to a debtor's estate. Furthermore, a stay will suspend any pending and future requests for commencing suspension of payments and bankruptcy proceedings.[597]

Even though a stay has a limited duration, courts may authorize individual creditors to exercise their rights or lift a stay *ex officio* or at the request of a debtor, a restructuring expert or third parties.[598] For instance, a stay can be terminated when it is no longer necessary to continue operating the business while preparing and negotiating the restructuring plan.[599] Furthermore, a court may lift a stay for one or more affected third parties for reason of deteriorating the position of these parties.[600]

4.5 *The Plan*

At its core, a WHOA process facilitates the drafting, negotiation, adoption and confirmation of a plan. As previously discussed, unless restructuring experts are appointed, debtors have the exclusive right to propose a plan in a WHOA process. However, when restructuring experts are involved, both a debtor and a restructuring expert may propose a plan.[601]

4.5.1 Scope of a Plan

A plan may be aimed at restructuring, in which case the legal entity will continue to exist, or liquidation, in which case it will involve a controlled winding-up upon which a legal entity will be dissolved.[602] Whether aimed at restructuring or liquidation, the proposer may determine which creditor and/or shareholder rights will be amended under a plan.[603]

The plan itself may modify obligations of a debtor towards creditors. A plan can do so with regard to creditors' claims, in particular either by deferring payment obligations,

594 Art. 376(4)(b) DBA.
595 Art. 376(2) and (5) DBA.
596 Art. 376(2)(a) DBA.
597 Art. 376(2)(b) and (c) DBA.
598 Art. 376(10) and (11) DBA.
599 Art. 376(11) DBA.
600 Art. 376(2)(a) DBA.
601 Arts. 370(1) and 371(1) DBA; *Kamerstukken II* 2019-20, 35 249, nr. 7, pp. 2-3. See also Section 4.3.2 above.
602 *Kamerstukken II* 2018/19, 35 249, nr. 3 (Explanatory memorandum to the WHOA), p. 2.
603 Arts. 369(2), 370(1) and 381(2) DBA.

imposing a (partial) haircut releasing a debtor from payment obligations or by converting debts into equity (debt-for-equity swap). Furthermore, a plan may also modify the rights of shareholders, this can be done for instance by issuing new shares, which can be part of a debt-for-equity swap.[604] The rights of employees are excluded from the scope of any plan. Their rights under the employment contract, including pension entitlements claimed by pension funds,[605] cannot be affected by a plan.[606] Also excluded from the scope of a plan are financial collateral agreements and close-out netting agreements, nor can a WHOA plan interfere with specific financial law regulations.[607] However, other types of executory contracts can be affected during a WHOA process. Debtors may pursue to alter such contracts consensually or alternatively request termination simultaneous to requesting confirmation of a plan (see Section 4.8).[608]

4.5.2 Contents of Plan

A restructuring plan must include all information necessary to ensure that those creditors and shareholders that are affected by the plan and are eligible to vote can form an informed opinion on the plan.[609] As a minimum requirement, the plan should include in particular the name and an email address of the debtor and (if appointed) the restructuring expert, the (criteria for) class formation, the financial consequences of the plan (per class of creditors and shareholders), the value that is expected to be realized under the restructuring plan as well as the proceeds expected in case of a liquidation in bankruptcy proceedings (along with the calculations and assumptions used), the procedure for voting on the plan, and how creditors and shareholders may obtain further information on the plan.[610] Furthermore, attached to the plan should be further detailed financial information on the debtor, the plan, and the affected creditors and shareholders. This involves financial statements of the debtor, a list of all claims and names of the affected creditors and shareholders, a description of the financial distress of the debtor and in what way and to what extent this is resolved under the plan.[611]

The plan and all annexes must be presented to the affected creditors and shareholders for a reasonable period of time. This will depend on the complexity of a plan as well as the prior involvement of creditors during negotiations. As a minimum, a plan must be

604 *Kamerstukken II* 2018/19, 35 249, nr. 3 (Explanatory memorandum to the WHOA), pp. 9-10, 34.

605 Dutch Supreme Court 25 February 2022, ECLI:NL:HR:2022:328 (*AHG/Pensioenfonds HC*), at 3.5. The bill on the Act Implementing the PRD 2019 has amended Art. 369(4), last sentence, DBA accordingly to include also pension claims and derivative contracts.

606 Art. 369(4)(a), (b) and last sentence DBA.

607 Art. 369(4)(b) and (11) DBA.

608 Art. 373(1) and (2) DBA.

609 Art. 381(1) DBA; *Kamerstukken II* 2018/19, 35 249, nr. 3 (Explanatory memorandum to the WHOA), p. 12.

610 Art. 375(1) DBA.

611 Art. 375(2) DBA.

submitted to the affected creditors and shareholders 8 days before the voting takes place.[612] When appointed, a restructuring expert will submit the plan or plans to the affected creditors and shareholders. Any conflicts concerning a debtor refusing to give such permission can be raised with the court, who might grant the permission if a debtor lacks reasonable grounds for refusing the permission.[613]

In drafting and negotiating a plan, disputes may arise between a debtor or restructuring expert and the affected creditors and shareholders. Affected creditors and shareholders are required to raise any grounds for rejecting confirmation of a plan within a reasonable time, after they became aware or should have been aware of such matters.[614] This should promote that a debtor or restructuring expert is urged to timely resolve these issues before confirmation is requested.[615] When needed, debtors and restructuring experts can get certainty early on by asking the court for an interim decision, possibly leading to bespoke measures. This is limited to matters which are relevant to obtaining court confirmation of a plan.[616]

4.6 *Adoption and Confirmation of a Plan*

4.6.1 Class Formation

Voting on a restructuring plan takes place in classes of affected creditors and shareholders. Separate classes of creditors and shareholders are formed when either their current rights in bankruptcy or their rights as offered under a restructuring plan are highly distinct.[617] This includes, in principle, a distinction between secured creditors, creditors with a right of retention of title, preferential creditors, ordinary unsecured creditors, subordinated creditors and shareholders, but may also be within the group of ordinary unsecured creditors, provided that the rights offered under the plan are sufficiently distinct. A restructuring plan should state how the rights of each class of affected creditors and shareholders are modified under the plan.[618] In case a restructuring plan modifies the rights of ordinary, unsecured SME creditors who have trade or tort claims, they must be placed in a separate class. This class should also receive at least 20% of the value of their original claim under the proposed plan, unless there are compelling grounds to refrain from doing so.[619]

612 Art. 381(1) DBA.
613 Art. 378(1)(g) DBA.
614 Art. 383(9) DBA.
615 *Kamerstukken II* 2018/19, 35 249, nr. 3 (Explanatory memorandum to the WHOA), p. 67.
616 Art. 378 DBA.
617 Art. 374(1) DBA.
618 Art. 375(1)(d) DBA.
619 Arts. 374(2) and 375(2)(f) DBA.

Furthermore, as discussed above, the WHOA introduced bifurcation of secured claims. To the extent that a claim of secured creditors – based on the liquidation value[620] of their secured claim in a bankruptcy proceeding – is covered by the security, their claim will be placed in a class of secured creditors. The remaining part of their claim will be placed in the class of ordinary, unsecured claims.[621] As a consequence, for the secured part of their claim, they can receive no more than the liquidation value under a restructuring plan. This enables that the reorganization surplus realized under the plan is distributed among all parties involved in a plan, disregarding any pre-existing security rights.[622]

4.6.2 Voting and Adoption of a Plan by Creditors and Shareholders

The WHOA is rather flexible with its procedure for the actual voting on a plan. All affected creditors and shareholders have a right to vote, which will take place per class. The proposer of a plan may determine how the voting occurs; it can take place through different means, including a physical meeting, a digital meeting or in writing.[623]

A class of creditors has adopted a restructuring plan if a group representing at least two thirds of the total amount of claims of creditors who voted on the plan have voted in favour of the plan.[624] Similarly, a class of shareholders has adopted a restructuring plan if a group representing at least two thirds of the total amount of issued capital of shareholders who voted on the plan have adopted the plan.[625] Following the voting, a request for confirmation of a restructuring plan can be made when at least one class of creditors has approved the plan. However, unless all classes would be 'out of the money' in a liquidation in bankruptcy, this class should be an 'in the money' class of creditors.[626]

4.6.3 Court Confirmation of a Plan

A court will confirm a restructuring plan, unless it finds that there are grounds to reject confirmation pursuant to Article 384 DBA. For affected creditors or shareholders to invoke a specific ground for rejection of confirmation, it is required that they could not have reasonably discovered these grounds earlier on, in particular, once they were involved in the negotiations on a restructuring plan and/or the contents of a restructuring plan. If they were aware or could have reasonably been aware, they should also have notified these

620 The liquidation value should be established on the likeliness of either a piece meal liquidation or going-concern sale in bankruptcy.

621 Art. 374(3) DBA.

622 *Kamerstukken II* 2019/20, 35 249, nr. 25.

623 Art. 381(5) DBA.

624 Art. 381(6) DBA.

625 Art. 381(7) DBA.

626 Art. 383(1) DBA. Similar to requesting a restructuring expert (Art. 371(15) DBA), if not all classes approved the restructuring plan, a restructuring expert requires the consent of a debtor if he was not appointed at the request of a debtor and the debtor itself qualifies as an SME (Art. 383(2) DBA).

grounds to the debtor or restructuring expert within a reasonable time. If they have not done so, they lose their right to invoke the ground to request the court to reject confirmation.[627] The legislator has introduced this rule to promote the efficiency of a WHOA process and to prevent affected creditors and shareholders from using rejection grounds strategically, and instead facilitating a debtor to timely resolve any disputes or issues with a plan.[628]

The legislator distinguishes between two sets of grounds for rejecting confirmation: general and additional grounds. The general grounds relate to a sound decision-making process. A court will reject confirmation on these grounds *ex officio* or at the request of creditors or shareholders. This is the case when it finds that the debtor does not or no longer meet the pre-insolvency test or affected creditors and shareholders have not been given sufficient time to vote or the date of the confirmation hearing.[629] It is also the case when not all affected creditors or shareholders have been duly notified of a plan, a plan does not meet the information requirements of Article 375 DBA, the classes of affected creditors or shareholders have not been correctly formed, or when the vote of affected creditors or shareholders is based on an incorrect amount of their claim.[630] Furthermore, a court will reject confirmation when the performance of a plan is not sufficiently guaranteed, when attracting new finance or entering into certain transactions is not (directly) necessary or is substantially detrimental to the interests of the general body of creditors. The plan will neither be confirmed when the plan has been concluded by deceit, preferential treatment or one or more creditors or shareholders or other unfair means.[631] Finally, there is a catch-all provision allowing a court to reject confirmation when it finds that there are any other reasons to do so.[632] In some cases a rejection ground will not automatically result in a court rejecting confirmation if the shortcoming did not result in a different outcome of the vote. For instance, this is the case when a court finds there has been a lack of information or the class formation was not correct.[633]

The additional rejection grounds relate to the substantive fairness of a plan. These grounds can be invoked only by dissenting creditors and shareholders, in some cases only when they are in a dissenting class. Firstly, confirmation can be rejected if the plan fails to meet the 'best interest test'. A court may do so when it is summarily proven that dissenting creditors or shareholders will be worse off under a restructuring plan than they would be

627 Art. 383(9) DBA.
628 *Kamerstukken II* 2018/19, 35 249, nr. 3 (Explanatory memorandum to the WHOA), pp. 67-68.
629 Art. 384(2)(a)-(b) DBA.
630 Art. 384(2)(c)-(d) DBA.
631 Art. 384(2)(e)-(g) DBA.
632 Art. 384(2)(g) DBA.
633 Art. 384(2)(c) DBA.

in case of liquidation in bankruptcy.[634] The liquidation value can be the value obtained with a piecemeal sale in bankruptcy; however, it might also be the value obtained in a (partial) going-concern sale in bankruptcy. Depending on the specifics of the case, a court – importantly – may reject confirmation when this liquidation value exceeds the reorganization value for this creditor or shareholder.[635]

Furthermore, dissenting creditors and shareholders in a class that rejected a restructuring plan may also oppose confirmation when the reorganization value is distributed unfairly under a restructuring plan. In principle, the WHOA adopts the APR, according to which the distribution of the reorganization value should follow the ranking of claims in bankruptcy. However, there are several exceptions to this rule which effectively turn it into a relaxed APR.[636] Firstly, the Dutch legislator introduced that as a minimum, ordinary SME creditors with a trade or tort claim should receive at least 20% in cash or a right to the value of their original claim. The court will reject confirmation if they receive less than 20%, unless a debtor or restructuring expert has compelling grounds to deviate from this threshold.[637] Secondly, a plan may deviate from the APR if (i) there is a reasonable ground to do so and (ii) the affected creditors or shareholders are not harmed in their interests.[638] Lastly, deviation from the APR is also permitted when all classes are consenting classes.

Another additional ground to reject confirmation is when dissenting creditors in a dissenting class do not have the right to a cash-out payment from the debtor of the liquidation value of their claim.[639] However, this is different for secured creditors financing the debtor's business. They do not have such a statutory right at a cash-out option. Instead, they may request the court to reject confirmation if their rights are amended or they are offered shares or depositary receipts under the plan, but have not been given the right to

634 Art. 384(3) DBA. Furthermore, this rejection ground may also be invoked by creditors or shareholders who have wrongly been refused to vote on the restructuring plan.

635 *Kamerstukken II* 2018/19, 35 249, nr. 3 (Explanatory memorandum to the WHOA), pp 50-51.

636 Compare Art. 11(2) PRD 2019.

637 Art. 384(4)(a) DBA, see also *Kamerstukken II* 2019/20, 35 249, nr. 23. There is more detail to this rule for ordinary SME creditors. For instance, it does not apply to claims from group companies, ordinary (subordinated) shareholder loans, unsecured subordinated claims of financiers and bondholders.

638 Art. 384(4)(b) DBA. The courts have decided on deviations from the APR a few times now, see for instance: District Court Amsterdam 28 February 2021, ECLI:NL:RBAMS:2021:886, at 6.15-6.15.1; District Court Rotterdam 3 March 2021, ECLI:NL:RBROT:2021:1769, at 3.9-3.11; District Court Den Haag 23 July 2021, ECLI:NL:RBDHA:2021:8121, at 4.8-4.13; District Court Limburg 22 November 2021, ECLI:NL:RBLIM:2021:8857, at 3.5.3-3.5.4; District Court Midden-Nederland 31 March 2022, ECLI:NL:RBMNE:2022:1329, 4.43-4.53; District Court Limburg 21 June 2022, ECLI:NL:RBLIM:2022:4990, at 4.5-4.7

639 Art. 384(4)(c) DBA. A question pending with the Dutch Supreme Court relates to what extent this exception is applicable to the unsecured part – due to the bifurcation (Art. 374(3) DBA) – of the claims of secured creditors (District Court Noord-Nederland 31 March 2022, ECLI:NL:RBMNE:2022:1329, at 4.25-4.35).

choose an alternative form of distribution. This may still involve an option for deferral of payment, but it does not include choosing for a cash-out payment.[640]

Absent grounds to reject confirmation, a court will order the confirmation of a plan. This will make the plan binding on all affected creditors and shareholders.[641] The WHOA amends the rights of affected creditors and shareholders but does not provide for a discharge of a debtor. Typically, the plan will provide for this upon completion. Furthermore, in principle, it may be possible for a restructuring plan to be dissolved, for instance if it later appears to be the result of deceit or in case of default and breach of a plan. However, a restructuring plan may provide that dissolution of a plan is excluded; this will be particularly relevant in debt-for-equity swaps.

4.7 *Possibilities for a Debt-for-Equity Swap*

The Dutch legislator opted for the option in Article 12 PRD 2019 enabling that a restructuring plan can affect the rights of shareholders.[642] When shareholders' rights are affected, they must be involved in the WHOA process and have a right to vote on a plan.[643] As discussed before, the WHOA allows for a debt-for-equity swap. This can take place in different ways, although generally involving the conversion of debt into equity. While the prior shareholders maintain their shares and rights, it does result in a dilution of the shareholding. It is generally held that shareholders therefore have a right to vote on a plan when new shares are issued in the course of such a swap.[644]

Since shareholders are not just capital providers but also part of the corporate structure of the debtor, they have specific corporate law rights. To prevent shareholders from interfering with a WHOA process by using their voting rights, the legislator has imposed limitations on their corporate law rights. For instance, a decision from the General Assembly is not required to issue new shares to execute the debt-for-equity-swap. The legislator argued that this is reasonable since affected shareholders – like affected creditors – have sufficient other options to be involved in a WHOA process. Therefore, at several instances, the legislator has limited shareholders and sometimes even prohibited shareholders from taking unreasonable steps to prevent adoption and confirmation of a

640 Art. 384(4)(d) DBA.

641 Art. 385 DBA.

642 *Kamerstukken II* 2018/19, 35 249, nr. 3 (Explanatory memorandum to the WHOA), p. 4.

643 Art. 381(1) and (2) DBA.

644 *Kamerstukken II* 2018/19, 35 249, nr. 3 (Explanatory memorandum to the WHOA), p. 62; S.C.E.F. Moulen Jansen, *De positie van aandeelhouders bij preventieve herstructureringen*, Serie Van der Heijden Instituut nr. 163 (diss. Nijmegen), Deventer: Wolters Kluwer, 2020, Para. 6.5.11.1. See A. Mennens, *Het dwangakkoord buiten surseance en faillissement*, Onderneming en Recht, nr. 118 (diss. Nijmegen), Deventer: Wolters Kluwer, 2020, Para. 7.3.4.1 arguing that shareholders have no right to vote on a plan in this case.

restructuring plan.[645] In addition, a debt-for-equity-swap may invoke certain change-of-control provisions. To prevent this and other types of *ipso facto* clauses from interfering with an envisaged restructuring, the legislator has provided that such clauses are rendered ineffective in the course of a WHOA process.[646]

4.8 *Executory Contracts*

Although treatment of executory contracts technically falls outside the scope of a restructuring plan, a debtor or restructuring expert may request termination of executory contracts (*lopende overeenkomsten*) along with the request for confirmation of a restructuring plan.[647] This can be requested only after an informal proposal to modify or terminate the executory contract was rejected by the counterparty. The court will only terminate a contract when it will also confirm the restructuring plan itself.[648] In principle, the termination of executory contracts will be effective upon the day when the court confirms the plan. However, there can be reasons to extend the termination with up to 3 months after the confirmation day.[649]

The unilateral termination of executory contracts may result in an obligation for a debtor to pay damages to the counterparty. The legislator has stated specifically that these claims for future damages under such executory contracts may be included in a plan and, for instance, be subject to a haircut or deferred payment.[650]

4.9 *Jurisdiction for and Recognition of Court Decisions in Europe*

4.9.1 Jurisdiction for Dutch Courts

As discussed before, a WHOA is designed as a dual-track process, which can be either public or private.[651] This distinction has particular relevance for international jurisdiction and, with respect to the court, decisions to be taken in the course of a WHOA process. Because the European Insolvency Regulation (EIR) 2015[652] includes only public insolvency

645 Arts. 370(5), 371(15) and 383(2) DBA. The bill on the Act Implementing the PRD 2019 introduces a further general rule prohibiting shareholders from unreasonably impeding the board of directors in a WHOA process (*Kamerstukken II* 2021/22, 36 040, nr. 3 (Explanatory memorandum to the bill on the Act Implementing the PRD 2019), p. 24; *Kamerstukken II* 2021/22, 36 040, nr. 7).

646 Art. 373(3) DBA; *Kamerstukken II* 2018/19, 35 249, nr. 3 (Explanatory memorandum to the WHOA), p. 46.

647 Art. 383(7) DBA.

648 Arts. 383(7) and 384(5) DBA.

649 Art. 373(1) DBA.

650 Art. 373(2) DBA.

651 Art. 369(6) DBA; see also Section 4.1 above.

652 Regulation (EU) 2015/838 of the European Parliament and of the Council of 20 May 2015 on insolvency proceedings (recast), O.J. L 141/19.

proceedings within its scope, it cannot apply to private WHOA processes.[653] This is different for the public WHOA processes, which were added to Annex A (insolvency proceedings) and the restructuring experts and observers in such processes to Annex B (insolvency practitioners).[654] Since January 2022, in line with the EIR 2015,[655] Dutch courts have jurisdiction to 'open' public WHOA processes when (a) debtors have their centre of main interests (COMI) in a European Union Member State (excluding Denmark),[656] and (b)(i) for a main proceeding debtors have their COMI in the Netherlands or (ii) for a secondary proceeding debtors have an establishment in the Netherlands.[657]

In cases where the EIR 2015 is not applicable to a public WHOA process, for instance when a debtor's COMI lies outside the EU, international jurisdiction is determined in the same way as for a private WHOA process. Because the EIR 2015 does not apply to a private WHOA, the legal basis for international jurisdiction is less clear. The Dutch legislator has taken the position that this is to be determined based on domestic private international law. It holds that a Dutch court can assume jurisdiction to take decisions during a private WHOA process when (a) an applicant (or at least one of the applicants) or one or more of the related parties has its (habitual) residence in the Netherlands or (b) that the case is otherwise sufficiently connected with the Netherlands.

The latter ground is the so-called Dutch sufficient-connection-test. This test is satisfied when, for instance, COMI or establishment of the debtor is in the Netherlands, when the debtor has (a substantial amount of its) assets in the Netherlands or a large part of the group of companies to which the debtor belongs are Dutch companies. Furthermore, the Dutch court can assume jurisdiction when a (substantial) part of the debt that is restructured under the plan arises from obligations subject to Dutch law or are subject to a forum choice for the Dutch courts. Jurisdiction can be assumed when a debtor is liable for debts owed to a party which is subject to the jurisdiction of Dutch courts.[658]

4.9.2 Foreign Recognition of Decisions in WHOA Processes

Similar to the matter of jurisdiction, the legal basis for foreign recognition of decisions of Dutch courts in a WHOA process depends on whether the EIR 2015 is applicable. When

---

653 Art. 1(1) EIR 2015.

654 Art. 369(7)(a) DBA; *Kamerstukken II* 2018/19, 35 249, nr. 3 (Explanatory memorandum to the WHOA), pp. 7 and 32.

655 Regulation (EU) 2015/838 of the European Parliament and of the Council of 20 May 2015 on insolvency proceedings (recast), O.J. L 141/19.

656 Recital 25 EIR 2015.

657 Art. 3(1) and (2) EIR 2015.

658 Art. 369(7)(b) DBA and Art. 3 Dutch Civil Procedure (*Wetboek van Burgerlijke Rechtsvordering*); *Kamerstukken II* 2018/19, 35 249, nr. 3 (Explanatory memorandum to the WHOA), pp. 7 and 32; Regulation (EU) 2021/2260 of the European Parliament and the Council of 15 December 2021 amending Regulation (EU) 2015/848 on insolvency proceedings to replace Annexes A and B, O.J. L 455/20.

this is the case for a public WHOA process, the court decisions will be automatically recognized in the EU (except Denmark) without further formalities.[659] This is different when the EIR 2015 does not apply, as is the case for private WHOA processes and outside the EU. Recognition of decisions of Dutch courts will in that case depend on – as far as they are available – bilateral agreements and treaties, but mostly the domestic private international law rules in the jurisdictions where recognition is sought.[660]

4.9.3 Discussion in Dutch Legal Doctrine

The approach of the Dutch legislator is based on the premise that public and private WHOA processes fall within the scope of the so-called 'bankruptcy exception' of the Brussels I bis Regulation, which therefore does not apply.[661] Adopting this approach to private WHOA processes has received some support,[662] but has also been criticized. There is general support that because of the lack of publicity in a private WHOA process, it cannot qualify as an 'insolvency proceeding' under the EIR 2015. However, some authors have argued – us included – that in line with case law of the CJEU, which reiterated the principle of dovetailing between the Brussels I bis Regulation and the EIR 2015, for a private WHOA process the bankruptcy exception should not apply. Consequently, decisions taken in the course of a private WHOA process should therefore fall within the scope of the Brussels I bis Regulation.[663] Given the legal uncertainty, this will be a matter for the Court of Justice of the European Union to decide on or the EU legislator to take action on.[664] So far, Dutch courts follow the approach discussed in Section 4.9.1 in case the EIR 2015 does not apply.[665]

659 Arts. 19, 20 and 32 EIR 2015. See further P.M. Veder, 'Internationale aspecten van de WHOA: de openbare en de besloten akkoordprocedure buiten faillissement', *FIP* 2019/219, p. 58 et seq.

660 See also P.M. Veder, 'Internationale aspecten van de WHOA: de openbare en de besloten akkoordprocedure buiten faillissement', *FIP* 2019/219, p. 62.

661 Art. 1(2)(b) Regulation (EU) No 1215/2012 of the European Parliament and of the Council of 12 December 2012 on jurisdiction and the recognition and enforcement of judgments in civil and commercial matters, O.J. L 351/20. Notably, the DBA nor the parliamentary history to the WHOA makes any reference to the Brussels I bis Regulation.

662 See, for instance, P.M. Veder, 'Internationale aspecten van de WHOA: de openbare en de besloten akkoordprocedure buiten faillissement', *FIP* 2019/219; A. Mennens, *Het dwangakkoord buiten surseance en faillissement*, Onderneming en Recht, nr. 118 (diss. Nijmegen), Deventer: Wolters Kluwer, 2020, p. 627.

663 See, for instance, W.J.E. Nijnens, 'IPR aspecten van de WHOA', *TvI* 2019/34, pp. 264-265; J.M G.J. Boon, R.D. Vriesendorp & R. Sijbesma, 'Netherlands Commercial Court als mogelijke WHOA-rechter bij internationale herstructureringen', *HERO* 2021/W-001, Para. 3.1; R.D. Vriesendorp, W. van Kesteren, E. Vilarin-Seivane & S. Hinse, 'Automatic recognition for the Dutch undisclosed WHOA procedure in the European Union', *NIPR* 2021/1, at 4.2.4.

664 Consider also CERIL Statement and Report 202202 on Cross-Border Effects in European Preventive Restructuring, 6 July 2022, available at: www.ceril.eu/news/ceril-report-2022-2-on-cross-border-effects-in-european-preventive-restructuring.

665 For private WHOA process, see for instance, District Court Limburg 11 February 2021, ECLI:NL:RBLIM:2021:8854, at 3.1; District Court Zeeland-West-Brabant 17 February 2021, ECLI:NL:RBZWB:2021:6911, at

5 What Has the WHOA Brought Us So Far?

Both academia and practice have anticipated the entry into force of the WHOA. Furthermore, the legislator also noted the importance of the WHOA as a tool to mitigate the financial distress faced by many debtors that was caused by the COVID-19 pandemic, and categorized the WHOA as part of the COVID-19 emergency legislation to be adopted in 2020.[666] Since the WHOA entered into force, courts have published over 120 decisions, including over 10 confirmed plans.[667] In all, it is reported that so far there have been over 100 cases;[668] by far most are private WHOA cases.[669] Although considered an *ultimum remedium*, the WHOA has surely established a foothold in the Dutch restructuring and insolvency practice. Whereas some expected WHOA processes to be of limited relevance for SME debtors, this was disproved by the various cases in the first year. WHOA processes have also been used for large debtors, including WHOA restructurings of enterprise groups, although they form a smaller part of the cases. Allegedly, large debtors involved in restructuring processes seem to benefit from the WHOA as a 'stick' to discipline non-cooperating creditors or shareholders.

Whereas the WHOA is designed as an expedient and efficient process, concerns have been raised over the costs involved, including the court fees.[670] With the modular approach of the WHOA, a debtor might easily face a number of requests in a WHOA process, such as requests for granting and extending a stay, interim decisions and confirmation. Also, for affected creditors or shareholders with a limited claim, the court fees for raising grounds for rejection may easily exceed their financial interests in the case.[671] If the restructuring involves several enterprise group members, for debtors and affected creditors and shareholders, court fees may become considerable. To improve accessibility and therewith effectiveness of WHOA processes for more debtors, in its recently published draft bill

3.3; District Court Gelderland 31 May 2022, ECLI:NL:RBGEL:2022:3062, at 4.3; District Court Amsterdam 3 September 2021, ECLI:NL:RBAMS:2021:6770, at 3.2.

666 *Kamerstukken II* 2019/20, 35 300 VI, nr. 118 and Annex 930000.

667 Not all decisions are (instantly) published by the courts in the online repository of the Dutch judiciary, the actual number of decisions will therefore be higher. See also L.S.E. Prickartz & R.W.A. Brunninkhuis, 'De WHOA: de stand van zaken na ruim één jaar', *Bb* 2022/17 and M. Knapen, 'Wow, de WHOA doet wat ie moet doen!', *Mr.* 2022/3, reporting on the first year of WHOA cases.

668 M. Knapen, 'Wow, de WHOA doet wat ie moet doen!', *Mr.* 2022/3, p. 55.

669 To date, there have been six public WHOA processes, see the register of WHOA cases of the Dutch Judiciary, available at: www.rechtspraak.nl/Registers/Paginas/whoa.aspx.

670 M. Kroezen, 'De toegankelijkheid van de WHOA voor het mkb: een beschouwing aan de hand van de Small Business Reorganization Act', *TvI* 2021/4, at 4.2; H.J. de Kloe, 'Het WHOA-akkoord en schuldeisers: een pleidooi voor meer zeggenschap', *TvOB* 2022/2, at 5 and 7.

671 These court fees are circa EUR 2.000. See also District Court Noord-Holland 15 April 2021, ECLI:NL:RBNHO:2021:3085, at 2.2 and 3.5-3.7; District Court Midden-Nederland 11 May 2022, ECLI:NL:RBMNE:2022:1936, at 2.7-2.10.

amending court fees, the Dutch legislator has proposed to substantially reduce court fees for requests for confirmation in WHOA processes.[672]

Furthermore, the WHOA is premised to be a tool apt for cross-border application.[673] This is reflected in several features of the WHOA, including (i) the dual-track nature of the WHOA,[674] (ii) the procedural consolidation for restructuring of domestic and foreign members of an enterprise group,[675] (iii) third-party releases in an enterprise group context[676] and (iv) the possibilities for appointment of a foreign 'insolvency practitioner' (under the EIR 2015) as a restructuring expert.[677] However, application in the cross-border context is still surrounded by legal uncertainty. To some extent, this is inherent in a new legal instrument which must be tried and tested. On the other hand, there are cross-border elements which have been criticized for their inconsistency with private international law. Consider for instance the above-mentioned discussion on the legal basis for assuming jurisdiction and recognition of court decisions in WHOA cases.[678] However, this also relates to applying the rules on procedural consolidation in a cross-border context. In this respect, mere domestic legislation cannot overrule or interfere with jurisdictional rules of the EIR 2015 and Brussels I bis Regulation.[679] Furthermore, the requisite use of Dutch language in court proceedings may impede the choice for the WHOA by foreign parties; in this regard the Netherlands Commercial Court (NCC) could play a more prominent role as it facilitates court cases to be conducted fully in the English language.[680]

The Dutch legislator has deliberately chosen to exclude rights deriving from employment contracts from a WHOA process.[681] During the first preliminary questioning on the WHOA, this was broadly interpreted, to also include the claims of pension funds

672 This would be reduced to EUR 676, see *Voorontwerp wet verlaging griffierechten* (draft bill on the Act reduction of court fees) available at: www.internetconsultatie.nl/wetverlaginggriffierechten. Notably, this draft bill does not yet reduce the court fees for affected creditors or shareholders requesting the court to reject confirmation of a restructuring plan. See also: H. Loonstein, 'Griffierechten en WHOA-procedures', *TvI* 2022/33.

673 *Kamerstukken II* 2019/20, 35 225, nr. 20, pp. 12 and 24.

674 Arts. 369(6)-(9), 370(4) and 371(1) DBA.

675 Art. 372 DBA.

676 Art. 370(2) DBA.

677 *Kamerstukken II* 2018/19, 35 249, nr. 3 (Explanatory memorandum to the WHOA), p. 42.

678 See above Section 4.9.3 above.

679 W.J.E. Nijnens, 'De WHOA en het internationaal privaatrecht inclusief de herstructurering van groepen', in: C.M. Harmsen & M.L.H. Reumers (eds), *De WHOA: van wet naar recht (Recht & Praktijk, nr. InsR18)*, Deventer: Wolters Kluwer, 2021, Para. 12.6.

680 See J.M.G.J. Boon, R.D. Vriesendorp & R. Sijbesma, 'Netherlands Commercial Court als mogelijke WHOA-rechter bij internationale herstructureringen', *HERO* 2021/W-001, arguing that the NCC is able to decide on requests in the course of both public and private WHOA cases, although procedural requirements of cases before the NCC will make it particularly well-suited for larger cross-border (financial) restructurings.

681 Art. 369(4)(a), (b), and last sentence, DBA.

for pension entitlements.[682] This has been received with mixed responses, as it may make not only restructuring more complicated, but might leave employees worse off in the end.[683] At this point, it is up to the legislator to reconsider how the interest of employees is best kept in the context of restructuring and insolvency.[684]

6 Conclusion

The WHOA is a promising addition to the Dutch restructuring toolbox, and until now, it has lived up to the expectations. This preventive restructuring framework is designed in line with Chapter 2 of the PRD 2019, while also drawing on features of the Chapter 11 US Bankruptcy Code (reorganization) and UK Scheme of Arrangement. The result is a framework of its own kind, characterized by a high degree of flexibility, expediency and cost-efficiency. There has been an overall positive response to the WHOA. Although it is too early for any thorough conclusions, so far, the WHOA seems to function well and deliver on its promise: providing for an effective framework to prevent bankruptcy.

---

682 Dutch Supreme Court 25 February 2022, ECLI:NL:HR:2022:328 (*AHG/Pensioenfonds H C*), at 3.5. See also Art. 369(4), last sentence, DBA.

683 Dutch Supreme Court 25 February 2022, ECLI:NL:HR:2022:328 (*AHG/Pensioenfonds H C*), with annotation J. van der Pijl, *JAR* 2022/88, P.R.W. Schaink, *TvI* 2022/17, F.M.J. Verstijlen, *NJ* 2022/150, S.B.A. Heumakers, *JOR* 2022/163; J. van der Pijl, 'Tijd voor conclusies', *TvI* 2022/1. Prior to the decision of the Dutch Supreme Court it was discussed *inter alia* by G. de Gruijter, 'Prejudiciële vraag aan de Hoge Raad: vallen pensioenpremies van verplicht gestelde bedrijfstakpensioenfondsen onder de werknemersuitzondering van de WHOA?', *HERO* 2021/B-073; M. Mouthaan, 'WHOA en pensioenpremie', *HERO* 2021/B-055; M.H. Visscher, 'Van bange bestuurders naar creatieve bestuurders als het om pensioenschulden gaat?', *TvOB* 2020/6; R. van den Sigtenhorst & P. Jahan, 'Prejudiciële vragen over de reikwijdte van de WHOA: vorderingen van bedrijfspensioenfondsen uitgezonderd?', *TvI* 2021/49; R.J. van Gaal, T.H.D. Struycken & S.B.A. Heumakers, 'De WHOA, pensioen en de rechten van werknemers', *MvV* 2021/12.

684 This matter has also been raised in response to two preliminary decisions on the position of employees in pre-packaged bankruptcies, see CJEU 22 June 2017, ECLI:EU:C:2017:489 (*FNV c.s./Smallsteps*); CJEU 28 April 2022, ECLI:EU:C:2022:321 (*FNV/Heiploeg*). See for an introduction J.H. Plomp, 'Revival of the Dutch pre-pack by the CJEU', *Leiden Law Blog*, 16 May 2022, available at: www.leidenlawblog.nl/articles/revival-of-the-dutch-pre-pack-by-the-cjeu.

8 United Kingdom

Eugenio Vaccari and Jennifer Gant[*]

1 Introduction

Despite withdrawing from the EU, the UK has continued to align its corporate insolvency framework with international best practices, including the recent European Preventive Restructuring Directive 2019/1023 (EU PRD 2019). As the UK was not required to implement the EU PRD 2019, this law has only influenced an ongoing debate on optimal preventive restructuring procedures. Additional European statutory instruments rumoured to be forthcoming in the near future are likely to have a similar impact on the UK framework.

This chapter assesses the degree of cross-fertilization between the EU and UK preventive restructuring frameworks. 'Cross-fertilization' refers to the practice of importing ideas from different legal frameworks and mixing these provisions with the existing domestic framework and legal culture to produce better outcomes for domestic stakeholders.

The chapter provides an overview of the English pre-reform restructuring framework (Section 2) and the regulatory debate following the enactment of the EU PRD 2019 (Section 3). It then analyses the statutory changes to key aspects of the English preventive restructuring framework (Section 4), and offers a detailed analysis of the growing case law on Pt 26A restructuring plans (Section 5). Its purpose is to assess the impact that recent reforms have had on professional practice and identify areas ripe for further regulatory reforms (Section 6). The chapter concludes with an overall evaluation of the effectiveness of the British legislator's regulatory reform efforts in the area of preventive restructuring frameworks.

---

* Part of the material included in this chapter is sourced from a manual written by E. Vaccari & E. Ghio, *English Corporate Insolvency Law: A Primer*, Edward Elgar Publishing: Cheltenham, 2022. The Chapter expands the content of a previous publication by the same authors: E. Vaccari & J.L. Gant, 'The UK Preventive Restructuring Framework after Brexit: Acknowledging EU's Supremacy?', *HERO*, 2022/W-002. The Chapter covers literature and case law published before 1 December 2022. The usual disclaimer applies.

2 OVERVIEW OF DOMESTIC PRE-REFORM RESTRUCTURING AND INSOLVENCY LAW REGIME

Before the most recent reforms, the UK corporate restructuring toolkit included:
1. Informal workouts;
2. Administration procedures, including pre-packaged plans and 'light-touch' administrations;[685]
3. Company voluntary arrangements (CVAs);[686] and
4. Pt 26 schemes of arrangement.[687]

Informal workouts are private contractual arrangements between debtors and creditors. They are confidential and thereby allow debtors to avoid the stigma of insolvency, but they only bind the signatory parties.

Administration is a practitioner-in-possession (PIP) procedure designed to rescue a company as a going concern.[688] If this is not possible, administrators must try to achieve a better result for the company's creditors than in a liquidation, or as a final hierarchical alternative, to distribute the company's assets and proceeds to the creditors. An administration procedure can be triggered by the company, its directors or its creditors, as well as by the Secretary of State and some other regulatory authorities. The administrator – a qualified insolvency practitioner (IP) – can be appointed by a court, by the debtor or by a qualified creditor out of court. The creditors vote on the plan proposed by the administrator, who is responsible for running the business and implementing the plan. *Sui generis* forms of administration are pre-packaged sales and light-touch administrations.[689] The latter is a debtor-in-possession (DIP) procedure,[690] where the existing directors run a company under the supervision of a qualified IP.

Other rescue mechanisms have traditionally been CVAs and Pt 26 schemes of arrangement. CVAs are agreements between a registered company (not necessarily

685 Part II Insolvency Act 1986 (IA 1986) and Schedule B1.

686 Part 1 IA 1986.

687 Part 26 Companies Act 2006 (CA 2006).

688 Para. 3, Sch. B1, IA 1986.

689 Pre-packs are administration procedures where the sale of the debtor's assets or business are effected shortly after the appointment of an administrator. Light-touch administrations are procedures where the debtor's directors remain in possession of the company during administration, even if they operate under the supervision of an administrator. For more details on light-touch administrations (and a preliminary assessment of Pt 26A restructuring plans), see: E. Vaccari, 'Corporate Insolvency Reforms in England: Rescuing a "Broken Bench"? A Critical Analysis of Light Touch Administrations and New Restructuring Plans', *International Company and Commercial Law Review*, 2020, 31(12), pp. 645-667.

690 Para. 64, Sch. B1 IA 1986. There is a parallel with section 103 IA 1986, which provides that on the appointment of the liquidator, the directors' powers cease. However, the liquidation committee or the creditors can sanction their continuance.

insolvent), its shareholders and its creditors. The IP acts as a nominee and provides an opinion on the viability of the proposal. If the plan obtains the statutory majority (75% by value of voting creditors), it is then implemented by the directors. The CVA is therefore a DIP procedure under the supervision of an IP.

Pt 26 schemes of arrangement are a company law procedure available to companies that are not yet insolvent and "liable to be wound up under the Insolvency Act 1986",[691] including foreign entities with a limited connection to the UK. Creditors and members[692] are divided into classes and vote on the plan. Thereafter, a court may sanction the Pt 26 scheme if it is fair and reasonable to do so.

The English corporate insolvency framework was already quite sophisticated before the enactment of the EU PRD 2019.[693] Despite this, consultations launched in 2016[694] and 2018[695] suggested that further reforms were needed. The harmonization process in the European Union[696] and the need to address the unique issues arising from the COVID-19 pandemic made these changes more urgent.[697]

3 EU PRD 2019: Reforming/Introducing Domestic Preventive Restructuring Laws

The insolvency industry has supported many governmental proposals,[698] except on the identification of 'essential supply contracts' and the introduction under English

691 Section 895(2)(b) CA 2006. A company 'liable to be wound up' is a company eligible to enter into a liquidation procedure governed by English law.

692 These are either the shareholders or the owners of the company.

693 Directive (EU) 2019/1023 of the European Parliament and of the Council of 20 June 2019 on preventive restructuring frameworks, on discharge of debt and disqualifications, and on measures to increase the efficiency of procedures concerning restructuring, insolvency and discharge of debt, and amending Directive (EU) 2017/1132 (Directive on restructuring and insolvency), O.J. L 172/13.

694 The Insolvency Service, A Review of the Corporate Insolvency Framework. A consultation on options for reform, available at: https://assets.publishing.service.gov.uk/government/uploads/system/uploads/attachment_data/file/525523/A_Review_of_the_Corporate_Insolvency_Framework.pdf (last viewed 1 December 2022).

695 Department for Business, Energy and Industrial Strategy, Insolvency and Corporate Governance, available at: https://assets.publishing.service.gov.uk/government/uploads/system/uploads/attachment_data/file/691857/Condoc_-_Insolvency_and_Corporate_Governance_FINAL_.pdf (last viewed 1 December 2022).

696 E. Vaccari & D. Ehmke, 'Harmonising Restructuring Frameworks: Top-Down, Bottom-Up, or Both?', Chapter 10 in: E. Ghio & E Vaccari (eds), *Insolvency Law: Back to the Future*, Nottingham: INSOL Europe, 2022, pp. 111-120.

697 E. Vaccari, 'Changes to the UK Insolvency Rules in the Wake of Covid-19: A Much-Needed Help for Businesses or an Unjustified Harm to the Rule of Law?' in: C. Ferstman & A. Fagan (eds), *Covid-19, Law and Human Rights: Essex Dialogues*, University of Essex: Online, 2020, pp. 127-136.

698 Department for Business, Energy and Industrial Strategy, Insolvency and Corporate Governance: Government Response, available at: https://assets.publishing.service.gov.uk/government/uploads/system/

restructuring law of the absolute priority rule (APR). The UK government has since acted on these proposals by means of the Corporate Insolvency and Governance Act 2020 (CIGA 2020) and the Administration (Restrictions on Disposal etc. to Connected Persons) Regulations 2021 (2021 Regulations).

Besides temporary changes to address the challenges arising from the COVID-19 pandemic, CIGA 2020 introduced a general prohibition on the validity of contractual termination clauses as well as the new Pt 26A restructuring plan procedure and the Pt A1 statutory moratorium. The 2021 Regulations introduced revised rules on pre-packs, preventing administrators from disposing of all or substantially the whole of a company to a connected buyer in the first 8 weeks of the procedure unless one of two conditions are satisfied: (1) the creditors have approved the sale, and (2) an independent 'qualifying' report has been written by an evaluator. Despite requirements for the evaluator to be independent, they may not necessarily be a qualified IP.

Further reforms are being considered.[699] However, CIGA 2020 and the 2021 Regulations represent the most direct and comprehensive answers to the features covered by the EU PRD 2019. Academia, professional bodies and legal practice have been supportive of the changes implemented, except for the reintroduction of the preferential treatment of some categories of tax claims.[700] An Interim Report on the implementation of CIGA 2020 seems to support the view from these stakeholders.[701]

4 MAIN FEATURES INTRODUCED BY UK REFORMS ALIGNING WITH THE EU PRD 2019

4.1 *Objective and Scope of the Framework/Proceeding*

The purpose of the compromise or arrangement in Pt 26A restructuring plans is to eliminate, reduce, prevent or mitigate the effect of any of the debtor's financial difficulties.[702] There are no specific provisions on the treatment of debtors who are part of an enterprise

uploads/attachment_data/file/736163/ICG_-_Government_response_doc_-_24_Aug_clean_version__with_Minister_s_photo_and_signature__AC.pdf (last viewed 1 December 2022) p. 41.

699 The Insolvency Service, The Future of Insolvency Regulation, available at: https://www.gov.uk/government/consultations/the-future-of-insolvency-regulation (last viewed 1 December 2022).

700 HM Revenue & Customs, Protecting Your Taxes in Insolvency. Summary of Responses, available at: https://assets.publishing.service.gov.uk/government/uploads/system/uploads/attachment_data/file/816290/Protecting_your_taxes_in_insolvency_-_summary_of_responses.pdf (last viewed 1 December 2022).

701 P. Walton & L. Jacobs, Corporate Insolvency and Governance Act 2020 – Interim Report March 2020 (21 June 2022), available at: https://www.gov.uk/government/publications/corporate-insolvency-and-governance-act-2020-interim-report-march-2022/corporate-insolvency-and-governance-act-2020-interim-report-march-2022 (last viewed 1 December 2022).

702 Section 901A(3)(b) CA 2006.

group, and there are no time limits for the plan to be implemented. However, the timetable is similar to that of Pt 26 schemes of arrangement (6-8 weeks from launch to completion). The approved plan will then need to be implemented by the parties.

Like Pt 26A plans, CVAs may include a composition in satisfaction of the company's debts or a scheme of arrangement of its affairs.[703] In contrast to the CVA, Pt 26 schemes have broader eligibility criteria, as they can be used by companies that are not (yet) in financial difficulties. However, they are potentially narrower in their content, as no mention is made in the law of the possibility of reaching a 'compromise' with the company's creditors.[704]

4.2 *Criteria/Test to Enter the New Framework/Proceeding*

According to Article 4(1) EU PRD 2019, the threshold for utilizing the new preventive restructuring framework should be the likelihood of insolvency and the company's long-term viability.

4.2.1 Likelihood of Insolvency[705]

Under English law, insolvency is generally understood as the 'inability to pay debts'.[706]

There are two general tests to determine whether a company is unable to pay debts: the cash flow and the balance sheet tests. These tests work simultaneously, meaning that if a company is able to pay its debts as they fall due (adequate cash flow), it can still be declared balance sheet insolvent if its liabilities are greater in value than its assets. The opposite is also true.[707]

Traditionally, under English law the definition of 'inability to pay debts' is only relevant for non-voluntary liquidation petitions and administration orders made by a court.[708] In CVAs and Pt 26 schemes, the petitioner does not need to prove the debtor to be insolvent.

703 Section 1(1), Pt I IA 1986.

704 For a comparison between Pt 26A restructuring plans and CVAs, and for a persuasive explanation of the decline in the use of CVAs, see: E. Nolan, K. Stephenson & Z Stembridge, 'Operational Restructurings: To RP or Not to RP, That Is the Question', *Corporate Rescue & Insolvency*, 2022, 15(4), pp. 111-115. For a comparison between CVAs, Pt 26 schemes and Pt 26A restructuring plans, see: M. Firrie, J. Houghton & I. Jack, 'Corporate Restructuring in the UK: the Old or the New?', *International Corporate Rescue*, 2022, 19(4) pp. 190-193.

705 The 'likelihood of insolvency' test is also mentioned in other parts of EU PRD 2019, such as recitals 24, 79 and 96, and Arts 1(a), 2(b) and 3(1) of the main body of the directive. Article 19 deals with the duties of the directors where there is likelihood of insolvency.

706 Section 123 IA 1986.

707 Re Casa Estates (UK) Ltd (in liq.) [2014] EWCA Civ 383; and Re HLC Environmental Projects Ltd [2013] EWHC 2876 (Ch).

708 Section 122(1)(f) IA 1986 for liquidations and Para. 11, Sch. B1 IA 1986 for administrations.

Pt 26 schemes are frequently used to restructure a company's debt as part of takeover and merger transactions outside insolvency or general financial distress.[709]

Pt 26A plans are the only procedures to fully comply with the 'likelihood of insolvency' requirement dictated by EU PRD 2019, as they are only available to companies that are encountering or are likely to encounter financial difficulties that either are affecting, will affect or may affect their ability to carry on business as a going concern (eligibility condition 'A').[710] The petitioner needs to show that the debtor's liquidity will reach critical levels or they will run out of cash soon after the commencement of the restructuring procedure.[711] Being in administration is not by itself proof that this condition is met.[712] It follows that, absent a 'burning platform'[713] and where a restructuring could reasonably be undertaken at a later stage, junior stakeholders (shareholders and unsecured creditors) might have an arguable case against the commencement or sanctioning of a Pt 26A plan that wipes out almost all of their equitable interests in or claims against the company.[714]

4.2.2 Viability Test[715]

The second eligibility condition requires that the proposed 'compromise or arrangement' is aimed to "eliminate, reduce or prevent, or mitigate the effect of, any of the financial difficulties" (condition 'B').[716] Whilst this requirement falls short of introducing a proper 'viability' test in Pt 26A plans,[717] it closely reflects the European provisions on viability.

709 On takeovers, see: Re Savoy Hotel Ltd [1981] Ch. 351; Re Jelf Group Plc [2015] EWHC 3857 (Ch); Re SABMiller Plc [2016] 10 WLUK 31.

710 Section 901A(2) CA 2006.

711 Re Virgin Atlantic Airways Ltd [2020] EWHC 2376 (Ch) (sanction) (where the debtor showed that certain bondholders were about to initiate enforcement processes against the company's landing and departure slots at Heathrow airport by 21 September 2020 and that, in any case, the company would run out of cash by 5 October 2020); Re Pizza Express Financing 2 Plc [2020] EWHC 2873 (Ch) (convening) (where the company demonstrated that its cash-flow forecast was negative).

712 Re Amicus Finance Plc [2021] EWHC 2255 (Ch) (convening). Snowden J also observed at Para. 70 that 'it will be a rare case in which the fact of being in administration will not mean that a company is experiencing financial difficulties, particularly (as in the instant case) where the administrators are pursuing the second statutory purpose of achieving a better result for creditors as a whole than would be likely in an immediate liquidation'.

713 This is a term used to describe the situation in which the company's insolvency is imminent and unavoidable.

714 Re Hurricane Energy Plc [2021] EWHC 1759 (Ch) (sanction). For an analysis, see: K. Stephenson & Z. Stembridge, 'Sanctioning a Restructuring Plan: Not a Port for Every Storm', *PLC Magazine*, 2021, 32(7) pp. 10-11; K. Crinson et al., 'UK Cross-Class Cram-Down Rejected in Hurricane Energy', *Corporate Rescue & Insolvency*, 2021, 14(4), pp. 124-126.

715 Similar to the 'likelihood of insolvency' test, also the 'viability' test is frequently mentioned in many other parts of EU PRD 2019.

716 Section 901A(3) CA 2006.

717 Under this test, the petitioner must show that the debtor's business is sound and has chances of thriving once the company's economic and financial issues have been addressed.

English courts have refused to sanction plans that did not meet this requirement.[718] Courts require proof that the statutory majority of members and creditors are acting *bona fide* and not coercing the minority in order to promote interests adverse to those of the class they purport to represent ('fairness and reasonable' test).[719] This does not mean that courts will impose their own opinion. It only means that the proposal must be one that a competent and honest person could fairly endorse.[720] English law, therefore, broadly aligns with the viability standard advocated by the EU PRD 2019.

4.3 *Involved Actors*

This section focuses on the role, powers and duties of the actors involved in Pt A1 moratoria, Pt 26 schemes and Pt 26A restructuring plans. Although Pt 26 schemes do not technically align with the EU PRD as do the Pt 26A schemes, the jurisprudence around Pt 26 schemes, some of which is discussed below, is also relevant to Pt 26A plans due to the closeness of their drafting. In addition, the Pt A1 moratorium may accompany a Pt 26A plan. Therefore, it is worth including in the discussion that follows as regards the preventive restructuring framework in the UK insofar as it aligns with the EU PRD 2019.

Debtors have the right to propose a Pt 26 scheme or a Pt 26A restructuring plan. They must also implement the plan and obtain preliminary approval of any variation to it. If the debtor applies for a Pt A1 moratorium, the company's activity is overseen by a monitor for its duration.

Creditors may have a leading role in petitioning for the opening of a Pt 26A restructuring plan. Creditors must ensure that the directors are acting in the best interest of the company[721] and in compliance with the law. Creditors may set up a creditors' committee and all types of claims can be compromised by Pt 26 schemes and Pt 26A plans.[722] If the creditors are dissatisfied with the way the procedure was conducted or its outcome, they may petition the court to challenge it.

Under English law, there are no formally appointed practitioners in the field of restructuring (PIFOR). There is, however, a category of unregulated turnaround professionals who may assist the debtors in formulating a scheme or restructuring plan. Pt 26 schemes and Pt 26A plans may be submitted by liquidators and administrators, who have to be a qualified IP.

718 Discussed below in Section 4.6.

719 Re Hawk Insurance Co Ltd [2001] EWCA Civ 241.

720 Virgin Atlantic (sanction) above note 711.

721 On directors' duties, see the recent ruling in BTI 2014 LLC v Sequana SA and others [2022] UKSC 25.

722 Section 901F(5) CA 2006.

Courts are key actors in Pt 26A plans and Pt 26 schemes. They have different roles in different stages of these procedure. In *Re Noble Group Ltd*,[723] it was held that in convening hearings the following elements must be considered:
1. Adequate notice of meetings;
2. Jurisdictional issues, particularly whether the company can be wound up under IA 1986;
3. Creditor (and member) class composition;
4. Arrangements for ensuring the members and creditors can participate in the vote; and
5. Potential obstacles to the implementation or the sanctioning of the plan.

In the sanction hearing, courts will sanction the vote and approve the plan if the statutory conditions for approval are met (see Section 4.6.1), and it is just and equitable to do so. The court order needs to be delivered to the Registrar of Companies.[724]

4.4 *Stay*

The provisions of a stay are included in Article 6 EU PRD 2019. It is prescribed that the initial duration should not exceed 4 months[725] and the overall duration cannot exceed 12 months.[726] The consequences of the moratorium are dealt with by Article 7 EU PRD 2019.

4.4.1 The Pt A1 Moratorium

Chapters 1-3, Pt A1 IA 1986, have introduced a general moratorium on executory actions against companies that are not subject or, in the previous 12 months, have not been subject to a similar stay;[727] are not subject to an outstanding winding-up petition;[728] and are not incorporated abroad.[729]

The Pt A1 moratorium is triggered by the directors of an ailing company (out-of-court process) or by an order of a court following the debtor's application (in-court process). The directors must state that their company is or is likely to become unable to pay its debts.[730]

723 [2018] EWHC 2911 (Ch).
724 Section 901F(6) CA 2006.
725 Art. 6(6) EU PRD 2019.
726 Art. 6(7) EU PRD 2019.
727 Para. 2, Sch. ZA1 IA 1986.
728 Despite this, the courts may use their discretion to grant a stay upon a petition from the directors of a company subject to an outstanding winding-up petition (Section A4, Pt A1 IA 1986) or an overseas Company (Section A5, P A1 IA 1986).
729 Section A3, Pt A1 IA 1986.
730 Section A6(1)(d), Pt A1 IA 1986.

The Pt A1 moratorium is overseen by one or more monitors[731] who are IPs and officers of the court.[732] Nevertheless, this is a DIP procedure. The monitor(s) must remain of the view that rescue of a company as a going concern is possible.[733] Otherwise, the Pt A1 moratorium must be terminated early.[734]

The Pt A1 moratorium must be notified to the monitor(s), the known creditors and the Registrar of Companies.[735] The 20-business-day initial period can be extended by the directors without creditor consent for an analogous period.[736] In case of an agreement with the creditors, the extension is granted for the agreed date.[737] Courts also have the power to grant one or more extensions upon petition from the directors.[738]

A free-standing Pt A1 moratorium can be terminated in three circumstances:

1. Expiry due to time passing;[739]
2. Where a company enters into a compromise or arrangement with its creditors or any other formal insolvency procedure;[740]
3. If the monitor files a notice to a court in which they state that:[741]
    a. it is the monitor's opinion the Pt A1 moratorium is no longer likely to result in the rescue of a company as a going concern; or
    b. the rescue has been achieved; or
    c. they cannot carry out their functions or believe that a company cannot pay the debts it is required to pay.

4.4.2 Effects of the Stay

During the moratorium, no legal action can be taken against the debtor or its assets without leave of the court. This includes enforcement of security (except financial collateral

731 The Parliament's proposals (2016) originally referred to 'supervisor'. The term 'monitor' was adopted in 2018 to avoid confusion with a CVA supervisor. In earlier proposals, there was to be no requirement for the new form of office holder to be a licensed IP. Guidance on the role and powers of the monitors was published by the Insolvency Service on 26 June 2020 it is available here: https://www.gov.uk/government/publications/insolvency-act-1986-part-a1-moratorium-guidance-for-monitors/test-doc (Last viewed 1 December 2022).

732 Section A34, Pt A1 IA 1986. Guidance on how to act in these procedures has been drafted by the Insolvency Service (26 June 2020) and it is available here: https://www.gov.uk/government/publications/insolvency-act-1986-part-a1-moratorium-guidance-for-monitors/test-doc#role-and-functions-of-monitor (Last viewed 1 December 2022).

733 Section A6(e), Pt A1 IA 1986.

734 Section A38, Pt A1 1986.

735 Section A8, Pt A1 IA 1986.

736 Section A10, Pt A1 Ia 1986.

737 Section A11, Pt A1 1986.

738 Section A13, Pt A1 IA 1986.

739 Section 9(1), Pt A1 IA 1986.

740 Section A16, Pt A1 IA 1986.

741 Section A38, Pt A1 IA 1986.

or collateral security charges)[742] and repossession of goods under hire-purchase agreements (or retention-of-title clauses).[743] No insolvency proceedings can be commenced against the company during the moratorium, unless the petition is submitted by the directors.[744]

Floating charge holders are prohibited from giving notice that would have the effect of either (i) causing the floating charge to crystallize or (ii) restricting the disposal of the property of a company.[745] Landlords cannot exercise their rights of forfeiture and may be forced to accept a reduction in their rents.[746]

Whilst the European legislator did not introduce explicit exceptions to the stay, the English provision relies on several carve-outs.

Firstly, there are restrictions on the transactions that companies can complete during a Pt A1 moratorium. For instance, new security can only be granted where the monitor consents and believes that granting security will support the rescue of a company.[747] The debtor is prohibited from entering into contracts such as market contracts or financial collateral arrangements.[748] Disposal of a company's property is only admissible if made in the ordinary course of business with the monitor's consent or following a court order.[749] Other restrictions apply to loans of more than £500[750] and payments of pre-moratorium debts.[751]

Secondly, certain moratorium debts are not subject to a payment holiday. These include goods or services supplied during the moratorium; rents in respect of the period during the moratorium; wages, salaries and redundancy payments; liabilities arising under a contract involving financial services.[752] Additionally, all debts incurred during the Pt A1 moratorium must be paid in full as they fall due. These include the monitor's remuneration and expenses.

The carve-out of such debts means that a company could still require access to significant funds during a Pt A1 moratorium. Finally, debts incurred under the Pt A1 moratorium are given priority ranking if the debtor falls into a formal insolvency procedure within 12 weeks after the end of the moratorium.[753]

742 Section A21(1)(c), Pt A1 IA 1986.
743 Section A21(1)(d), Pt A1 IA 1986.
744 Section A20, Pt A1 IA 1986.
745 Section A21(3)-22, Pt A1 IA 1986.
746 Section A21(10(a), Pt A1 IA 1986.
747 Section A26, Pt A1 IA 1986.
748 Section A27, Pt A1 IA 1986.
749 Section A29, Pt A1 IA 1986.
750 Section A25, Pt A1 IA 1986.
751 Section A28, Pt A1 IA 1986.
752 Section A18(3), Pt A1 IA 1986. The words 'contract or other instrument involving financial services' has the meaning given by Sch. ZA2 IA 1986.
753 Para. 64A, Sch. B1 IA 1986 (administration) and Section 174A IA 1986 (liquidation).

4.5 The Pt 26A Restructuring Plan

4.5.1 Application and Information Requirements

Pt 26A restructuring plans are triggered by an application to a competent court to convene a meeting of the creditors or a class of creditors, or of the members of the company or class of members.[754] The application can only be submitted by the company and its directors; any creditor or member of the company; a liquidator or an administrator.[755] There is no need for the involvement of an IP or a PIFOR.

Courts have the jurisdiction to make a convening order in respect of a company that is liable to be wound up under IA 1986.[756] The creditors and members must be allowed to participate,[757] unless the court is satisfied that none of the members of that class has a genuine economic interest in the company.[758]

When a meeting is summoned, the creditors and the members shall receive a notice of the meeting and an explanatory statement under Section 901D CA 2006.[759] The explanatory statement must outline the effects of the compromise or arrangement; any material interests of the directors of the company; and the effect on those interests of the compromise or arrangement, insofar as it is different from the effect on the like interests of other persons.[760] Explanations must also be given if the compromise or arrangement affects the rights of the debenture holders.[761]

Any failure to comply with these notice requirements constitutes an offence,[762] unless "the default was due to the refusal of a director or trustee for debenture holders to supply the necessary particulars of the director's or (as the case may be) the trustee's interests".[763] If the latter fails to provide this information, they are the ones who commit an offence.[764]

4.5.2 The Plan

English law does not replicate the detailed requirements for the content of the restructuring plan outlined in Article 8 EU PRD. This means that parties have *de facto* unrestricted freedom, provided that the plan results in a compromise with the debtor's creditors and/

754 Section 901C(1) CA 2006.
755 Section 901C(2) CA 2006.
756 Section 901A(4)(b) CA 2006.
757 Section 901C(3) CA 2006.
758 Section 901C(4) CA 2006.
759 The Pension Regulator and the Pension Protection Fund also need to be informed of the procedure in the cases outlined in Section 901I CA 2006.
760 Section 901D(2) CA 2006.
761 Section 901D(3) CA 2006.
762 Section 901D(5) CA 2006.
763 Section 901D(7) CA 2006.
764 Section 901E CA 2006.

or an arrangement of its financial liabilities.[765] It is also possible to propose a plan with some but not all of the debtor's creditors, provided that it is not arbitrary or manipulated to exclude some trade creditors from one of the classes.[766]

Both Pt 26A restructuring plans and CVAs may be asset- or trade-based, depending on whether the money for the implementation of the plan is collected predominantly from the sale of assets or from proceeds arising in the ordinary course of business.

Should the Pt 26A plan not be approved by all classes of impaired creditors, the compromise or arrangement can be sanctioned by the court only if none of the members of the dissenting class would be any worse off than they would be in the event of the relevant alternative.[767] The 'relevant alternative' is whatever the court considers would be most likely to occur in relation to the company if the compromise or arrangement were not sanctioned.[768] There is, however, no explicit APR under English law.

The sanctioned plan is binding on both secured and unsecured creditors,[769] and any changes will need to be approved by them. The court order needs to be delivered to the Registrar of Companies.[770]

Usually, Pt 26 schemes are implemented shortly after the court's sanction, as they entail the transfer of assets and shares to one or more new companies. CVAs and Pt 26A restructuring plans may require more time for their implementation.

4.5.3 The Composition of Members' and Creditors' Classes

The overall commonality between Pt 26 schemes and Pt 26A restructuring plans allows the courts to draw on the existing case law on Pt 26 schemes. Courts have long refrained from offering guidance on what constitutes a class of members or creditors at the application stage.[771]

Both in Pt 26A plans and in Pt 26 schemes, stakeholders should vote in the class where their rights are "not so dissimilar as to make it impossible for them to consult together

765 Among others, see: Re Virgin Atlantic [2020] EWHC 2191 (Ch) (convening), at Para. 38; Pizza Express (convening), above note 711, at Para. 27.

766 Virgin Atlantic (sanction), above note 711. The question in front of the court was whether adding 1,000 creditors owed less than £50,000 to the plan would have materially changed the return to the other creditors or simply created additional administrative complexity to the procedure.

767 Section 901G(3) CA 2006.

768 Section 901G(4) CA 2006.

769 Section 901F(5) CA 2006.

770 Section 901F(6) CA 2006.

771 V. Finch & D. Milman, *Corporate Insolvency Law. Perspectives and Principles* (3rd ed.), Cambridge CUP, 2017, p. 412.

with a view to their common interest".[772] This assessment is conducted at the convening, rather than the sanction hearing.[773]

Courts have interpreted this requirement with a 'degree of pragmatism', and creditors have been treated as a single class when their interests were "sufficiently closely aligned".[774] Courts have generally refrained from the creation of small classes of creditors to avoid granting to their members either a potential power of veto on the Pt 26 plan or unequal bargaining powers.[775]

Issues might arise where it appears that the chosen classes were artificially formed to obtain the majorities required by the law to approve the plan.[776] If the artificial formation of the classes only becomes apparent at the sanction hearing, "that may be a ground on which the court will be prepared to revisit the conclusion that it reached on classes at the convening hearing"[777] and refuse the sanctioning of a creditors' vote. However, "where the terms of the restructuring would demonstrably benefit the affected creditors, there was a powerful argument that the artificiality should not prevent the company and its creditors from being able to take advantage of the English scheme jurisdiction."[778] These decisions suggest that English courts will continue adopting a light-touch approach to second-guessing the composition of members' and creditors' classes.

4.6 *Adoption and Confirmation of the Pt 26A Plan*

4.6.1 Adoption of Pt 26A Restructuring Plans

A Pt 26A plan is approved if 75% in value of the creditors or class or creditors, members or class of members affected by the compromise or arrangement vote in favour of it.[779] Despite the broad reading of the word 'affected' in *Hurricane Energy*,[780] it is understood that a creditor does not fall into this category if their claims are not impacted in form and substance or otherwise *negatively* affected by the compromise or arrangement, as they

772 Sovereign Life Assurance v. Dodd [1892] 2 Q.B. 573, p. 583; Re BTR Plc [2000] 1 B.C.L.C. 740; Re Sovereign Marine & General Insurance Co. Ltd [2006] B.C.C. 774 (with reference to Pt 26 schemes); Virgin Atlantic (sanction), above note 711, at para. 44 (with reference to Pt 26A plans).

773 Above note 712, at Para. 22.

774 Re APCOA Parking Holdings GmbH [2014] EWHC 3849 (Ch); Re Obrascon Huarte Lain SA [2021] EWHC 859 (Ch) at para. 25; Re Smile Telecoms Holdings Ltd [2022] EWHC 337 (Ch) (convening).

775 Re Provident SPV Ltd [2021] EWHC 1341 (Ch), where the Court held that a single class meeting could be convened, because borrowers and guarantors were not being treated differently in principle under the proposed plan, and guarantors comprised only 0.024% of potential claims.

776 Re DeepOcean 1 UK Ltd [2021] EWHC 138 (Ch) (sanction).

777 Ibid., at Para. 41.

778 Re Gategroup Guarantee Ltd [2021] EWHC 775 (Ch) (sanction), at Para. 14, citing Para. 174 of the convening judgement.

779 Section 901F(1) CA 2006.

780 Re Hurricane Energy Plc [2021] EWHC 1418 (Ch) (convening), at Paras. 27-34.

would have no need that justifies being protected through their participation in the Pt 26A plan.[781]

Crucially, two requirements applicable to Pt 26 schemes and CVAs have not been replicated in the new restructuring plan procedure, thus making it easier to achieve the requisite majority. These are the requirements that more than half in value of unconnected creditors ('unconnected creditors test') and that the majority in number ('numerosity test')[782] vote in favour of the plan.

4.6.2 Cross-Class Cram-Down Provisions

To further facilitate the approval of a plan, the new restructuring procedure features a cross-class cram-down.[783] This allows dissenting classes of creditors to be bound by the plan if a court sanctions it where they consider it fair and equitable, and two conditions are met. First (condition 'A'), a court must be satisfied that, if the compromise or arrangement is sanctioned, none of the members of the dissenting class would be any **worse off** than in the event of the **relevant alternative.** The relevant alternative is whatever a court considers most likely to occur in relation to the company if the compromise or arrangement is not sanctioned ('no worse off' test).[784]

The 'no worse off' test is the English equivalent of the best-interest-of-creditors test. This does not create an obligation to comply with the APR, as deviations from it have been sanctioned by competent courts. For instance, in *DeepOcean*,[785] the Court noted that the Pt 26A plan may provide differential treatment for some creditors that are 'out of the money', if such differential treatment is justified. In *Virgin Active*, the Court ruled that shareholders could receive some value in the new company because they provided new money under the plan, whilst more senior-ranking creditors (landlords) had their obligations compromised and were crammed-down.[786]

Finding the relevant alternative is analogous to establishing a suitable comparator for class purposes in the context of a Pt 26 scheme.[787] It is also comparable to the analysis that a court may be asked to perform when applying a 'vertical' comparison for an unfair

781 S. Paterson & A. Walters, 'Selective Corporate Restructuring Strategy', available at: https://ssrn.com/abstract=3924225 (last viewed 1 December 2022) p. 10.

782 Section 899(1) CA 2006.

783 Section 901G CA 2006.

784 Section 901G(3) and (4) CA 2006. On this, see: Y. Bazinas, 'Restructuring Plans in the Eye of the Hurricane: The "No Worse Off" Test and the Application of the Cramdown Tool in the Aftermath of Re Hurricane Energy Plc', *International Corporate Rescue*, 2022, 19(1), pp. 10-14.

785 Above note 776.

786 Re Virgin Active Holdings Ltd [2021] EWHC 1246 (Ch) (sanction).

787 Above note 776, at Para. 29. See also: Re Telewest Telecommunications Plc [2004] B.C.C. 342, p. 351; Re The British Aviation Insurance Co. Ltd [2006] B.C.C. 14, at Paras. 82, 88; and Re ColourOz Investment 2 LLC [2020] EWHC 1864 (Ch) at Para. 74.

prejudice challenge to a CVA.[788] In a vertical comparison, courts identify the projected outcome of a realistically available alternative process and use it as the boundary below which a CVA (and in this case, the Pt 26A restructuring plan) cannot go.[789] English courts are not afraid to challenge the debtor's evidence as to the relevant alternative. If the petitioning creditors can prove that the company is not hopelessly insolvent, the court will not consider liquidation as the adequate comparator.[790]

Second (condition 'B'), the plan must receive the consent of at least one class of creditors who would receive a payment or have a **genuine economic interest** in the company in the relevant alternative ('economic interest' test).[791]

Virgin Active[792] marked the first time a Pt 26A restructuring plan had been used to compromise landlord claims despite the opposition of this class of creditors to the plan. In the sanction hearing, the Court held that, provided that the statutory requirements are met, it was for a company and its creditors who were 'in the money' to decide how the value of the business and assets of the company should be divided.

Overall, courts have claimed that the test is "a broad concept taking into account the impact of the restructuring plan on all incidents of the liability to the creditor, but primarily focused upon anticipated returns based upon assumptions and projections and comparing them with a counterfactual based upon the relevant alternative".[793]

4.6.3 Confirmation of Pt 26A Restructuring Plans

Even if the statutory conditions are satisfied, courts retain discretion over whether to sanction a restructuring plan pursuant to Section 901F(1) CA 2006. In exercising this discretion, courts evaluate factors such as (i) the support for the plan from other classes of creditors; (ii) the benefits provided by other companies in the group; (iii) any issues regarding the fair representation of the category of dissenting creditors; (iv) the relative treatment of creditors under the proposals, similar to the 'horizontal comparison' carried out when considering an unfair challenge to a CVA;[794] and (v) whether the plan operates

788 Above note 776, at Para. 30.

789 See Re T N Ltd [2004] EWHC 2361 (Ch) at Para. 82; and Prudential Assurance Co. v. PRG Powerhouse Ltd [2007] EWHC 1002 (Ch) at Paras. 75-81.

790 Hurricane Energy (sanction), above note 714.

791 Section 901G(5) CA 2006.

792 Above note 786. For a comment, see: L. Linklater, 'Virgin Active and New Look: A New Dawn for the Rescue Culture?', *Insolvency Intelligence*, 2021, 34(3), pp. 55-57; N. Cooper et al., 'Landlord's Day in Court? Lessons Learned from the New Look CVA and Virgin Atlantic Restructuring Plan Judgments', *International Corporate Rescue*, 2021, 18(4), p. 253; A. Cohen et al., 'Imposing a Restructuring Plan: A Sign of Times?', *PLC Magazine*, 2021, 32(5), pp. 4-5; C. Lamont, 'A New Look at Leasehold Restructuring', *L. & T. Review*, 2021, 25(5), pp. 192-195.

793 Re Amicus Finance plc (in admin.) [2021] EWHC 3036 (Ch) (sanction), at Para. 50.

794 Above note 776, at para. 63: "justice may require the court to look at questions of horizontal comparability in the context of a cross-class cram down to see whether a restructuring plan provides for differences in

as "a mechanism for varying creditor rights and effecting a distribution of the available assets".[795]

It is generally accepted that courts will not exercise their discretion if, overall, an intelligent and honest person would have voted in the same way as the majority of creditors.[796] Nevertheless, they used their discretion where there had been alleged negligent or fraudulent misconduct from the proponents of the plan; unfairness towards the dissenting creditors; unreasonable breach of the order of priority of distribution; or multiple and similar concerns raised by a variety of creditors.[797]

4.6.4 Analysis with Respect to Articles 9-11 EU PRD 2019

As evidenced above, UK law is broadly compliant with the EU directive. For the moment, the legislator has not opted for the introduction of special rules applicable to workers and MSME debtors. With reference to workers, a partial reason can be found in the preferential treatment that some of their claims have under employment and insolvency law. Regarding MSMEs, R3 (the UK Association of Business Recovery Professionals) is working on a 'model' Pt 26A plan to reduce costs and complexities for these claimants.

Additionally, there are no specific provisions on new financing as set out in Article 17 of the EU PRD 2019. New financing is possible in the UK, and may give rise to entitlements to some returns even though these may be contrary to a strict interpretation of the APR.[798] However, there is no provision for super-priority status in an ensuing insolvency procedure.

4.7 Possibilities for a Debt-for-Equity Swap

Pursuant to Section 895(2) CA 2006, 'arrangement' includes a reorganization of the company's share capital by the consolidation of shares of different classes or by the division of shares into different classes, or by both of those methods. As a result, debt-for-equity swaps are allowed under the law.

The first Pt 26A restructuring plan to utilize a debt-for-equity swap was *Hurricane Energy*.[799] The fact that the plan was not sanctioned in this case does not mean that debt-for-equity swaps might not work in future Pt 26A restructuring plans.

---

treatment of creditors *inter se*, and if so whether those differences are justified".

795 Ibid., at Para. 66.

796 Ibid., at Para. 61.

797 Above note 712, at para. 78.

798 Above note 786.

799 Hurricane Energy (sanction), above note 714.

4.8 Executory Contracts

Provisions on the treatment of executory contracts are included in Article 7(4) EU PRD 2019. Whilst the UK has long refused to curtail the parties' autonomy to vary or terminate contracts by reason of insolvency,[800] there was evidence of a more rescue-oriented approach even before the enactment of EU PRD 2019. Since 1986, the suppliers of goods and services (such as gas, electricity and water) to insolvent companies could not make a condition for further supplies that the office holder personally guaranteed for their payment, or that pre-insolvency charges were paid.[801] The Insolvency (Protection of Essential Supplies) Order 2015 (SI 2015/989) expanded the list of contracts subject to this regime to the supply of communications services. However, such provisions only applied to companies that entered into administration, liquidation or a CVA.

After CIGA 2020,[802] if the debtor is subject to any relevant insolvency procedure, a creditor cannot terminate the supply of any goods or services or do 'any other thing' by reason of the commencement of the relevant insolvency procedure.[803] Additionally, a supplier shall not make it a condition of any supply of goods and services after the time when the company becomes subject to the relevant insolvency procedure that any outstanding charges in respect of a supply made to the company before that time are paid.[804]

It would be incorrect to hold that *ipso facto* clauses can no longer be enforced under English law. This is so for five reasons. Firstly, the list of relevant procedures does not include Pt 26 schemes of arrangement.[805] Secondly, invalidation of the enforceability of *ipso facto* clauses is much narrower in scope than the equivalent US provision.[806] Thirdly, the prohibition excludes several types of suppliers or contracts (*e.g.* contracts for the supply of goods or services from banks, insurers and financial providers). Fourthly, the supplier can obtain the consent of the office holder or a court to terminate the supply.[807]

800 E. Vaccari, 'National Report for England and Wales', in: J. Chuah and E. Vaccari (eds), *Executory Contracts in Insolvency Law: A Global Guide*, Cheltenham: EE Publishing, 2019; E. Vaccari, 'Conceptualising the Anti-Deprivation Principle *Vis-à-Vis* Freedom of Contract', *International Insolvency Review*, 2022, 31(2), pp. 235-274; E. Vaccari, 'A Modular Approach to Restructuring and Insolvency Law: Executory Contracts and Onerous Property in England and Italy', *Norton Journal of Bankruptcy Law and Practice (West)*, 2022, 31(5), pp. 534-589.

801 Section 233-233A IA 1986.

802 This provision included a temporary exclusion for small suppliers, which expired on 30 June 2021. This date has been extended by The Corporate Insolvency and Governance Act 2020 (Coronavirus) (Extension of the Relevant Period) Regulations 2021.

803 Section 233B(4) IA 1986.

804 Section 233B(7) IA 1986.

805 Section 233B(2) IA 1986.

806 §.541(c), 11 U.S. Code.

807 Section 233B(5) IA 1986. The court's consent is subject to the proof that the supplier would suffer hardship if termination was not granted.

Finally, under certain circumstances, the supplier may also require additional guarantees to continue performing.[808]

Suppliers can be relieved of the requirement to supply if it causes hardship to their business. Suppliers also retain the power to terminate these contracts for breaches that occur after the commencement of the relevant procedure. Permanent exclusions still apply for the benefit of certain financial contracts and institutions.

The creditor's prohibition to terminate a contract is mirrored by an analogous prohibition on the debtor to disclaim it,[809] at least in restructuring procedures. However, in all UK restructuring procedures the debtor can unilaterally change the terms of the contract, although without creating new obligations[810] and provided that other conditions are met.

4.9 *Jurisdiction for and Recognition of Court Decisions in Europe*

Following the UK's withdrawal from the EU (Brexit), the regulation on insolvency proceedings (EIR 2015)[811] is no longer applicable to the UK.[812] Consequently, English courts no longer automatically recognize insolvency judgements from EU Member States, and vice versa.

The relationship is now regulated by the EU-UK Trade and Cooperation Agreement (24 December 2020), implemented in the UK via the European Union (Future Relationship) Act 2020. These documents fail to replicate the seamless and straightforward system for the recognition of civil and insolvency judgements outlined by the EIR 2015 for insolvency judgements and the Brussels Recast Regulation 2012 (Brussels Recast Regulation)[813] for civil and commercial judgements.

Starting with insolvency procedures, the easiest way to recognize an English insolvency judgement in another EU Member State is if such country has adopted the UNCITRAL Model Law on Cross-Border Insolvency (MLCBI).[814] MLCBI results in merely streamlined

808 Section 233A(s) IA 1986.

809 Re Instant Cash Loans Ltd [2019] EWHC 2795 (Ch).

810 APCOA Parking, above note 774, at Paras. 133-167.

811 Regulation (EU) 2015/838 of the European Parliament and of the Council of 20 May 2015 on insolvency proceedings (recast), O.J. L 141/19.

812 E. Vaccari, 'WHOA, Brexit! Which Future for London as Europe's (Largest) Insolvency Forum?', *Journal of International Banking Law & Regulation*, 2022, 37(2), pp. 46-68; J. Payne, ''Debt Restructuring in Transition', *Law Quarterly Review*, 2023, 139(Jan), pp. 101-125 (arguing that Brexit and the changes introduced by CIGA 2020 have resulted in 'lack of commercial certainty for the parties').

813 Regulation (EU) No 1215/2012 of the European Parliament and of the Council of 12 December 2012 on jurisdiction and the recognition and enforcement of judgments in civil and commercial matters [2012] OJ L 351/1.

814 U.N. Comm'n on Int'l Trade Law, 'UNCITRAL Model Law on Cross-Border Insolvency with Guide to Enactment and Interpretation', U.N. Sales No. E.14.V.2 (2014), available at: https://uncitral.un.org/sites/

rather than automatic recognition of foreign insolvency proceedings. In all other cases, the recognition of English insolvency proceedings is dependent on the domestic private international law governing recognition of foreign judgements in a particular Member State.

With reference to inbound recognition of those insolvency proceedings that are listed and could be listed in 'Annex A' EIR 2015, there are two alternative options. Irish practitioners can rely on the broad assistance granted under Section 426(4) IA 1986. Assistance is not automatic; however, if required, it can only be denied if it would be improper to grant such assistance,[815] if such assistance would impinge on the UK's public policy[816] or cause oppression.[817] A more limited but equally effective form of assistance is the streamlined recognition granted by the Cross-Border Insolvency Regulations 2006 (CBIR 2006), which enacts the MLCBI in the UK.

Whilst Pt 26 schemes of arrangement are not formal insolvency procedures, the decision in *gategroup*[818] established that Pt 26A restructuring plans are. As a result, the recognition of Pt 26A restructuring plans by European Member States should follow the rules outlined above with reference to insolvency proceedings. Outside Europe, Pt 26A plans will be recognized under Chapter 15 of the U.S. Bankruptcy Code.

Special rules apply to the outbound recognition of Pt 26 schemes of arrangement, and to the inbound recognition of all restructuring proceedings that fall outside the scope of 'Annex A' EIR 2015. It used to be possible to recognize Pt 26 schemes based on the Brussels Recast Regulation. The case of *Lecta Paper*[819] validated this practice. However, reliance on the Brussels Recast Regulation is no longer possible.[820] The alternative route has traditionally been to utilize Regulation (EC) No 593/2008 (Rome I Regulation).[821]

---

uncitral.un.org/files/media-documents/uncitral/en/1997-model-law-insol-2013-guide-enactment-e.pdf (last viewed 1 December 2022).

815 Re Focus Insurance Co. Ltd [1996] B.C.C. 659; New Cap Reinsurance Corp. Ltd (in liq.) v. Grant [2011] EWHC 677 (Ch).

816 Re Levy's Trusts (1885) 30 Ch. D. 119; Galbraith v. Grimshaw [1910] A.C. 508; Re Osborn Ex p. Tree [1931-32] B. & C.R. 189; Re Jackson [1973] N.I. 67; Re Dallhold Estates (UK) Pty Ltd [1992] B.C.C. 394; Re Bank of Credit and Commerce International SA (No.9) [1994] 2 B.C.L.C. 636; Focus Insurance, above note 815; Hughes v. Hannover [1997] B.C.C. 921.

817 Focus Insurance, above note 815; England v Smith [2001] Ch. 419.

818 Re Gategroup Guarantee Ltd [2021] EWHC 304 (Ch) (convening), at Paras. 85-137.

819 Re Lecta Paper UK Ltd [2020] EWHC 382 (Ch), at Para. 45 ('I shall adopt what has become the usual practice of assuming without deciding, that Chapter II of the (Brussels Recast Regulation) applies to this application on the basis that the scheme creditors are sued by the company and, that they are defendants to the scheme application').

820 The regulation was repealed pursuant to *The Civil Jurisdiction and Judgments (Amendment) (EU Exit) Regulations 2019*, which also revoked the Brussels Regulation, the Lugano Convention and certain other frameworks.

821 Regulation (EC) No 593/2008 of the European Parliament and of the Council of 17 June 2008 on the law applicable to contractual obligations (Rome I) [2008] OJ L 177/6. For Denmark, reference should be made

However, this alternative route applies only in case the restructuring plan involved a compromise of contracts governed by English law.

It may have been possible to rely on the 2007 Lugano Convention on Jurisdiction and the Recognition and Enforcement of Judgments (Lugano Convention)[822] for restructuring plans submitted by distressed but not yet insolvent companies, and which do not result in the liquidation of the debtor's assets. The UK applied to join the Lugano Convention in April 2020. Acceding to the Lugano Convention requires unanimous consent from all parties, including the EU. Whilst EFTA Member States supported the UK's application, the EU formally blocked the UK's accession. This means that outbound recognition of Pt 26 schemes is subject to local private international laws.

Beyond Lugano and bilateral agreements with EU Member States, it might be possible in future to rely on the 2019 Hague Convention on the Recognition and Enforcement of Foreign Judgments in Civil or Commercial Matters.[823] When ratified by enough states, it will establish an international framework for the recognition and enforcement of such judgements. However, the 2019 Hague Convention is not yet in force, and it is unlikely it will be ratified by enough states in the near future.

5 Case Law on Pt 26A Restructuring Plans

As of 30 September 2022, a total of 14 companies incorporated in England and Wales and 2 companies incorporated in Scotland had a Pt 26A restructuring plan registered at the Companies House.[824] Two applications (*Virgin Active* and *DeepOcean*) were from companies in a group. The average time between confirmation and sanction hearing varies between 10 (*Amicus Finance*) and 44 (*DeepOcean 1 Ltd*) days, even if courts acknowledged that shorter rimes are possible in case of urgency.[825]

Some of the key findings by the courts in the convening and sanction hearings will be discussed in what follows. The purpose of this case law analysis is twofold. Firstly, the interpretation given by the courts of the statutory provisions described above will be analysed whilst the extent to which the cross-fertilization process has resulted in the UK's

to the 1980 Rome Convention on the law applicable to contractual obligations (consolidated version) [1998] OJ C 27.

822 Convention on Jurisdiction and the Recognition and Enforcement of Judgments [2007] OJ L 339/3.

823 HCCH, 'Convention on the Recognition and Enforcement of Foreign Judgments in Civil or Commercial Matters', available at: https://assets.hcch.net/docs/806e290e-bbd8-413d-b15e-8e3e1bf1496d.pdf (last viewed 1 December 2022).

824 This information was provided in an answer to a freedom-of-information request submitted to the Insolvency Service by one of the authors of this piece.

825 Re Virgin Active Holdings Ltd [2021] EWHC 814 (Ch) (convening), at Paras. 135-150.

approximation of EU laws in the context of preventive restructuring will then also be assessed.

5.1 Convening Hearing

Since *Gategroup*,[826] English courts have consistently held that the following issues will need to be addressed at the convening hearing:

1. Adequacy of notice of the convening hearing to plan creditors;
2. Jurisdictional requirements;
3. Threshold conditions 'A' and 'B';
4. Class composition;
5. Any other issues not going to merits or fairness which might cause the court to refuse to sanction the restructuring plans;
6. Practical issues regarding the adequacy of notice, documentation and proposals for the meetings of creditors;
7. Whether there are any blots on the scheme or any roadblock in the way of its implementation.

5.1.1 Notice

Creditors must be given adequate notice of the convening hearing to creditors affected by the plan. When adequate notice is not provided, courts have followed an established line of precedents,[827] giving creditors the right to challenge the procedure for issues of class composition and jurisdiction at the sanction hearing.[828] It is permissible for debtors not to involve some creditors in the preliminary negotiations. If the choice is motivated by a rational assessment of the situation, for example by the nature of the creditors' claims and the number of creditors as occurred in *Virgin Atlantic*,[829] the courts will uphold the company's decision. However, courts will carefully scrutinize whether the notice given to them later was sufficient in the circumstances.[830]

With reference to the explanatory statement, which should be more detailed than notice letters,[831] courts have held that its adequacy should be assessed at the sanction

826 Gategroup (convening), above note 818.
827 Port Finance Investment Limited [2021] EWHC 378 (Ch).
828 Virgin Active (convening), above note 825.
829 The nature of the creditors' claims, and the number of creditors suggested against sending the notice to this group of creditors.
830 Virgin Atlantic (convening), above note 786, at Para. 27.
831 Re ED & F Man Holdings Ltd [2022] EWHC 433 (Ch) (convening), at Para. 42. In this case, the 'concise' Practice Statement letter was 35 pages long and contained 115 paragraphs. However, explanatory statements can run for thousands of pages, as they include all the plan documents, and the reports as to the relevant alternative and the plan outcome.

hearing.[832] However, where a court at a convening hearing detects or has its attention drawn to a manifest deficiency in the draft explanatory statement, it is entitled, if it thinks fit, to decline to convene the meetings unless and until that manifest defect is corrected.[833]

Even if courts can order that additional documents are made available to the creditors, a debtor cannot be forced to include commercially confidential information in the statement. The judgement in *Virgin Active* outlines in detail the documents that should be included in the explanatory statement.

5.1.2 Jurisdictional Requirements

Where companies are incorporated in England and Wales, they are inherently liable to be wound up under the IA 1986 should that be required and, therefore, they are an entity in relation to which the provisions of Pt 26A apply.[834] This is so even if the applicant has only recently been incorporated and entered into the deed of indemnity for the purposes of the plan.[835]

It is well established that a foreign company may be wound up under IA 1986 as an unregistered company. There is, nonetheless, in general, a requirement for there to be a sufficient connection with this jurisdiction in order for a foreign company to be wound up as an unregistered company.[836] Questions of sufficiency of connection (where applicable) and international effectiveness are for the sanction hearing,[837] unless there are obvious roadblocks to the company being able to establish a sufficient connection.[838]

5.1.3 Threshold Conditions

Where the purpose of the compromise or arrangement is to mitigate the effect of the financial difficulties referred to in condition 'A', courts must identify what constitutes such 'effect'. They also have to determine whether the compromise or arrangement has, as its purpose, a lessening or reduction in the gravity or seriousness of such effect.[839]

As for condition 'B', courts have argued that the broad language of the legislator needs to be 'expansively construed'.[840] As a result, the compromise or arrangement requires some

832 Virgin Active (convening), above note 825, at Para. 99.

833 Indah Kiat International Finance Co BV [2016] BCC 418. However, see also Virgin Active (convening), above note 825, at para. 46, saying that this would be a rare case.

834 Virgin Atlantic (convening), above note 786, at Para. 36.

835 Gategroup (convening), above note 818.

836 Smile Telecoms (convening), above note 774, at Para. 58; Re Drax Holdings [2004] 1 WLR 1049.

837 Virgin Atlantic (convening), above note 786, at Para. 57; DeepOcean 1 UK Ltd [2020] EWHC 3549 (Ch) (convening), at Para. 58.

838 Smile Telecoms (convening), above note 774, at Para. 60.

839 DeepOcean 1 (convening), above note 837, at Para. 46.

840 Gategroup (convening), above note 818, at Para. 110.

element of give and take between a company and its scheme creditors, but a definition is neither necessary nor desirable.[841]

5.1.4 Class Composition

It is well established that classes must be confined to those persons whose rights are not so dissimilar as to make it impossible for them to consult together with a view to their common interest.[842] In this area, courts do follow the case law developed under Pt 26 schemes, even if they may depart from a rigid application of those rules[843] as a 'degree of pragmatism' is needed.[844] Courts look at the legal rights of the creditors to determine the appropriate constitution of a class.[845] The rights of those included in a single class can be subject to material differences.[846]

This means that, where appropriate, courts will approve a request to convene a meeting of only one class of creditors for the purpose of considering and approving a proposed Pt 26A restructuring plan.[847] It is not necessary to summon meetings of classes of creditors or members if their rights against the company are not directly varied, or if they would be 'out of the money' in the relevant alternative.

The question of whether consultation is possible depends in large part on whether, ignoring any personal or extraneous interests, there is more that unites the relevant creditors than divides them.[848] A class meeting of a single entity is possible,[849] and issues of cross-holding shares do not necessarily result in a need for separate classes. In any case, determining the composition of each class is mainly a factual exercise, and courts will refrain from an unnecessary proliferation of classes even if there are material differences between creditors.[850]

---

841 Virgin Atlantic (convening), above note 786, at Para. 38, citing by way of example Savoy, above note 702, p. 359; and Re Lehman Brothers International (Europe) [2019] BCC 115, at Para. 64. See also: ED & F Man (convening), above note 831, at Paras. 55-56.

842 Sovereign Life, above note 765, p. 583; Re UDL Holdings Ltd [2002] 1 HKC 172, at Para. 27; Re Hawk Insurance Company Ltd [2002] BCC 300, at Para. 30; Virgin Atlantic (convening), above note 786, at Para. 41; DeepOcean 1 (convening), above note 837, at Para. 50; Virgin Active (convening), above note 825, at Paras. 61, 66.

843 Amicus Finance (convening), above note 712.

844 Re Houst Ltd [2022] EWHC 1765 (Ch) (convening), at Para. 41. In this case, the Court held that they were not persuaded of the need to separate ordinary from preferred shareholders for voting purposes.

845 Virgin Atlantic (convening), above note 786, at Para. 42; Amicus Finance (convening), above note 712.

846 Neuberger J said in Re Anglo American Insurance Co Ltd [2001] 1 BCLC 755, p. 764: 'if one gets too picky about different classes, one could end up with virtually as many classes as there are members of a particular group'.

847 Smile Telecoms (convening), above note 774.

848 APCOA Parking Holdings GmbH [2015] Bus LR 374, at Para. 52 (with reference to Pt 26 schemes); Virgin Atlantic (convening), above note 786, at Para. 47 (with reference to Pt 26A plans)

849 Re Altitude Scaffolding [2006] BCC 904, at Paras. 12, 18; Smile Telecoms (convening), above note 774, at Para. 85.

850 ED & F Man (convening), above note 831, at Para. 62.

To assess the adequacy of the proposed composition of the classes, courts consider the treatment of creditors in the relevant alternative ('relevant counterfactual comparator').[851] The question of class composition can be revisited at the sanction hearing,[852] if new evidence is brought to the attention of the court. At the convening hearing, decisions on class composition are based on the evidence adduced by the debtor.

5.1.5 Practical Issues

Courts have on more than one occasion reminded parties that "it is well-established … that the[ir] function … at this stage is emphatically not to consider the merits or fairness of the proposed"[853] plan. Other matters which could make it pointless to convene the meetings (because they cast a blot on the scheme or present a roadblock in the way of its approval) are also worthy of consideration, at least on a provisional basis.[854]

5.2 Sanction Hearing

At sanction hearings, English courts do consider the following issues:

- Compliance with statutory provisions;
- Specific requirements for cross-class cram-down;
- Representation and voting at plan meeting;
- Fairness of the scheme;
- Blots or defects in the scheme;
- Jurisdiction and international effectiveness.

Issues related to the existence of the conditions for commencing a Pt 26A plan, on class constitution and on jurisdiction should not be considered again in the sanction hearing unless there are valid reasons to do it.[855]

5.2.1 Statutory Provisions

Where all the classes have approved the plan with the **statutory majorities**, the courts are in a similar position as in a Pt 26 scheme of arrangement.[856] Accordingly, the approach to

851 Virgin Atlantic (convening), above note 786, at Para. 43; Virgin Active (convening), above note 825, at Para. 69.

852 Virgin Active (convening), above note 825, at Para. 70.

853 Virgin Atlantic (convening), above note 786, at Para. 35. See also: Telewest Communications [2004] B.C.C. 342, at Para. 14 (for the case law on Pt 26 schemes of arrangement); Pizza Express (convening), above note 711, at Para. 23; DeepOcean 1 (convening), above note 837, at Para. 58.

854 Pizza Express (convening), above note 711, at Para. 23.

855 DeepOcean 1 (sanction), above note 776.

856 Re Noble [2018] EWHC 2092 (Ch), at Para. 17.

sanctioning is the same.[857] This includes adhering to the tried-and-tested approach to discretion.[858] Courts exercise an independent role, and the absence of objection does not relieve them of the burden of scrutiny.[859]

5.2.2 Cross-Class Cram-Down

Courts need to assess the existence of conditions 'A' and 'B' described in Section 4.6.2. Artificial attempts to create an in-the-money class for the purposes of providing the anchor to activate the cross-class cram-down power should be resisted, particularly where such a class is not impaired by the plan.[860] At the same time, where creditors or members would receive no payment or have no economic interest in the company in the relevant alternative, little regard is paid to their views.[861]

Identifying the 'relevant alternative' is similar to the process provided for the Pt 26 scheme.[862] Courts are not required to satisfy themselves that a particular alternative would definitely occur. The critical words in the section are what is 'most likely' to occur.[863] Courts recognize that the directors are normally in the best position to identify what will happen if a Pt 26A plan fails. Where the evidence appears on its face to reflect a rational and considered view of the company's board, courts will require sufficient reason for doubting that evidence.[864]

Having identified the relevant alternative scenario, the court is also required to identify its consequences for the members of the dissenting classes. This exercise is inherently uncertain because it involves the court in considering a hypothetical counterfactual, which may be subject to contingencies and which will, inevitably, be based upon assumptions that are themselves uncertain.[865]

The starting point will normally be a comparison of the value of the likely dividend, or the amount of any discount to the par value of each creditor's debt. However, the phrase used is 'any worse off', which is a broad concept and appears to contemplate the need to take into account the impact of the restructuring plan on all incidents of the liability to the

857 Virgin Atlantic (sanction), above note 711, at Para. 46.

858 As summarised by Richards J in Re Telewest Communications plc (No. 2) [2005] B.C.C. 36, at Paras. 20-22.

859 Re Pizza Express Financing 2 plc [2020] EWHC 3933 (Ch) (sanction), at Para. 4.

860 Re Houst Ltd [2022] EWHC 1941 (Ch) (sanction), at Para. 20.

861 Ibid., at Para. 27.

862 Telewest Telecommunications, above note 787, p. 351; British Aviation Insurance, above note 787, at Paras. 82, 88; ColourOz Investment 2, above note 787, at Para. 74.

863 Virgin Active (sanction), above note 786, at Para. 107; Amicus Finance (sanction), above note 793, at Para. 57: 'when assessing the relevant alternative, the relevant balance of proof for the proponents of the scheme was the balance of probabilities. The proponents of the scheme did not have to demonstrate that there was no real prospect of a better outcome for the creditors'.

864 Re ED & F Man Holdings Ltd [2022] EWHC 687 (Ch) (sanction), at Para. 39.

865 Virgin Active (sanction), above note 786, at Para. 108.

creditor concerned, including matters such as timing and the security of any covenant to pay.[866]

The attempt to preserve the interests of dissenting creditors cannot result in lengthy valuation disputes that operate for the interest of no one (except the lawyers).[867] It follows that there is no absolute obligation to conduct a full market testing[868] under the law. However, where practicable, market testing should be conducted. Valuations will invariably produce a range of possible outcomes, and professional advisers will need to identify the most likely one. The mere existence of a broad range is not *per se* unreliable.[869]

5.2.3 Courts' Discretion

In exercising their powers, courts can rely on the **discretion** granted by Section 901F(1) CA 2006.[870] As little guidance is provided by the law, courts will generally follow the approach adopted for Pt 26 schemes.[871]

Where the evidence is that the members of the dissenting class are out of the money and that their exclusion would in any event have been achievable in the relevant alternative, the receipt of any benefits under the terms of the proposed Pt 26A restructuring plan is in itself sufficient to demonstrate that they are unlikely to have been treated in a manner that is not just and equitable.[872] Additionally, courts tend to exercise their discretion to sanction a plan if a significant majority (even if not the statutory one) voted in favour of it; none of the opposing creditors appears to oppose the sanction of the plan; and none of them have explained in evidence why it is that the terms of the plan might be considered unfair to them.[873]

Besides this, as a general rule, a court will not exercise their discretion not to sanction a plan if an intelligent and honest man would vote in favour of it.[874] Courts will also carry out an 'horizontal comparison' among creditors of the same class, similar to the approach followed in fairness challenges to CVAs to determine whether they should exercise their discretion not to sanction a plan.[875]

Whilst there is no prohibition on differential treatment of creditors, this behaviour must be justified.[876] Differential treatment can be explained by reference to the profitability

---

866 DeepOcean 1 (sanction), above note 776, at Para. 35.
867 Virgin Active (sanction), above note 786, at Para. 130.
868 Saltri III Ltd v MD Mezzanine SA Sicar [2012] EWHC 3025 (Comm).
869 Virgin Active (sanction), above note 786, at Para. 157.
870 DeepOcean 1 (sanction), above note 776, at Para. 21.
871 Ibid., at Para. 44.
872 Ibid., at Para. 51; ED & F Man (sanction), above note 864, at Para. 48.
873 ED & F Man (sanction), above note 864, at Paras. 55-56.
874 DeepOcean 1 (sanction), above note 776, at Para. 61.
875 Ibid., at Para. 62.
876 Virgin Active (sanction), above note 786, at Para. 259. See, for instance, the case of critical suppliers: SEA Assets Ltd v. PT Garuda Indonesia [2001] EWCA Civ 1696.

and commercial importance that the debtors attached to particular creditors and to the desire of the debtor to eliminate contingent liabilities arising in connection with key contracts. In general, shareholders should pay new money for their retention of equity rights.[877]

The last discretionary factor is whether there is anything in the formulation of the plan that causes concern as to how it will operate in practice as a mechanism for varying creditor rights and effecting a distribution of the available assets.[878]

Courts have not been reluctant to cram-down a dissenting class, even if 100% of its members have voted against the plan.[879] In general, an applicant company will have a fair wind behind it if it seeks a cram-down order where conditions 'A' and 'B' in Section 901G CA 2006 are met.[880] This is because para. 192 of the Explanatory Notes to CIGA 2020 is drafted in a way that it suggests that, where the conditions have been met, the court will focus on the negative question as to whether a refusal to sanction is appropriate on the grounds that the restructuring plan is not just and equitable.

5.2.4 Representation and Voting

Distressed companies can propose a compromise or arrangement with some but not necessarily all company creditors.[881] Despite this, debtors should refrain from carrying out an 'arbitrary selection' of creditors because they have to obtain not only their approval but also the sanction of the court.[882] Courts will generally abide by the commercial judgement of the debtor's creditors if they have been 'properly consulted', meaning that they were given sufficient time and information to reach an informed decision.[883]

5.2.5 Fairness

As explained by Richards J in *Telewest*,[884] the requirement that a scheme be 'fair' does not mean that the court imposes its own view of what is in the interests of creditors or even what is the 'best' scheme. Fairness in this context means that the scheme must be one that an intelligent and honest man, a member of the class concerned and acting in respect of their interest, might reasonably approve.[885] This stage of the *Buckley* test[886] is closely

877 Virgin Active (sanction), above note 786, at Paras. 265-278.

878 DeepOcean 1 (sanction), above note 776, at Para. 66.

879 Virgin Active (sanction), above note 786, at Para. 214.

880 Ibid., at Para. 217.

881 Virgin Atlantic (sanction), above note 711, at Para. 60.

882 Ibid., at Para. 62.

883 Ibid., at Para. 63.

884 Telewest Communications, above note 853.

885 Re English, Scottish and Australian Charter Bank [1893] 3 Ch 385, p. 409; Pizza Express (sanction), above note 859, at Para. 17.

886 J.B. Lindon, G.B. Parker, H.R. Williams & Lord Wrenbury, *Buckley on the Companies Acts* (13th ed.), London: Butterworth & Co, 1957.

connected with the issue of representation and voting, because if the Court is satisfied that the class was fairly represented and properly consulted, it will be slow to differ from the result at the meeting.[887]

The low turnout of the representatives of one class may also suggest that the vote is not fair and representative. However, where extensive efforts had been made to ensure the creditors had notice of the meetings, and there was no reason to think that those who attended and voted had any interest that was averse to or different from the class as a whole, it is unlikely a court will conclude that the vote was obtained by coercion of the minority.[888]

5.2.6 Concluding Matters

With reference to the existence of any blot or defect in the plan, the use of an artificial structure to engage the court's jurisdiction was not in itself a reason to claim that the plan is compromised.[889] As for international effectiveness, this is an issue that is mainly investigated in the sanction hearing, where a court needs to be satisfied that the plan is likely to achieve its purpose. The recognized test is whether there is a reasonable prospect that the restructuring plan will be recognized in the jurisdictions in which it is necessary for it to be effective.[890]

The test on the international effectiveness of the plan is an important one, and courts take it seriously. In *Smile Telecoms*, Snowden J observed that compliance with the requirements of the Civil Procedure Rules (CPR) as to the provision of expert evidence in court proceedings in England is important in a case raising novel points of international restructuring practice that involved an overseas company and in which some plan participants had expressed dissent. In that case, the Court only sanctioned the Pt 26A plan after having received CPR-compliant reports from the experts.[891]

5.3 General Comments/Observations

From the legislative background to Pt 26A restructuring plans and having regard to the Explanatory Notes to CIGA 2020,[892] courts have a general discretion whether to sanction a restructuring plan under Pt 26A CA 2006. It is also envisaged that the authorities under

887 Virgin Atlantic (sanction), above note 711, at Para. 68.

888 Gategroup (sanction), above note 778.

889 Ibid., at Paras. 14-15, referring in particular to the notion of 'good forum shopping' identified by Newey J in Re Codere [2015] EWHC 3778 (Ch), at Paras. 18-19.

890 ED & F Man (sanction), above note 864, at para. 67.

891 Re Smile Telecoms Holdings Ltd [2022] EWHC 740 (Ch) (sanction), at Paras. 75-76, 100-101.

892 Available here: https://www.legislation.gov.uk/ukpga/2020/12/pdfs/ukpgaen_20200012_en.pdf (last viewed 1 December 2022).

Pt 26 may, where appropriate, assist the courts in deciding how to exercise its discretion under Pt 26A restructuring plans.

In the case of *Virgin Atlantic*, the court sanctioned a plan even though some creditors were excluded from it (and paid in full). This is because they provided services that were essential for the continuation of the company's business or to the implementation of the recapitalization plan. This shows once again that English courts do not feel constrained by a strict observance to the APR.

Courts clarified that Pt 26A plans can be undertaken not simply to ensure that a company continues operating, but also to mitigate the severity of the losses that creditors could face.[893] They generally exercise their powers in a flexible manner, in line with the guidance provided by paragraph 10 of the Practice Statement.[894] However, courts expect any objecting creditor who first raises any issue relating to the threshold conditions at the sanction stage to show good reason why they did not raise the issue earlier at the convening hearing.[895]

Excluding annexes, the approved Pt 26A restructuring plans are brief documents (ca. 20 pages) considering the complex capital structure of many of the companies involved in these procedures. The approved plans generally[896] include the following headings/sections:

1. Scope of the plan/definitions;
2. Creditors and distribution;
3. Role of the plan administrators and authority to execute the plan;
4. Implementation/plan steps;
5. Miscellaneous (new articles of association and shares, execution, registration, interests, currency, submissions of claims and their determination);
6. Compromissory clauses and application of set-offs;
7. Expenses and distribution of dividends.
8. The rights and duties of administrators (if not covered above), experts and board;
9. Stay of proceedings, termination and completion of the plan;
10. Miscellaneous (payments, modification, costs, exercise of discretion, notices);
11. Governing law.

893 DeepOcean 1 (convening), above note 837, at Para. 49.

894 It was noted that this paragraph "is intended to discourage parties who disagree with a scheme or plan from playing a tactical game of keeping their powder dry at the convening stage and only appearing to raise jurisdictional points at the sanction hearing" (Smile Telecoms (sanction), above note 891, at Para. 48).

895 DeepOcean 1 (convening), above note 837, at Para. 30.

896 The only marked departure from this approach is the plan submitted by *DeepOcean 1*, partly by reason of the fact that the debtor was a holding company.

6 OUTLOOK: FOCUS POINTS FOR DOMESTIC PRACTICE

The UK's approach to preventive restructuring mechanisms is not fully aligned with the EU PRD 2019, especially due to the UK government's decision not to introduce any form of absolute or relative priority rule or any special category of PIFORs. Nevertheless, the British restructuring community is largely supportive of the new rules.[897] The case law analysed in this chapter suggests that parties are making proper use of the statutory provisions, and that the judiciary is exercising their powers to ensure this remains the case.[898] At the same time, all that glitters is not gold.

6.1 *Objective and Scope of the Framework*

The uptake number of Pt 26A plans has so far fallen short of the government's expectations of between 50 and 100 cases per year.[899] The low number can be explained by a variety of reasons, including costs, the general fall in restructuring procedures caused by the COVID-19 pandemic and the uncertainties associated with Brexit. Additionally, it might take time for practitioners to leave tried-and-tested measures for the newly enacted Pt 26A plans.

Conflicting guidance on the interpretation of key aspects of the Pt 26A plans may have also contributed to this slow start. For instance, in *DeepOcean*,[900] Trower J held that where the cram-down conditions are met, the plan is likely to be sanctioned unless a court considers it unjust and inequitable. However, in *Virgin Active*, Snowden J cautioned against the use of too much discretion and invited courts to rely on the rationality test for sanctioning a Pt 26 scheme.[901]

6.2 *Eligibility Criteria*

Whilst some commentators argued that the 'financial difficulties' threshold is too low,[902] there is evidence that courts adopt a case-by-case approach to determine whether

897 Linklater above note 792; J. Walker and J. Hollingshead, 'The Future of CVAs for Restructuring Lease Liabilities: Is Part 26A Restructuring Plan the New Tool of Choice?', *Corporate Rescue and Insolvency*, 2021, 14(4), pp. 115-117.

898 Virgin Atlantic (sanction), above note 711, at para. 45.

899 Corporate Governance and Insolvency Bill Impact Assessment, available at: https://publications.parliament.uk/pa/bills/cbill/58-01/0146/SIGNED%20-%20IA%20Insolvency%20and%20Corporate%20Governance%20Enactment%20Stage.pdf (last viewed 1 December 2022), at Para. 6.92.

900 Above note 776, at Para. 48.

901 Above note 779, at Para. 221.

902 I. West, 'Reflections on a Year of Restructuring Plans', *Insolvency Intelligence*, 2021, 34(3), pp. 62-67, p. 63.

sanctioning a plan is in the best interest of the creditors. It is unfortunate that courts seem to be willing to exercise such discretion only at the sanction hearing and mainly upon a petition from crammed-down creditors rather than on their own motion.[903]

6.3 *Players in Restructuring*

Courts have not refrained from using their discretion to refuse sanctioning plans that fell short of the statutory requirements,[904] as in *Hurricane Energy*.[905] Some commentators observed that in Pt 26 schemes and Pt 26A plans, UK courts have moved towards a quasi-inquisitorial approach in which they undertake a holistic review of the inclusion and treatment of creditors, even if no specific objections are raised.[906]

Besides the enhanced judicial supervision in these restructuring procedures, there are still areas where further judicial guidance is awaited. This is particularly around the treatment of crammed-down shareholders and on other innovations introduced pursuant to the EU PRD 2019, such as the ban on the enforceability of *ipso facto* clauses. With reference to the latter, the interim report on CIGA 2020[907] observed that, despite the limited implementation of this provision due to the suspension of insolvency filings during the COVID-19 pandemic, the measure is seen as effective in preventing companies in insolvency procedures from being held hostage by suppliers. The same report observed that previously IPs would negotiate with suppliers when the need arose. The measure makes communication with suppliers a priority matter, and it is likely to result in savings in time and in fees due to a more certain approach to disputes in the area.

6.4 *Preparation and Confirmation of the Plan*

When Pt 26A restructuring plans were first launched, there was much speculation and criticism of the deliberate omission of any form of absolute or relative priority rule from the UK restructuring rescue framework. Clearly, the lack of stringent requirements such as the APR is good news for the experienced British restructuring profession and judiciary, who have been proven to thrive on the flexibility granted in the implementation of Pt 26 schemes. Additionally, the strong links between Pt 26 schemes and Pt 26A plans suggest

903 Hurricane Energy (sanction), above note 714.

904 On the increasing role of the judiciary in Pt 26 schemes and Pt 26A plans, see: J. Watson & T. Smyth, 'All Rise: Increasing Judicial Scrutiny in Recent Restructurings?', *Corporate Rescue and Insolvency*, 2021, 14(5), pp. 160-162.

905 Hurricane Energy (sanction), above note 714.

906 Above note 774.

907 Above note 694, at Para. 4.4.

that parties have reasonable expectations as to how courts will exercise their discretion in given cases.

However, this also results in restructuring procedures treating impaired creditors differently,[908] as evidenced when discussing the treatment of executory contracts in restructuring procedures.[909] The cross-class cram-down power heightens the risks that a selected group of debtors and creditors "may be tempted to use the cram-down feature to write off debts in ways which generate too much unfair value for other stakeholders".[910] This is even if courts have declared – and put into practice[911] – that they will not be reluctant to differ from the vote at class meeting[912] whilst not imposing their views of what is 'fair' or 'just and equitable' in exercising their discretion.[913]

6.5 *Jurisdiction*

The jury is still out on determining whether treating Pt 26A restructuring plans as insolvency procedures may restrict their use and the prospects of successful recognition in other EU Member States. Arguably, the fact that Pt 26A plans fall within the scope of Chapter 15 of the U.S. Bankruptcy Code should promote their use from financially distressed European companies, especially in the current wake of uncertainties surrounding the recognition of Pt 26 schemes.

Despite this, it is evident that the degree of cross-fertilization in the area is still quite marked. See, for instance, the recent reasoning given by Snowden J in *Re Smile Telecoms* in the matter of jurisdiction:

> "Although the concept of COMI under the EU Insolvency Regulation is no longer relevant to the exercise of the English court's winding-up jurisdiction, and COMI was not one of the bases for the exercise of scheme jurisdiction considered in *Re Drax Holdings Ltd* [2004] 1 WLR 1049, there can be little doubt that in the modern era the presence of a company's COMI in England gives a legitimate basis for a finding of sufficient connection for the purposes of entertaining a restructuring plan."[914]

908 Ibid.
909 See above Section 4.8 of this article.
910 Above note 781, p. 9.
911 Hurricane Energy (convening), above note 780.
912 Above note 786, at Para. 214.
913 Ibid., at Para. 221.
914 Smile Telecoms (sanction), above note 891, at Para. 60.

6.6 Concluding Remarks

Moving forwards, despite the recent case of *Houst*, more should be done to encourage the use of Pt 26A plans by MSMEs. The key aspects of Pt 26A plans that need to be reformed to ensure widespread use among MSMEs are: (i) the cost of devising the plan; (ii) the degree of control over the process exercised by courts; and (iii) the longer time to the sanction of the plan compared to other rescue mechanisms.[915]

The sanctioning of the restructuring plan in *Houst* – especially the authorization on the use of cross-class cram-down powers against a powerful dissenting creditor like the HMRC – may encourage other medium and smaller enterprises to use this mechanism. However, practice shows that the use of Pt 26A restructuring plans is limited to those cases where there is the need or strong likelihood to cram down dissenting classes of creditors. In any event, the costs associated with these procedures are still too high for ensuring their widespread use among small and micro enterprises.

Another significant and positive development in the area is the recent announcement by the UK government[916] to implement two additional UNCITRAL model laws, one that facilitates the recognition of insolvency-related judgements,[917] and one that facilitates the management and co-ordination of group insolvencies.[918] This move has been hailed as a much-needed improvement on the current policy framework by most practitioners,[919] especially with reference to group insolvencies.[920] However, the fact that recognition of insolvency-related judgements cannot affect the rights of defendants that did not submit to the foreign jurisdiction and relied on contracts governed by English law (essentially preserving the 'rule in *Gibbs*')[921] may have a chilling effect in promoting co-operation with foreign courts and recognition of their judgements.

915 Linklater above note 792, p. 56.

916 The Insolvency Service, 'Implementation of Two UNCITRAL Model Laws on Insolvency: Consultation' (7 July 2022) https://www.gov.uk/government/consultations/implementation-of-two-uncitral-model-laws-on-insolvency/implementation-of-two-uncitral-model-laws-on-insolvency-consultation (last viewed 1 December 2022).

917 UNCITRAL Model Law on Recognition and Enforcement of Insolvency-Related Judgments (2018) https://uncitral.un.org/sites/uncitral.un.org/files/media-documents/uncitral/en/ml_recognition_gte_e.pdf (last viewed 1 December 2022).

918 UNCITRAL Model Law on Enterprise Group Insolvency with Guide to Enactment (2019) https://uncitral.un.org/sites/uncitral.un.org/files/media-documents/uncitral/en/19-11346_mloegi.pdf (last viewed 1 December 2022).

919 See, among others: Norton Rose Fulbright, UK Government moves to adopt two new UNCITRAL Model Laws on Cross-Border Insolvency (August 2022), available at: https://www.nortonrosefulbright.com/en/knowledge/publications/fd10b6c3/uk-government-moves-to-adopt-new-uncitral-model-laws-on-crossborder-insolvency (last viewed 1 December 2022).

920 K. Stephenson, 'UK Consultation on New UNCITRAL Model Laws: *Gibbs* Survives (for Now)', *International Corporate Rescue*, 2022, 19(5), pp. 243-246.

921 *Antony Gibbs & Sons v. La Société Industrielle et Commerciale des Métaux* (1890) LR 25 QBD 399. The 'rule in *Gibbs*' has formed an integral part of English common law since the 19th century. The rule provides that

7 Conclusion

Construction of new provisions, especially formidable and potentially disruptive ones, requires a careful and balanced approach. So far, the British restructuring profession and judiciary has proven capable of exercising a firm but creative use of these powerful mechanisms, particularly in those procedures such as Pt 26 schemes and Pt 26A plans where the court's supervision is a necessary part of the restructuring process.[922] However, questions have been and are still being raised as to whether the English system can further be improved.[923]

This chapter has shown the degree to which the UK has been influenced and 'fertilized' by the regulatory debate in international fora. It has also shown that the UK has not become a passive recipient of innovations devised elsewhere. The UK is looking to its own unique way to deal with increasingly global challenges, whilst not dismissing the importance of established principles and the common law, including controversial rules such as those in *Gibbs*[924] and *Dicey*.[925]

---

a debt governed by English law cannot be discharged or altered by foreign law (including a foreign insolvency proceeding).

922 Above note 781, p. 30.

923 See the recommendations in Walton & Jacobs' report, above note 701. See also: R. Elford, 'Is the UK Restructuring Regime Fit for Purpose?', *Estates Gazette*, 2022, 2241, pp. 56-57.

924 Gibbs, above note 921.

925 Dicey et al., Conflict of Laws, Sweet & Maxwell: London, 1896. This rule dictates that the enforcement of foreign judgements *in personam* is possible only where the person against whom the foreign judgement has been entered meets certain criteria, including taking part to the foreign procedure or otherwise submitting to that jurisdiction.

9 Conclusion

Gert-Jan Boon, Harold Koster and Reinout Vriesendorp[*]

1 Introduction

Upon the adoption by the Council and the European Parliament of the Preventive Restructuring Directive (2019/1023) (PRD 2019) in June 2019,[926] it was up to the national legislators to ensure its timely transposition[927] into domestic restructuring and insolvency laws.[928] Besides provisions on a debt discharge to over-indebted entrepreneurs (Title III) and measures to improve efficiency of restructuring, insolvency and discharge procedures (Title IV), a key part of the PRD 2019 entails the so-called preventive restructuring frameworks (also PRFs) in Title II. This Title lays down a set of provisions that enable debtors that face financial distress to restructure by amending their capital structure, while continuing their business.

Although the PRD 2019 provides for minimum harmonization, also for the PRFs, the EU legislator has not refrained from setting ambitious objectives. As part of its endeavour to build a European Capital Markets Union (CMU),[929] the PRD 2019 aims to contribute not only to reducing legal uncertainty and the costs of cross-border investments, but also to "enable debtors to restructure effectively at an early stage and to avoid insolvency, thus limiting the unnecessary liquidation of viable enterprises".[930] Has the PRD 2019 succeeded in achieving such objectives? The expectations have been diverse: some expect that it may result only in a very limited degree of harmonization;[931] others expect that reforms in national laws may benefit the economies of specific jurisdictions, in particular those

* We thank the authors of the preceding chapters reporting on the domestic transposition of the PRD 2019, as well as Pien Kets (lecturer at Leiden University) for her assistance with the research for this Chapter. All sources have been checked on 1 August 2023. This chapter is a more extensive version of a paper that was published before: J.M.G.J. Boon, H. Koster, & R.D. Vriesendorp, 'Implementation of the Preventive Restructuring Directive 2019 in Review: A Directive Delivering on Its Promise?', *HERO* 2023/W-002.

926 Directive (EU) 2019/1023 of the European Parliament and of the Council of 20 June 2019 on preventive restructuring frameworks, on discharge of debt and disqualifications, and on measures to increase the efficiency of procedures concerning restructuring, insolvency and discharge of debt, and amending Directive (EU) 2017/1132 (Directive on restructuring and insolvency), O.J. L 172/18.

927 In this Chapter, transposition is used synonymously to implementation.

928 Arts 34 and 35 PRD 2019.

929 Recital 8 PRD 2019.

930 See for instance recitals 2, 7 and 9 PRD 2019.

931 D.C. Ehmke, J.L.L. Gant, J.M.G.J. Boon, L. Langkjaer & E. Ghio, 'The European Union Preventive Restructuring Framework: A Hole in One?', *International Insolvency Review*, 2019, 28(2), Para. 5.

lacking a PRF.[932] This chapter reviews the objectives of the PRD 2019 and focuses on the question as to whether and to what extent the transpositions (already) deliver on the policy objectives. We do so by focussing at one part of the PRD 2019: the provisions on PRFs, as laid down in Title II PRD 2019. We adopt a 'law at the books' approach concerning the PRFs in Austria, Denmark, France, Germany, Greece, the Netherlands and the United Kingdom, even though after Brexit the latter is not part of the EU anymore and, consequently, was not bound to implement the PRD 2019.[933]

The EU legislator has left considerable discretion to the Member States in transposing the PRD 2019. At first glance this seems commendable, as it allows national legislators to accommodate for the extensive difference between domestic laws. For instance, for some Member States, like France, it was commented that transposition would require limited reforms because already a more extensive domestic PRF was in place. However, for other Member States the PRD 2019 would require revision of existing restructuring regimes, or – as was the case with Denmark and the Netherlands – even the introduction of new frameworks.[934] However, the degree of minimum harmonization is also a direct impediment to any real harmonization of PRFs. It leaves much discretion to Member States to design their own, diverse PRFs, limiting the *de facto* convergence.[935]

The rules on PRFs have brought about ample legal and academic debate.[936] In this regard, the PRD 2019 has been referred to positively as "a milestone in the harmonisation movement",[937] but also more critically or negatively, as "a radical and substantive reform",[938] or even "a refuge for failing firms".[939] The PRD 2019 suggests that even in restructuring and insolvency law, as "one of the last vestiges of a nationalistic, codified approach to private law on the European continent",[940] harmonization is not a 'mission impossible'. However,

932 European Bank for Reconstruction and Development, *EBRD Insolvency Assessment on Reorganisation Procedures*, 2022, p. 4, 10; R.P. Freitag, 'General Aspects of the Directive on Restructuring and Insolvency', *Zeitschrift für Vergleichende Rechtswissenschaft*, 2022, 121, pp. 243-244.

933 This Chapter provides a synthesis and analysis of Chapters 2-8.

934 D.C. Ehmke, J.L.L. Gant, J.M.G.J. Boon, L. Langkjaer & E. Ghio, above note 931, Para. 4.1 and 5.

935 Ibid., Para. 5.

936 Consider for instance: H. Eidenmüller, 'Contracting for a European insolvency regime', *European Business Organization Law Review*, 2017/18, p. 273-304; R.J. de Weijs, A. Jonkers & M. Malakotipour, 'The Imminent Distortion of European Insolvency Law: How the European Union Erodes the Basic Fa'ric of Private La' by Allowing 'Relative Priority' (RPR)', *Tijdschrift voor Belgisch Handelsrecht*, 2019/*125*(4), pp. 477-493; D.C. Ehmke, J.L.L. Gant, J.M.G.J. Boon, L. Langkjaer & E. Ghio, above note 931, pp. 208-209.

937 M. Vanmeenen, 'Pre-Insolvency Arrangements: The Belgian Experience', in: R. Parry and P.J. Omar (eds), *Reimaging Rescue*, Nottingham: INSOL Europe 2016, p. 162.

938 D.C. Ehmke, J.L.L. Gant, J.M.G.J. Boon, L. Langkjaer & E. Ghio, above note 931, Para. 1.

939 H. Eidenmüller, 'The Rise and Fall of Regulatory Competition in Corporate Insolvency Law in the European Union', *European Business Organization Law Review*, 2019/20, p. 559.

940 J.H. Dalhuisen, 'Harmonization of Substantive Insolvency Law in the EU', *Maandblad voor Vermogensrecht*, 2021/5, p. 159, who uses this quote to refer to the more recent publication by the European Commission, Proposal for a Directive of the European Parliament and the Council harmonising certain aspects of insolvency law, 7 December 2022, COM(2022) 702 final.

that depends not merely on the adoption of a directive, but even more so on its transposition. This study shows that to date, the results of the transpositions have only partially reached the PRD 2019's objectives. This is important, as a next wave of harmonization is forthcoming with the proposal for a directive harmonizing certain aspects of insolvency law,[941] and lessons may be learned of what the PRD 2019 did and did not deliver to further effective efforts at harmonization.

This chapter is structured as follows. Section 2 sets out the background of the PRD 2019 and discusses the objectives set by the EU legislator. Section 3 analyses the so-called 'logic and limits' of minimum harmonization on any implementation efforts of the PRD 2019. Subsequently, the chapter contains a substantive comparison of seven domestic PRFs, analysing the extent to which there is convergence among these PRFs (Section 4), followed by an analysis showing that the PRD 2019 has only partially delivered on its promises (Section 5) and some final concluding remarks (Section 6).

2 BACKGROUND OF PRD 2019

2.1 *The EU's Efforts for a Shared Business Rescue Culture*

Legislative efforts of some eight years culminated in the PRD 2019. The European Parliament can be seen as the instigator, with its Resolution in November 2011.[942] In this Resolution, the European Parliament called upon the Commission to bring forward legislative proposals that would also touch upon restructuring plans, as corporate rescue had emerged as an alternative to liquidation.[943] The EU legislator has taken several steps towards what became the PRD 2019. Including a In subsequent Communications of the Commission in 2012, in which the Commission stated that EU laws should better "facilitate the survival of businesses and present a second chance for entrepreneurs",[944] and

941 European Commission, Proposal for a Directive of the European Parliament and of the Council harmonising certain aspects of insolvency law, 7 December 2022, COM(2022) 702 final.

942 European Parliament resolution of 15 November 2011 with recommendations to the Commission on insolvency proceedings in the context of EU company law (2011/2006(INI)). The Resolution built on two studies that were commissioned by the European Parliament: European Parliament 'Harmonisation of insolvency law at EU level, note', European Parliament 2010, PE419.633, and European Parliament, 'Harmonisation of insolvency law at EU level with respect to opening of proceedings, claims filing and verification and reorganisation plans, note', 2011, PE 432.766.

943 European Parliament resolution of 15 November 2011 with recommendations to the Commission on insolvency proceedings in the context of EU company law (2011/2006(INI)), recitals I, J and L, and Annex at 1.1 and 1.5.

944 Communication from the Commission to the European Parliament, the Council, the European Economic and Social Committee and the Committee of the Regions, Single Market Act II, Together for new growth, 3 October 2012, COM(2012) 573 final, at 11.

that the EU should take steps to develop a "rescue and recovery culture across the Member States".[945]

Following public consultations and meetings with stakeholders, in 2014 the Commission published its Recommendation on a new approach to business failure and insolvency (Commission Recommendation 2014).[946] It laid down objectives and key topics that would be amalgamated and elaborated along in much more detail in the later PRD 2019, including the adoption of a PRF that enables financially distressed but viable business to restructure at an early stage and give honest bankrupt entrepreneurs a second chance.[947] The next steps were embedded in the Commission's new initiative for a European CMU.[948] In furthering a CMU, the widely differing insolvency regimes in the EU were considered to inhibit cross-border investment and prevent timely restructuring.[949] To this end, the Commission published a proposal (Proposal PRD 2016)[950] that commenced the legislative process that resulted in the PRD 2019. Whereas harmonization of core aspects of insolvency is considered a so-called 'bridge too far',[951] the Commission held that preventive restructuring is an area where harmonization is possible.[952] The Commission

945 Communication from the Commission to the European Parliament, the Council and the European Economic and Social Committee, A new European approach to business failure and insolvency, 12 December 2012, COM(2012) 742 final, Para. 1 and 2.

946 Commission Recommendation on a new approach to business failure and insolvency, 12 March 2014, C(2014) 1500 final.

947 Recital 1 Commission Recommendation 2014. The Recommendation introduced a PRF with the following main features: (a) enable a debtor to restructure at an early stage, (b) a debtor to keep control over the day-to-day operation of its business, (c) enable a debtor to request a stay, (d) provide for confirmation of a restructuring plan adopted by the required majority, (e) facilitate a debtor to acquire new financing which is would not be declared void, voidable or unenforceable as an act detrimental to the general body of creditors, and (f) require limited court involvement (Commission Recommendation 2014, at 6 and 7).

948 Communication from the Commission to the European Parliament, the Council, the European Economic and Social Committee and the Committee of the Regions, Action Plan on Building a Capital Markets Union, 30 September 2015, COM(2015) 468 final, p. 3.

949 Communication from the Commission to the European Parliament, the Council, the European Economic and Social Committee and the Committee of the Regions, Action Plan on Building a Capital Markets Union, 30 September 2015, COM(2015) 468 final, pp. 6, 24-25.

950 Proposal for a Directive of the European Union and the Council on preventive restructuring frameworks, second chance and measures to increase the efficiency of restructuring, insolvency and discharge procedures and amending Directive 2012/30/EU of 22 November 2016, COM(2016) 723 final (Proposal PRD 2016).

951 Explanatory Memorandum to Proposal PRD 2016, p. 6. Notably, in the meantime the Commission has changed its mind this regard and recently published the Proposal for a Directive of the European Parliament and the Council harmonising certain aspects of insolvency law, 7 December 2022, COM(2022) 702 final.

952 European Parliament resolution of 15 November 2011 with recommendations to the Commission on insolvency proceedings in the context of EU company law (2011/2006(INI)), Paras. A, C and D; Explanatory Memorandum to Proposal PRD 2016, p. 6.

observed that only a few Member States lack a form of preventive restructuring, while others have a PRF, but it is not always an effective tool to enable debtors to restructure.[953]

Whereas the PRD 2019 is the first real binding legal instrument in the area of substantive European restructuring and insolvency law, it is the result of a long-running legislative process. By means of minimum harmonization it introduces a framework – or toolbox – for Member States to introduce in its domestic legislation tools important to facilitate preventive restructuring. Therefore, the PRD 2019 functions as an important step for the EU to contribute to a paradigm shift at the European and domestic levels promoting a shift away "... from the sacrosanct 'pay what you owe' to the balanced promotion of the continuity of companies in distress ...",[954] and therewith contributing towards a shared European rescue culture.[955]

2.2 *Objectives of Harmonized Preventive Restructuring Frameworks*

Before we review whether the PRD 2019 is delivering on its promise, it should be made clear what the EU legislator – so to say – has 'promised'. As has been reiterated many times, domestic insolvency regimes are widely differing;[956] this difference also regards restructuring frameworks. As noted in the Commission Recommendation 2014:

953 European Commission, Commission Staff Working Document, Impact Assessment, Accompanying the document Proposal for a Directive of the Parliament and of the Council on preventive restructuring frameworks, second chance and measures to increase the efficiency of restructuring, insolvency and discharge procedures and amending Directive 20212/30/EU, SWD(2016) 357 final (Impact Assessment Proposal PRD 2016), pp. 14-15.

954 B. Wessels, 'On the Future of European Insolvency Law', in: Rebecca Parry (ed), *European Insolvency Law: Prospects for Reform*, Nottingham: INSOL Europe 2014, p. 157.

955 See for instance: J.M.G.J. Boon & S. Madaus, 'Toward a European Business Rescue Culture', in: J.A.A Adriaanse & J.I., van der Rest (eds), *Turnaround Management and Bankruptcy: A Research Companion* (Routledge Advances in Management and Business Studies), Routledge: New York 2017; B. Wessels & S. Madaus, *Instrument of the European Law Institute on Rescue of Business in Insolvency Law*, 2017, p. 6, available at: https://ssrn.com/abstract=3032309; E. Ghio, J.M.G.J. Boon, D.C. Ehmke, J.L. Gant, L. Langkjaer & E. Vaccari, 'Harmonising Insolvency Law in the EU: New Thoughts on Old Ideas in the Wake of the COVID-19 Pandemic', *International Insolvency Review*, 2021, 30(3), pp. 424-435.

956 See for instance: Recital 11 Council Regulation (EC) No 1346/2000 of 29 May 2000 on insolvency proceedings, O.J. L 160; Recital 22 Regulation (EU) 2015/848 of the European Parliament and of the Council of 20 May 2015 on insolvency proceedings (recast), O.J. L 141/19; European Parliament resolution of 15 November 2011 with recommendations to the Commission on insolvency proceedings in the context of EU company law (2011/2006(INI)), recitals A; Communication from the Commission to the European Parliament, the Council and the European Economic and Social Committee, A new European approach to business failure and insolvency, 12 December 2012, COM(2012) 742 final, Para. 5; Communication from the Commission to the European Parliament, the Council, the European Economic and Social Committee and the Committee of the Regions, Action Plan on Building a Capital Markets Union, 30 September 2015, COM(2015) 468 final, Para. 6.1; European Commission, Commission staff working document, Economic analysis, Accompanying the document Communication from the Commission to the European Parliament, the Council, the European Economic and Social Committee and the Committee of the Regions, Action

> [n]ational insolvency rules vary greatly in respect of the range of the procedures available to debtors facing financial difficulties in order to restructure their business. Some Member States have a limited range of procedures meaning that businesses are only able to restructure at a relatively late stage, in the context of formal insolvency proceedings. In other Member States, restructuring is possible at an earlier stage but the procedures available are not as effective as they could be or involve varying degrees of formality, in particular in relation to the use of out-of-court processes.[957]

As an area that had benefited hardly from harmonization before,[958] this is not surprising. At the same time, the Commission repeatedly pointed out that these differences cause problems to the internal market:

> [t]he discrepancies between the national restructuring frameworks, and between the national rules giving honest entrepreneurs a second chance lead to increased costs and uncertainty in assessing the risks of investing in another Member State, fragment conditions for access to credit and result in different recovery rates for creditors. They make the design and adoption of consistent restructuring plans for cross-border groups of companies more difficult. More generally, the discrepancies may serve as disincentives for businesses wishing to establish themselves in different Member States.[959]

Whereas the European Parliament recognized a need for harmonization of restructuring and insolvency law in 2011, the Commission brought it within the scope of the CMU. Here, the disparity between national restructuring and insolvency laws has been regarded as one of the key bottlenecks hampering cross-border investment in the European single market.[960] In this regard, insolvency laws play a key role in addressing financial distress. However, most domestic "frameworks seem unclear, inflexible and costly", according to

Plan on Building a Capital Markets Union, 30 September 2015, SWD(2015) 183 final, pp. 73-74; Proposal PRD 2016, p. 2; Recital 4 PRD 2019.

957 Recital 2 Commission Recommendation 2014.

958 See also B. Wessels, above note 954, pp. 131-158; J.M.G.J. Boon, 'Harmonising European Insolvency Law: The Emerging Role of Stakeholders', *International insolvency Review*, 2018, 27(2), pp. 162-163.

959 Recital 4 Commission Recommendation 2014.

960 Communication from the Commission to the European Parliament, the Council, the European Economic and Social Committee and the Committee of the Regions, Action Plan on Building a Capital Markets Union, 30 September 2015, COM(2015) 468 final, Para. 6; European Commission, Commission staff working document, Economic analysis, Accompanying the document Communication from the Commission to the European Parliament, the Council, the European Economic and Social Committee and the Committee of the Regions, Action Plan on Building a Capital Markets Union, 30 September 2015, SWD(2015) 183 final, pp. 74-77.

the European Parliament.[961] Therefore, harmonization of restructuring law was aimed not only to contribute to creating more legal certainty for cross-border investors but also to encourage that debtors will pursue restructuring timely.[962]

These two key objectives, as stated in the Action Plan for the CMU, were reiterated in the Proposal PRD 2016 and elaborated in the accompanying Impact Assessment.[963] The Proposal PRD 2016 states that:

> [t]he aim is for all Member States to have in place key principles on effective preventive restructuring and second chance frameworks, and measures to make all types of insolvency procedures more efficient by reducing their length and associated costs and improving their quality. More specifically, such frameworks aim to help increase investment and job opportunities in the single market, reduce unnecessary liquidations of viable companies, avoid unnecessary job losses, prevent the build-up of non-performing loans facilitate cross-border restructurings, and reduce costs and increase opportunities for honest entrepreneurs to be given a fresh start.[964]

This is done because "a higher degree of harmonisation in insolvency law is thus essential for a well-functioning single market and for a true Capital Markets Union".[965] However, from a more practical viewpoint, the Proposal PRD 2016 does not have the objective "to interfere with what works well, but to establish a common EU-wide framework to ensure effective restructuring, second chance and efficient procedures both at national and cross-border level".[966]

The final text as adopted in the PRD 2019 finds its legal basis in Article 114 TFEU,[967] which regards private law harmonization of direct and indirect obstacles to the internal market.[968] In this regard, recital 1 PRD 2019 lays down the main objective of the Directive:

---

961 European Commission, Commission staff working document, Economic analysis, Accompanying the document Communication from the Commission to the European Parliament, the Council, the European Economic and Social Committee and the Committee of the Regions, Action Plan on Building a Capital Markets Union, 30 September 2015, SWD(2015) 183 final, p. 73.

962 Communication from the Commission to the European Parliament, the Council, the European Economic and Social Committee and the Committee of the Regions, Action Plan on Building a Capital Markets Union, 30 September 2015, COM(2015) 468 final, Para. 6.

963 Proposal PRD 2016, p. 2; Impact Assessment Proposal PRD 2016, p. 13 et seq.

964 Proposal PRD 2016, pp. 5-6.

965 Ibid., p. 2.

966 Ibid., p. 7.

967 Treaty on the Functioning of the European Union, O.J. C 326/47.

968 See further E. Ghio, J.M.G.J. Boon, D.C. Ehmke, J.L.L. Gant, L. Langkjaer & E. Vaccari, above note 955, pp. 431, 435-436.

> [t]he objective of this Directive is to contribute to the proper functioning of the internal market and remove obstacles to the exercise of fundamental freedoms, such as the free movement of capital and freedom of establishment, which result from differences between national laws and procedures concerning preventive restructuring, insolvency, discharge of debt, and disqualifications.[969]

In order to reach this objective, the PRD 2019 provides for minimum harmonization of PRFs, in addition to separate rules on the debt discharge for honest and insolvent or over-indebted entrepreneurs.[970] Especially with regard to PRFs, it is stated that they should "enable debtors to restructure effectively at an early stage and to avoid insolvency, thus limiting the unnecessary liquidation of viable enterprises".[971] In addition, the PRFs should also serve other objectives, such as (i) preventing job losses, (ii) preventing the loss of know-how and skills, (iii) maximizing the total value not only to creditors but also to the owners and the economy as a whole, (iv) maintaining business activity and (v) preventing the build-up of non-performing loans.[972]

In concluding, the above puts forward two overall key objectives of the PRD 2019 with respect to PRFs. Firstly, that is to create more legal certainty for cross-border investment, by reducing the divergences between Member States. Secondly, it aims to enable debtors to restructure at an early stage, in order to avoid increasing losses and consequently, prevent unnecessary insolvency proceedings. This brings us to the next question: what can we expect of the PRD 2019?

3 What Can Be Expected from Implementing the PRD 2019?

3.1 *Introduction*

When discussing harmonization, we must first note that harmonization as a concept is remarkably vague. As pointed out by Tadic: "[t]he open nature of the term harmonisation and the resultant indeterminacy enables people to say something without really saying anything".[973] There are in fact various descriptions of what harmonization (and related

969 Recital 1 PRD 2019.

970 Recitals 1 and 8 PRD 2019.

971 Recitals 2 and 15 PRD 2019.

972 Recitals 2, 3 and 16 and Art. 4(1) PRD 2019; Impact Assessment Proposal PRD 2016, p. 13 et seq; R.D. Vriesendorp, 'How to Measure the Success of National Implementations of the Restructuring Directive?' in: E. Vaccari & E. Ghio (eds), *Insolvency Law in Times of Crisis*, Nottingham: INSOL Europe, 2023, pp. 96-97.

973 F. Tadic, 'How Harmonious Can Harmonisation Be? A Theoretical Approach Towards Harmonisation of (Criminal) Law', in: A. Klip & H. van der Wilt (eds), *Harmonisation and Harmonising Measures in Criminal*

concepts) mean. In line with Ghio, we consider harmonization within the EU as an act making laws more similar across the Member States so that the national legal frameworks can work better together.[974] Before assessing the harmonization that is achieved by the PRD 2019, it is important to consider what generally can be expected by its transposition. In this section, we review factors which may impact the harmonization that can be achieved by Member States, by looking at three meta dimensions of harmonization processes. We (i) review the limitations imposed by the EU's 'harmonisation strategy' which has opted for minimum harmonization, (ii) elaborate on the perils of harmonization by means of a directive and (iii) look back on prior experience from harmonization efforts in the field of restructuring and insolvency law.

3.2 *The Implications of Minimum Harmonization of Preventive Restructuring Frameworks*

According to the Treaty on the Functioning of the European Union (TFEU), harmonization aims at "establishing or ensuring the functioning of the internal market".[975] This shapes the legislative action of the EU in the internal market, also for preventive restructuring. To pursue this aim, in recent years the EU legislator has shifted to an approach of 'differentiated integration'.[976] Under this approach towards European integration, more discretion is left to Member States in implementing legislation. As a consequence, the extent to which an integral market can be effectively realized is of course limited, because Member States have more discretion to shape legislation when transposing EU law. This seems to have impacted the PRD 2019 too.[977]

In preparing the Proposal PRD 2016, the Commission considered different approaches to come to more harmonization. In addition to maintaining the status quo, it considered to (i) set up a fully harmonized PRF; (ii) introduce an alternative, optional EU restructuring regime for cross-border cases; and (iii) set up a minimum harmonized legal framework in the area of restructuring.[978] The Commission chose the latter option.[979] While noting that restructuring and insolvency law is regulated nearly exclusively at the national level and

Law, Amsterdam: Koninklijke Nederlandse Akademie van Wetenschappen, 2002, p. 21.

974 Adaptation after the definition proposed by E. Ghio, *Redefining Harmonisation: Lessons From EU Insolvency Law*, Cheltenham: Edward Elgar, 2022, p. 141.

975 Art. 26(1) TFEU.

976 European Parliament, Committee on Constitutional Affairs, Report on Differentiated Integration (2018/2093(INI)), 27 November 2018, A8-0402/2018. See further: E. Ghio, above note 974, Paras. 7.3.1-7.3.4.

977 See further E. Ghio, J.M.G.J Boon, D.C. Ehmke, J.L.L. Gant, L. Langkjaer & E. Vaccari, above note 955, pp. 430-431.

978 Impact Assessment Proposal PRD 2016, pp. 48-51.

979 See Impact Assessment Proposal PRD 2016, pp. 51-55; Recitals 12, 13 and 16 PRD 2019.

that it is strongly embedded in other areas of law, the Commission considered in its Proposal PRD 2016 that "[m]inimum standards are therefore the most appropriate means to ensure a coherent framework in all Member States while also enabling Member States to go beyond the Directive's provisions."[980] This has been reflected in the PRD 2019 itself, stating that:

> [t]here is therefore a need to go beyond matters of judicial cooperation and to establish substantive minimum standards for preventive restructuring procedures as well as for procedures leading to a discharge of debt for entrepreneurs.[981]

Whereas full harmonization would be able to address the legal uncertainty caused by fragmented restructuring and insolvency laws, it would result in an overly complex legislative endeavour for three reasons. Firstly, such harmonization would have to give full consideration to the domestic insolvency regimes. Secondly, it would have to consider various connected areas of domestic law. Thirdly, it may not be in conformity with the principles of subsidiarity and proportionality. Instead, allowing for some flexibility would enable Member States to better integrate the reform into national law, although not resolving all legal uncertainty.[982] Still, the Commission considered that this would:

> ensure major progress towards the functioning of the internal market. Under such a convergent framework, cross-border investment would no longer be inhibited by concerns that, for example, preventive restructuring of the debtor is not effectively possible in all Member States or that shareholders may bloc a plan which is supported by creditors.[983]

Various scholars have criticized that, despite the EU legislator's ambition at harmonization, the PRD 2019 has become a directive that provides for minimum harmonization at most.[984] Eïdenmüller commented that a:

980 Proposal PRD 2016, p. 16.

981 Recital 12 PRD 2019.

982 Impact Assessment Proposal PRD 2016, p. 51.

983 Ibid., p. 51.

984 See for instance R.P. Freitag, above note 932, p. 229; D.C. Ehmke, J.L.L. Gant, J.M.G.J. Boon, L. Langkjaer & E. Ghio, above note 931, Para. 4.1 and 5; H. Eidenmüller, above note 939, Para. 6; J.L.L. Gant, J.M.G.J. Boon, D.C. Ehmke, E. Ghio, L. Langkjaer, E. Vaccari & P.J. Omar, 'The EU preventive restructuring framework: in extra time?', *Fizetésképtelenségi Jog (Insolvency Law)*, 2022, Para. 1, available at: https://jogaszvilag.hu/szakma/the-eu-preventive-restructuring-framework-in-extra-time.

> 'political price' the European law-maker had to pay for getting the [PRD 2019] adopted is a serious compromise to the harmonisation goal that was driving the project from the beginning. The Directive contains more than 70 regulatory options for the Member States.[985]

Furthermore, Ehmke et al. remarked that:

> [t]he Directive leaves so much open to the Member States that the effects of the directive's implementation are difficult to foresee. Minimum harmonization requirements may not lead to the convergence envisaged by the [Commission Recommendation 2014] or the early discussions on the purpose of the Directive and its eventual form as a Preventive Restructuring Directive. The wording in the Directive tends to take an almost optional approach, using the word 'may' instead of something more prescriptive that would present a more obligatory implementation parameter. The impression left by the wording in the Articles is vague and even voluntary.[986]

A thorough analysis of the many policy options offered by the PRD 2019 was made by the IMF, noting that the PRD 2019's "harmonization effect will be limited given multiple options for implementation, likely leading to divergent restructuring models in Europe".[987] In fact, the IMF sees not just upsides to minimum harmonization but points at the downsides. This approach to harmonization may result in substantial differences on how preventive restructuring regimes treat debtors and creditors. At the same time, it is stated that:

> [s]ome countries may compete with each other in implementing the most effective restructuring framework, but this 'race to the top' may also produce some dysfunctional effects, and in some cases, there may even be a 'race to the bottom'.[988]

It is best to consider the PRD 2019 as a toolbox, with Articles 4-19 PRD 2019 stating the tools that any PRF should have. In this regard it is important to emphasize that PRFs are not to be seen as 'proceedings' or 'procedures'. Article 4(5) PRD 2019 clarifies that a PRF can "consist of one or more procedures, measures or provisions". In fact, they can be both

985 H. Eidenmüller, above note 939, Para. 6.

986 D.C. Ehmke, J.L.L. Gant, J.M.G.J. Boon, L. Langkjaer & E. Ghio, above note 931, p. 208

987 J. Garrido, C. DeLong, A. Rasekh & A. Rosha, Restructuring and Insolvency in Europe: Policy Options in the Implementation of the EU Directive, IMF Working Paper, 2021/152, p. 3 and 5.

988 Ibid., p. 5.

in- or out-of-court, reiterating that the PRF of Title II PRD 2019 can be best regarded as a toolbox allowing for different tools.[989] Although many policy options are available within this toolbox, there is limited guidance for Member States in implementing the PRD 2019. Instead, some guidance in reviewing the many options in the PRD 2019 comes from other institutions and experts.[990]

Lastly, the room for harmonization is limited by the personal and substantive scope of the PRD 2019 itself. In particular for PRFs, the personal scope regards debtors, but excludes financial institutions.[991] In line with its objective, the material scope of the PRD 2019 focuses on those debtors that are businesses which are in financial difficulties.[992] More specifically, with respect to PRFs, the PRD 2019 is restricted to those debtors that are not yet insolvent (pre-insolvency).[993] As regards the substantive scope of the PRD 2019, various other topics that were considered for harmonization (conditions for filing for insolvency (definition of insolvency), ranking of claims, the wider issue of avoidance actions, the length of formal insolvency proceedings, directors' responsibilities relating to insolvency)[994] that would contribute to reducing the legal uncertainty for investors have been left out of this first initiative for substantive harmonization. Instead, the PRD 2019 has been restricted in scope and aims to contribute to the EU legislator's objectives with the CMU in a specific area only.

989 Compare also: R.P. Freitag, above note 932, p. 229.

990 Guides have been prepared informing Member States of the policy options, see Guidance Notes of INSOL Europe, Touching Upon Several Aspects of the PRD 2019, available at: www.insol-europe.org/publications/guidance-notes; S. Madaus, A Simple Guide to the Relative Priority Rule, 2020, available at: https://stephanmadaus.de/2020/01/20/a-simple-guide-to-the-relative-priority-rule/; J. Garrido, C. DeLong, A. Rasekh & A. Rosha, above note 987.

991 Art. 1(1)(a) and 1(2) PRD 2019.

992 Art. 1(1)(a) PRD 2019.

993 Recital 24 and Arts 1(1)(a) and 4(1) PRD 2019; Impact Assessment Proposal PRD 2016, pp. 14, 58, 59, 131. See also European Commission, Commission Staff Working Document, Impact Assessment, Accompanying the document Proposal for a Directive of the Parliament and of the Council harmonising certain aspects of insolvency law, 7 December 2022, SWD(2022) 395 final, pp. 8 and 13-14.

994 Impact Assessment Proposal PRD 2016, pp. 23-25. Compare also European Parliament resolution of 15 November 2011 with recommendations to the Commission on insolvency proceedings in the context of EU company law (2011/2006(INI)) where most of these topics were raised for a legislative proposal by the Commission. Notably, several of the topics for harmonization have now become part a recent legislative proposal (European Commission, Proposal for a Directive of the European Parliament and the Council harmonising certain aspects of insolvency law, 7 December 2022, COM(2022) 702 final).

3.3 The Limits of Directives and Top-Down Harmonization

After the Commission Recommendation 2014 had not delivered sufficient results,[995] the Commission followed up with the Proposal PRD 2016, a directive. Within the legislative tools of the EU legislator, a directive is stronger than a recommendation because it is a legal instrument which binds Member States to the result that is to be achieved. Directives require domestic implementation in the Member States to whom it is left to decide about the form and the methods to be used.[996] Directives leave a margin to manoeuvre for Member States.[997] Depending on the respective minimum or maximum harmonization of the directive, it should at least increase the degree of harmonization in the Union.[998] The discretion in implementing directives is not unlimited. Also for directives like the PRD 2019 that bring minimum harmonization, a Member State is:

> obliged to adopt, within the framework of its national legal system, all the measures necessary to ensure that the directive is fully effective, in accordance with the objective that it pursues.[999]

In this regard, Member States are bound to a transposition which is "sufficiently precise and clear to enable the individuals concerned to know the extent of their rights and obligations".[1000]

Whereas the PRD 2019 is a directive providing for minimum harmonization, the EU legislator's narrative on the PRD 2019 and objectives shows an approach that is focussed primarily on achieving top-down harmonization. The need for EU legislation on PRFs is presented as the sole driver for achieving its policy objectives.[1001] However, harmonization is not necessarily or solely a process that results from top-down legislative action of the EU

995 Directorate-General Justice & Consumers of the European Commission, 'Evaluation of the implementation of the Commission Recommendation of 12.3.2014 on a new approach to business failure and insolvency', 30 September 2015, pp. 2 and 5. The same conclusion was repeated in the Communication from the Commission to the European Parliament, the Council, the European Economic and Social Committee and the Committee of the Regions, Action Plan on Building a Capital Markets Union, 30 September 2015, COM(2015) 468 final, p. 25.

996 Art. 288 TFEU.

997 See also CJEU 16 June 2005, C—456/03, ECLI:EU:C:2005:388, at 50-51 (*Commission v. Italy*); CJEU 5 July 2007, C-321/05, ECLI:EU:C:2007:408 (*Kofoed*), at 43. Compare EUR-Lex, EU Legal Instruments, available at: https://eur-lex.europa.eu/EN/legal-content/glossary/eu-legal-instruments.html.

998 Compare recital 8 PRD 2019.

999 CJEU 5 July 2007, C-321/05, ECLI:EU:C:2007:408 (*Kofoed*), at 41. See also: ECJ 17 June 1999, C-336-97, ECLI:EU:C:1999:314, at 19 (*European Commission/Italy*); CJEU 30 November 2006, C-32/05, ECLI:EU:C:2006:749, at (*European Commission/Luxemburg*); CJEU 8 May 2008, C-491/06, ECLI:EU:C:2008:263, at 28 (*Danske Svineproducenter*).

1000 CJEU 16 June 2005, C 456/03, ECLI:EU:C:2005:388, at 51 (*Commission v. Italy*).

1001 Impact Assessment Proposal PRD 2016, p. 47 et seq.

legislator. Instead, it may also result from bottom-up reforms driven by Member States, for instance due to regulatory competition. Furthermore, as argued by Ghio et al., harmonization may even rely on both strategies, simultaneously and/or subsequently.[1002] As such, focussing on the transposition of the PRD 2019 itself is important, but presents a partial view of what harmonization is as it neglects that it is the result of a multi-layered process.

Previous information indicates that Member States have considerable discretion in implementing the PRD 2019 in their domestic legal frameworks. It leaves much leeway for diverse approaches among jurisdictions. Whereas this study focuses on the transposition of the PRD 2019 in domestic laws, the focus on top-down harmonization alone may not suffice to achieve the PRD 2019's objectives, in particular due to the minimum harmonization provided by the PRD 2019 itself.

3.4 *Prior Experiences in Harmonizing Restructuring and Insolvency Laws*

A third reason why expectations of harmonization should not be overly optimistic relates to the prior reluctance of Member States towards harmonization of restructuring and insolvency laws. This was demonstrated in the process leading to the European Insolvency Regulation 1346/2000 (EIR 2000)[1003] and the PRD 2019. The EIR 2000 had to overcome several political hurdles before it was adopted, involving prior legislative initiatives including the Convention on Certain international Aspects of Bankruptcy (1990)[1004] and the Convention on Insolvency Proceedings (1995) that did not succeed.[1005] Although these initiatives regarded cross-border insolvency law and occurred in a different time frame, it took several decades to develop.

There was seemingly limited appetite for pursuing harmonization of PRFs from Member States.[1006] In 2013, the Commission already envisaged a directive; however, this was later converted into a non-binding recommendation with a more limited scope. In addition, it regarded only in part the topics that were pointed out by the European

1002 E. Ghio, J.M.G.J Boon, D.C. Ehmke, J.L.L. Gant, L. Langkjaer & E. Vaccari, above note 955, pp. 429, 444 and 450.

1003 Council Regulation (EC) No 1346/2000 of 29 May 2000 on insolvency proceedings, O.J. L 160.

1004 Council of Europe, Convention on Certain International Aspects of Bankruptcy, 1990 (Istanbul Convention), available at: https://rm.coe.int/168007b3d0. See further B. Wessels & J.M.G.J Boon, *Cross-Border Insolvency, International Instruments and Commentary*, Alphen aan den Rijn: Kluwer Law International, 2015, at p. 39.

1005 Council of the European Union, Convention on Insolvency Proceedings, 1995, available at: http://aei.pitt.edu/2840/. See further B. Wessels & J.M.G.J Boon, above note 1004, at p. 34.

1006 This was clear in particular from the responses of Member States to the public consultations, see further J.M.G.J Boon, above note 958, pp. 169-172.

Parliament in 2011.[1007] The evaluation of the Commission Recommendation 2014 showed disappointment, as it had "not succeeded in having the desired impact in facilitating the rescue of businesses in financial difficulty".[1008] Or as observed in the 2015 'Leeds study', a study commissioned by the European Commission, it "appears to be the incomplete and inconsistent implementation of the Recommendation".[1009]

The Proposal PRD 2016 was adopted by the European Parliament and the Council at its first reading, even though Member States were initially reluctant with the proposed harmonization and preferred a principle-based approach.[1010] It raises the question of:

> whether the [PRD 2019] has introduced provisions of an obligatory enough nature to go beyond what was set out in the original [Commission Recommendation 2014], which did not see a major change among the Member State[s]. If the [Commission Recommendation 2014] failed to encourage reform, will a watered-down Preventive Restructuring Directive allowing massive margins of appreciation in its implementation result in member state implementation that actually bridges the gap between procedures, fomenting European harmonisation in member state approaches to preventive restructuring?[1011]

4 IMPLEMENTATIONS OF THE PRD 2019: AN OVERVIEW

4.1 *Introduction*

To date, a majority of Member States have completed the implementation of the PRD 2019. In the prior seven successive chapters, the domestic PRFs of Austria, Denmark, France, Germany, Greece, the Netherlands and the United Kingdom (UK) have been examined. Apart from the first six countries, after Brexit, the UK was no longer under an obligation to implement the PRD 2019. However, their legislative reforms in this area closely resemble features of the PRFs under the PRD 2019. Furthermore, the UK still has

1007 European Parliament resolution of 15 November 2011 with recommendations to the Commission on insolvency proceedings in the context of EU company law (2011/2006(INI)).

1008 Directorate-General Justice & Consumers of the European Commission, 'Evaluation of the implementation of the Commission Recommendation of 12.3.2014 on a new approach to business failure and insolvency', 30 September 2015, p. 5.

1009 G. McCormack, A. Keay, S. Brown & J. Dalgreen, *Study on a New Approach to Business Failure and Insolvency, Comparative Legal Analysis of the Member States' Relevant Provisions and Practices* (Tender No. JUST/2014/JCOO/PR/CIVI/0075), 2016, p. 18.

1010 J.M.G.J Boon, above note 958, pp. 171-172.

1011 D.C. Ehmke, J.L.L. Gant, J.M.G.J. Boon, L. Langkjaer & E. Ghio, above note 931, p. 209

a prominent role in the European restructuring and insolvency sector. Consequently, it has been included in this analysis of how the PRD 2019 has influenced domestic European restructuring laws.[1012]

Per jurisdiction, the prior chapters analysed in detail the most important parts of the PRD 2019's PRFs. Here, we present a comparative study focussing on a selected number of these topics: the domestic approach to implementation (Section 4.2), the criteria or test to access PRFs (Section 4.3), the actors involved in PRFs (Section 4.4), the stay of individual enforcement actions (Section 4.5), the adoption and confirmation of restructuring plans (Section 4.6), and the jurisdiction for and recognition of court decisions relating to PRFs (Section 4.7).

4.2 Domestic Approach towards Implementation

Jurisdictions are free to choose the form and method to implement directives.[1013] Furthermore, the PRD 2019 also allows Member States to design PRFs to consist of a single or multiple "procedures, measures or provisions".[1014] Adopting such measures may, but does not have to, impinge on other solutions available in the domestic restructuring regimes to avoid insolvency.[1015] This grants considerable discretion to national legislators in (re)shaping their PRFs (Table 1).

Table 1 Approach to implementing preventive restructuring framework (PRF) in the respective Member States.

Jurisdiction and PRFs	Form of Implementation
Austria	Introduction of new PRFs with the adoption of the *Restrukturierungsordnung (ReO)*, introducing the regular (private), European (public) and simplified (private) *Restrukturierungsverfahren*
Denmark (*Preventive restructuring procedure*)	Introduction of a new PRF in a new chapter of the Danish Bankruptcy Act, introducing the preventive restructuring procedure (*forebyggende rekonstruktion*)

1012 Where references are made to implementation, for the UK this must be read as drawing inspiration from the PRD 2019, without being formally required to do so.

1013 See above Section 3.3.

1014 Art. 4(5) PRD 2019, see also above Section 3.2.

1015 Art. 4(1) PRD 2019.

Jurisdiction and PRFs	Form of Implementation
France (*Ad hoc mandate, conciliation, safeguard, accelerated safeguard*)	The implementing act introduced amendments to three already existing procedures: the safeguard (*sauvegarde*), the accelerated safeguard (*sauvegarde accélérée*) and the judicial reorganization (*redressement judiciaire*)
Germany (*Restrukturierungssache*)	Introduction of new PRFs with the adoption of the *Unternehmensstabilisierungs-und-restrukturierungsgesetz* (StaRUG), introducing the private and public *Restrukturierungssache*
Greece (*Διαδικασία Εξυγίανσης* (*Pre-insolvency rehabilitation*))	Introduction of a revised PRF with the adoption of the Debt Settlement and Facilitation of a Second Chance (resulting in a new Greek Insolvency Law), including a chapter that modifies the provisions on the pre-insolvency rehabilitation procedure
The Netherlands (*WHOA*)	Introduction of new PRFs with the adoption of the *Wet Homologatie Onderhands Akkoord* (WHOA), introducing a public (disclosed) and a non-public (undisclosed) *onderhands akkoord* (also referred to as a 'WHOA')
United Kingdom (*Pt 26A restructuring plan, Pt A1 moratorium*)	Introduction of a new PRF with the adoption of the Corporate Insolvency and Governance Act (CIGA) 2020, introducing the Restructuring Plan (Pt 26A Companies Act 2006), and Moratorium (Pt A1 Insolvency Act 1986)

The forms of implementing the PRD 2019 in the various Member States show some divergences. Except for France and Greece, all jurisdictions in this study introduced new PRFs, adding it to their current restructuring and insolvency regime(s). In the Netherlands, there was some discussion on possibly amending the existing suspension of payments, even while the Dutch WHOA was being drafted.[1016] However, ultimately it was decided to consider the Dutch WHOA as the partial implementation of the PRD 2019.[1017] For Greece, implementation of the PRD 2019 was part of a general overhaul of its insolvency laws,[1018] whereas for the other jurisdictions the reform focussed (primarily) on implementation of the PRD 2019 as such. The UK introduced a new PRF with two stand-alone measures, incorporated in the Companies Act 2006 and the Insolvency Act 1986. France too adopted features from the PRD 2019 in multiple processes, amending in particular the already existing safeguard and accelerated safeguard.

1016 *Kamerstukken II* 2017/18, 33 695, nr. 17, p. 4; *Kamerstukken II* 2018/19, 35 249, nr. 3, p. 4; *Kamerstukken II* 2018/19, 33 695, nr. 18, p. 3. See on this matter also S. Schreurs, 'Implementatie van de Herstructureringsrichtlijn: wellicht beter in de surseance dan in de WHOA?', *Tijdschrift voor Insolventierecht*, 2019/33, Para. 1 and 4.

1017 Chapter 7, Section 3.2.

1018 See also D. Skauradszun & G. Tsignopoulou, 'The Transposition of the Directive on Preventive Restructuring Frameworks Into Greek Law', *Nottingham Insolvency and Business Law E-Journal*, 2022, 10(1), Para. IV.

At the same time, most jurisdictions have maintained their existing restructuring and insolvency regime. This is explicitly permitted under the PRD 2019, stating that:

> [t]his Directive should allow Member States flexibility to apply common principles while respecting national legal systems. Member States should be able to maintain or introduce in their national legal systems preventive restructuring frameworks other than those provided for by this Directive.[1019]

In sum, the implementation of the PRD 2019 has mostly broadened the pre-existing regimes by extending the scope of restructuring tools available to debtors in financial distress.

4.3 *Criteria and Tests to Access Preventive Restructuring Frameworks*

Under the PRD 2019, PRFs should enable debtors "to restructure, with a view to preventing insolvency and ensuring their viability".[1020] To avoid the risk of preventive restructuring being misused to clear debts, the PRD 2019 requires that:

> the financial difficulties of the debtor should indicate a likelihood of insolvency and the restructuring plan should be capable of preventing the insolvency of the debtor and ensuring the viability of the business.[1021]

A PRF should furthermore be available to debtors at their request, but may also be available at the request of creditors and employees' representatives.[1022] This presented national legislators with various policy options in shaping the entry to the PRFs (Table 2).

1019 Recital 16 PRD 2019.
1020 Art. 4(1) PRD 2019. Compare also Art. 1(1)(a) PRD 2019.
1021 Recital 24 PRD 2019.
1022 Art. 4(1) and (8) PRD 2019.

Table 2 Commencement of preventive restructurings.

Jurisdiction and PRFs	Commenced by/at the Request of	Criteria to Enter Preventive Restructuring Framework
Austria[1023] (*Restrukturierungs-verfahren*)	Debtor	Likelihood of insolvency (warscheinliche Insolvenz) is present when the debtor's viability would be threatened without restructuring, in particular in case of imminent illiquidity. Under certain financial conditions, likelihood of insolvency is presumed. The court can deny an application for Restrukturierungsverfahren only when there is obviously no likelihood of insolvency. There is no explicit viability test. However, a debtor may not be illiquid at the time when the application for Restrukturierungsverfahren is made.
Denmark[1024] (*Preventive restructuring procedure*)	Debtor	Likelihood of insolvency is undefined and will be assumed if not disputed. There is no viability test to enter the preventive restructuring procedure.
France[1025] (*Ad hoc mandate, conciliation, safeguard, accelerated safeguard*)	Debtor	In ad hoc mandate, a debtor must face legal, economic or financial difficulties while not being insolvent yet. Conciliation is available to debtors facing legal, economic or financial difficulties, while not being insolvent for more than 45 days. The safeguard is available to debtors that are unable to pay debts that have become due (in *cessation des paiements*) or merely face difficulties that cannot be overcome, but which may later result in an inability to pay debts as they fall due (likelihood of insolvency). The accelerated safeguard is available to debtors who are not insolvent or insolvent not for more than 45 days before requesting the preceding conciliation procedure for negotiating a restructuring plan. Except for the accelerated safeguard, there is no viability test applicable for entering these procedures. In the accelerated safeguard, the debtor must show that the proposed restructuring plan will receive support from the involved creditors.

1023 Chapter 2, Section 4.2.

1024 Chapter 3, Section 4.2.

1025 Chapter 4, Section 3.1.

Jurisdiction and PRFs	Commenced by/at the Request of	Criteria to Enter Preventive Restructuring Framework
Germany[1026] (*Restrukturierungs-sache*)	Debtor	Likelihood of insolvency is transposed as imminent or prospective insolvency (drohende Zahlungsunfähigkeit). This is the case when it is more likely than not that the debtor will not be able to cover all debts once they fall due with the available liquidity within a forecast-period of 24 months. The StaRUG does not allow debtors to access the private or public *Restrukturierungssache* if they are already unable to pay their debts as they fall due or over-indebted[1027] (but they may continue the procedure if such inability to pay debts due/over-indebtedness occurs during the procedure provided continuation is in the best interest of creditors). There is no viability test to in the StaRUG to initiate the procedure.
Greece[1028] (*Διαδικασία Εξυγίανσης* (*Pre-insolvency rehabilitation*))	Debtor or individual creditors	Pre-insolvency rehabilitation is available to debtors (excluding consumers) meeting one of the statutory criteria, which range from a likelihood of insolvency to a general and permanent inability to pay debts as they fall due.
The Netherlands[1029] (*WHOA*)	Debtor, individual creditors, individual shareholders, the Works Council, and the Employee Representative Body	Debtors can enter a WHOA process when they are in a situation in which it can reasonably be assumed that they will be unable to continue paying their debts. There is not an explicit viability test to enter a WHOA.

1026 Chapter 5, Section 4.2.

1027 A debtor is considered to be over-indebted if (i) liabilities exceed asset value and (ii) the debtor is more likely than not to be unable to pay its debts within a forecast period of 12 months (shortened to 4 months until 31 December 2023).

1028 Chapter 6, Section 4.2.2.

1029 Chapter 7, Section 4.2.

Jurisdiction and PRFs	Commenced by/at the Request of	Criteria to Enter Preventive Restructuring Framework
United Kingdom (*Pt 26A restructuring plan, Pt A1 moratorium*)	Pt 26A restructuring plan Company and its directors, individual creditors,[1030] individual members of the company, and the liquidator (when the company is being wound up) and administrator (in administration).[1031] Pt A1 moratorium Company directors[1032]	In Pt 26A restructuring plans likelihood of insolvency requires that they "are only available to companies that are encountering or are likely to encounter financial difficulties that either are affecting, will affect, or may affect their ability to carry on business as a going concern".[1033] There is not a full viability test, still it is required that the petitioner shows the restructuring plan's compromise or arrangement is aimed at "eliminate, reduce or prevent, or mitigate the effect of, any of the financial difficulties".[1034] In a Pt A1 moratorium, a stand-alone stay is available when the directors believe that a company is or is likely to become unable to pay its debts.[1035]

Lacking a definition of what 'likelihood of insolvency' entails in the PRD 2019,[1036] the various jurisdictions have taken different approaches. Some have clearly described time frames within which such a likelihood should be present (like Germany and France), others leave it more open for case-by-case assessment (the Netherlands), whereas again others do not give any indications (Denmark) or take a fluid approach by opening the frameworks not exclusively to debtors that are facing a likelihood of insolvency (Greece and the UK). Although the PRD 2019 gives much flexibility to the Member States to define likelihood of insolvency, it is unclear whether certain approaches fall within the envisaged scope of the PRD 2019, in particular when they include debtors that face formal insolvency. Then again, leaving the desirability of such varied approaches aside, the minimum harmonization of the PRD 2019 does not explicitly preclude Member States from introducing a broader application of its PRFs.[1037]

To achieve more uniformity of the entry test, when debtors can access PRFs, the EU legislator should take action. In the PRD 2019 it has intentionally been left to Member States themselves to define what 'insolvency' as well as 'likelihood of insolvency' are.[1038] As

1030 Although in practice it is difficult for a creditor to do so without the involvement of the company.

1031 Chapter 8, Section 4.5.1.

1032 Chapter 8, Section 4.4.1.

1033 Chapter 8, Section 4.2.1; Section 901A(2) Companies Act 2006.

1034 Chapter 8, Section 4.2.2; Section 901A(3) Companies Act 2006.

1035 Chapter 8, Section 4.4.1.

1036 The EU legislator left the meaning of this concept, explicitly to the discretion of Member States, see Art. 2(2)(b) PRD 2019.

1037 This may be inferred from the lack of provisions regarding non-applicability to insolvent debtors, and at various points furthering general flexibility with implementing the PRD 2019 is reiterated, including in Recitals 13 and 16, and Arts 2(2)(a) and (b), 4(3) and (5) PRD 2019.

1038 Art. 2(2)(a) and (b) PRD 2019.

the above discussion shows, the results are divergent and possibly at odds with the objective of the PRD 2019 itself: creating more legal certainty for cross-border investment, by reducing the divergences between Member States and enabling debtors to restructure at an early stage, in order to avoid increasing losses and consequently, preventing unnecessary insolvency proceedings.

In its recent Proposal to harmonize certain aspects of insolvency law, the European Commission provides further guidance on the intended scope of PRFs under the PRD 2019. The Commission emphasizes that the scope of preventive restructuring processes – as provided for by the PRD 2019 – is confined to 'pre-insolvency'; this is to be distinguished from actual insolvency as well as post-insolvency.[1039] However, once again driven by opposition from Member States, the Commission stays away from proposing any form of definition of these concepts in the Proposal itself.[1040]

4.4 *Actors Involved in Preventive Restructuring Frameworks*

Article 5(1) PRD 2019 makes a clear choice regarding the governance of PRFs with the debtor remaining fully or at least partially in possession over its assets and day-to-day operation of the business, the so-called 'Debtor-in-Possession' (DIP). The recitals reiterate that debtors should "in principle, be left in control of their assets and the day-to-day operation of their business".[1041]

The involvement of other actors and specialized practitioners – the so-called 'Practitioner in the Field of Restructuring' (PIFOR) – is optional on a case-by-case basis, subject to limited exceptions where mandatory appointment is warranted to protect the interests of the creditors.[1042] This includes in particular the following situations: when its appointment is necessary to protect the creditors' rights while a debtor benefits from a stay, in case of a confirmation of a restructuring plan which requires cross-class cram-down, and when a majority of the creditors request the appointment of a PIFOR. [1043] Optional appointment of a PIFOR, on a case-by-case basis only, is possible when a

1039 European Commission Proposal for a Directive of the European Parliament and the Council harmonising certain aspects of insolvency law, 7 December 2022, COM(2022) 702 final, p. 4; European Commission, Commission Staff Working Document, Impact Assessment, Accompanying the document Proposal for a Directive of the Parliament and of the Council harmonising certain aspects of insolvency law, 7 December 2022, SWD(2022) 395 final, p. 8, 13 and 14-15.

1040 European Commission, Commission Staff Working Document, Impact Assessment, Accompanying the document Proposal for a Directive of the Parliament and of the Council harmonising certain aspects of insolvency law, 7 December 2022, SWD(2022) 395 final, p. 89. There was similar opposition on this matter when the PRD 2019 was prepared, see Impact Assessment Proposal PRD 2016, pp. 23, 60 and 93.

1041 Recital 30 PRD 2019.

1042 Recital 30 and Art. 5(2) and (3) PRD 2019.

1043 Recital 31 and Art. 5(3) PRD 2019.

restructuring plan affects the rights of workers or when a debtor's management has acted criminally, fraudulently or otherwise detrimental in business relations.[1044] Furthermore, Article 4(6) PRD 2019 provides that the involvement of a judicial or administrative authority may be limited to where it is necessary to protect the rights of affected parties and relevant stakeholders.

Compared to certain other parts of the PRD 2019, the EU legislator left limited room for divergence in transposing the Directive with respect to the involvement of actors, which is also demonstrated in the implementations in various jurisdictions (Table 3).

Table 3 Overview of involved actors in preventive restructuring frameworks.

Jurisdiction and PRFs	DIP	PIFOR(s)
Austria[1045] (*Restrukturierungs-verfahren*)	A debtor is, in principle, fully in possession, but may be partially divested when for certain decisions a debtor requires consent of the court or a PIFOR.	A PIFOR is appointed at the request of a debtor, the majority of creditors or at the court's own motion. A PIFOR is appointed mandatorily if one of the conditions of Article 5(3) PRD 2019 applies. In addition, a PIFOR is mandatory when leaving a debtor-in-possession may be detrimental to the creditors. The court may also appoint a PIFOR when this is required to examine new finance, to report on the results of the alternative scenario to the offered restructuring plan, or to review contested claims. The tasks of a PIFOR are determined by the court and may comprise, in particular, (i) support of the debtor or the creditors in relation to the restructuring plan, (ii) supervision of the debtor and report to the court and (iii) partially taking over control of the debtor's assets and business.
Denmark[1046] (*Preventive restructuring procedure*)	A debtor is, in principle, fully in possession, but may be partially divested when a PIFOR is appointed.	A PIFOR is appointed at the request of a debtor. A PIFOR is appointed mandatorily when a debtor is granted a stay. A PIFOR will assist and supervise a debtor. A debtor also requires the consent of a PIFOR for entering into transactions with material significance.

1044 Recital 30 PRD 2019.
1045 Chapter 2, Section 4.3.
1046 Chapter 3, Section 4.3.

Jurisdiction and PRFs	DIP	PIFOR(s)
France (*Ad hoc mandate, conciliation, safeguard, accelerated safeguard*)	A debtor is, in principle, fully in possession in the ad hoc mandate, conciliation, safeguard and accelerated safeguard. In the safeguard and accelerated safeguard a PIFOR is mandatory in certain circumstances.	The respective French processes provide for different types of practitioners (which may qualify as PIFORs): In ad hoc mandate, a court mandatorily appoints an ad hoc representative, who will assist with the negotiations between the debtor and its main creditors. The debtor remains fully in possession.[1047] In conciliation, a court mandatorily appoints a conciliator, who will pursue to reach an agreement between the debtor and the main creditors. A conciliator does not divest the debtor.[1048] In a safeguard and accelerated safeguard, an administrator (*administrateur judiciaire*) is in principle mandatorily appointed to supervise and/or assist the debtor when meeting a threshold of 20 employees or turnover of EUR 3 million. The administrator will assist in preparing a plan together with the debtor. The debtor requires consent from the administrator to enter into agreements and dispose of assets. A creditor's representative (*mandataire judiciaire*) is in principle mandatorily appointed to represent the interests of the creditors and to assess proof of claims.[1049]
Germany[1050] (*Restrukturierungs-sache*)	A debtor is, in principle, fully in possession and control of the operative business and the restructuring procedure. The role of the PIFOR is limited. A debtor has the exclusive right to commence a process, to propose a restructuring plan, and to request the court to sanction a stay or confirm a restructuring plan.	A PIFOR is appointed at the request of a debtor, creditor(s) holding more than 25% of voting rights or at the court's own discretion. A PIFOR is appointed mandatorily if one of the conditions of Article 5(3) PRD 2019 applies. There is an exception when there is a cross-class cram-down for a plan involving only financial creditors. Furthermore, courts may appoint a PIFOR also at their own motion to conduct certain examinations. A PIFOR monitors the process, advises the debtor and reports to the court. A PIFOR may be given the power to (dis)approve exceptional payments of the debtor and to preside over the voting process.

1047 Chapter 4, Section 3.1.

1048 Chapter 4, Section 3.1 and 4.1.1.

1049 Chapter 4, Section 3.2.

1050 Chapter 5, Section 4.3.

Jurisdiction and PRFs	DIP	PIFOR(s)
Greece[1051] (*Διαδικασία Εξυγίανσης* (*Pre-insolvency rehabilitation*))	A debtor is, in principle, fully in possession, but may be partially or fully divested when a PIFOR is appointed.	A PIFOR can be appointed at the request of anyone with a 'legitimate interest'. A PIFOR can be appointed when a debtor has delayed the filing of an insolvency application or has intentionally caused the insolvency, when there have been fraudulent transfers of assets, or in cases when a debtor abusively refuses to participate in negotiations for a rehabilitation agreement. An appointment can take place only after confirmation of the rehabilitation agreement has been requested. Furthermore, a PIFOR can also be appointed after confirmation of the rehabilitation agreement to protect the debtor's assets or implement the agreement. A PIFOR can partially or fully exercise the debtor's powers.
The Netherlands[1052] (*WHOA*)	A debtor is fully in possession, also when a PIFOR is appointed.	A PIFOR is appointed at the request of a debtor, creditors, shareholders, Works Council, Employee Representative Body or at the court's own motion. A PIFOR will be mandatorily appointed if one of the conditions of Article 5(3) PRD 2019 applies. There are two types of PIFORS: observers and restructuring experts. An observer is limited to supervising the debtor, preparing a plan and informing the court. A restructuring expert will prepare a plan (with the debtor) and supervises the debtor and the preparations for a plan and will inform the court.
United Kingdom[1053] (*Pt 26A restructuring plan, Pt A1 moratorium*)	In a Pt 26A restructuring plan, the debtor remains fully in possession. In a Pt A1 moratorium, a debtor is fully in possession, also when a monitor is appointed.	In a Pt 26A restructuring plan, no appointment of a PIFOR is envisaged. In a Pt A1 moratorium, a monitor will be appointed mandatorily. A monitor is tasked with supervising the company's activities during the moratorium.

As Table 3 demonstrates, the various implementations show considerable convergence with respect to the PRD 2019's 'DIP Principle', in which the debtor is left in full or at least in partial control of its assets and affairs. For the Netherlands and the UK Pt A1 moratorium, a debtor stays fully in possession also when a PIFOR is appointed. However, most other jurisdictions in this study provide that a debtor may be divested in case a PIFOR is

1051 Chapter 6, Section 4.3.1.

1052 Chapter 7, Section 4.3.

1053 Chapter 8, Section 4.3.

appointed. Such appointments entail in Austria, Denmark, France and Germany only partial divestment of a debtor. Only in Greece the debtor may be fully divested in pre-insolvency rehabilitation, deviating from the DIP Principle.

In most jurisdictions, the involvement of a PIFOR is decided on a case-by-case basis, which is the case in Austria, Denmark, Germany, Greece and the Netherlands. Deviating from the PRD 2019, others provide for mandatory appointment of PIFORs. For instance in France, if certain conditions are met, PIFORs are appointed mandatorily (ad hoc mandate, conciliation, safeguard and accelerated safeguard). Even though these French PIFORs do not always divest the debtor, it is not consistent with the PRD 2019. In the UK Pt A1 moratorium, a PIFOR is appointed mandatorily; however, this falls within the exception of Article 5(3)(A) PRD 2019.

According to the exception of Article 5(3) PRD 2019, the appointment of a PIFOR is envisaged typically (if necessary) when a stay is granted, when confirmation involves a cross-class cram-down or when (a majority of) the creditors request its appointment. Germany and the Netherlands follow these minimum grounds strictly. On the other end of the spectrum, Austria and Greece take a much more 'generous' approach for appointing a PIFOR, while in France it is mandatory in every case. This is opposed to the Danish approach, where mandatory appointment of a PIFOR is available only in case of a stay. A notable exception is the UK, where Pt 26A restructuring plan does not envisage the appointment of a PIFOR at all, similar to the UK Scheme of Arrangement. In sum, most jurisdictions in this study require appointment of a PIFOR, at least in the categories listed in Article 5(3) PRD 2019. However, there are still some considerable divergences, even deviating from the PRD 2019. It is also problematic that the role of the PIFOR seems to lack clear articulation in some jurisdictions. In Greece, the relevant provision merely states that a PIFOR may be assigned partial or full administration over the debtor's estate. This is different in the Netherlands and Germany, which have introduced different types of PIFORs, with more elaborate provisions on their respective rights and duties.

For all jurisdictions, the involvement of the court or an administrative authority in the governance of the restructuring process is generally limited. Court involvement relates mostly to responding to requests from the debtor (such as granting a stay or confirming a plan), and sometimes also from other (affected) parties (*e.g.* to appoint a PIFOR). This is less so in some court-supervised processes in France, such as the (accelerated) safeguard, where each case involves a supervisory judge.[1054]

1054 Chapter 4, Section 3.2.

4.5 Stay of Individual Enforcement Actions

The PRD 2019 requires availability of a stay "to support the negotiations of a restructuring plan".[1055] It provides, however, extensive policy options to national legislators in shaping the stay, including the scope of a stay (who is affected), the effects of stay (what does it entail), duration of stay (how long) and how a stay can be lifted (under which conditions).[1056] Under the PRD 2019, a stay should be available at the request of debtors, for an initial duration of not more than four months and in total not more than twelve months. This has been implemented in various ways (Table 4).[1057]

Table 4 Requesting and duration of a stay of individual enforcement actions.

Jurisdiction and PRFs	Availability of a Stay	Duration of a Stay
Austria[1058] (*Restrukturierungs-verfahren*)	In regular and European proceedings: a stay is available upon request of a debtor. In simplified proceedings: no stay available.	In regular and European proceedings: Initial duration: max. 3 months Total duration: max. 6 months
Denmark[1059] (*Preventive restructuring procedure*)	A stay is available upon request of a debtor.	Initial duration: max. 4 weeks Total duration: max. 12 months
France[1060] (*Conciliation, safeguard, accelerated safeguard*)	In conciliation, a stay is available upon request of a debtor. In a safeguard and accelerated safeguard, a stay is granted automatically.	In conciliation: Max. duration of 2 years for debts due and payable pre-petition Max. duration 5 months for debts that are not yet due and payable In safeguard: Initial duration: max. 6 months Total duration: max. 12 months In accelerated safeguard: Initial duration: max 2 months Total duration: max. 4 months
Germany[1061] (*Restrukturierungs-sache*)	A stay is available upon request of a debtor.	Initial duration: max. 3 months Total duration: max. 8 months

1055 Art. 6(1) PRD 2019.

1056 See for a detailed overview of the different policy options J. Garrido, C. DeLong, A. Rasekh & A. Rosha, above note 987, p. 13 et seq.

1057 Art. 6(1) and (6) PRD 2019.

1058 Chapter 2, Section 4.4.1.

1059 Chapter 3, Section 4.4.

1060 Chapter 4, Sections 3.1, 3.2, 4.1.1.

1061 Chapter 5, Section 4.4.

Jurisdiction and PRFs	Availability of a Stay	Duration of a Stay
Greece[1062] (*Διαδικασία Εξυγίανσης* (*Pre-insolvency rehabilitation*))	During negotiations, a stay is available upon request of a debtor or creditor. During the confirmation phase, a stay is granted automatically.	During negotiations: Initial duration: max. 4 months Total duration: max. 6 months Duration of automatic stay is unclear from statute, but it is presumed to be: Initial duration: max. 4 months Total duration: max. 12 months
The Netherlands[1063] (*WHOA*)	A stay is available upon request of a debtor or PIFOR.	Initial duration: max. 4 months Total duration: max. 8 months
United Kingdom[1064] (*Pt 26A restructuring plan; Pt A1 moratorium*)	Pt 26A restructuring plan: there is no (automatic) stay for the restructuring plan; this is provided as a stand-alone tool by the Pt 1A moratorium. Pt 1A moratorium: a stay is available upon request of the directors of a company.	Pt 1A moratorium Initial duration: 20 business days Total duration: max. 12 months

It follows from Table 4 that each jurisdiction in this study offers a stay, mostly within a PRF. The UK stands out as it has a stand-alone stay, separate from its PRFs. A stay is typically available at the request of a debtor, although in the Netherlands, it is also available at the request of a PIFOR.

In line with the PRD 2019, the initial duration is not more than four months (although varying between 20 business days and four months). The total duration is capped at 12 months in Denmark, France (safeguard), Greece (stay upon request for confirmation) and the UK. However, several jurisdictions have opted to limit the maximum duration to eight (Germany and the Netherlands), six (Austria) or even just four months (France, in the accelerated safeguard). Looking at these minimum standards for stays and noting still considerable differences in the duration of stays, most jurisdictions offer at least one stay in line with the PRD 2019.

4.6 *Adoption and Confirmation of Restructuring Plans*

Chapter 3 of the PRD 2019 regulates the restructuring plan, including the contents of a plan, class formation, as well as the voting, adoption and confirmation of plans, including

1062 Chapter 6, Section 4.4.
1063 Chapter 7, Section 4.4.
1064 Chapter 8, Section 4.4.2.

grounds for rejecting confirmation. There is a plethora of options for legislators. For instance, whether class formation is mandatory for SME debtors, whether shareholders' and workers' rights can be affected, and how reorganization value should be distributed under the plan.[1065] As the IMF pointed out, the intricacy for the EU legislator was balancing a framework that maximizes legal flexibility without necessitating full legal scrutiny by a court.[1066] Whereas the PRD 2019 lays down many minimum standards and policy options, in this section we focus our analysis on four features of restructuring frameworks: (i) who can propose a plan and who can be affected by the plan, (ii) what is the threshold for intra-class adoption of a plan, (iii) what is the threshold for a plan to be eligible for cross-class cram-down and (iv) what fairness test applies in a cross-class cram-down (Table 5).

As a minimum, the PRD 2019 requires that a debtor is able to propose a plan, but creditors and/or PIFORs may be granted the right to submit competing plans.[1067] The PRD 2019 gives national legislators considerable discretion in considering who will be affected by the plan. However, all affected parties must have the right to vote on the plan.[1068] A class of such affected creditors and/or shareholders will have adopted a plan if there is majority in value of claims or interests. National legislators may not require a majority exceeding 75%.[1069] If all classes adopt the plan with the required majority, the plan may – subject to other criteria including the best-interest-of-creditors test – be confirmed.[1070]

When a plan has not been adopted by all classes, it may still be confirmed by the court by means of a cross-class cram-down. A plan will be eligible for confirmation subject to several requirements. A plan must have been adopted (i) by a majority of all voting classes (including one secured class or class senior to the unsecured creditors class) or (ii) at least one class of creditors that would be 'in-the-money' in case of either a going-concern sale or in a liquidation proceeding.[1071]

Besides the best-interest-of-creditors test, in this case also the fairness test must be adhered to for dissenting classes. The EU legislator has introduced – which resulted in a vivid academic debate[1072] – that this could be based on the so-called relative priority rule (RPR), the absolute priority rule (APR) or a relaxed version of the APR. The RPR entails

1065 Consider for instance Arts 9(4), 11, 12 and 13.

1066 J. Garrido, C. DeLong, A. Rasekh & A. Rosha, above note 987, p. 16.

1067 Art. 9(1) PRD 2019.

1068 Art. 9(2) AND (3) PRD 2019.

1069 Art. 9(6) PRD 2019.

1070 Arts 9(6) and 10 PRD 2019.

1071 Art. 11(1)(b) PRD 2019.

1072 See for instance: S. Madaus, 'Leaving the shadows of US Bankruptcy Law: A Proposal to Divide the Realms of Insolvency and Restructuring Law', *European Business Organization Law Review*, 2019, pp. 615-647; R.J. de Weijs, A. Jonkers & M. Malakotipour, above note 936, 2019/*125*(4); G. Ballerini, 'The Priorities Dilemma in the EU Restructuring Directive: Absolute or Relative Priority Rule?', *International Insolvency Review*, 2020, 30(1), pp. 7-33; R.P. Freitag, above note 932, para. 2(b).

that in distributing the reorganization value (the excess value compared to the next best alternative to the restructuring), any dissenting class of creditors should be treated at least as favourable as classes of an equal rank and more favourable than any junior class.[1073] This is much more flexible than the APR, under which a lower ranking class can receive value only when any higher ranking class is paid in full.[1074] Whereas the latter can be rather strict, implementations may also provide for a 'relaxed APR' or 'relaxed RPR', where limited deviations from the APR or RPR are acceptable when they are necessary to achieve the aims of an restructuring.[1075]

Table 5 Adoption and confirmation of plans.

Jurisdiction and PRFs	Proposing a Plan	Threshold for Intra-Class Adoption	Threshold for Cross-Class Cram-Down and Fairness Test
Austria[1076] (*Restrukturierungs-verfahren*)	By the debtor to the affected creditors	In regular and European proceedings: simple majority of affected creditors (in number) and qualified majority of 75% of creditors (in value), both based on creditors present at the meeting. In simplified proceedings: 75% of creditors in value.	In regular and European proceedings: Threshold: simple majority of classes including secured creditors or simple majority of the 'in-the-money' classes Fairness test: RPR In simplified proceedings: no cross-class cram-down.
Denmark[1077] (*Preventive restructuring procedure*)	By the debtor to the affected creditors	Simple majority of the affected creditors (in value) present at the meeting.	Threshold: simple majority of classes. Fairness test: APR.

1073 Art. 11(1)(c) PRD 2019.
1074 Art. 11(2), first sentence, PRD 2019.
1075 Art. 11(2), last sentence, PRD 2019.
1076 Chapter 2, Sections 4.5.2, 4.6.1, 4.6.2 and 4.6.4.
1077 Chapter 3, Sections 4.3, 4.5 and 4.6.

Jurisdiction and PRFs	Proposing a Plan	Threshold for Intra-Class Adoption	Threshold for Cross-Class Cram-Down and Fairness Test
France[1078] (*Conciliation, safeguard, accelerated safeguard*)	By the debtor to the affected creditors and shareholders	Qualified majority of two thirds of the affected creditors (in value). Similar requirements apply to classes of shareholders.	Threshold: (i) simple majority of classes voting in favour, including at least one class of secured creditors or a class senior to the ordinary unsecured creditors, or (ii) at least one class of affected parties has voted in favour of the plan, which is a class which is 'in-the-money' in judicial liquidation. Fairness test: APR.
Germany[1079] (*Restrukturierungs-sache*)	By the debtor to the affected creditors and shareholders	Qualified majority of 75% (in value) of all affected creditors entitled to vote; qualified majority of 75% of all affected shareholders entitled to vote.	Threshold: simple majority of classes. Fairness test: – horizontal: no discrimination of a class ranking equally in a liquidation; – flexible composition of classes and different treatment of different classes possible with sound economic justification; – vertical: relaxed APR.
Greece[1080] (*Διαδικασία Εξυγίανσης (Pre-insolvency rehabilitation)*)	By the debtor or the affected creditors	Simple majority of the affected secured creditors (in value) and simple majority of all other (non-secured) affected creditors (in value).	Threshold: qualified majority of 60% of the creditors (in value), of which at least 50% of the secured creditors (in value). Fairness test: a form of RPR, applied to individual creditors.

1078 Chapter 4, Sections 4.2 and 4.3.
1079 Chapter 5, Section 4.6.
1080 Chapter 6, Section 4.6.3.

Jurisdiction and PRFs	Proposing a Plan	Threshold for Intra-Class Adoption	Threshold for Cross-Class Cram-Down and Fairness Test
The Netherlands[1081] (*WHOA*)	By the debtor and restructuring expert to the affected creditors and shareholders	Qualified majority of two thirds of the affected creditors (in value) present and voting and a qualified majority of two thirds of the affected shareholders (based on issued capital), based on those affected creditors/ shareholders present at the meeting/having cast their vote.	Threshold: at least one class of creditors (in principle an 'in-the-money' class in case of liquidation in bankruptcy). Fairness test: relaxed APR
United Kingdom[1082] (*Pt 26A restructuring plan*)	By directors, the company, creditors, liquidator or administrator to the affected creditors and shareholders	Qualified majority of 75% of the affected creditors (in value) present and voting. Similar requirement for classes of shareholders (members).[1083]	Condition A is that none of the members of a dissenting class would be any worse off than they would be in the event of the 'relevant alternative'.[1084] Condition B is that the compromise or arrangement has been agreed by a class of members or creditors who have a genuine economic interest in the company.[1085]

All jurisdictions in this study allow a debtor to propose a plan, but in Greece, the Netherlands and the UK it has been extended to certain other parties, such as creditors and/or practitioners. Noticeable is the Greek option in the pre-insolvency rehabilitation where creditors may pursue a restructuring without any direct involvement of a debtor.[1086]

The threshold for intra-class adoption of restructuring plans shows much diversity, and it is doubtful whether the PRD 2019 succeeded in any actual harmonization. The required majority differs between a simple majority, or a qualified two-thirds majority or

1081 Chapter 7, Sections 4.6.2 and 4.6.3.

1082 Chapter 8, Sections 4.6.1, 4.6.2 and 4.6.3.

1083 Section 901F(1) CA 2006.

1084 Whatever the court considers would be most likely to occur in relation to the company if the compromise or arrangement were not sanctioned under section 901F.

1085 Section 901g(3) and (4) CA 2006. There is no APR under English law, English courts have recently clarified that they are not persuaded by arguments relying on APR or RPR narratives because the introduction of these concepts in the law was rejected by the consultations leading to the CIGA

1086 Chapter 6, Section 4.2.1.

75% of the value of the claims of creditors and/or interests of shareholders. However, Austria also requires a majority in the number of affected parties that voted. Furthermore, Germany requires the majority to be calculated based on all affected parties in a class, whereas most other jurisdictions allow for the majority to be calculated based on the affected parties present and voting. With regard to the threshold for requesting a cross-class cram-down, there is also some divergence, but several jurisdictions remain close to the requirements as listed in Article 11(1)(b) PRD 2019.

In addition, the applied fairness tests show great diversity among jurisdictions. Denmark and France strictly apply the APR; Germany and the Netherlands have opted for the relaxed APR. Austria and Greece have opted for the RPR, and the UK has not adopted a statutory fairness test. It goes without saying that the features reviewed here with respect to adoption and confirmation of restructuring plans show it is hard to detect any clear convergence in Europe as regards adoption and confirmation of plans in PRFs. Much will depend on how the courts will apply these tests in practice.

4.7 *Jurisdiction for and Recognition of Court Decisions in Europe*

Whereas the PRD 2019 is introduced to reduce the costs for cross-border investors, the EU legislator has given limited consideration for the cross-border aspects of PRFs. It must be noted that the EIR 2015 covers PRFs that meet its requirements, including that it is a 'public' collective proceeding.[1087] The PRD 2019 is without prejudice to this EIR 2015, thus enabling that within the EU (excluding Denmark), PRFs listed on Annex A of the EIR 2015 would benefit from its framework for jurisdiction, recognition and enforcement of judicial decisions as well as its mechanism protecting against abusive relocation of the centre of main interests of debtors.[1088]

A notable feature, which has arisen also in implementations of the PRD 2019, is that PRFs do not necessarily meet the requirements of an 'insolvency proceeding' under the EIR 2015. This relates in particular to the requirement of publicity for insolvency proceedings falling within the scope of the EIR 2015.[1089] The EU legislator has remained silent on questions of jurisdiction and recognition in this regard, which has resulted in considerable uncertainty across Europe.[1090] Therefore, it remains unclear whether

1087 Art. 1(1) EIR 2015.

1088 Recitals 12-14 PRD 2019. Cross-border insolvency aspects of PRFs also appear in in Art. 6(8) PRD 2019 limiting the duration of a stay in case (i) a process does not meet the requirements being subject to the EIR 2015 and (ii) debtors have moved their centre of main interests within three months prior to requesting 'for the opening of preventive restructuring proceedings'.

1089 Recital 13 PRD 2019.

1090 Recital 13 and Art. 1(1) EIR 2015. See on this among others: W.J.E. Nijnens, 'Internationaal privaatrechtelijke aspecten van de WHOA', *Tijdschrift voor Insolventierecht* 2019/34; P.M. Veder, 'Internationale aspecten van

questions of jurisdiction, recognition and enforcement of decisions in such PRFs are subject to the Brussels Ibis Regulation (Brussels Ibis)[1091] or fall within the scope of domestic private international rules. As a result, diverse and sometimes hesitant approaches have been taken on this matter, as is reflected in Table 6 dealing with the question of jurisdiction for (rendering decisions in) PRFs.

Table 6 Jurisdiction of (decisions taken in) preventive restructuring frameworks.

Jurisdiction and PRFs	PRFs Listed on Annex A EIR 2015	PRFs Not Listed on Annex A EIR 2015 and Legal Basis for Courts to Exercise Jurisdiction[1092]
Austria[1093] (*Restrukturierungs-verfahren*)	*Das Europäische*	Regular restructuring proceedings and simplified restructuring proceedings. Statute remains silent on whether jurisdiction and recognition for such proceedings is based on Brussels Ibis or domestic rules. For jurisdiction, the domestic *Jurisdiktionsnorm* requires debtors using regular or simplified restructuring proceedings to operate their business or have their habitual residence in Austria. In addition, even appreciable assets in Austria suffice.
Denmark[1094] (*Preventive restructuring procedure*)	(EIR 2015 does not apply)	Preventive restructuring procedure. Statute remains silent on whether jurisdiction and recognition of decisions in the Danish preventive restructuring proceeding are based on Brussels Ibis or on domestic rules.

de WHOA: de openbare en de besloten akkoordprocedure buiten faillissement', *Tijdschrift Financiering, Zekerheden en Insolventierechtpraktijk*, 2019/6; J.M.G.J. Boon, R.D. Vriesendorp & R. Sijbesma, 'Netherlands Commercial Court als mogelijke WHOA-rechter bij internationale herstructureringen', *HERO*, 2021/W-001, Para. 3.1; J. Schmidt, 'Präventiver Restrukturierungsrahmen: Internationale Zuständigkeit, Anerkennung und anwendbares Recht', *Zeitschrift für das gesamte Insolvenzrecht*, 2021/654, at 654-656; R.D. Vriesendorp, W. van Kesteren, E. Vilarin-Seivane & S. Hinse, 'Automatic Recognition for the Dutch Undisclosed WHOA Procedure in the European Union', *NIPR*, 2021/1. See also S. Madaus & B. Wessels, CERIL Report 2022-2 on Cross-Border Effects in European Preventive Restructuring, 2022, available at: www.ceril.eu/news/ceril-report-2022-2-on-cross-border-effects-in-european-preventive-restructuring.

1091 Regulation (EU) No 1215/2012 of the European Parliament and of the Council of 12 December 2012 on jurisdiction and the recognition and enforcement of judgments in civil and commercial matters (recast), O.J. L 351/20.

1092 This category also applies to cases where the debtor's centre of main interest is located in a third country, to which the EIR 2015 does not apply (compare recital 25 EIR 2015).

1093 Chapter 2, Section 4.9 and 4.10.

1094 Chapter 3, Section 4.9.

Jurisdiction and PRFs	PRFs Listed on Annex A EIR 2015	PRFs Not Listed on Annex A EIR 2015 and Legal Basis for Courts to Exercise Jurisdiction[1092]
France[1095] (*Ad hoc mandate, conciliation, safeguard, accelerated safeguard*)	*Sauvegarde* (safeguard) and *sauvegarde accélérée* (accelerated safeguard)	Ad hoc mandate and conciliation. Statute remains silent on whether jurisdiction and recognition of decisions in ad hoc mandate and conciliation are based on Brussels Ibis or on domestic rules.
Germany[1096] (*Restrukturierungs-sache*)	*Die öffentliche Restrukturierungssache* (public Restrukturierungs-sache)	Private *Restrukturierungssache*. The Statute gives no clear guidance on the matter of international jurisdiction. German courts should be expected to assume jurisdiction provided the debtor's centre of main interest is in Germany.
Greece[1097] (*Διαδικασία Εξυγίανσης (Pre-insolvency rehabilitation)*)	*Διαδικασία Εξυγίανσης* (rehabilitation procedure)	-
The Netherlands[1098] (*WHOA*)	Public WHOA	Private WHOA The Dutch Bankruptcy Code provides that jurisdiction and recognition of decisions in a private WHOA are based on domestic rules. A sufficient connection test is applied for a Dutch court to assume jurisdiction.
United Kingdom[1099] (*Pt 26A restructuring plan; Pt A1 moratorium*)	(EIR 2015 does not apply)	Pt 26A restructuring plan and Pt A1 moratorium Jurisdiction and recognition are based on domestic PIL rules.

It is clear that – except for Denmark and the UK to which the EIR 2015 does not apply – various PRFs have been listed as 'insolvency proceeding' on Annex A of the EIR 2015. Whereas the EIR 2015 provides a well-functioning framework for cross-border effect of insolvency proceedings, it is criticized as incompatible with preventive restructuring.[1100] When it comes to jurisdiction and recognition for those preventive frameworks that are not on Annex A or when it regards third countries (and the EIR 2015 does not apply), it is clear that not only the EU legislator but also national legislators have left considerable uncertainty to the market. The Dutch legislator has made a clear choice, but most

1095 INSOL Europe/LexisPSL joint project on the implementation analysis of the Directive (EU) 2019/1023 in the EU Member States, France, 2022, p. 4.

1096 Chapter 5, Section 4.9.

1097 Chapter 6, Section 4.7.

1098 Chapter 7, Section 4.9.

1099 Chapter 8, Section 4.9 and 5.6.

1100 S. Madaus & B. Wessels, CERIL Report 2022-2 on Cross-Border Effects in European Preventive restructuring, 2022, p. 7, available at: www.ceril.eu/news/ceril-report-2022-2-on-cross-border-effects-in-european-preventive-restructuring.

jurisdictions have remained silent. If the EU legislator will not address this itself, which for now seems to be the case, it appears to be left ultimately to the CJEU to resolve.

In the recitals to the PRD 2019, it is rightly emphasized that the EIR 2015 was not able to resolve disparities between domestic PRFs. In addition, it is stated that

> an instrument limited only to cross-border insolvencies would not remove all obstacles to free movement, nor would it be feasible for investors to determine in advance the cross-border or domestic nature of the potential financial difficulties of the debtor in the future.[1101]

Our analysis suggests that the opposite may also be true. By ignoring the implications of preventive restructuring in a European market and leaving untouched the need for an adequate cross-border insolvency regime, the PRD 2019 leaves ample uncertainty for jurisdiction, recognition and enforcement of decisions during a PRF. As a result, the EU legislator may effectively have created an impediment to the free movement of capital, contrary to the objectives of the PRD 2019.

5 DOES THE PRD 2019 DELIVER ON ITS PROMISE?

5.1 *Introduction*

The discussion in Section 4 shows that the implementations of the PRD 2019 in the various jurisdictions in this study bring about a rather divergent picture. It is clear that in considering the policy alternatives of the PRD 2019, national legislators have taken different choices. The variety in outcomes is a serious impediment in formulating an answer to the question whether the approach adopted by the EU legislator – minimum harmonization of preventive restructuring by means of a directive – has been successful in achieving the aforementioned key objectives of reducing legal uncertainty for cross-border investment and promoting early restructuring of financially distressed debtors. Or to put it differently, whether the introduction of or amendments to domestic PRFs have been effective. There are several considerations to take into account.

Firstly, what can we justifiably assess at this moment, with for some jurisdictions some two years, but for most jurisdictions less of experience with a new or amended legal framework? An analysis of the effectiveness will therefore be done based predominantly on a so-called 'law at the books' approach. Although a further analysis of the 'law in action'

1101 Recital 12 PRD 2019.

will certainly provide more insights, that remains difficult to achieve shortly after the implementation.

Secondly, the high degree of minimum harmonization – including the possibility to introduce preventive restructuring tools in multiple procedures, measures or provisions – complicates any assessment of effectiveness. Although there is an obligation that restructuring frameworks must provide a coherent protection of the rights of the affected parties, such as debtors, creditors, shareholders and workers,[1102] this in itself is insufficient to guarantee the effectiveness of the frameworks. However, an understanding of how the implementation has been used to shape PRFs in the respective jurisdictions is needed first.

Thirdly, one might be critical about the PRD 2019's assumptions, including the presumed economic effects of the availability of PRFs.[1103] This draws indeed to limitations of the PRD 2019 as a tool to reach certain policy objectives. For instance, (i) PRFs are merely one indicator among many that are relevant for the (costs of a) cross-border investment climate in Europe, and (ii) the minimum standards laid down in the PRD 2019 provide mostly for a formal legal framework for preventive restructuring. One must be aware that the impact of PRFs on cross-border investment has not been substantively quantified.[1104] Similarly, the effectiveness of the preventive restructuring tools will also depend on their implementation and application in domestic law, the coherence between the different tools, as well as the domestic legal culture including the expertise and experience of judges and practitioners.[1105] In short, effectiveness may be a very different concept in practice than it is in the law.[1106]

The next two sections contain a discussion about the extent to which the PRD 2019 has (already) achieved its objectives. Firstly, we investigate whether and to what extent the PRD 2019 has reduced legal uncertainty on PRFs (Section 5.2). Secondly, we review the

---

1102 Art. 4(5), second sentence, PRD 2019.

1103 R.P. Freitag, above note 932, pp. 229-231 and 243-244.

1104 See Recital 6 Proposal PRD 2016 and Proposal PRD 2016, p. 2 where the Commission only states that '[m]any investors mention uncertainty over insolvency rules or the risk of lengthy or complex insolvency procedures in another country as a main reason for not investing or not entering into a business relationship outside their own country.'

1105 Compare H. Eidenmüller, above note 939, Para. 6; R.P. Freitag, above note 932, pp. 229-231 and 244; R. Dammann & M. Gerrer, 'The Transposition of the EU Directive on Early Corporate Restructuring and Second Chance into French Law', *Revista General de Insolvencias & Reestructuraciones*, 2022(5), p. 401. Although left outside of the scope of this study and having received limited discussion so far, the EU legislator has considered the role of judges and practitioners in Arts 26 and 27 PRD 2019. See on this B. Wessels, 'EU has High Expectations of Judges in Restructuring Cases', *International Corporate Rescue*, 2020, 17, p. 253 et seq. On how this has been implemented in the Netherlands, see: S. Boot, M.C. Bosch, J.C.A.T. Frima & H.J. van Harten, 'Duidelijk, transparant en rechtvaardig', *Tijdschrift voor Insolventierecht*, 2023/1, p. 4 et seq.

1106 Compare also European Bank for Reconstruction and Development, EBRD Insolvency Assessment on Reorganisation Procedures, 2022, p. 4 and the discussion in Section 3.

extent to which the PRD 2019 has succeeded in promoting early restructuring by debtors (Section 5.3).

5.2 *PRD 2019 as a Means to Reduce Legal Uncertainty over Preventive Restructuring*

Section 4.2 dealt with the approaches that several national legislators took in implementing the PRD 2019. Except for France and Greece, the other jurisdictions introduced new PRFs as an addition to the pre-existing domestic restructuring and insolvency regime. However, compared to the poor follow-up to the Commission Recommendation 2014 by the Member States, the PRD 2019 can be considered all in all to have succeeded in bringing top-down harmonization amending the 'law at the books'.

Furthermore, there are also some traces of regulatory competition between European legislators. We draw on two examples: firstly, although no longer a Member State, also the UK has introduced in recent years its new restructuring plan and stand-alone moratorium. Although this legislative initiative commenced before the PRD 2019 was adopted, as pointed out by Vaccari and Gant, the reform shows resemblance to the PRD 2019.[1107] It illustrates that the PRD 2019 had a prospective and broader standard-setting influence. In addition, some jurisdictions introduced features to their new PRFs, which were not explicitly provided for by the PRD 2019. This is the case in particular with the dual track preventive restructuring. Under this approach, proposed first in the Netherlands, PRF is available both as a private (not listed on Annex A the EIR 2015) and public process (listed on Annex A to the EIR 2015), has been taken on board also in Germany and Austria. This suggests that legislators have considered each other's implementation on these and possibly other features too.

Does this also lead to the conclusion that the PRD 2019 has succeeded broadly in harmonizing PRFs? Based on our study, for now, we come to answer that question in the negative. Reviewing the implementation of the PRD 2019 in six Member States clearly shows that national legislators took ample use of the flexibility offered by the PRD 2019,[1108] and sometimes even seem to have gone beyond.[1109] The divergences are reflected both in forms in which the provisions on preventive restructuring have been implemented, introducing one or multiple new "procedures, measures or provisions",[1110] and in taking different choices on the policy options provided by specific provisions of the PRD 2019. This results not only in quite disparate legal regimes, but possibly also in different dynamics

1107 Chapter 8, Sections 1, 3 and 4.

1108 Consider for instance the introduction of non-public processes in the Netherlands, Germany and Austria.

1109 Consider for instance the involvement of practitioners in Austria and France, or Greece.

1110 Art. 4(5) PRD 2019.

within processes themselves. For one, most poignantly, this relates to the effective usability of the preventive frameworks, which for certain jurisdictions has already received severe critiques. The Commission has deliberately chosen for this minimum harmonization, as this would not "interfere with what works well".[1111] That fits our perception, where the national legislators designed PRFs typically in addition to the existing framework, while making use of the many policy options the PRD 2019 offers. At the same time, this does not match with the Commission's objective to "ensure major progress towards the functioning of the internal market".[1112] As a consequence, we must be cautious about concluding whether the EU legislator's aim to reduce barriers to cross-border investments by minimizing legal uncertainty on preventive restructuring, has been achieved. Further research, especially on the 'law in action', will be necessary to determine how cross-border investors assess the investment risks with PRFs across Europe.

Ehmke et al. predicted already that the amount of actual harmonization among Member States might be limited as the PRD 2019's toolbox allowed for (too) many options.[1113] In a comparison of implementations of the PRD 2019 and commentaries on Austria, Germany, Italy, Spain and the UK, Thole observes a considerable convergence among jurisdictions, despite noticing various differences.[1114] Bork and Mangano, on the other hand, express concerns for these differences, noting that this in fact leads to 'disharmonizing' restructuring law. It must be noted that they do so in particular from a cross-border insolvency perspective, noting that for different reasons several new PRFs are not included on Annex A of the EIR 2015.[1115] However, Gant et al. reiterated that the national transposition efforts take different speeds, also depending on varying domestic circumstances. Therefore, it may take some time before we can draw conclusions.[1116]

Nonetheless, we also note that some steps in the direction of further harmonization have been made. Firstly, the PRD 2019 introduced a shared European terminology of preventive restructuring vocabulary. It also created common ground for various concepts, which have become part now in domestic regimes. Secondly, it was aimed that the PRD 2019 would bring convergence such that "cross-border investment would no longer be inhibited by concerns that, for example, preventive restructuring of the debtor is not

1111 Proposal PRD 2016, p. 7.

1112 Impact Assessment Proposal PRD 2016, p. 51.

1113 D.C. Ehmke, J.L.L. Gant, J.M.G.J. Boon, L. Langkjaer & E. Ghio, above note 931, Para. 4.1 and 5.

1114 C. Thole, 'Die Umsetzungsgesetzgebung zur Restrukturierungsrichtlinie in Europa – Gemeinsames und Trennendes – Synthese aus den Beiträgen des Heftes 3/2022 der ZVglRWiss', *Zeitschrift für Vergleichende Rechtswissenschaft*, 2022, 121, p. 396.

1115 R. Bork & R. Mangano, *European Cross-Border Insolvency Law* (2nd ed.), Oxford: Oxford University Press, 2022, p. 38.

1116 J.L.L. Gant, J.M.G.J Boon, D.C. Ehmke, E. Ghio, L. Langkjaer, E. Vaccari and P.J. Omar, above note 984, Para. 4.

effectively possible in all Member States".[1117] The PRD 2019 has indeed contributed to such convergence by introducing a more shared framework for preventive restructuring among Member States. Although, as previously discussed, the significant and substantive differences between jurisdictions downplay the level of harmonization, it nevertheless resulted in a more shared, common ground for preventive restructuring. Thirdly, the PRD 2019 has shown that substantive harmonization in restructuring and insolvency law is not impossible, an assumption that – based on the very diverse domestic regimes – over a long time played a dominant role in inhibiting efforts to bring convergence in this area.

5.3 PRD 2019 as a Means to Promote Early Restructuring by Debtors

The PRD 2019 requires that all Member States will have a PRF in place. To date, most Member States have done so already. Although the implementation deadline – including extension – has passed, in some Member States full implementation and notification of the implementation measures to the Commission is still pending.[1118] Upon completion, *de jure*, this will promote the availability of early restructuring for debtors in all Member States, as aimed for by the EU legislator. However, it remains to be seen whether this will also practically result in more early restructuring. As the Greek contributors stated: "It still remains to be seen whether the new framework will prove up to the task of addressing the issues faced by debtors and creditors and the economy at large."[1119] A difficulty is the limited uptake of PRFs in several Member States. Different from the Netherlands,[1120] no cases have been reported in Austria.[1121] In Germany and the UK, the number of cases is lower than expected.[1122] In the UK, they expected between 50 and 100 cases, with only 9 in the first year.[1123] Although this may give an indication of the *de facto* success of the PRD 2019, its limited use may be impacted by various factors. This has no doubt been influenced by the overall decline in the number of insolvency proceedings since the COVID-19 pandemic due to massive government liquidity support schemes,[1124] which were already

1117 Impact Assessment Proposal PRD 2016, p. 51.

1118 For an overview of the implementation measures reported to the Commission (Art. 34(3) PRD 2019), see: https://eur-lex.europa.eu/legal-content/EN/NIM/?uri=celex:32019L1023. Some of these Member States – who have not notified the transposition measures – may have already a preventive restructuring framework in place.

1119 Chapter 6, Section 5.

1120 Chapter 7, Section 5.

1121 Chapter 2, Section 5.

1122 Chapter 5, Section 5; Chapter 8, Section 5.1; C. Thole, above note 1114, p. 391.

1123 Chapter 8, Section 5.1.

1124 Compare E. Inacio, 'Record Low Number of Insolvencies, Calm Before the Storm?', *Eurofenix*, Autumn, 2020, pp. 13-14; Dun & Bradstreet Worldwide Network, Global Bankruptcy Report, 2020, p. 4 et seq; Dun & Bradstreet Worldwide Network, Global Bankruptcy Report, 2021, p. 4 et seq.

rather low in years before. Furthermore, it is not clear to what extent PRFs have rather promoted informal, consensual restructurings, and where PRFs are effectively a 'stick' for when these approaches do not succeed.

The authors of the seven national chapters have pointed already at several areas to improve the domestic preventive restructuring regimes. There have been some suggestions regarding aspects that go beyond the scope of Title II of PRD 2019. This relates to not only jurisdiction, recognition and enforcement of (decisions taken in) PRFs (Section 4.7),[1125] but also the training and expertise of practitioners and judges.[1126] However, there are more critical observations by several authors. Some have stated that their domestic PRF could benefit from further legal clarity.[1127] Some have pointed at specific features, including the entry test to commence a PRF, treatment of executory contracts and availability of a debt-for-equity swap.[1128] Others more generally stated that "there is certainly need to still improve the [Austrian PRF] in several aspects."[1129] These issues may result, in particular, in time and cost inefficiencies for the involved parties, which may cause barriers, especially for micro-, small- and medium-sized debtors to enter such frameworks.[1130] Or even more drastically, some concerns were raised on the actual usefulness of the new PRF.[1131] Although further research is necessary, it suggests that mere implementation itself may not be sufficient to achieve the EU legislator's aim to promote early restructuring of debtors.

6 Concluding Remarks

The PRD 2019 has not become, what some expected it to be, a "[p]rocrustean bed that rules out radical innovations with respect to corporate restructuring regimes".[1132] Neither can it be considered the panacea for a European business rescue culture. The minimum harmonization of the PRD 2019 has resulted in – quite literally – minimum harmonization in Europe. In transposing the PRD 2019, a plethora of divergences have emerged, however, mostly within the PRD 2019's policy options. Taking a 'law at the books' approach in reviewing recent reforms in Austria, Denmark, France, Germany, Greece, the Netherlands and the United Kingdom shows that 'what you see is what you get'.

1125 See for instance Chapter 5, Sections 4.9 and 5 ; Chapter 3; Chapter 7, Section 5.
1126 See for instance Chapter 4, Section 6; Chapter 3, Section 5; Chapter 8, Section 5.7.
1127 See for instance, Chapter 2, Section 5; Chapter 3, Section 5; Chapter 6, Section 5.
1128 Chapter 2, Section 5; Chapter 5, Section 5.
1129 Chapter 2, Section 5.
1130 Chapter 2, Section 5, compare also Chapter 8, Section 5.7.
1131 Chapter 2, Section 5; Chapter 3, Section 5.
1132 H. Eidenmüller, above note 939, Para. 6.

The approach of minimum harmonization has delivered on 'its' promise, but that does not match the overall objectives of the PRD 2019. The conclusion of this study, reviewing whether the EU legislator has succeeded in fully achieving objectives, must be answered in the negative. At this point, it is at least doubtful whether the EU legislator's objective to reduce legal uncertainties in (preventive) restructuring for cross-border investments has succeeded. Although a baseline for preventive restructuring has been established, the 'law at the books' shows extensive differences. We observe that much uncertainty between jurisdictions remains, where key concepts have not been harmonized since uniform definitions lack and due to the many policy options national legislators can choose from. This has hampered the objective to effectively address legal uncertainty for cross-border investors.

Nevertheless, we can be more optimistic about the objective to promote restructuring at an early stage and avoid unnecessary liquidation. Nearly all Member States have – some still have to implement the PRD 2019 – a PRF in place, which works along certain minimum standards. This will contribute to restructuring at an early stage. However, the actual success of the PRD 2019 is to be reviewed by looking also at the 'law in action': are the PRFs effective and efficient? Are the courts, DIPs and PIFORs able to deliver on the promises of the frameworks? To what extent do PRFs promote restructuring in the shadow of the law?

Whereas several jurisdictions report that their new PRF has been used only limitedly to date, it is interesting to observe what uptake they will get in the aftermath of the COVID-19 pandemic and also to what extent this may drive harmonization through regulatory competition. However, this may be impeded because of the lack of cross-border effects of decisions in preventive restructuring cases. At this stage, there are too little data – including actual cases – to say that the PRD 2019 has succeeded in achieving its objectives.[1133] Our analysis shows that also in practice this may be a 'tough nut to crack'.

In addition to critically assessing the harmonization brought about for preventive restructuring, we also observe that the PRD 2019 has opened Europe's view on harmonization in restructuring and insolvency. No longer is this an area where substantive harmonization is unattainable, merely because of the large divergences. In that observation lies a promise for future initiatives. As we are at the start of a next wave of harmonization of EU insolvency with the recent EU Proposal for a directive to harmonize certain aspects of insolvency law,[1134] this paradigm shift that results from the PRD 2019 may prove to be

1133 Vriesendorp has launched a call for a more extensive analysis on implementations of the PRD 2019, see R.D. Vriesendorp, above note 972, p. 101.

1134 European Commission, Proposal for a Directive of the European Parliament and the Council harmonising certain aspects of insolvency law, 7 December 2022, COM(2022) 702 final.

of more significance and relevance than the current state of harmonization of preventive restructuring laws does credit to the PRD 2019.

Annex: Preventive Restructuring Directive

DIRECTIVE (EU) 2019/1023 OF THE EUROPEAN PARLIAMENT AND OF THE COUNCIL

of 20 June 2019

on preventive restructuring frameworks, on discharge of debt and disqualifications, and on measures to increase the efficiency of procedures concerning restructuring, insolvency and discharge of debt, and amending Directive (EU) 2017/1132 (Directive on restructuring and insolvency)

(Text with EEA relevance)

THE EUROPEAN PARLIAMENT AND THE COUNCIL OF THE EUROPEAN UNION,

Having regard to the Treaty on the Functioning of the European Union, and in particular Articles 53 and 114 thereof,

Having regard to the proposal from the European Commission,

After transmission of the draft legislative act to the national parliaments,

Having regard to the opinion of the European Economic and Social Committee ([1]),

Having regard to the opinion of the Committee of the Regions ([2]),

Acting in accordance with the ordinary legislative procedure ([3]),

Whereas:

(1) The objective of this Directive is to contribute to the proper functioning of the internal market and remove obstacles to the exercise of fundamental freedoms, such as the free movement of capital and freedom of establishment, which result from

1 OJ C 209, 30.6.2017, p. 21.
2 OJ C 342, 12.10.2017, p. 43.
3 Position of the European Parliament of 28 March 2019 (not yet published in the Official Journal) and decision of the Council of 6 June 2019.

differences between national laws and procedures concerning preventive restructuring, insolvency, discharge of debt, and disqualifications. Without affecting workers' fundamental rights and freedoms, this Directive aims to remove such obstacles by ensuring that: viable enterprises and entrepreneurs that are in financial difficulties have access to effective national preventive restructuring frameworks which enable them to continue operating; honest insolvent or over-indebted entrepreneurs can benefit from a full discharge of debt after a reasonable period of time, thereby allowing them a second chance; and that the effectiveness of procedures concerning restructuring, insolvency and discharge of debt is improved, in particular with a view to shortening their length.

(2) Restructuring should enable debtors in financial difficulties to continue business, in whole or in part, by changing the composition, conditions or structure of their assets and their liabilities or any other part of their capital structure — including by sales of assets or parts of the business or, where so provided under national law, the business as a whole — as well as by carrying out operational changes. Unless otherwise specifically provided for by national law, operational changes, such as the termination or amendment of contracts or the sale or other disposal of assets, should comply with the general requirements that are provided for under national law for such measures, in particular civil law and labour law rules. Any debt-to-equity swaps should also comply with safeguards provided for by national law. Preventive restructuring frameworks should, above all, enable debtors to restructure effectively at an early stage and to avoid insolvency, thus limiting the unnecessary liquidation of viable enterprises. Those frameworks should help to prevent job losses and the loss of know-how and skills, and maximise the total value to creditors — in comparison to what they would receive in the event of the liquidation of the enterprise's assets or in the event of the next-best-alternative scenario in the absence of a plan — as well as to owners and the economy as a whole.

(3) Preventive restructuring frameworks should also prevent the build-up of non-performing loans. The availability of effective preventive restructuring frameworks would ensure that action is taken before enterprises default on their loans, thereby helping to reduce the risk of loans becoming non-performing in cyclical downturns and mitigating the adverse impact on the financial sector. A significant percentage of businesses and jobs could be saved if preventive frameworks existed in all the Member States in which businesses' places of establishment, assets or creditors are situated. In restructuring frameworks the rights of all parties involved, including workers, should be protected in a balanced manner. At the same time, non-viable businesses with no prospect of survival should be liquidated as quickly as possible.

Where a debtor in financial difficulties is not economically viable or cannot be readily restored to economic viability, restructuring efforts could result in the acceleration and accumulation of losses to the detriment of creditors, workers and other stakeholders, as well as the economy as a whole.

(4) There are differences between Member States as regards the range of the procedures available to debtors in financial difficulties in order to restructure their business. Some Member States have a limited range of procedures that allow the restructuring of businesses only at a relatively late stage, in the context of insolvency procedures. In other Member States, restructuring is possible at an earlier stage but the procedures available are not as effective as they could be, or they are very formal, in particular because they limit the use of out-of-court arrangements. Preventive solutions are a growing trend in insolvency law. The trend favours approaches that, unlike the traditional approach of liquidating a business in financial difficulties, have the aim of restoring it to a healthy state or, at least, saving those of its units which are still economically viable. That approach, among other benefits to the economy, often helps to maintain jobs or reduce job losses. Moreover, the degree of involvement of judicial or administrative authorities, or the persons appointed by them, varies from no involvement or minimal involvement in some Member States to full involvement in others. Similarly, national rules giving entrepreneurs a second chance, in particular by granting them discharge from the debts they have incurred in the course of their business, vary between Member States in respect of the length of the discharge period and the conditions for granting such a discharge.

(5) In many Member States, it takes more than three years for entrepreneurs who are insolvent but honest to be discharged from their debts and make a fresh start. Inefficient discharge of debt and disqualification frameworks result in entrepreneurs having to relocate to other jurisdictions in order to benefit from a fresh start in a reasonable period of time, at considerable additional cost to both their creditors and the entrepreneurs themselves. Long disqualification orders, which often accompany a procedure leading to discharge of debt, create obstacles to the freedom to take up and pursue a self-employed, entrepreneurial activity.

(6) The excessive length of procedures concerning restructuring, insolvency and discharge of debt in several Member States is an important factor triggering low recovery rates and deterring investors from carrying out business in jurisdictions where procedures risk taking too long and being unduly costly.

(7) Differences between Member States in relation to procedures concerning restructuring, insolvency and discharge of debt translate into additional costs for

investors when assessing the risk of debtors getting into financial difficulties in one or more Member States, or of investing in viable businesses in financial difficulties, as well as additional costs of restructuring enterprises that have establishments, creditors or assets in other Member States. This is most notably the case with restructuring international groups of companies. Investors mention uncertainty about insolvency rules or the risk of lengthy or complex insolvency procedures in another Member State as being one of the main reasons for not investing or not entering into a business relationship with a counterpart outside the Member State where they are based. That uncertainty acts as a disincentive which obstructs the freedom of establishment of undertakings and the promotion of entrepreneurship and harms the proper functioning of the internal market. Micro, small and medium-sized enterprises ('SMEs') in particular do not, for the most part, have the resources needed to assess risks related to cross-border activities.

(8) The differences among Member States in procedures concerning restructuring, insolvency and discharge of debt lead to uneven conditions for access to credit and to uneven recovery rates in the Member States. A higher degree of harmonisation in the field of restructuring, insolvency, discharge of debt and disqualifications is thus indispensable for a well-functioning internal market in general and for a working Capital Markets Union in particular, as well as for the resilience of European economies, including for the preservation and creation of jobs.

(9) The additional cost of risk-assessment and of cross-border enforcement of claims for creditors of over-indebted entrepreneurs who relocate to another Member State in order to obtain a discharge of debt in a much shorter period of time should also be reduced. The additional costs for entrepreneurs stemming from the need to relocate to another Member State in order to benefit from a discharge of debt should also be reduced. Furthermore, the obstacles stemming from long disqualification orders linked to an entrepreneur's insolvency or over-indebtedness inhibit entrepreneurship.

(10) Any restructuring operation, in particular one of major size which generates a significant impact, should be based on a dialogue with the stakeholders. That dialogue should cover the choice of the measures envisaged in relation to the objectives of the restructuring operation, as well as alternative options, and there should be appropriate involvement of employees' representatives as provided for in Union and national law.

(11) The obstacles to the exercise of fundamental freedoms are not limited to purely cross-border situations. An increasingly interconnected internal market, in which goods, services, capital and workers circulate freely, and which has an ever-stronger digital dimension, means that very few enterprises are purely national if all relevant elements

are considered, such as their client base, supply chain, scope of activities, investor and capital base. Even purely national insolvencies can have an impact on the functioning of the internal market through the so-called domino effect of insolvencies, whereby a debtor's insolvency may trigger further insolvencies in the supply chain.

(12) Regulation (EU) 2015/848 of the European Parliament and of the Council ([4]) deals with issues of jurisdiction, recognition and enforcement, applicable law and cooperation in cross-border insolvency proceedings as well as with the interconnection of insolvency registers. Its scope covers preventive procedures which promote the rescue of economically viable debtors as well as discharge procedures for entrepreneurs and other natural persons. However, that Regulation does not tackle the disparities between national laws regulating those procedures. Furthermore, an instrument limited only to cross-border insolvencies would not remove all obstacles to free movement, nor would it be feasible for investors to determine in advance the cross-border or domestic nature of the potential financial difficulties of the debtor in the future. There is therefore a need to go beyond matters of judicial cooperation and to establish substantive minimum standards for preventive restructuring procedures as well as for procedures leading to a discharge of debt for entrepreneurs.

(13) This Directive should be without prejudice to the scope of Regulation (EU) 2015/848. It aims to be fully compatible with, and complementary to, that Regulation, by requiring Member States to put in place preventive restructuring procedures which comply with certain minimum principles of effectiveness. It does not change the approach taken in that Regulation of allowing Member States to maintain or introduce procedures which do not fulfil the condition of publicity for notification under Annex A to that Regulation. Although this Directive does not require that procedures within its scope fulfil all the conditions for notification under that Annex, it aims to facilitate the cross-border recognition of those procedures and the recognition and enforceability of judgments.

(14) The advantage of the application of Regulation (EU) 2015/848 is that it provides for safeguards against abusive relocation of the debtor's centre of main interests during cross-border insolvency proceedings. Certain restrictions should also apply to procedures not covered by that Regulation.

(15) It is necessary to lower the costs of restructuring for both debtors and creditors. Therefore, the differences between Member States which hamper the early

4 Regulation (EU) 2015/848 of the European Parliament and of the Council of 20 May 2015 on insolvency proceedings (OJ L 141, 5.6.2015, p. 19).

restructuring of viable debtors in financial difficulties and the possibility of a discharge of debt for honest entrepreneurs should be reduced. Reducing such differences should bring greater transparency, legal certainty and predictability across the Union. It should maximise the returns to all types of creditors and investors and encourage cross-border investment. Greater coherence of restructuring and insolvency procedures should also facilitate the restructuring of groups of companies irrespective of where the members of the group are located in the Union.

(16) Removing the barriers to effective preventive restructuring of viable debtors in financial difficulties contributes to minimising job losses and losses of value for creditors in the supply chain, preserves know-how and skills and hence benefits the wider economy. Facilitating a discharge of debt for entrepreneurs would help to avoid their exclusion from the labour market and enable them to restart entrepreneurial activities, drawing lessons from past experience. Moreover, reducing the length of restructuring procedures would result in higher recovery rates for creditors as the passing of time would normally only result in a further loss of value of the debtor or the debtor's business. Finally, efficient preventive restructuring, insolvency and discharge procedures would enable a better assessment of the risks involved in lending and borrowing decisions and facilitate the adjustment for insolvent or over-indebted debtors, minimising the economic and social costs involved in their deleveraging process. This Directive should allow Member States flexibility to apply common principles while respecting national legal systems. Member States should be able to maintain or introduce in their national legal systems preventive restructuring frameworks other than those provided for by this Directive.

(17) Enterprises, and in particular SMEs, which represent 99 % of all businesses in the Union, should benefit from a more coherent approach at Union level. SMEs are more likely to be liquidated than restructured, since they have to bear costs that are disproportionately higher than those faced by larger enterprises. SMEs, especially when facing financial difficulties, often do not have the necessary resources to cope with high restructuring costs and to take advantage of the more efficient restructuring procedures available only in some Member States. In order to help such debtors restructure at low cost, comprehensive check-lists for restructuring plans, adapted to the needs and specificities of SMEs, should be developed at national level and made available online. In addition, early warning tools should be put in place to warn debtors of the urgent need to act, taking into account the limited resources of SMEs for hiring experts.

(18) When defining SMEs, Member States could give due consideration to Directive 2013/34/EU of the European Parliament and of the Council ([5]) or the Commission Recommendation of 6 May 2003 concerning the definition of micro, small and medium-sized enterprises ([6]).

(19) It is appropriate to exclude from the scope of this Directive debtors which are insurance and re-insurance undertakings as defined in points (1) and (4) of Article 13 of Directive 2009/138/EC of the European Parliament and of the Council ([7]), credit institutions as defined in point (1) of Article 4(1) of Regulation (EU) No 575/2013 of the European Parliament and of the Council ([8]), investment firms and collective investment undertakings as defined in points (2) and (7) of Article 4(1) of Regulation (EU) No 575/2013, central counterparties as defined in point (1) of Article 2 of Regulation (EU) No 648/2012 of the European Parliament and of the Council ([9]), central securities depositories as defined in point (1) of Article 2(1) of Regulation (EU) No 909/2014 of the European Parliament and of the Council ([10]) and other financial institutions and entities listed in the first subparagraph of Article 1(1) of Directive 2014/59/EU of the European Parliament and of the Council ([11]). Such debtors are subject to special arrangements and the national supervisory and resolution authorities have wide-ranging powers of intervention in relation to them. Member States should be able to exclude other financial entities providing financial services which are subject to comparable arrangements and powers of intervention.

5 Directive 2013/34/EU of the European Parliament and of the Council of 26 June 2013 on the annual financial statements, consolidated financial statements and related reports of certain types of undertakings, amending Directive 2006/43/EC of the European Parliament and of the Council and repealing Council Directives 78/660/EEC and 83/349/EEC (OJ L 182, 29.6.2013, p. 19).

6 Commission Recommendation of 6 May 2003 concerning the definition of micro, small and medium-sized enterprises (OJ L 124, 20.5.2003, p. 36).

7 Directive 2009/138/EC of the European Parliament and of the Council of 25 November 2009 on the taking-up and pursuit of the business of Insurance and Reinsurance (Solvency II) (OJ L 335, 17.12.2009, p. 1).

8 Regulation (EU) No 575/2013 of the European Parliament and of the Council of 26 June 2013 on prudential requirements for credit institutions and investment firms and amending Regulation (EU) No 648/2012 (OJ L 176, 27.6.2013, p. 1).

9 Regulation (EU) No 648/2012 of the European Parliament and of the Council of 4 July 2012 on OTC derivatives, central counterparties and trade repositories (OJ L 201, 27.7.2012, p. 1).

10 Regulation (EU) No 909/2014 of the European Parliament and of the Council of 23 July 2014 on improving securities settlement in the European Union and on central securities depositories and amending Directives 98/26/EC and 2014/65/EU and Regulation (EU) No 236/2012 (OJ L 257, 28.8.2014, p. 1).

11 Directive 2014/59/EU of the European Parliament and of the Council of 15 May 2014 establishing a framework for the recovery and resolution of credit institutions and investment firms and amending Council Directive 82/891/EEC, and Directives 2001/24/EC, 2002/47/EC, 2004/25/EC, 2005/56/EC, 2007/36/EC, 2011/35/EU, 2012/30/EU and 2013/36/EU, and Regulations (EU) No 1093/2010 and (EU) No 648/2012, of the European Parliament and of the Council (OJ L 173, 12.6.2014, p. 190).

(20) For similar considerations, it is also appropriate to exclude from the scope of this Directive public bodies under national law. Member States should also be able to limit the access to preventive restructuring frameworks to legal persons, since the financial difficulties of entrepreneurs may be efficiently addressed not only by means of preventive restructuring procedures but also by means of procedures which lead to a discharge of debt or by means of informal restructurings based on contractual agreements. Member States with different legal systems, where the same type of entity has a different legal status in those legal systems, should be able to apply one uniform regime to such entities. A preventive restructuring framework laid down pursuant to this Directive should not affect claims and entitlements against a debtor that arise from occupational pension systems if those claims and entitlements accrued during a period prior to the restructuring.

(21) Consumer over-indebtedness is a matter of great economic and social concern and is closely related to the reduction of debt overhang. Furthermore, it is often not possible to draw a clear distinction between the debts incurred by entrepreneurs in the course of their trade, business, craft or profession and those incurred outside those activities. Entrepreneurs would not effectively benefit from a second chance if they had to go through separate procedures, with different access conditions and discharge periods, to discharge their business debts and other debts incurred outside their business. For those reasons, although this Directive does not include binding rules on consumer over-indebtedness, it would be advisable for Member States to apply also to consumers, at the earliest opportunity, the provisions of this Directive concerning discharge of debt.

(22) The earlier a debtor can detect its financial difficulties and can take appropriate action, the higher the probability of avoiding an impending insolvency or, in the case of a business the viability of which is permanently impaired, the more orderly and efficient the liquidation process would be. Clear, up-to-date, concise and user-friendly information on the available preventive restructuring procedures as well as one or more early warning tools should therefore be put in place to incentivise debtors that start to experience financial difficulties to take early action. Early warning tools which take the form of alert mechanisms that indicate when the debtor has not made certain types of payments could be triggered by, for example, non-payment of taxes or social security contributions. Such tools could be developed either by Member States or by private entities, provided that the objective is met. Member States should make information about early warning tools available online, for example on a dedicated website or webpage. Member States should be able to adapt the early warning tools depending on the size of the enterprise and to lay down

specific provisions on early warning tools for large-sized enterprises and groups that take into account their peculiarities. This Directive should not impose any liability on Member States for potential damage incurred through restructuring procedures which are triggered by such early warning tools.

(23) In an effort to increase the support of employees and their representatives, Member States should ensure that employees' representatives are given access to relevant and up-to-date information regarding the availability of early warning tools and it should also be possible for them to provide support to employees' representatives in assessing the economic situation of the debtor.

(24) A restructuring framework should be available to debtors, including legal entities and, where so provided under national law, natural persons and groups of companies, to enable them to address their financial difficulties at an early stage, when it appears likely that their insolvency can be prevented and the viability of the business can be ensured. A restructuring framework should be available before a debtor becomes insolvent under national law, namely before the debtor fulfils the conditions under national law for entering collective insolvency proceedings, which normally entail a total divestment of the debtor and the appointment of a liquidator. In order to avoid restructuring frameworks being misused, the financial difficulties of the debtor should indicate a likelihood of insolvency and the restructuring plan should be capable of preventing the insolvency of the debtor and ensuring the viability of the business.

(25) Member States should be able to determine whether claims that fall due or that come into existence after an application to open a preventive restructuring procedure has been submitted or after the procedure has been opened are included in the preventive restructuring measures or the stay of individual enforcement actions. Member States should be able to decide whether the stay of individual enforcement actions has an effect on the interest due on claims.

(26) Member States should be able to introduce a viability test as a condition for access to the preventive restructuring procedure provided for by this Directive. Such a test should be carried out without detriment to the debtor's assets, which could take the form of, among other things, the granting of an interim stay or the carrying out without undue delay of the test. However, the absence of detriment should not prevent Member States from requiring debtors to prove their viability at their own cost.

(27) The fact that Member States can limit access to a restructuring framework with regard to debtors that have been sentenced for serious breaches of accounting or book-keeping obligations should not prevent Member States from also limiting the access of debtors to preventive restructuring frameworks where their books and records are incomplete or deficient to a degree that makes it impossible to ascertain the business and financial situation of the debtors.

(28) Member States should be able to extend the scope of preventive restructuring frameworks provided for by this Directive to situations in which debtors face non-financial difficulties, provided that such difficulties give rise to a real and serious threat to a debtor's actual or future ability to pay its debts as they fall due. The time frame relevant for the determination of such threat may extend to a period of several months, or even longer, in order to account for cases in which the debtor is faced with non-financial difficulties threatening the status of its business as a going concern and, in the medium term, its liquidity. This may be the case, for example, where the debtor has lost a contract which is of key importance to it.

(29) To promote efficiency and reduce delays and costs, national preventive restructuring frameworks should include flexible procedures. Where this Directive is implemented by means of more than one procedure within a restructuring framework, the debtor should have access to all rights and safeguards provided for by this Directive with the aim of achieving an effective restructuring. Except in the event of mandatory involvement of judicial or administrative authorities as provided for under this Directive, Member States should be able to limit the involvement of such authorities to situations in which it is necessary and proportionate, while taking into consideration, among other things, the aim of safeguarding the rights and interests of debtors and of affected parties, as well as the aim of reducing delays and the cost of the procedures. Where creditors or employees' representatives are allowed to initiate a restructuring procedure under national law and where the debtor is an SME, Member States should require the agreement of the debtor as a precondition for the initiation of the procedure, and should also be able to extend that requirement to debtors which are large enterprises.

(30) To avoid unnecessary costs, to reflect the early nature of preventive restructuring and to encourage debtors to apply for preventive restructuring at an early stage of their financial difficulties, they should, in principle, be left in control of their assets and the day-to-day operation of their business. The appointment of a practitioner in the field of restructuring, to supervise the activity of a debtor or to partially take over control of a debtor's daily operations, should not be mandatory in every case, but made on a case-by-case basis depending on the circumstances of the case or on the debtor's

specific needs. Nevertheless, Member States should be able to determine that the appointment of a practitioner in the field of restructuring is always necessary in certain circumstances, such as where: the debtor benefits from a general stay of individual enforcement actions; the restructuring plan needs to be confirmed by means of a cross-class cram-down; the restructuring plan includes measures affecting the rights of workers; or the debtor or its management have acted in a criminal, fraudulent, or detrimental manner in business relations.

(31) For the purpose of assisting the parties with negotiating and drafting a restructuring plan, Member States should provide for the mandatory appointment of a practitioner in the field of restructuring where: a judicial or administrative authority grants the debtor a general stay of individual enforcement actions, provided that in such case a practitioner is needed to safeguard the interests of the parties; the restructuring plan needs to be confirmed by a judicial or administrative authority by means of a cross-class cram-down; it was requested by the debtor; or it is requested by a majority of creditors provided that the creditors cover the costs and fees of the practitioner.

(32) A debtor should be able to benefit from a temporary stay of individual enforcement actions, whether granted by a judicial or administrative authority or by operation of law, with the aim of supporting the negotiations on a restructuring plan, in order to be able to continue operating or at least to preserve the value of its estate during the negotiations. Where so provided by national law, it should also be possible for the stay to apply for the benefit of third-party security providers, including guarantors and collateral givers. However, Member States should be able to provide that judicial or administrative authorities can refuse to grant a stay of individual enforcement actions where such a stay is not necessary or where it would not fulfil the objective of supporting the negotiations. Grounds for refusal might include a lack of support by the required majorities of creditors or, where so provided under national law, the debtor's actual inability to pay debts as they fall due.

(33) In order to facilitate and accelerate the course of proceedings, Member States should be able to establish, on a rebuttable basis, presumptions for the presence of grounds for refusal of the stay, where, for example, the debtor shows conduct that is typical of a debtor that is unable to pay debts as they fall due — such as a substantial default vis-à-vis workers or tax or social security agencies — or where a financial crime has been committed by the debtor or the current management of an enterprise which gives reason to believe that a majority of creditors would not support the start of the negotiations.

(34) A stay of individual enforcement actions could be general, in that it affects all creditors, or it could apply only to some individual creditors or categories of creditors. Member States should be able to exclude certain claims or categories of claims from the scope of the stay, in well-defined circumstances, such as claims which are secured by assets the removal of which would not jeopardise the restructuring of the business or claims of creditors in respect of which a stay would cause unfair prejudice, such as by way of an uncompensated loss or depreciation of collateral.

(35) In order to provide for a fair balance between the rights of the debtor and those of creditors, a stay of individual enforcement actions should apply for a maximum period of up to four months. Complex restructurings may, however, require more time. Member States should be able to provide that, in such cases, extensions of the initial period of the stay can be granted by the judicial or administrative authority. Where a judicial or administrative authority does not take a decision on the extension of a stay before it lapses, the stay should cease to have effect upon expiry of the stay period. In the interest of legal certainty, the total period of the stay should be limited to 12 months. Member States should be able to provide for an indefinite stay where the debtor becomes insolvent under national law. Member States should be able to decide whether a short interim stay pending a judicial or administrative authority's decision on access to the preventive restructuring framework is subject to the time limits under this Directive.

(36) To ensure that creditors do not suffer unnecessary detriment, Member States should provide that judicial or administrative authorities can lift a stay of individual enforcement actions if it no longer fulfils the objective of supporting negotiations, for example if it becomes apparent that the required majority of creditors does not support the continuation of the negotiations. The stay should also be lifted if creditors are unfairly prejudiced by it, where Member States provide for such a possibility. Member States should be allowed to limit the possibility to lift the stay to situations where creditors have not had the opportunity to be heard before it came into force or before it was extended. Member States should also be allowed to provide for a minimum period during which the stay cannot be lifted. In establishing whether there is unfair prejudice to creditors, judicial or administrative authorities should be able to take into account whether the stay would preserve the overall value of the estate, and whether the debtor acts in bad faith or with the intention of causing prejudice or generally acts against the legitimate expectations of the general body of creditors.

(37) This Directive does not cover provisions on compensation or guarantees for creditors of which the collateral is likely to decrease in value during the stay. A single creditor

or a class of creditors would be unfairly prejudiced by the stay if, for example, their claims would be made substantially worse-off as a result of the stay than if the stay did not apply, or if the creditor is put more at a disadvantage than other creditors in a similar position. Member States should be able to provide that, whenever unfair prejudice is established in respect of one or more creditors or one or more classes of creditors, the stay can be lifted in respect of those creditors or classes of creditors or in respect of all creditors. Member States should be able to decide who is entitled to request the lifting of the stay.

(38) A stay of individual enforcement actions should also result in the suspension of a debtor's obligation to file for, or the opening at a creditor's request of, an insolvency procedure which could end in liquidation of the debtor. Such insolvency procedures should, in addition to those limited by law to having as the only possible outcome the liquidation of the debtor, also include procedures that could lead to a restructuring of the debtor. The suspension of the opening of an insolvency procedure at the request of creditors should apply not only where Member States provide for a general stay of individual enforcement actions covering all creditors, but also where Member States provide for the option of a stay of individual enforcement actions covering only a limited number of creditors. Nevertheless, Member States should be able to provide that insolvency proceedings can be opened at the request of public authorities which are not acting in a creditor capacity, but in the general interest, such as a public prosecutor.

(39) This Directive should not prevent debtors from paying, in the ordinary course of business, claims of unaffected creditors, and claims of affected creditors that arise during the stay of individual enforcement actions. To ensure that creditors with claims that came into existence before the opening of a restructuring procedure or a stay of individual enforcement actions do not put pressure on the debtor to pay those claims, which otherwise would be reduced through the implementation of the restructuring plan, Member States should be able to provide for the suspension of the obligation on the debtor with respect to payment of those claims.

(40) When a debtor enters an insolvency procedure, some suppliers can have contractual rights, provided for in so- called ipso facto clauses, entitling them to terminate the supply contract solely on account of the insolvency, even if the debtor has duly met its obligations. Ipso facto clauses could also be triggered when a debtor applies for preventive restructuring measures. Where such clauses are invoked when the debtor is merely negotiating a restructuring plan or requesting a stay of individual enforcement actions or invoked in connection with any event connected with the stay, early termination can have a negative impact on the debtor's business and the

successful rescue of the business. Therefore, in such cases, it is necessary to provide that creditors are not allowed to invoke ipso facto clauses which make reference to negotiations on a restructuring plan or a stay or any similar event connected to the stay.

(41) Early termination can endanger the ability of a business to continue operating during restructuring negotiations, especially when contracts for essential supplies such as gas, electricity, water, telecommunication and card payment services are concerned. Member States should provide that creditors to which a stay of individual enforcement actions applies, and whose claims came into existence prior to the stay and have not been paid by a debtor, are not allowed to withhold performance of, terminate, accelerate or, in any other way, modify essential executory contracts during the stay period, provided that the debtor complies with its obligations under such contracts which fall due during the stay. Executory contracts are, for example, lease and licence agreements, long- term supply contracts and franchise agreements.

(42) This Directive lays down minimum standards for the content of a restructuring plan. However, Member States should be able to require additional explanations in the restructuring plan, concerning for example the criteria according to which creditors have been grouped, which may be relevant in cases where a debt is only partially secured. Member States should not be obliged to require an expert opinion regarding the value of assets which need to be indicated in the plan.

(43) Creditors affected by a restructuring plan, including workers, and, where allowed under national law, equity- holders, should have a right to vote on the adoption of a restructuring plan. Member States should be able to provide for limited exceptions to this rule. Parties unaffected by the restructuring plan should have no voting rights in relation to the plan, nor should their support be required for the approval of any plan. The concept of 'affected parties' should only include workers in their capacity as creditors. Therefore, if Member States decide to exempt the claims of workers from the preventive restructuring framework, workers should not be considered as affected parties. The vote on the adoption of a restructuring plan could take the form of a formal voting process or of a consultation and agreement with the required majority of affected parties. However, where the vote takes the form of an agreement with the requisite majority, affected parties which were not involved in the agreement could nevertheless be offered the opportunity to join the restructuring plan.

(44) To ensure that rights which are substantially similar are treated equitably and that restructuring plans can be adopted without unfairly prejudicing the rights of affected parties, affected parties should be treated in separate classes which correspond to the

class formation criteria under national law. 'Class formation' means the grouping of affected parties for the purposes of adopting a plan in such a way as to reflect their rights and the seniority of their claims and interests. As a minimum, secured and unsecured creditors should always be treated in separate classes. Member States should, however, be able to require that more than two classes of creditors are formed, including different classes of unsecured or secured creditors and classes of creditors with subordinated claims. Member States should also be able to treat types of creditors that lack a sufficient commonality of interest, such as tax or social security authorities, in separate classes. It should be possible for Member States to provide that secured claims can be divided into secured and unsecured parts based on collateral valuation. It should also be possible for Member States to lay down specific rules supporting class formation where non- diversified or otherwise especially vulnerable creditors, such as workers or small suppliers, would benefit from such class formation.

(45) Member States should be able to provide that debtors that are SMEs, can, on account of their relatively simple capital structure, be exempted from the obligation to treat affected parties in separate classes. In cases where SMEs have opted to create only one voting class and that class votes against the plan, it should be possible for debtors to submit another plan, in line with the general principles of this Directive.

(46) Member States should in any case ensure that adequate treatment is given in their national law to matters of particular importance for class formation purposes, such as claims from connected parties, and that their national law contains rules that deal with contingent claims and contested claims. Member States should be allowed to regulate how contested claims are to be handled for the purposes of allocating voting rights. The judicial or administrative authority should examine class formation, including the selection of creditors affected by the plan, when a restructuring plan is submitted for confirmation. However, Member States should be able to provide that such authority can also examine class formation at an earlier stage should the proposer of the plan seek validation or guidance in advance.

(47) Requisite majorities should be established by national law to ensure that a minority of affected parties in each class cannot obstruct the adoption of a restructuring plan which does not unfairly reduce their rights and interests. Without a majority rule binding dissenting secured creditors, early restructuring would not be possible in many cases, for example where a financial restructuring is needed but the business is otherwise viable. To ensure that parties have a say on the adoption of restructuring plans proportionate to the stakes they have in the business, the required majority should be based on the amount of the creditors' claims or equity holders' interests in

any given class. Member States should, in addition, be able to require a majority in the number of affected parties in each class. Member States should be able to lay down rules in relation to affected parties with a right to vote which do not exercise that right in a correct manner or are not represented, such as rules allowing those affected parties to be taken into account for a participation threshold or for the calculation of a majority. Member States should also be able to provide for a participation threshold for the vote.

(48) Confirmation of a restructuring plan by a judicial or administrative authority is necessary to ensure that the reduction of the rights of creditors or interests of equity holders is proportionate to the benefits of the restructuring and that they have access to an effective remedy. Confirmation is particularly necessary where: there are dissenting affected parties; the restructuring plan contains provisions on new financing; or the plan involves a loss of more than 25 % of the work force. Member States should, however, be able to provide that confirmation by a judicial or administrative authority is necessary also in other cases. A confirmation of a plan which involves the loss of more than 25 % of the work force should only be necessary where national law allows preventive restructuring frameworks to provide for measures that have a direct effect on employment contracts.

(49) Member States should ensure that a judicial or administrative authority is able to reject a plan where it has been established that it reduces the rights of dissenting creditors or equity holders either to a level below what they could reasonably expect to receive in the event of the liquidation of the debtor's business, whether by piecemeal liquidation or by a sale as a going concern, depending on the particular circumstances of each debtor, or to a level below what they could reasonably expect in the event of the next-best-alternative scenario where the restructuring plan is not confirmed. However, where the plan is confirmed through a cross-class cram-down, reference should be made to the protection mechanism used in such scenario. Where Member States opt to carry out a valuation of the debtor as a going concern, the going-concern value should take into account the debtor's business in the longer term, as opposed to the liquidation value. The going-concern value is, as a rule, higher than the liquidation value because it is based on the assumption that the business continues its activity with the minimum of disruption, has the confidence of financial creditors, shareholders and clients, continues to generate revenues, and limits the impact on workers.

(50) While compliance with the best-interests-of-creditors test should be examined by a judicial or administrative authority only if the restructuring plan is challenged on that ground in order to avoid a valuation being made in every case, Member States

should be able to provide that other conditions for confirmation can be examined ex officio. Member States should be able to add other conditions which need to be complied with in order to confirm a restructuring plan, such as whether equity holders are adequately protected. Judicial or administrative authorities should be able to refuse to confirm restructuring plans which have no reasonable prospect of preventing the insolvency of the debtor or ensuring the viability of the business. However, Member States should not be required to ensure that such assessment is made ex officio.

(51) Notification to all affected parties should be one of the conditions for confirmation of a restructuring plan. Member States should be able to define the form of the notification, to identify the time when it is to be made, as well as to lay down provisions for the treatment of unknown claims as regards notification. They should also be able to provide that non-affected parties have to be informed about the restructuring plan.

(52) Satisfying the 'best-interest-of-creditors' test should be considered to mean that no dissenting creditor is worse off under a restructuring plan than it would be either in the case of liquidation, whether piecemeal liquidation or sale of the business as a going concern, or in the event of the next-best-alternative scenario if the restructuring plan were not to be confirmed. Member States should be able to choose one of those thresholds when implementing the best-interest-of-creditors test in national law. That test should be applied in any case where a plan needs to be confirmed in order to be binding for dissenting creditors or, as the case may be, dissenting classes of creditors. As a consequence of the best-interest-of-creditors test, where public institutional creditors have a privileged status under national law, Member States could provide that the plan cannot impose a full or partial cancellation of the claims of those creditors.

(53) While a restructuring plan should always be adopted if the required majority in each affected class supports the plan, it should still be possible for a restructuring plan which is not supported by the required majority in each affected class to be confirmed by a judicial or administrative authority, upon the proposal of a debtor or with the debtor's agreement. In the case of a legal person, Member States should be able to decide if, for the purpose of adopting or confirming a restructuring plan, the debtor is to be understood as the legal person's management board or a certain majority of shareholders or equity holders. For the plan to be confirmed in the case of a cross-class cram-down, it should be supported by a majority of voting classes of affected parties. At least one of those classes should be a secured creditor class or senior to the ordinary unsecured creditors class.

(54) It should be possible that, where a majority of voting classes does not support the restructuring plan, the plan can nevertheless be confirmed if it is supported by at least one affected or impaired class of creditors which, upon a valuation of the debtor as a going concern, receive payment or keep any interest, or, where so provided under national law, can reasonably be presumed to receive payment or keep any interest, if the normal ranking of liquidation priorities is applied under national law. In such a case, Member States should be able to increase the number of classes which are required to approve the plan, without necessarily requiring that all those classes should, upon a valuation of the debtor as a going concern, receive payment or keep any interest under national law. However, Member States should not require the consent of all classes. Accordingly, where there are only two classes of creditors, the consent of at least one class should be deemed to be sufficient, if the other conditions for the application of a cross-class cram-down are met. The impairment of creditors should be understood to mean that there is a reduction in the value of their claims.

(55) In the case of a cross-class cram-down, Member States should ensure that dissenting classes of affected creditors are not unfairly prejudiced under the proposed plan and Member States should provide sufficient protection for such dissenting classes. Member States should be able to protect a dissenting class of affected creditors by ensuring that it is treated at least as favourably as any other class of the same rank and more favourably than any more junior class. Alternatively, Member States could protect a dissenting class of affected creditors by ensuring that such dissenting class is paid in full if a more junior class receives any distribution or keeps any interest under the restructuring plan (the 'absolute priority rule'). Member States should have discretion in implementing the concept of 'payment in full', including in relation to the timing of the payment, as long as the principal of the claim and, in the case of secured creditors, the value of the collateral are protected. Member States should also be able to decide on the choice of the equivalent means by which the original claim could be satisfied in full.

(56) Member States should be able to derogate from the absolute priority rule, for example where it is considered fair that equity holders keep certain interests under the plan despite a more senior class being obliged to accept a reduction of its claims, or that essential suppliers covered by the provision on the stay of individual enforcement actions are paid before more senior classes of creditors. Member States should be able to choose which of the above-mentioned protection mechanisms they put in place.

(57) While shareholders' or other equity holders' legitimate interests should be protected, Member States should ensure that they cannot unreasonably prevent the adoption of restructuring plans that would bring the debtor back to viability. Member States

should be able to use different means to achieve that goal, for example by not giving equity holders the right to vote on a restructuring plan and by not making the adoption of a restructuring plan conditional on the agreement of equity holders that, upon a valuation of the enterprise, would not receive any payment or other consideration if the normal ranking of liquidation priorities were applied. However, where equity holders have the right to vote on a restructuring plan, a judicial or administrative authority should be able to confirm the plan by applying the rules on cross-class cram down notwithstanding the dissent of one or more classes of equity holders. Member States that exclude equity holders from voting should not be required to apply the absolute priority rule in the relationship between creditors and equity holders. Another possible means of ensuring that equity holders do not unreasonably prevent the adoption of restructuring plans would be to ensure that restructuring measures that directly affect equity holders' rights, and that need to be approved by a general meeting of shareholders under company law, are not subject to unreasonably high majority requirements and that equity holders have no competence in terms of restructuring measures that do not directly affect their rights.

(58) Several classes of equity holders can be needed where different classes of shareholdings with different rights exist. Equity holders of SMEs that are not mere investors, but are the owners of the enterprise and contribute to the enterprise in other ways, such as managerial expertise, might not have an incentive to restructure under such conditions. For this reason, the cross-class cram-down should remain optional for debtors that are SMEs.

(59) The restructuring plan should, for the purposes of its implementation, make it possible for equity holders of SMEs to provide non-monetary restructuring assistance by drawing on, for example, their experience, reputation or business contacts.

(60) Throughout the preventive restructuring procedures, workers should enjoy full labour law protection. In particular, this Directive should be without prejudice to workers' rights guaranteed by Council Directives 98/59/EC ([12]) and 2001/23/EC ([13]),

12 Council Directive 98/59/EC of 20 July 1998 on the approximation of the laws of the Member States relating to collective redundancies (OJ L 225, 12.8.1998, p. 16).

13 Council Directive 2001/23/EC of 12 March 2001 on the approximation of the laws of the Member States relating to the safeguarding of employees' rights in the event of transfers of undertakings, businesses or parts of undertakings or businesses (OJ L 82, 22.3.2001, p. 16).

and Directives 2002/14/EC ([14]), 2008/94/EC ([15]) and 2009/38/EC ([16]) of the European Parliament and of the Council. The obligations concerning information and consultation of employees under national law transposing those Directives remain fully intact. This includes obligations to inform and consult employees' representatives on the decision to have recourse to a preventive restructuring framework in accordance with Directive 2002/14/EC.

(61) Employees and their representatives should be provided with information regarding the proposed restructuring plan in so far as provided for in Union law, in order to allow them to undertake an in-depth assessment of the various scenarios. Furthermore, employees and their representatives should be involved to the extent necessary to fulfil the consultation requirements laid down in Union law. Given the need to ensure an appropriate level of protection of workers, Member States should be required to exempt workers' outstanding claims from any stay of individual enforcement actions, irrespective of the question of whether those claims arise before or after the stay is granted. A stay of enforcement of workers' outstanding claims should be allowed only for the amounts and for the period for which the payment of such claims is effectively guaranteed at a similar level by other means under national law. Where national law provides for limitations on the liability of guarantee institutions, either in terms of the length of the guarantee or the amount paid to workers, workers should be able to enforce any shortfall in their claims against the employer even during the stay period. Alternatively, Member States should be able to exclude workers' claims from the scope of the preventive restructuring frameworks and provide for their protection under national law.

(62) Where a restructuring plan entails the transfer of a part of an undertaking or business, workers' rights arising from a contract of employment or from an employment relationship, in particular the right to wages, should be safeguarded in accordance with Articles 3 and 4 of Directive 2001/23/EC, without prejudice to the specific rules applying in the event of insolvency proceedings under Article 5 of that Directive and in particular the possibilities provided for in Article 5(2) of that Directive. This Directive should be without prejudice to the rights to information and consultation,

14 Directive 2002/14/EC of the European Parliament and of the Council of 11 March 2002 establishing a general framework for informing and consulting employees in the European Community (OJ L 80, 23.3.2002, p. 29).

15 Directive 2008/94/EC of the European Parliament and of the Council of 22 October 2008 on the protection of employees in the event of the insolvency of their employer (OJ L 283, 28.10.2008, p. 36).

16 Directive 2009/38/EC of the European Parliament and of the Council of 6 May 2009 on the establishment of a European Works council or a procedure in Community-scale undertakings and community-scale groups of undertakings for the purpose of informing and consulting employees (OJ L 122, 16.5.2009, p. 28).

which are guaranteed by Directive 2002/14/EC, including on decisions likely to lead to substantial changes in work organisation or in contractual relations with a view to reaching an agreement on such decisions. Furthermore, under this Directive, workers whose claims are affected by a restructuring plan should have the right to vote on the plan. For the purposes of voting on the restructuring plan, Member States should be able to decide to place workers in a class separate from other classes of creditors.

(63) Judicial or administrative authorities should only decide on the valuation of a business — either in liquidation or in the next-best-alternative scenario, if the restructuring plan was not confirmed — if a dissenting affected party challenges the restructuring plan. This should not prevent Member States from carrying out valuations in another context under national law. However, it should be possible that such a decision also consists of an approval of a valuation by an expert or of a valuation submitted by the debtor or another party at an earlier stage of the process. Where the decision to carry out a valuation is taken, Member States should be able to provide for special rules, separate from general civil procedural law, for a valuation in restructuring cases, with a view to ensuring that it is carried out in an expedited manner. Nothing in this Directive should affect the rules on burden of proof under national law in the case of a valuation.

(64) The binding effects of a restructuring plan should be limited to the affected parties that were involved in the adoption of the plan. Member States should be able to determine what it means for a creditor to be involved, including in the case of unknown creditors or creditors of future claims. For example, Member States should be able to decide how to deal with creditors that have been notified correctly but that did not participate in the procedures.

(65) Interested affected parties should be able to appeal a decision on the confirmation of a restructuring plan issued by an administrative authority. Member States should also be able to introduce the option of appealing a decision on the confirmation of a restructuring plan issued by a judicial authority. However, in order to ensure the effectiveness of the plan, to reduce uncertainty and to avoid unjustifiable delays, appeals should, as a rule, not have suspensive effects and therefore not preclude the implementation of a restructuring plan. Member States should be able to determine and limit the grounds for appeal. Where the decision on the confirmation of the plan is appealed, Member States should be able to allow the judicial authority to issue a preliminary or summary decision that protects the execution and implementation of the plan against the consequences of the pending appeal being upheld. Where an appeal is upheld, judicial or administrative authorities should be able to consider, as an alternative to setting aside the plan, an amendment of the plan, where Member

States provide for such a possibility, as well as a confirmation of the plan without amendments. It should be possible for any amendments to the plan to be proposed or voted on by the parties, on their own initiative or at the request of the judicial authority. Member States could also provide for compensation for monetary losses for the party whose appeal was upheld. National law should be able to deal with a potential new stay or extension of the stay in event of the judicial authority deciding that the appeal has suspensive effect.

(66) The success of a restructuring plan often depends on whether financial assistance is extended to the debtor to support, firstly, the operation of the business during restructuring negotiations and, secondly, the implementation of the restructuring plan after its confirmation. Financial assistance should be understood in a broad sense, including the provision of money or third-party guarantees and the supply of stock, inventory, raw materials and utilities, for example through granting the debtor a longer repayment period. Interim financing and new financing should therefore be exempt from avoidance actions which seek to declare such financing void, voidable or unenforceable as an act detrimental to the general body of creditors in the context of subsequent insolvency procedures.

(67) National insolvency laws providing for avoidance actions of interim and new financing or providing that new lenders may incur civil, administrative or criminal sanctions for extending credit to debtors in financial difficulties could jeopardise the availability of financing necessary for the successful negotiation and implementation of a restructuring plan. This Directive should be without prejudice to other grounds for declaring new or interim financing void, voidable or unenforceable, or for triggering civil, criminal or administrative liability for providers of such financing, as laid down in national law. Such other grounds could include, among other things, fraud, bad faith, a certain type of relationship between the parties which could be associated with a conflict of interest, such as in the case of transactions between related parties or between shareholders and the company, and transactions where a party received value or collateral without being entitled to it at the time of the transaction or in the manner performed.

(68) When interim financing is extended, the parties do not know whether the restructuring plan will be eventually confirmed or not. Therefore, Member States should not be required to limit the protection of interim finance to cases where the plan is adopted by creditors or confirmed by a judicial or administrative authority. To avoid potential abuses, only financing that is reasonably and immediately necessary for the continued operation or survival of the debtor's business or the preservation or enhancement of the value of that business pending the confirmation of that plan

should be protected. Furthermore, this Directive should not prevent Member States from introducing an ex ante control mechanism for interim financing. Member States should be able to limit the protection for new financing to cases where the plan is confirmed by a judicial or administrative authority and for interim financing to cases where it is subject to ex ante control. An ex ante control mechanism for interim financing or other transactions could be exercised by a practitioner in the field of restructuring, by a creditor's committee or by a judicial or administrative authority. Protection from avoidance actions and protection from personal liability are minimum guarantees that should be granted to interim financing and new financing. However, encouraging new lenders to take the enhanced risk of investing in a viable debtor in financial difficulties could require further incentives such as, for example, giving such financing priority at least over unsecured claims in subsequent insolvency procedures.

(69) In order to promote a culture that encourages early preventive restructuring, it is desirable that transactions which are reasonable and immediately necessary for the negotiation or implementation of a restructuring plan also be given protection from avoidance actions in subsequent insolvency procedures. Judicial or administrative authorities should be able, when determining the reasonableness and immediate necessity of costs and fees, for instance, to consider projections and estimates submitted to affected parties, a creditor's committee, a practitioner in the field of restructuring or the judicial or administrative authority itself. To this end, Member States should also be able to require debtors to provide and update relevant estimates. Such protection should enhance certainty in respect of transactions with businesses that are known to be in financial difficulties and remove the fear of creditors and investors that all such transactions could be declared void in the event that the restructuring fails. Member States should be able to provide for a point in time prior to the opening of a preventive restructuring procedure and to the granting of the stay of individual enforcement actions, from which fees and costs of negotiating, adopting, confirming or seeking professional advice for the restructuring plan start to benefit from protection against avoidance actions. In the case of other payments and disbursements and the protection of the payment of workers' wages, such a starting point could also be the granting of the stay or the opening of the preventive restructuring procedure.

(70) To further promote preventive restructuring, it is important to ensure that directors are not dissuaded from exercising reasonable business judgment or taking reasonable commercial risks, particularly where to do so would improve the chances of a restructuring of potentially viable businesses. Where the company experiences

financial difficulties, directors should take steps to minimise losses and to avoid insolvency, such as: seeking professional advice, including on restructuring and insolvency, for instance by making use of early warning tools where applicable; protecting the assets of the company so as to maximise value and avoid loss of key assets; considering the structure and functions of the business to examine viability and reduce expenditure; refraining from committing the company to the types of transaction that might be subject to avoidance unless there is an appropriate business justification; continuing to trade in circumstances where it is appropriate to do so in order to maximise going-concern value; holding negotiations with creditors and entering preventive restructuring procedures.

(71) Where the debtor is close to insolvency, it is also important to protect the legitimate interests of creditors from management decisions that may have an impact on the constitution of the debtor's estate, in particular where those decisions could have the effect of further diminishing the value of the estate available for restructuring efforts or for distribution to creditors. It is therefore necessary to ensure that, in such circumstances, directors avoid any deliberate or grossly negligent actions that result in personal gain at the expense of stakeholders, and avoid agreeing to transactions at below market value, or taking actions leading to unfair preference being given to one or more stakeholders. Member States should be able to implement the corresponding provisions of this Directive by ensuring that judicial or administrative authorities, when assessing whether a director is to be held liable for breaches of duty of care, take the rules on duties of directors laid down in this Directive into account. This Directive is not intended to establish any hierarchy among the different parties whose interests need to be given due regard. However, Member States should be able to decide on establishing such a hierarchy. This Directive should be without prejudice to Member States' national rules on the decision-making processes in a company.

(72) Entrepreneurs exercising a trade, business, craft or independent, self-employed profession can run the risk of becoming insolvent. The differences between the Member States in terms of opportunities for a fresh start could incentivise over-indebted or insolvent entrepreneurs to relocate to a Member State other than the Member State where they are established, in order to benefit from shorter discharge periods or more attractive conditions for discharge, leading to additional legal uncertainty and costs for the creditors when recovering their claims. Furthermore, the effects of insolvency, in particular the social stigma, the legal consequences, such as disqualifying entrepreneurs from taking up and pursuing entrepreneurial activity, and the continual inability to pay off debts, constitute important disincentives for entrepreneurs seeking to set up a business or have a second chance, even if evidence

shows that entrepreneurs who have become insolvent have more chances of being successful the next time.

(73) Steps should therefore be taken to reduce the negative effects of over-indebtedness or insolvency on entrepreneurs, in particular by allowing for a full discharge of debt after a certain period of time and by limiting the length of disqualification orders issued in connection with a debtor's over-indebtedness or insolvency. The concept of 'insolvency' should be defined by national law and it could take the form of over-indebtedness. The concept of 'entrepreneur' within the meaning of this Directive should have no bearing on the position of managers or directors of a company, which should be treated in accordance with national law. Member States should be able to decide how to obtain access to discharge, including the possibility of requiring the debtor to request discharge.

(74) Member States should be able to provide for the possibility to adjust the repayment obligations of insolvent entrepreneurs when there is a significant change in their financial situation, regardless of whether it improves or deteriorates. This Directive should not require that a repayment plan be supported by a majority of creditors. Member States should be able to provide that entrepreneurs are not prevented from starting a new activity in the same or different field during the implementation of the repayment plan.

(75) A discharge of debt should be available in procedures that include a repayment plan, a realisation of assets, or a combination of both. In implementing those rules, Member States should be able to choose freely among those options. If more than one procedure leading to discharge of debt is available under national law, Member States should ensure that at least one of those procedures gives insolvent entrepreneurs the opportunity of having a full discharge of debt within a period that does not exceed three years. In the case of procedures which combine a realisation of assets and a repayment plan, the discharge period should start, at the latest, from the date the repayment plan is confirmed by a court or starts being implemented, for example from the first instalment under the plan, but it could also start earlier, such as when a decision to open the procedure is taken.

(76) In procedures that do not include a repayment plan, the discharge period should start, at the latest, from the date when a decision to open the procedure is taken by a judicial or administrative authority, or the date of the establishment of the insolvency estate. For the purposes of calculating the duration of the discharge period under this Directive, Member States should be able to provide that the concept of 'opening of procedure' does not include preliminary measures, such as preservation measures or

the appointment of a preliminary insolvency practitioner, unless such measures allow for the realisation of assets, including the disposal and the distribution of assets to creditors. The establishment of the insolvency estate should not necessarily entail a formal decision or confirmation by a judicial or administrative authority, where such decision is not required under national law, and could consist in the submission of the inventory of assets and liabilities.

(77) Where the procedural path leading to a discharge of debt entails the realisation of an entrepreneur's assets, Member States should not be prevented from providing that the request for discharge is treated separately from the realisation of assets, provided that such request constitutes an integral part of the procedural path leading to the discharge under this Directive. Member States should be able to decide on the rules on the burden of proof in order for the discharge to operate, which means that it should be possible for entrepreneurs to be required by law to prove compliance with their obligations.

(78) A full discharge of debt or the ending of disqualifications after a period no longer than three years is not appropriate in all circumstances, therefore derogations from this rule which are duly justified by reasons laid down in national law might need to be introduced. For instance, such derogations should be introduced in cases where the debtor is dishonest or has acted in bad faith. Where entrepreneurs do not benefit from a presumption of honesty and good faith under national law, the burden of proof concerning their honesty and good faith should not make it unnecessarily difficult or onerous for them to enter the procedure.

(79) In establishing whether an entrepreneur was dishonest, judicial or administrative authorities might take into account circumstances such as: the nature and extent of the debt; the time when the debt was incurred; the efforts of the entrepreneur to pay the debt and comply with legal obligations, including public licensing requirements and the need for proper bookkeeping; actions on the entrepreneur's part to frustrate recourse by creditors; the fulfilment of duties in the likelihood of insolvency, which are incumbent on entrepreneurs who are directors of a company; and compliance with Union and national competition and labour law. It should also be possible to introduce derogations where the entrepreneur has not complied with certain legal obligations, including obligations to maximise returns to creditors, which could take the form of a general obligation to generate income or assets. It should furthermore be possible to introduce specific derogations where it is necessary to guarantee the balance between the rights of the debtor and the rights of one or more creditors, such as where the creditor is a natural person who needs more protection than the debtor.

(80) A derogation could also be justified where the costs of the procedure leading to a discharge of debt, including the fees of judicial and administrative authorities and of practitioners, are not covered. Member States should be able to provide that the benefits of that discharge can be revoked where, for example, the financial situation of the debtor improves significantly due to unexpected circumstances, such as winning a lottery, or coming in the possession of an inheritance or a donation. Member States should not be prevented from providing additional derogations in well-defined circumstances and when duly justified.

(81) Where there is a duly justified reason under national law, it could be appropriate to limit the possibility of discharge for certain categories of debt. It should be possible for Member States to exclude secured debts from eligibility for discharge only up to the value of the collateral as determined by national law, while the rest of the debt should be treated as unsecured debt. Member States should be able to exclude further categories of debt when duly justified.

(82) Member States should be able to provide that judicial or administrative authorities can verify, either ex officio or at the request of a person with a legitimate interest, whether entrepreneurs have fulfilled the conditions for obtaining a full discharge of debt.

(83) If an entrepreneur's permit or licence to carry on a certain craft, business, trade or profession has been denied or revoked as a result of a disqualification order, this Directive should not prevent Member States from requiring the entrepreneur to submit an application for a new permit or licence after the disqualification has expired. Where a Member State authority adopts a decision concerning a specifically supervised activity, it should be possible to also take into account, even after the expiry of the disqualification period, the fact that the insolvent entrepreneur has obtained a discharge of debt in accordance with this Directive.

(84) Personal and professional debts that cannot be reasonably separated, for example where an asset is used in the course of the professional activity of the entrepreneur as well as outside that activity, should be treated in a single procedure. Where Member States provide that such debts are subject to different insolvency procedures, coordination of those procedures is needed. This Directive should be without prejudice to Member States being able to choose to treat all the debts of an entrepreneur in a single procedure. Member States in which entrepreneurs are allowed to continue their business on their own account during insolvency proceedings should not be prevented from providing that such entrepreneurs can be

made subject to new insolvency proceedings, where such continued business becomes insolvent.

(85) It is necessary to maintain and enhance the transparency and predictability of the procedures in delivering outcomes that are favourable to the preservation of businesses and to allowing entrepreneurs to have a second chance or that permit the efficient liquidation of non-viable enterprises. It is also necessary to reduce the excessive length of insolvency procedures in many Member States, which results in legal uncertainty for creditors and investors and low recovery rates. Finally, given the enhanced cooperation mechanisms between courts and practitioners in cross-border cases, set up under Regulation (EU) 2015/848, the professionalism of all actors involved needs to be brought to comparable high levels across the Union. To achieve those objectives, Member States should ensure that members of the judicial and administrative authorities dealing with procedures concerning preventive restructuring, insolvency and discharge of debt are suitably trained and have the necessary expertise for their responsibilities. Such training and expertise could be acquired also during the exercise of the duties as a member of a judicial or administrative authority or, prior to appointment to such duties, during the exercise of other relevant duties.

(86) Such training and expertise should enable decisions with a potentially significant economic and social impact to be taken in an efficient manner, and should not be understood to mean that members of a judicial authority have to deal exclusively with matters concerning restructuring, insolvency and discharge of debt. Member States should ensure that procedures concerning restructuring, insolvency and discharge of debt can be carried out in an efficient and expeditious manner. The creation of specialised courts or chambers, or the appointment of specialised judges in accordance with national law, as well as concentrating jurisdiction in a limited number of judicial or administrative authorities would be efficient ways of achieving the objectives of legal certainty and effectiveness of procedures. Member States should not be obliged to require that procedures concerning restructuring, insolvency and discharge of debt be prioritised over other procedures.

(87) Member States should also ensure that practitioners in the field of restructuring, insolvency, and discharge of debt that are appointed by judicial or administrative authorities ('practitioners') are: suitably trained; appointed in a transparent manner with due regard to the need to ensure efficient procedures; supervised when carrying out their tasks; and perform their tasks with integrity. It is important that practitioners adhere to standards for such tasks, such as obtaining insurance for professional liability. Suitable training, qualifications and expertise for practitioners could also be

acquired while practising their profession. Member States should not be obliged to provide the necessary training themselves, but this could be provided by, for example, professional associations or other bodies. Insolvency practitioners as defined in Regulation (EU) 2015/848 should be included in the scope of this Directive.

(88) This Directive should not prevent Member States from providing that practitioners are chosen by a debtor, by creditors or by a creditors' committee from a list or a pool that is pre-approved by a judicial or administrative authority. In choosing a practitioner, the debtor, the creditors or the creditors' committee could be granted a margin of appreciation as to the practitioner's expertise and experience in general and the demands of the particular case. Debtors who are natural persons could be exempted from such a duty altogether. In cases with cross-border elements, the appointment of the practitioner should take into account, among other things, the practitioner's ability to comply with the obligations, under Regulation (EU) 2015/848, to communicate and cooperate with insolvency practitioners and judicial and administrative authorities from other Member States, as well as their human and administrative resources to deal with potentially complex cases. Member States should not be prevented from providing for a practitioner to be selected by other methods, such as random selection by a software programme, provided that it is ensured that in using those methods due consideration is given to the practitioner's experience and expertise. Member States should be able to decide on the means for objecting to the selection or appointment of a practitioner or for requesting the replacement of the practitioner, for example through a creditors' committee.

(89) Practitioners should be subject to oversight and regulatory mechanisms which should include effective measures regarding the accountability of practitioners who have failed in their duties, such as: a reduction in a practitioner's fee; the exclusion from the list or pool of practitioners who can be appointed in insolvency cases; and, where appropriate, disciplinary, administrative or criminal sanctions. Such oversight and regulatory mechanisms should be without prejudice to provisions under national law on civil liability for damages for breach of contractual or non-contractual obligations. Member States should not be required to set up specific authorities or bodies. Member States should ensure that information about the authorities or bodies exercising oversight over practitioners is publicly available. For instance, a mere reference to the judicial or administrative authority should be sufficient as information. It should be possible, in principle, to attain such standards without the need to create new professions or qualifications under national law. Member States should be able to extend the provisions on the training and supervision of practitioners to other practitioners not covered by this Directive. Member States should not be

obliged to provide that disputes over remuneration of practitioners are to be prioritised over other procedures.

(90) To further reduce the length of procedures, to facilitate better participation of creditors in procedures concerning restructuring, insolvency and discharge of debt and to ensure similar conditions among creditors irrespective of where they are located in the Union, Member States should put in place provisions enabling debtors, creditors, practitioners and judicial and administrative authorities to use electronic means of communication. Therefore, it should be possible that procedural steps such as the filing of claims by creditors, the notification of creditors, or the lodging of challenges and appeals, can be carried out by electronic means of communication. Member States should be able to provide that notifications of a creditor can only be performed electronically if the creditor concerned has previously consented to electronic communication.

(91) Parties to procedures concerning restructuring, insolvency and discharge of debt should not be obliged to use electronic means of communication if such use is not mandatory under national law, without prejudice to Member States being able to establish a mandatory system of electronic filing and service of documents in procedures concerning restructuring, insolvency and discharge of debt. Member States should be able to choose the means of electronic communications. Examples of such means could include a purpose-built system for the electronic transmission of such documents or the use of email, without preventing Member States from being able to put in place features to ensure the security of electronic transmissions, such as electronic signature, or trust services, such as electronic registered delivery services, in accordance with Regulation (EU) No 910/2014 of the European Parliament and of the Council ([17]).

(92) It is important to gather reliable and comparable data on the performance of procedures concerning restructuring, insolvency and discharge of debt in order to monitor the implementation and application of this Directive. Therefore, Member States should collect and aggregate data that are sufficiently granular to enable an accurate assessment of how the Directive is working in practice and should communicate those data to the Commission. The communication form for the transmission of such data to the Commission should be established by the Commission assisted by a Committee within the meaning of Regulation (EU) No

17 Regulation (EU) No 910/2014 of the European Parliament and of the Council of 23 July 2014 on electronic identification and trust services for electronic transactions in the internal market and repealing Directive 1999/93/EC (OJ L 257, 28.8.2014, p. 73).

182/2011 of the European Parliament and of the Council ([18]). The form should provide a shortlist of the main outcomes of procedures that are common to all Member States. For example, in the case of a restructuring procedure, those main outcomes could be the following: the plan being confirmed by a court; the plan not being confirmed by a court; the restructuring procedures being converted to liquidation procedures or closed because of the opening of liquidation procedures before the plan was confirmed by a court. Member States should not be required to provide a break-down by types of outcome in respect of the procedures which end before any relevant measures are taken, but could instead provide a common number for all procedures which are declared inadmissible, rejected or withdrawn before being opened.

(93) The communication form should provide a list of options which could be taken into account by the Member States when determining the size of a debtor by reference to one or more of the elements of the definition of SMEs and large enterprises common to all Member States. The list should include the option of determining the size of a debtor based on the number of workers only. The form should: define the elements of average cost and average recovery rates for which Member States should be able to collect data voluntarily; provide guidance on elements which could be taken into account when Member States make use of a sampling technique, for example on sample sizes to ensure representativeness in terms of geographical distribution, size of debtors and industry; and include the opportunity for Member States to provide any additional information available, for example on the total amount of assets and liabilities of debtors.

(94) The stability of financial markets relies heavily on financial collateral arrangements, in particular, when collateral security is provided in connection with the participation in designated systems or in central bank operations and when margins are provided to central counterparties. As the value of financial instruments given as collateral security may be very volatile, it is crucial to realise their value quickly before it goes down. Therefore, the provisions of Directives 98/26/EC ([19]) and 2002/47/EC ([20]) of the European Parliament and of the Council and Regulation (EU) No 648/2012 should apply notwithstanding the provisions of this Directive. Member States should

18 Regulation (EU) No 182/2011 of the European Parliament and of the Council of 16 February 2011 laying down the rules and general principles concerning mechanisms for control by the Member States of the Commission's exercise of implementing powers (OJ L 55, 28.2.2011, p. 13).

19 Directive 98/26/EC of the European Parliament and of the Council of 19 May 1998 on settlement finality in payment and securities settlement systems (OJ L 166, 11.6.1998, p. 45).

20 Directive 2002/47/EC of the European Parliament and of the Council of 6 June 2002 on financial collateral arrangements (OJ L 168, 27.6.2002, p. 43).

be allowed to exempt netting arrangements, including close-out netting, from the effects of the stay of individual enforcement actions even in circumstances where they are not covered by Directives 98/26/EC, 2002/47/EC and Regulation (EU) No 648/2012, if such arrangements are enforceable under the laws of the relevant Member State even if insolvency proceedings are opened.

This could be the case for a significant number of master agreements widely used in the financial, energy and commodity markets, both by non-financial and financial counterparties. Such arrangements reduce systemic risks especially in derivatives markets. Such arrangements might therefore be exempt from restrictions that insolvency laws impose on executory contracts. Accordingly, Member States should also be allowed to exempt from the effects of the stay of individual enforcement actions statutory netting arrangements, including close-out netting arrangements, which operate upon the opening of insolvency procedures. The amount resulting from the operation of netting arrangements, including close-out netting arrangements should, however, be subject to the stay of individual enforcement actions.

(95) Member States that are parties to the Convention on international interests in mobile equipment, signed at Cape Town on 16 November 2001, and its Protocols should be able to continue to comply with their existing international obligations. The provisions of this Directive regarding preventive restructuring frameworks should apply with the derogations necessary to ensure an application of those provisions without prejudice to the application of that Convention and its Protocols.

(96) The effectiveness of the process of adoption and implementation of the restructuring plan should not be jeopardised by company law. Therefore, Member States should be able to derogate from the requirements laid down in Directive (EU) 2017/1132 of the European Parliament and of the Council ([21]) concerning the obligations to convene a general meeting and to offer on a pre-emptive basis shares to existing shareholders, to the extent and for the period necessary to ensure that shareholders do not frustrate restructuring efforts by abusing their rights under that Directive. For example, Member States might need to derogate from the obligation to convene a general meeting of shareholders or from the normal time periods, for cases where urgent action is to be taken by the management to safeguard the assets of the company, for instance through requesting a stay of individual enforcement actions and when there is a serious and sudden loss of subscribed capital and a likelihood of insolvency. Derogations from company law might also be required when the restructuring plan

21 Directive (EU) 2017/1132 of the European Parliament and of the Council of 14 June 2017 relating to certain aspects of company law (OJ L 169, 30.6.2017, p. 46).

provides for the emission of new shares which could be offered with priority to creditors as debt-to-equity swaps, or for the reduction of the amount of subscribed capital in the event of a transfer of parts of the undertaking. Such derogations should be limited in time to the extent that Member States consider such derogations necessary for the establishment of a preventive restructuring framework. Member States should not be obliged to derogate from company law, wholly or partially, for an indefinite or for a limited period of time, if they ensure that their company law requirements do not jeopardise the effectiveness of the restructuring process or if Member States have other, equally effective tools in place to ensure that shareholders do not unreasonably prevent the adoption or implementation of a restructuring plan which would restore the viability of the business. In this context Member States should attach particular importance to the effectiveness of provisions relating to a stay of individual enforcement actions and confirmation of the restructuring plan which should not be unduly impaired by calls for, or the results of, general meetings of shareholders. Directive (EU) 2017/1132 should therefore be amended accordingly. Member States should enjoy a margin of appreciation in assessing which derogations are needed in the context of national company law in order to effectively implement this Directive, and should also be able to provide for similar exemptions from Directive (EU) 2017/1132 in the case of insolvency proceedings not covered by this Directive but which allow for restructuring measures to be taken.

(97) In respect of the establishment of, and subsequent changes to, the data communication form, implementing powers should be conferred on the Commission. Those powers should be exercised in accordance with Regulation (EU) No 182/2011.

(98) A study should be carried out by the Commission in order to evaluate the necessity of submitting legislative proposals to deal with the insolvency of persons not exercising a trade, business, craft or profession, who, as consumers, in good faith, are temporarily or permanently unable to pay debts as they fall due. Such study should investigate whether access to basic goods and services needs to be safeguarded for those persons to ensure that they benefit from decent living conditions.

(99) In accordance with the Joint Political Declaration of 28 September 2011 of Member States and the Commission on explanatory documents ([22]), Member States have undertaken to accompany, in justified cases, the notification of their transposition measures with one or more documents explaining the relationship between the components of a directive and the corresponding parts of national transposition

22 OJ C 369, 17.12.2011, p. 14.

instruments. With regard to this Directive, the legislator considers the transmission of such documents to be justified.

(100) Since the objectives of this Directive cannot be sufficiently achieved by the Member States because differences between national restructuring and insolvency frameworks would continue to raise obstacles to the free movement of capital and the freedom of establishment, but can rather be better achieved at Union level, the Union may adopt measures, in accordance with the principle of subsidiarity as set out in Article 5 of the Treaty on European Union. In accordance with the principle of proportionality, as set out in that Article, this Directive does not go beyond what is necessary in order to achieve those objectives.

(101) On 7 June 2017, the European Central Bank delivered an opinion ([23]),

HAVE ADOPTED THIS DIRECTIVE:

TITLE I
GENERAL PROVISIONS

Article 1
Subject matter and scope

1. This Directive lays down rules on:
(a) preventive restructuring frameworks available for debtors in financial difficulties when there is a likelihood of insolvency, with a view to preventing the insolvency and ensuring the viability of the debtor;
(b) procedures leading to a discharge of debt incurred by insolvent entrepreneurs; and
(c) measures to increase the efficiency of procedures concerning restructuring, insolvency and discharge of debt.

2. This Directive does not apply to procedures referred to in paragraph 1 of this Article that concern debtors that are:
(a) insurance undertakings or reinsurance undertakings as defined in points (1) and (4) of Article 13 of Directive 2009/138/EC;
(b) credit institutions as defined in point (1) of Article 4(1) of Regulation (EU) No 575/2013;

23 OJ C 236, 21.7.2017, p. 2.

(c) investment firms or collective investment undertakings as defined in points (2) and (7) of Article 4(1) of Regulation (EU) No 575/2013;
(d) central counter parties as defined in point (1) of Article 2 of Regulation (EU) No 648/2012;
(e) central securities depositories as defined in point (1) of Article 2(1) of Regulation (EU) No 909/2014;
(f) other financial institutions and entities listed in the first subparagraph of Article 1(1) of Directive 2014/59/EU; (g) public bodies under national law; and
(g) natural persons who are not entrepreneurs.

3. Member States may exclude from the scope of this Directive procedures referred to in paragraph 1 that concern debtors which are financial entities, other than those referred to in paragraph 2, providing financial services which are subject to special arrangements under which the national supervisory or resolution authorities have wide-ranging powers of intervention comparable to those laid down in Union and national law in relation to the financial entities referred to in paragraph 2. Member States shall communicate those special arrangements to the Commission.

4. Member States may extend the application of the procedures referred to in point (b) of paragraph 1 to insolvent natural persons who are not entrepreneurs.
Member States may restrict the application of point (a) of paragraph 1 to legal persons.

5. Member States may provide that the following claims are excluded from, or are not affected by, preventive restructuring frameworks referred to in point (a) of paragraph 1:
(a) existing and future claims of existing or former workers;
(b) maintenance claims arising from a family relationship, parentage, marriage or affinity; or
(c) claims that arise from tortious liability of the debtor.

6. Member States shall ensure that preventive restructuring frameworks have no impact on accrued occupational pension entitlements.

Article 2
Definitions

1. For the purposes of this Directive, the following definitions apply:
(1) 'restructuring' means measures aimed at restructuring the debtor's business that include changing the composition, conditions or structure of a debtor's assets and liabilities or any other part of the debtor's capital structure, such as sales of assets or

parts of the business and, where so provided under national law, the sale of the business as a going concern, as well as any necessary operational changes, or a combination of those elements;

(2) 'affected parties' means creditors, including, where applicable under national law, workers, or classes of creditors and, where applicable, under national law, equity holders, whose claims or interests, respectively, are directly affected by a restructuring plan;

(3) 'equity holder' means a person that has an ownership interest in a debtor or a debtor's business, including a shareholder, in so far as that person is not a creditor;

(4) 'stay of individual enforcement actions' means a temporary suspension, granted by a judicial or administrative authority or applied by operation of law, of the right of a creditor to enforce a claim against a debtor and, where so provided for by national law, against a third-party security provider, in the context of a judicial, administrative or other procedure, or of the right to seize or realise out of court the assets or business of the debtor;

(5) 'executory contract' means a contract between a debtor and one or more creditors under which the parties still have obligations to perform at the time the stay of individual enforcement actions is granted or applied;

(6) 'best-interest-of-creditors test' means a test that is satisfied if no dissenting creditor would be worse off under a restructuring plan than such a creditor would be if the normal ranking of liquidation priorities under national law were applied, either in the event of liquidation, whether piecemeal or by sale as a going concern, or in the event of the next-best-alternative scenario if the restructuring plan were not confirmed;

(7) 'new financing' means any new financial assistance provided by an existing or a new creditor in order to implement a restructuring plan and that is included in that restructuring plan;

(8) 'interim financing' means any new financial assistance, provided by an existing or a new creditor, that includes, as a minimum, financial assistance during the stay of individual enforcement actions, and that is reasonable and immediately necessary for the debtor's business to continue operating, or to preserve or enhance the value of that business;

(9) 'entrepreneur' means a natural person exercising a trade, business, craft or profession;

(10) 'full discharge of debt' means that enforcement against entrepreneurs of their outstanding dischargeable debts is precluded or that outstanding dischargeable debts as such are cancelled, as part of a procedure which could include a realisation of assets or a repayment plan or both;

(11) 'repayment plan' means a programme of payments of specified amounts on specified dates by an insolvent entrepreneur to creditors, or a periodic transfer to creditors of a certain part of entrepreneur's disposable income during the discharge period;

(12) 'practitioner in the field of restructuring' means any person or body appointed by a judicial or administrative authority to carry out, in particular, one or more of the following tasks:

  (a) assisting the debtor or the creditors in drafting or negotiating a restructuring plan;
  (b) supervising the activity of the debtor during the negotiations on a restructuring plan, and reporting to a judicial or administrative authority;
  (c) taking partial control over the assets or affairs of the debtor during negotiations.

2. For the purposes of this Directive, the following concepts are to be understood as defined by national law:

(a) insolvency;
(b) likelihood of insolvency;
(c) micro, small and medium-sized enterprises ('SMEs').

Article 3

Early warning and access to information

1. Member States shall ensure that debtors have access to one or more clear and transparent early warning tools which can detect circumstances that could give rise to a likelihood of insolvency and can signal to them the need to act without delay.
For the purposes of the first subparagraph, Member States may make use of up-to-date IT technologies for notifications and for communication.

2. Early warning tools may include the following:

(a) alert mechanisms when the debtor has not made certain types of payments;
(b) advisory services provided by public or private organisations.
(c) incentives under national law for third parties with relevant information about the debtor, such as accountants, tax and social security authorities, to flag to the debtor a negative development.

3. Member States shall ensure that debtors and employees' representatives have access to relevant and up-to-date information about the availability of early warning tools as well as of the procedures and measures concerning restructuring and discharge of debt.

4. Member States shall ensure that information on access to early warning tools is publicly available online and that, in particular for SMEs, it is easily accessible and presented in a user-friendly manner.

5. Member States may provide support to employees' representatives for the assessment of the economic situation of the debtor.

TITLE II
PREVENTIVE RESTRUCTURING FRAMEWORKS

CHAPTER 1
Availability of preventive restructuring frameworks

Article 4
Availability of preventive restructuring frameworks

1. Member States shall ensure that, where there is a likelihood of insolvency, debtors have access to a preventive restructuring framework that enables them to restructure, with a view to preventing insolvency and ensuring their viability, without prejudice to other solutions for avoiding insolvency, thereby protecting jobs and maintaining business activity.

2. Member States may provide that debtors that have been sentenced for serious breaches of accounting or bookkeeping obligations under national law are allowed to access a preventive restructuring framework only after those debtors have taken adequate measures to remedy the issues that gave rise to the sentence, with a view to providing creditors with the necessary information to enable them to take a decision during restructuring negotiations.

3. Member States may maintain or introduce a viability test under national law, provided that such a test has the purpose of excluding debtors that do not have a prospect of viability, and that it can be carried out without detriment to the debtors' assets.

4. Member States may limit the number of times within a certain period a debtor can access a preventive restructuring framework as provided for under this Directive.

5. The preventive restructuring framework provided for under this Directive may consist of one or more procedures, measures or provisions, some of which may take place out of court, without prejudice to any other restructuring frameworks under national law.

Member States shall ensure that such restructuring framework affords debtors and affected parties the rights and safeguards provided for in this Title in a coherent manner.

6. Member States may put in place provisions limiting the involvement of a judicial or administrative authority in a preventive restructuring framework to where it is necessary and proportionate while ensuring that rights of any affected parties and relevant stakeholders are safeguarded.

7. Preventive restructuring frameworks provided for under this Directive shall be available on application by debtors.

8. Member States may also provide that preventive restructuring frameworks provided for under this Directive are available at the request of creditors and employees' representatives, subject to the agreement of the debtor. Member States may limit that requirement to obtain the debtor's agreement to cases where debtors are SMEs.

CHAPTER 2
Facilitating negotiations on preventive restructuring plans

Article 5
Debtor in possession

1. Member States shall ensure that debtors accessing preventive restructuring procedures remain totally, or at least partially, in control of their assets and the day-to-day operation of their business.

2. Where necessary, the appointment by a judicial or administrative authority of a practitioner in the field of restructuring shall be decided on a case-by-case basis, except in certain circumstances where Member States may require the mandatory appointment of such a practitioner in every case.

3. Member States shall provide for the appointment of a practitioner in the field of restructuring, to assist the debtor and creditors in negotiating and drafting the plan, at least in the following cases:
(a) where a general stay of individual enforcement actions, in accordance with Article 6(3), is granted by a judicial or administrative authority, and the judicial or administrative authority decides that such a practitioner is necessary to safeguard the interest of the parties;

(b) where the restructuring plan needs to be confirmed by a judicial or administrative authority by means of a cross- class cram-down, in accordance with Article 11; or
(c) where it is requested by the debtor or by a majority of the creditors, provided that, in the latter case, the cost of the practitioner is borne by the creditors.

Article 6
Stay of individual enforcement actions

1. Member States shall ensure that debtors can benefit from a stay of individual enforcement actions to support the negotiations of a restructuring plan in a preventive restructuring framework.
Member States may provide that judicial or administrative authorities can refuse to grant a stay of individual enforcement actions where such a stay is not necessary or where it would not achieve the objective set out in the first subparagraph.

2. Without prejudice to paragraphs 4 and 5, Member States shall ensure that a stay of individual enforcement actions can cover all types of claims, including secured claims and preferential claims.

3. Member States may provide that a stay of individual enforcement actions can be general, covering all creditors, or can be limited, covering one or more individual creditors or categories of creditors.
Where a stay is limited, the stay shall only apply to creditors that have been informed, in accordance with national law, of negotiations as referred to in paragraph 1 on the restructuring plan or of the stay.

4. Member States may exclude certain claims or categories of claims from the scope of the stay of individual enforcement actions, in well-defined circumstances, where such an exclusion is duly justified and where:
(a) enforcement is not likely to jeopardise the restructuring of the business; or
(b) the stay would unfairly prejudice the creditors of those claims.

5. Paragraph 2 shall not apply to workers' claims.
By way of derogation from the first subparagraph, Member States may apply paragraph 2 to workers' claims if, and to the extent that, Member States ensure that the payment of such claims is guaranteed in preventive restructuring frameworks at a similar level of protection.

6. The initial duration of a stay of individual enforcement actions shall be limited to a maximum period of no more than four months.

7. Notwithstanding paragraph 6, Member States may enable judicial or administrative authorities to extend the duration of a stay of individual enforcement actions or to grant a new stay of individual enforcement actions, at the request of the debtor, a creditor or, where applicable, a practitioner in the field of restructuring. Such extension or new stay of individual enforcement actions shall be granted only if well-defined circumstances show that such extension or new stay is duly justified, such as:
(a) relevant progress has been made in the negotiations on the restructuring plan;
(b) the continuation of the stay of individual enforcement actions does not unfairly prejudice the rights or interests of any affected parties; or
(c) insolvency proceedings which could end in the liquidation of the debtor under national law have not yet been opened in respect of the debtor.

8. The total duration of the stay of individual enforcement actions, including extensions and renewals, shall not exceed 12 months.
Where Member States choose to implement this Directive by means of one or more procedures or measures which do not fulfil the conditions for notification under Annex A to Regulation (EU) 2015/848, the total duration of the stay under such procedures shall be limited to no more than four months if the centre of main interests of the debtor has been transferred from another Member State within a three-month period prior to the filing of a request for the opening of preventive restructuring proceedings.

9. Member States shall ensure that judicial or administrative authorities can lift a stay of individual enforcement actions in the following cases:
(a) the stay no longer fulfils the objective of supporting the negotiations on the restructuring plan, for example if it becomes apparent that a proportion of creditors which, under national law, could prevent the adoption of the restructuring plan do not support the continuation of the negotiations;
(b) at the request of the debtor or the practitioner in the field of restructuring;
(c) where so provided for in national law, if one or more creditors or one or more classes of creditors are, or would be, unfairly prejudiced by a stay of individual enforcement actions; or
(d) where so provided for in national law, if the stay gives rise to the insolvency of a creditor.

Member States may limit the power, under the first subparagraph, to lift the stay of individual enforcement actions to situations where creditors had not had the opportunity

to be heard before the stay came into force or before an extension of the period was granted by a judicial or administrative authority.
Member States may provide for a minimum period, which does not exceed the period referred to in paragraph 6, during which a stay of individual enforcement actions cannot be lifted.

Article 7
Consequences of the stay of individual enforcement actions

1. Where an obligation on a debtor, provided for under national law, to file for the opening of insolvency proceedings which could end in the liquidation of the debtor, arises during a stay of individual enforcement actions, that obligation shall be suspended for the duration of that stay.

2. A stay of individual enforcement actions in accordance with Article 6 shall suspend, for the duration of the stay, the opening, at the request of one or more creditors, of insolvency proceedings which could end in the liquidation of the debtor.

3. Member States may derogate from paragraphs 1 and 2 in situations where a debtor is unable to pay its debts as they fall due. In such cases, Member States shall ensure that a judicial or administrative authority can decide to keep in place the benefit of the stay of individual enforcement actions, if, taking into account the circumstances of the case, the opening of insolvency proceedings which could end in the liquidation of the debtor would not be in the general interest of creditors.

4. Member States shall provide for rules preventing creditors to which the stay applies from withholding performance or terminating, accelerating or, in any other way, modifying essential executory contracts to the detriment of the debtor, for debts that came into existence prior to the stay, solely by virtue of the fact that they were not paid by the debtor. 'Essential executory contracts' shall be understood to mean executory contracts which are necessary for the continuation of the day-to-day operations of the business, including contracts concerning supplies, the suspension of which would lead to the debtor's activities coming to a standstill.
The first subparagraph shall not preclude Member States from affording such creditors appropriate safeguards with a view to preventing unfair prejudice being caused to such creditors as a result of that subparagraph.
Member States may provide that this paragraph also applies to non-essential executory contracts.

5. Member States shall ensure that creditors are not allowed to withhold performance or terminate, accelerate or, in any other way, modify executory contracts to the detriment of the debtor by virtue of a contractual clause providing for such measures, solely by reason of:
(a) a request for the opening of preventive restructuring proceedings;
(b) a request for a stay of individual enforcement actions;
(c) the opening of preventive restructuring proceedings; or
(d) the granting of a stay of individual enforcement actions as such.

6. Member States may provide that a stay of individual enforcement actions does not apply to netting arrangements, including close-out netting arrangements, on financial markets, energy markets and commodity markets, even in circumstances where Article 31(1) does not apply, if such arrangements are enforceable under national insolvency law. The stay shall, however, apply to the enforcement by a creditor of a claim against a debtor arising as a result of the operation of a netting arrangement.
The first subparagraph shall not apply to contracts for the supply of goods, services or energy necessary for the operation of the debtor's business, unless such contracts take the form of a position traded on an exchange or other market, such that it can be substituted at any time at current market value.

7. Member States shall ensure that the expiry of a stay of individual enforcement actions without the adoption of a restructuring plan does not, of itself, give rise to the opening of an insolvency procedure which could end in the liquidation of the debtor, unless the other conditions for such opening laid down by national law are fulfilled.

CHAPTER 3
Restructuring plans

Article 8
Content of restructuring plans

1. Member States shall require that restructuring plans submitted for adoption in accordance with Article 9, or for confirmation by a judicial or administrative authority in accordance with Article 10, contain at least the following information:
(a) the identity of the debtor;
(b) the debtor's assets and liabilities at the time of submission of the restructuring plan, including a value for the assets, a description of the economic situation of the debtor and the position of workers, and a description of the causes and the extent of the difficulties of the debtor;

(c) the affected parties, whether named individually or described by categories of debt in accordance with national law, as well as their claims or interests covered by the restructuring plan;
(d) where applicable, the classes into which the affected parties have been grouped, for the purpose of adopting the restructuring plan, and the respective values of claims and interests in each class;
(e) where applicable, the parties, whether named individually or described by categories of debt in accordance with national law, which are not affected by the restructuring plan, together with a description of the reasons why it is proposed not to affect them;
(f) where applicable, the identity of the practitioner in the field of restructuring;
(g) the terms of the restructuring plan, including, in particular:
    (i) any proposed restructuring measures as referred to in point (1) of Article 2(1);
    (ii) where applicable, the proposed duration of any proposed restructuring measures;
    (iii) the arrangements with regard to informing and consulting the employees' representatives in accordance with Union and national law;
    (iv) where applicable, overall consequences as regards employment such as dismissals, short-time working arrangements or similar;
    (v) the estimated financial flows of the debtor, if provided for by national law; and
    (vi) any new financing anticipated as part of the restructuring plan, and the reasons why the new financing is necessary to implement that plan;
(h) a statement of reasons which explains why the restructuring plan has a reasonable prospect of preventing the insolvency of the debtor and ensuring the viability of the business, including the necessary pre-conditions for the success of the plan. Member States may require that that statement of reasons be made or validated either by an external expert or by the practitioner in the field of restructuring if such a practitioner is appointed.

2. Member States shall make available online a comprehensive check-list for restructuring plans, adapted to the needs of SMEs. The check-list shall include practical guidelines on how the restructuring plan has to be drafted under national law.
The check-list shall be made available in the official language or languages of the Member State. Member States shall consider making the check-list available in at least one other language, in particular in a language used in international business.

Article 9

Adoption of restructuring plans

1. Member States shall ensure that, irrespective of who applies for a preventive restructuring procedure in accordance with Article 4, debtors have the right to submit restructuring plans for adoption by the affected parties.

Member States may also provide that creditors and practitioners in the field of restructuring have the right to submit restructuring plans, and provide for conditions under which they may do so.

2. Member States shall ensure that affected parties have a right to vote on the adoption of a restructuring plan.

Parties that are not affected by a restructuring plan shall not have voting rights in the adoption of that plan.

3. Notwithstanding paragraph 2, Member States may exclude from the right to vote the following:

(a) equity holders;

(b) creditors whose claims rank below the claims of ordinary unsecured creditors in the normal ranking of liquidation priorities; or

(c) any related party of the debtor or the debtor's business, with a conflict of interest under national law.

4. Member States shall ensure that affected parties are treated in separate classes which reflect sufficient commonality of interest based on verifiable criteria, in accordance with national law. As a minimum, creditors of secured and unsecured claims shall be treated in separate classes for the purposes of adopting a restructuring plan.

Member States may also provide that workers' claims are treated in a separate class of their own.

Member States may provide that debtors that are SMEs can opt not to treat affected parties in separate classes.

Member States shall put in place appropriate measures to ensure that class formation is done with a particular view to protecting vulnerable creditors such as small suppliers.

5. Voting rights and the formation of classes shall be examined by a judicial or administrative authority when a request for confirmation of the restructuring plan is submitted.

Member States may require a judicial or administrative authority to examine and confirm the voting rights and formation of classes at an earlier stage than that referred to in the first subparagraph.

6. A restructuring plan shall be adopted by affected parties, provided that a majority in the amount of their claims or interests is obtained in each class. Member States may, in addition, require that a majority in the number of affected parties is obtained in each class. Member States shall lay down the majorities required for the adoption of a restructuring plan. Those majorities shall not be higher than 75 % of the amount of claims or interests in each class or, where applicable, of the number of affected parties in each class.

7. Notwithstanding paragraphs 2 to 6, Member States may provide that a formal vote on the adoption of a restructuring plan can be replaced by an agreement with the requisite majority.

Article 10
Confirmation of restructuring plans

1. Member States shall ensure that at least the following restructuring plans are binding on the parties only if they are confirmed by a judicial or administrative authority:
(a) restructuring plans which affect the claims or interests of dissenting affected parties;
(b) restructuring plans which provide for new financing;
(c) restructuring plans which involve the loss of more than 25 % of the workforce, if such loss is permitted under national law.

2. Member States shall ensure that the conditions under which a restructuring plan can be confirmed by a judicial or administrative authority are clearly specified and include at least the following:
(a) the restructuring plan has been adopted in accordance with Article 9;
(b) creditors with sufficient commonality of interest in the same class are treated equally, and in a manner proportionate to their claim;
(c) notification of the restructuring plan has been given in accordance with national law to all affected parties;
(d) where there are dissenting creditors, the restructuring plan satisfies the best-interest-of-creditors test;
(e) where applicable, any new financing is necessary to implement the restructuring plan and does not unfairly prejudice the interests of creditors.

Compliance with point (d) of the first subparagraph shall be examined by a judicial or administrative authority only if the restructuring plan is challenged on that ground.

3. Member States shall ensure that judicial or administrative authorities are able to refuse to confirm a restructuring plan where that plan would not have a reasonable prospect of preventing the insolvency of the debtor or ensuring the viability of the business.

4. Member States shall ensure that where a judicial or administrative authority is required to confirm a restructuring plan in order for it to become binding, the decision is taken in an efficient manner with a view to expeditious treatment of the matter.

Article 11
Cross-class cram-down

1. Member States shall ensure that a restructuring plan which is not approved by affected parties, as provided for in Article 9(6), in every voting class, may be confirmed by a judicial or administrative authority upon the proposal of a debtor or with the debtor's agreement, and become binding upon dissenting voting classes where the restructuring plan fulfils at least the following conditions:

(a) it complies with Article 10(2) and (3);

(b) it has been approved by:

  (i) a majority of the voting classes of affected parties, provided that at least one of those classes is a secured creditors class or is senior to the ordinary unsecured creditors class; or, failing that,

  (ii) at least one of the voting classes of affected parties or where so provided under national law, impaired parties, other than an equity-holders class or any other class which, upon a valuation of the debtor as a going concern, would not receive any payment or keep any interest, or, where so provided under national law, which could be reasonably presumed not to receive any payment or keep any interest, if the normal ranking of liquidation priorities were applied under national law;

(c) it ensures that dissenting voting classes of affected creditors are treated at least as favourably as any other class of the same rank and more favourably than any junior class; and

(d) no class of affected parties can, under the restructuring plan, receive or keep more than the full amount of its claims or interests.

2. By way of derogation from the first subparagraph, Member States may limit the requirement to obtain the debtor's agreement to cases where debtors are SMEs.

Member States may increase the minimum number of classes of affected parties or, where so provided under national law, impaired parties, required to approve the plan as laid down in point (b)(ii) of the first subparagraph.

3. By way of derogation from point (c) of paragraph 1, Member States may provide that the claims of affected creditors in a dissenting voting class are satisfied in full by the same or equivalent means where a more junior class is to receive any payment or keep any interest under the restructuring plan.
Member States may maintain or introduce provisions derogating from the first subparagraph where they are necessary in order to achieve the aims of the restructuring plan and where the restructuring plan does not unfairly prejudice the rights or interests of any affected parties.

Article 12
Equity holders

1. Where Member States exclude equity holders from the application of Articles 9 to 11, they shall ensure by other means that those equity holders are not allowed to unreasonably prevent or create obstacles to the adoption and confirmation of a restructuring plan.

2. Member States shall also ensure that equity holders are not allowed to unreasonably prevent or create obstacles to the implementation of a restructuring plan.

3. Member States may adapt what it means to unreasonably prevent or create obstacles under this Article to take into account, inter alia: whether the debtor is an SME or a large enterprise; the proposed restructuring measures touching upon the rights of equity holders; the type of equity holder; whether the debtor is a legal or a natural person; or whether partners in a company have limited or unlimited liability.

Article 13
Workers

1. Members States shall ensure that individual and collective workers' rights, under Union and national labour law, such as the following, are not affected by the preventive restructuring framework:
(a) the right to collective bargaining and industrial action; and
(b) the right to information and consultation in accordance with Directive 2002/14/EC and Directive 2009/38/EC, in particular:
    (i) information to employees' representatives about the recent and probable development of the undertaking's or the establishment's activities and economic situation, enabling them to communicate to the debtor concerns about the situation of the business and as regards the need to consider restructuring mechanisms;

(ii) information to employees' representatives about any preventive restructuring procedure which could have an impact on employment, such as on the ability of workers to recover their wages and any future payments, including occupational pensions;

(iii) information to and consultation of employees' representatives about restructuring plans before they are submitted for adoption in accordance with Article 9, or for confirmation by a judicial or administrative authority in accordance with Article 10;

(c) the rights guaranteed by Directives 98/59/EC, 2001/23/EC and 2008/94/EC.

2) Where the restructuring plan includes measures leading to changes in the work organisation or in contractual relations with workers, those measures shall be approved by those workers, if national law or collective agreements provide for such approval in such cases.

Article 14

Valuation by the judicial or administrative authority

1. The judicial or administrative authority shall take a decision on the valuation of the debtor's business only where a restructuring plan is challenged by a dissenting affected party on the grounds of either:

(a) an alleged failure to satisfy the best-interest-of-creditors test under point (6) of Article 2(1); or

(b) an alleged breach of the conditions for a cross-class cram-down under point (ii) of Article 11(1)(b).

2. Member States shall ensure that, for the purpose of taking a decision on a valuation in accordance with paragraph 1, judicial or administrative authorities may appoint or hear properly qualified experts.

3. For the purposes of paragraph 1, Member States shall ensure that a dissenting affected party may lodge a challenge with the judicial or administrative authority called upon to confirm the restructuring plan.

Member States may provide that such a challenge can be lodged in the context of an appeal against a decision on the confirmation of a restructuring plan.

Article 15

Effects of restructuring plans

1. Member States shall ensure that restructuring plans that are confirmed by a judicial or administrative authority are binding upon all affected parties named or described in accordance with point (c) of Article 8(1).

2. Member States shall ensure that creditors that are not involved in the adoption of a restructuring plan under national law are not affected by the plan.

Article 16

Appeals

1. Member States shall ensure that any appeal provided for under national law against a decision to confirm or reject a restructuring plan taken by a judicial authority is brought before a higher judicial authority.
Member States shall ensure that an appeal against a decision to confirm or reject a restructuring plan taken by an administrative authority is brought before a judicial authority.

2. Appeals shall be resolved in an efficient manner with a view to expeditious treatment.

3. An appeal against a decision confirming a restructuring plan shall have no suspensive effects on the execution of that plan.
By way of derogation from the first subparagraph, Member States may provide that judicial authorities can suspend the execution of the restructuring plan or parts thereof where necessary and appropriate to safeguard the interests of a party.

4. Member States shall ensure that, where an appeal pursuant to paragraph 3 is upheld, the judicial authority may either:
(a) set aside the restructuring plan; or
(b) confirm the restructuring plan, either with amendments, where so provided under national law, or without amendments.

Member States may provide that, where a plan is confirmed under point (b) of the first subparagraph, compensation is granted to any party that incurred monetary losses and whose appeal is upheld.

CHAPTER 4
Protection for new financing, interim financing and other restructuring related transactions

Article 17
Protection for new financing and interim financing

1. Member States shall ensure that new financing and interim financing are adequately protected. As a minimum, in the case of any subsequent insolvency of the debtor:
(a) new financing and interim financing shall not be declared void, voidable or unenforceable; and
(b) the grantors of such financing shall not incur civil, administrative or criminal liability, on the ground that such financing is detrimental to the general body of creditors, unless other additional grounds laid down by national law are present.

2. Member States may provide that paragraph 1 shall only apply to new financing if the restructuring plan has been confirmed by a judicial or administrative authority, and to interim financing which has been subject to ex ante control.

3. Member States may exclude from the application of paragraph 1 interim financing which is granted after the debtor has become unable to pay its debts as they fall due.

4. Member States may provide that grantors of new or interim financing are entitled to receive payment with priority in the context of subsequent insolvency procedures in relation to other creditors that would otherwise have superior or equal claims.

Article 18
Protection for other restructuring related transactions

1. Without prejudice to Article 17, Member States shall ensure that, in the event of any subsequent insolvency of a debtor, transactions that are reasonable and immediately necessary for the negotiation of a restructuring plan are not declared void, voidable or unenforceable on the ground that such transactions are detrimental to the general body of creditors, unless other additional grounds laid down by national law are present.

2. Member States may provide that paragraph 1 only applies where the plan is confirmed by a judicial or administrative authority or where such transactions were subject to ex ante control.

3. Member States may exclude from the application of paragraph 1 transactions that are carried out after the debtor has become unable to pay its debts as they fall due.

4. Transactions referred to in paragraph 1 shall include, as a minimum:
(a) the payment of fees for and costs of negotiating, adopting or confirming a restructuring plan;
(b) the payment of fees for and costs of seeking professional advice closely connected with the restructuring;
(c) the payment of workers' wages for work already carried out without prejudice to other protection provided in Union or national law;
(d) any payments and disbursements made in the ordinary course of business other than those referred to in points (a) to (c).

5. Without prejudice to Article 17, Member States shall ensure that, in the event of any subsequent insolvency of the debtor, transactions that are reasonable and immediately necessary for the implementation of a restructuring plan, and that are carried out in accordance with the restructuring plan confirmed by a judicial or administrative authority, are not declared void, voidable or unenforceable on the ground that such transactions are detrimental to the general body of creditors, unless other additional grounds laid down by national law are present.

CHAPTER 5
Duties of directors

Article 19
Duties of directors where there is a likelihood of insolvency

Member States shall ensure that, where there is a likelihood of insolvency, directors, have due regard, as a minimum, to the following:
(a) the interests of creditors, equity holders and other stakeholders;
(b) the need to take steps to avoid insolvency; and
(c) the need to avoid deliberate or grossly negligent conduct that threatens the viability of the business.

TITLE III
DISCHARGE OF DEBT AND DISQUALIFICATIONS

Article 20
Access to discharge

1. Member States shall ensure that insolvent entrepreneurs have access to at least one procedure that can lead to a full discharge of debt in accordance with this Directive. Member States may require that the trade, business, craft or profession to which an insolvent entrepreneur's debts are related has ceased.

2. Member States in which a full discharge of debt is conditional on a partial repayment of debt by the entrepreneur shall ensure that the related repayment obligation is based on the individual situation of the entrepreneur and, in particular, is proportionate to the entrepreneur's seizable or disposable income and assets during the discharge period, and takes into account the equitable interest of creditors.

3. Member States shall ensure that entrepreneurs who have been discharged from their debts may benefit from existing national frameworks providing for business support for entrepreneurs, including access to relevant and up-to- date information about these frameworks.

Article 21
Discharge period

1. Member States shall ensure that the period after which insolvent entrepreneurs are able to be fully discharged from their debts is no longer than three years starting at the latest from the date of either:
(a) in the case of a procedure which includes a repayment plan, the decision by a judicial or administrative authority to confirm the plan or the start of the implementation of the plan; or
(b) in the case of any other procedure, the decision by the judicial or administrative authority to open the procedure, or the establishment of the entrepreneur's insolvency estate.

2. Member States shall ensure that insolvent entrepreneurs who have complied with their obligations, where such obligations exist under national law, are discharged of their debt on expiry of the discharge period without the need to apply to a judicial or administrative authority to open a procedure additional to those referred to in paragraph 1.

Without prejudice to the first subparagraph, Member States may maintain or introduce provisions allowing the judicial or administrative authority to verify whether the entrepreneurs have fulfilled the obligations for obtaining a discharge of debt.

3. Member States may provide that a full discharge of debt does not hinder the continuation of an insolvency procedure that entails the realisation and distribution of assets of an entrepreneur that formed part of the insolvency estate of that entrepreneur as at the date of expiry of the discharge period.

Article 22

Disqualification period

1. Member States shall ensure that, where an insolvent entrepreneur obtains a discharge of debt in accordance with this Directive, any disqualifications from taking up or pursuing a trade, business, craft or profession on the sole ground that the entrepreneur is insolvent, shall cease to have effect, at the latest, at the end of the discharge period.

2. Member States shall ensure that, on expiry of the discharge period, the disqualifications referred to in paragraph 1 of this Article cease to have effect without the need to apply to a judicial or administrative authority to open a procedure additional to those referred to in Article 21(1).

Article 23

Derogations

1. By way of derogation from Articles 20 to 22, Member States shall maintain or introduce provisions denying or restricting access to discharge of debt, revoking the benefit of such discharge or providing for longer periods for obtaining a full discharge of debt or longer disqualification periods, where the insolvent entrepreneur acted dishonestly or in bad faith under national law towards creditors or other stakeholders when becoming indebted, during the insolvency proceedings or during the payment of the debt, without prejudice to national rules on burden of proof.

2. By way of derogation from Articles 20 to 22, Member States may maintain or introduce provisions denying or restricting access to discharge of debt, revoking the benefit of discharge or providing for longer periods for obtaining a full discharge of debt or longer disqualification periods in certain well-defined circumstances and where such derogations are duly justified, such as where:

(a) the insolvent entrepreneur has substantially violated obligations under a repayment plan or any other legal obligation aimed at safeguarding the interests of creditors, including the obligation to maximise returns to creditors;
(b) the insolvent entrepreneur has failed to comply with information or cooperation obligations under Union and national law;
(c) there are abusive applications for a discharge of debt;
(d) there is a further application for a discharge within a certain period after the insolvent entrepreneur was granted a full discharge of debt or was denied a full discharge of debt due to a serious violation of information or cooperation obligations;
(e) the cost of the procedure leading to the discharge of debt is not covered; or
(f) a derogation is necessary to guarantee the balance between the rights of the debtor and the rights of one or more creditors.

3. By way of derogation from Article 21, Member States may provide for longer discharge periods in cases where:
(a) protective measures are approved or ordered by a judicial or administrative authority in order to safeguard the main residence of the insolvent entrepreneur and, where applicable, of the entrepreneur's family, or the essential assets for the continuation of the entrepreneur's trade, business, craft or profession; or
(b) the main residence of the insolvent entrepreneur and, where applicable, of the entrepreneur's family, is not realised.

4. Member States may exclude specific categories of debt from discharge of debt, or restrict access to discharge of debt or lay down a longer discharge period where such exclusions, restrictions or longer periods are duly justified, such as in the case of:
(a) secured debts;
(b) debts arising from or in connection with criminal penalties;
(c) debts arising from tortious liability;
(d) debts regarding maintenance obligations arising from a family relationship, parentage, marriage or affinity;
(e) debts incurred after the application for or opening of the procedure leading to a discharge of debt; and
(f) debts arising from the obligation to pay the cost of the procedure leading to a discharge of debt.

5. By way of derogation from Article 22, Member States may provide for longer or indefinite disqualification periods where the insolvent entrepreneur is a member of a profession:

(a) to which specific ethical rules or specific rules on reputation or expertise apply, and the entrepreneur has infringed those rules; or
(b) dealing with the management of the property of others.

The first subparagraph shall also apply where an insolvent entrepreneur requests access to a profession as referred to in point (a) or (b) of that subparagraph.

6. This Directive is without prejudice to national rules regarding disqualifications ordered by a judicial or administrative authority other than those referred to in Article 22.

Article 24

Consolidation of proceedings regarding professional and personal debts

1. Member States shall ensure that, where insolvent entrepreneurs have professional debts incurred in the course of their trade, business, craft or profession as well as personal debts incurred outside those activities, which cannot be reasonably separated, such debts, if dischargeable, shall be treated in a single procedure for the purposes of obtaining a full discharge of debt.

2. Member States may provide that, where professional debts and personal debts can be separated, those debts are to be treated, for the purposes of obtaining a full discharge of debt, either in separate but coordinated procedures or in the same procedure.

TITLE IV
MEASURES TO INCREASE THE EFFICIENCY OF PROCEDURES CONCERNING RESTRUCTURING, INSOLVENCY AND DISCHARGE OF DEBT

Article 25

Judicial and administrative authorities

Without prejudice to judicial independence and to any differences in the organisation of the judiciary across the Union, Member States shall ensure that:
(a) members of the judicial and administrative authorities dealing with procedures concerning restructuring, insolvency and discharge of debt receive suitable training and have the necessary expertise for their responsibilities; and
(b) procedures concerning restructuring, insolvency and discharge of debt are dealt with in an efficient manner, with a view to the expeditious treatment of procedures.

Article 26

Practitioners in procedures concerning restructuring, insolvency and discharge of debt

1. Member States shall ensure that:

(a) practitioners appointed by a judicial or administrative authority in procedures concerning restructuring, insolvency and discharge of debt ('practitioners') receive suitable training and have the necessary expertise for their responsibilities;

(b) the conditions for eligibility, as well as the process for the appointment, removal and resignation of practitioners are clear, transparent and fair;

(c) in appointing a practitioner for a particular case, including cases with cross-border elements, due consideration is given to the practitioner's experience and expertise, and to the specific features of the case; and

(d) in order to avoid any conflict of interest, debtors and creditors have the opportunity to either object to the selection or appointment of a practitioner or request the replacement of the practitioner.

2. The Commission shall facilitate the sharing of best practices between Member States with a view to improving the quality of training across the Union, including by means of the exchange of experiences and capacity building tools.

Article 27

Supervision and remuneration of practitioners

1. Member States shall put in place appropriate oversight and regulatory mechanisms to ensure that the work of practitioners is effectively supervised, with a view to ensuring that their services are provided in an effective and competent way, and, in relation to the parties involved, are provided impartially and independently. Those mechanisms shall also include measures for the accountability of practitioners who have failed in their duties.

2. Member States shall ensure that information about the authorities or bodies exercising oversight over practitioners is publicly available.

3. Member States may encourage the development of and adherence to codes of conduct by practitioners.

4. Member States shall ensure that the remuneration of practitioners is governed by rules that are consistent with the objective of an efficient resolution of procedures.
Member States shall ensure that appropriate procedures are in place to resolve any disputes over remuneration.

Article 28

Use of electronic means of communication

Member States shall ensure that, in procedures concerning restructuring, insolvency and discharge of debt, the parties to the procedure, the practitioner and the judicial or administrative authority are able to perform by use of electronic means of communication, including in cross-border situations, at least the following actions:
(a) filing of claims;
(b) submission of restructuring or repayment plans;
(c) notifications to creditors;
(d) lodging of challenges and appeals.

TITLE V
MONITORING OF PROCEDURES CONCERNING RESTRUCTURING, INSOLVENCY AND DISCHARGE OF DEBT

Article 29

Data collection

1. Member States shall collect and aggregate, on an annual basis, at national level, data on procedures concerning restructuring, insolvency and discharge of debt, broken down by each type of procedure, and covering at least the following elements:
(a) the number of procedures that were applied for or opened, where such opening is provided for under national law, and of procedures that are pending or were closed;
(b) the average length of procedures from the submission of the application, or from the opening thereof, where such opening is provided for under national law, to their closure;
(c) the number of procedures other than those required under point (d), broken down by types of outcome;
(d) the number of applications for restructuring procedures that were declared inadmissible, were rejected or were withdrawn before being opened.

2. Member States shall collect and aggregate, on an annual basis, at national level, data on the number of debtors which were subject to restructuring procedures or insolvency

procedures and which, within the three years prior to the submission of the application or the opening of such procedures, where such opening is provided for under national law, had a restructuring plan confirmed under a previous restructuring procedure implementing Title II.

3. Member States may collect and aggregate, on an annual basis, at national level, data on:
(a) the average cost of each type of procedure;
(b) the average recovery rates for secured and unsecured creditors and, where applicable, other types of creditors, separately;
(c) the number of entrepreneurs who, after having undergone a procedure under point (b) of Article 1(1), launch a new business;
(d) the number of job losses linked to restructuring and insolvency procedures.

4. Member States shall break down the data referred to in points (a) to (c) of paragraph 1 and, where applicable and available, the data referred to in paragraph 3 by:
(a) the size of the debtors that are not natural persons;
(b) whether debtors subject to procedures concerning restructuring or insolvency are natural or legal persons; and
(c) whether the procedures leading to a discharge of debt concern only entrepreneurs or all natural persons.

5. Member States may collect and aggregate the data referred to in paragraphs 1 to 4 through a sample technique that ensures that the samples are representative in terms of size and diversity.

6. Member States shall collect and aggregate the data referred to in paragraphs 1, 2, 4 and, where applicable, paragraph 3, for full calendar years ending on 31 December of each year, starting with the first full calendar year following the date of application of implementing acts referred to in paragraph 7. The data shall be communicated annually to the Commission, on the basis of a standard data communication form, by 31 December of the calendar year following the year for which data are collected.

7. The Commission shall establish the communication form referred to in paragraph 6 of this Article by way of implementing acts. Those implementing acts shall be adopted in accordance with the examination procedure referred to in Article 30(2).

8. The Commission shall publish on its website the data communicated in accordance with paragraph 6 in an accessible and user-friendly manner.

Article 30
Committee procedure

1. The Commission shall be assisted by a committee. That committee shall be a committee within the meaning of Regulation (EU) No 182/2011.
2. Where reference is made to this paragraph, Article 5 of Regulation (EU) No 182/2011 shall apply.
Where the committee delivers no opinion, the Commission shall not adopt the draft implementing act and the third subparagraph of Article 5(4) of Regulation (EU) No 182/2011 shall apply.

TITLE VI
FINAL PROVISIONS

Article 31
Relationship with other acts and international instruments

1. The following acts shall apply notwithstanding this Directive:
(a) Directive 98/26/EC;
(b) Directive 2002/47/EC; and
(c) Regulation (EU) No 648/2012.

2. This Directive shall be without prejudice to the safeguarding requirements of funds for payment institutions laid down under Directive (EU) 2015/2366 of the European Parliament and of the Council ([24]) and for electronic money institutions laid down under Directive 2009/110/EC of the European Parliament and of the Council ([25]).

3. This Directive shall be without prejudice to the application of the Convention on international interests in mobile equipment and its Protocol on matters specific to aircraft equipment, signed at Cape Town on 16 November 2001, to which some Member States are party at the time of the adoption of this Directive.

---

24 Directive (EU) 2015/2366 of the European Parliament and of the Council of 25 November 2015 on payment services in the internal market, amending Directives 2002/65/EC, 2009/110/EC and 2013/36/EU and Regulation (EU) No 1093/2010, and repealing Directive 2007/64/EC (OJ L 337, 23.12.2015, p. 35).

25 Directive 2009/110/EC of the European Parliament and of the Council of 16 September 2009 on the taking up, pursuit and prudential supervision of the business of electronic money institutions amending Directives 2005/60/EC and 2006/48/EC and repealing Directive 2000/46/EC (OJ L 267, 10.10.2009, p. 7).

Article 32

Amendment of Directive (EU) 2017/1132

In Article 84 of Directive (EU) 2017/1132, the following paragraph is added:

'4. Member States shall derogate from Article 58(1), Article 68, Articles 72, 73, and 74, point (b) of Article 79(1), Article 80(1) and Article 81 to the extent and for the period that such derogations are necessary for the establishment of the preventive restructuring frameworks provided for in Directive (EU) 2019/1023 of the European Parliament and of the Council (*).

The first subparagraph shall be without prejudice to the principle of equal treatment of shareholders.

(*) Directive (EU) 2019/1023 of the European Parliament and of the Council of 20 June 2019 on preventive restructuring frameworks, on discharge of debt and disqualifications and on measures to increase the efficiency of procedures concerning restructuring, insolvency and discharge of debt, and amending Directive (EU) 2017/1132 (Directive on restructuring and insolvency) (OJ L 172, 26.6.2019, p. 18).'

Article 33

Review clause

No later than 17 July 2026 and every five years thereafter, the Commission shall present to the European Parliament, the Council and the European Economic and Social Committee a report on the application and impact of this Directive, including on the application of the class formation and voting rules in respect of vulnerable creditors, such as workers. On the basis of that assessment, the Commission shall submit, if appropriate, a legislative proposal, considering additional measures to consolidate and harmonise the legal framework on restructuring, insolvency and discharge of debt.

Article 34

Transposition

1. Member States shall adopt and publish, by 17 July 2021, the laws, regulations and administrative provisions necessary to comply with this Directive, with the exception of the provisions necessary to comply with points (a), (b) and (c) of Article 28 which shall be adopted and published by 17 July 2024 and the provisions necessary to comply with point (d) of Article 28 which shall be adopted and published by 17 July 2026. They shall immediately communicate the text of those provisions to the Commission.

They shall apply the laws, regulations and administrative provisions necessary to comply with this Directive from 17 July 2021, with the exception of the provisions necessary to comply with points (a), (b) and (c) of Article 28, which shall apply from 17 July 2024 and of the provisions necessary to comply with point (d) of Article 28, which shall apply from 17 July 2026.

2. By way of derogation from paragraph 1, Member States that encounter particular difficulties in implementing this Directive shall be able to benefit from an extension of a maximum of one year of the implementation period provided for in paragraph 1. Member States shall notify to the Commission the need to make use of this option to extend the implementation period by 17 January 2021.

3. Member States shall communicate to the Commission the text of the main provisions of national law which they adopt in the field covered by this Directive.

Article 35

Entry into force

This Directive shall enter into force on the twentieth day following that of its publication in the Official Journal of the European Union.

Article 36

This Directive is addressed to the Member States.
Done at Brussels, 20 June 2019.

For the European Parliament	*For the Council*
The President	*The President*
A. TAJANI	G. CIAMBA

Business and Law Research Network Series

The following volumes have been published in the Business and Law Research Network Series:

1. J.M.G.J. Boon, H. Koster & R.D. Vriesendorp, *Implementation of the EU Preventive Restructuring Directive, Volume I, Business and Law Research Network Series No 1*, Den Haag: Eleven, 2023.

www.ingramcontent.com/pod-product-compliance
Lightning Source LLC
Chambersburg PA
CBHW061354240926
51846CB00007B/1401